**CHILTON'S** Repair and Tune-Up Guide

# Datsun 240-Z/ 260-Z

ILLUSTRATED

Prepared by the

**Automotive Editorial Department**

Chilton Book Company

Chilton Way

Radnor, Pa. 19089

215—687-8200



**CHILTON BOOK COMPANY** RADNOR, PENNSYLVANIA

First Edition

Published in Radnor, Pa. by Chilton Book Company
and simultaneously in Ontario, Canada
by Thomas Nelson & Sons, Ltd.

Manufactured in the United States of America

*Library of Congress Cataloging in Publication Data*

Chilton Book Company. Automotive Editorial Dept.
Chilton's repair and tune-up guide, Datsun 240-Z and 260-Z.

1. Datsun automobile. I. Title. II. Title:
Repair and tune-up guide, Datsun 240-Z and 260-Z.
TL215.D35C54 1975 629.28'7'22 74-34240
ISBN 0-8019-6214-5
ISBN 0-8019-6215-3 pbk.



## ACKNOWLEDGMENTS

Chilton Book Company expresses appreciation to the following for their generous assistance:

Nissan Motor Corporation in U.S.A.
18501 S. Figueroa St.
Carson, California
P.O. Box 191
Gardena, California 90247

Bob Sharp Racing
Route 7
Danbury Road
Georgetown, Connecticut 06829

Devon Datsun, Inc.
459 W. Lancaster Ave.
Devon, Pennsylvania 19333

Although the information in this guide is based on industry sources and is as complete as possible at the time of publication, the possibility exists that the manufacturer made later changes which could not be included here. While striving for total accuracy, Chilton Book Company cannot assume responsibility for any errors, changes, or omissions that may occur in the compilation of this data.

# *Contents*

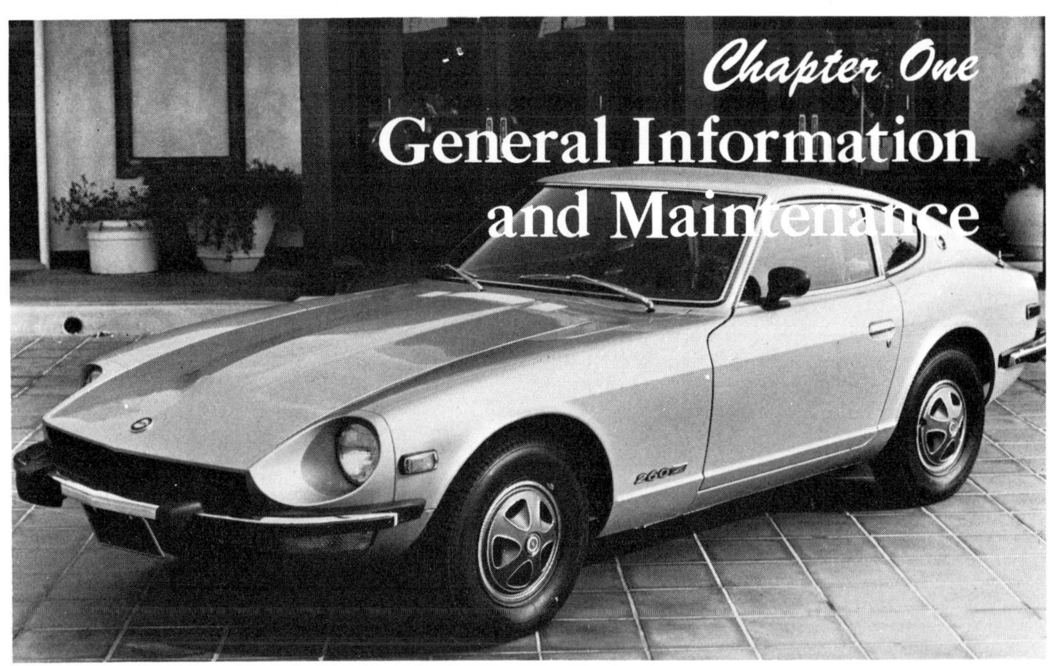

# Chapter One
# General Information and Maintenance

## How To Use This Book

This book is organized so that the most often used portions appear at the front, the least used portions at the rear. The first chapter covers all the information that may be required at a moment's notice—information like the locations of the various serial numbers, and proper towing instructions. Chapter 1 will probably be the most often used part of the book because of the need to carefully follow the maintenance schedule which it includes to ensure good performance and long component life. Chapter 2 covers tune-up and troubleshooting and will be used regularly to keep the engine running at peak performance and to restore operation in case of failure of any of the more delicate components. Chapters 3 through 10 cover repairs (rather than maintenance) for various portions of the car, with each chapter covering either one system or two related systems. The appendix then lists general information which may be useful in rebuilding the engine or performing some other operation on any car.

In using the Table of Contents, refer to the bold listings for the beginning of the chapter. See the smaller listings for information on a particular component or specifications.

In general, there are three things a proficient mechanic has which must be allowed for when a nonprofessional does work on his car. These are:

1. A sound knowledge of the construction of the parts he is working with, their order of assembly, etc.
2. A knowledge of potentially hazardous situations.
3. Manual dexterity, which includes the ability to put the right amount of torque on a part to ensure that it will not be damaged or warped.

This book provides step-by-step instructions and illustrations wherever possible. Use them carefully and wisely—do not just jump headlong into disassembly. Where you are not sure about being able to readily reassemble something, make a careful drawing of it before beginning to take it apart. Assembly always looks simple when everything is still assembled.

Cautions and notes will be provided where appropriate to help keep you from injuring yourself or damaging the car. Therefore, you should read through the entire procedure before beginning work, and make sure that you are aware of the warnings. Since no number of warnings could cover every possible situation, you should work slowly and try to envision what is going to happen in each operation ahead of time.

When it comes to tightening things, there is generally a slim area between too loose to properly seal or resist vibration and so tight as to risk damage or warping. When dealing with major engine parts, or with any aluminum component, it pays to procure a torque wrench and go by the recommended figures.

*TOOLS AND EQUIPMENT*

The suggested list of tools below is what you would have under ideal conditions. If your budget won't allow such a complete tool kit, you can probably make do without the tools that are marked with an asterisk.

1. A set of metric sockets, including a deep well socket suitable for spark plug removal. Includes socket drive and, if possible, various socket drive extensions.

*2. A set of metric combination (open-end and box) wrenches.

3. Feeler gauges (both blade and wire type).

4. A spark plug cleaning tool.

5. Various standard and phillips head screwdrivers.

*6. Various angled standard and phillips head screwdrivers.

7. A timing light (preferably battery powered).

8. A dwell meter.

*9. A special valve pivot locking nut adjusting tool ST 10640001, if you wish to do your own valve adjustments.

*10. An airflow meter for carburetor balancing.

*11. A torque wrench.

12. A grease gun, preferably with a flexible hose.

13. An oil filter wrench.

14. An oil can spout.

## History

It was not long after the introduction of the Datsun 240-Z in 1969 that the term "Z-car" became a part of the language. For many, the Z-car represented a perfect compromise between the large size of American "personal" cars and the primitiveness of the traditional sports car. The 240-Z was within the financial reach of many who could not afford a traditional grand touring car, and yet it sported the overhead cam, fully independent suspension, and exciting appearance and performance which they had dreamed of.

Datsun calls the 260-Z an "encore" to the 240-Z. While it is not a radical departure from the 240-Z, it represents a surprising change in direction. While most cars simply continue to sport more and more modest performance, the 260-Z's slight increase in displacement and fully redesigned emission control system means full performance with a minimal penalty in fuel economy, hitting the Z-car owner or potential owner right where he wants to be hit.

The 260-Z 2+2 allows the Z-car to become an exciting alternative to the con-

The 260-Z 2+2

ventional family sedan, while formerly it sometimes had to be dismissed because the entire family could not be accommodated.

## Model Identification

The 240-Z and 260-Z models are virtually identical, except for minor changes in trim on the latter, which include a new "260-Z" nameplate. The 260-Z 2+2 may be identified by its more nearly flat roofline.

## Serial Number Identification

*VEHICLE*

On all cars, the identification number is located on the top of the instrument panel so that it can be seen from outside the vehicle. This number also appears on the car identification plate, which is located on the right front strut housing on 1970–72 models, and on the right panel of the hood ledge on later models.

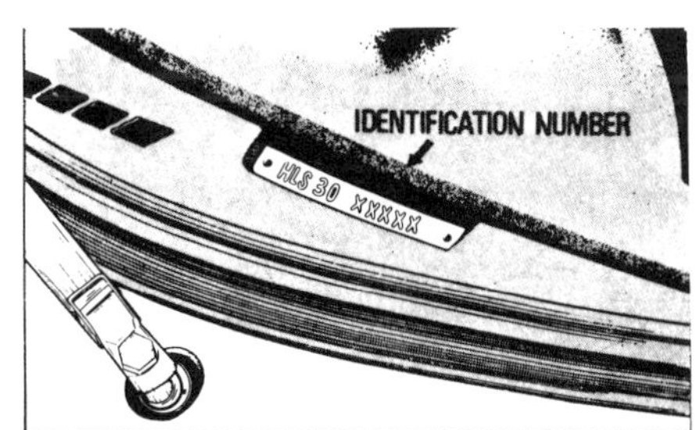

Vehicle serial number location

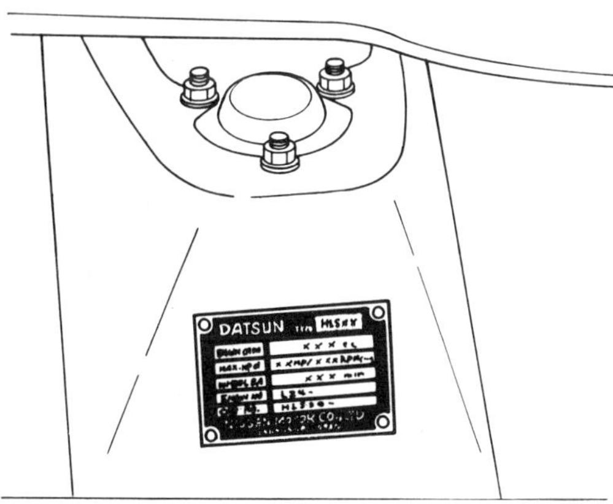

Car identification plate location

The model identification prefix of the serial number may be interpreted as follows:

1. The first letter will be either an "H" (for L24 engine) or "R" (for L26 engine).
2. Following this, an "L" will appear if the vehicle is left-hand drive.
3. Then the designation "S30" will appear for all 240-Z or 260-Z models.
4. If the vehicle has an automatic transmission, an "A" will then appear.
5. The letter "U" will then appear for all vehicles designed for U.S. and Canadian markets.
6. An "N" will then appear for Canadian vehicles.
7. If the vehicle is air conditioned, a "C" will appear at the end of the prefix.
8. On pre-1973 vehicles, a dash will follow the S30 designation. The L24 engine is the 2400 cc engine used in the 240-Z while the L26 engine refers to the 2600 cc engine used in the 260-Z.

Thus, a 260-Z designed for Canadian use only and equipped with automatic transmission and air conditioning would have the prefix:

"RLS30AUNC"

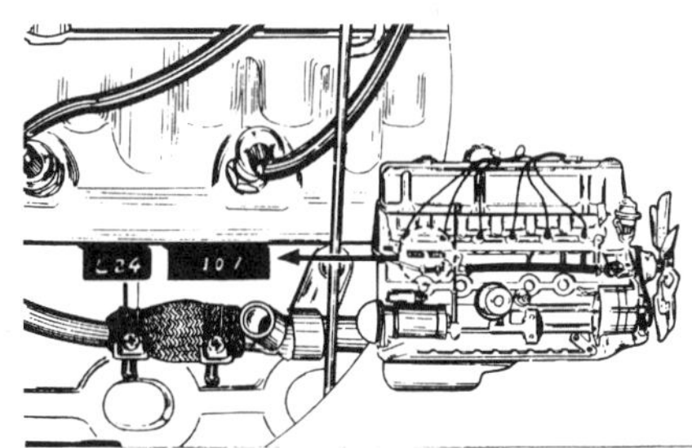

Engine serial number location

*ENGINE*

The engine serial number is located on the right rear of the block at the cylinder head contact surface. The prefix will be "L24" or "L26," depending on the engine displacement, and the three-digit (1973 and earlier) or four-digit (1974) serial number will appear just below.

*BODY COLOR*

A body color number plate is attached to the top face of the radiator core support on 1973 and 1974 vehicles. This number may be interpreted as follows:

| 1973 | |
|---|---|
| 110 | Red |
| 112 | Yellow |
| 113 | Green Metallic |
| 114 | Brown Metallic |
| 115 | Blue Metallic |
| 901 | Silver Metallic |
| 904 | White (except Canada) |
| 918 | Orange |

| 1974 | |
|---|---|
| 110 * | Red |
| 214 | Brown Metallic |
| 301 | Brown Metallic |
| 302 | Leaf Green Metallic |
| 303 | Green Metallic |
| 304 | Gold Metallic |
| 305 | Light Blue Metallic |
| 306 | Silver Metallic |
| 307 | Blue Metallic |
| 904 * | White |

* For 1974, the factory specifies two coats of paint except for the colors which are marked with an asterisk.

## Routine Maintenance

### *AIR CLEANER*

An air cleaner is used to keep airborne dirt and dust out of the air flowing through the engine. Proper maintenance is vital, as a clogged element will undesirably richen the fuel mixture, restrict airflow and power, and allow excessive contamination of the oil with abrasives. To remove the air cleaner, simply remove the two or three thumbscrews and pull off the air cleaner cover. Then, pull out the element.

The element must be replaced every 24,000 miles, or more often if the car is driven in dusty areas. The condition of the element should be checked at every tune-up. Replace the element if it is so heavily coated with dust that you cannot see light through it. The element has been specially treated to eliminate the need for cleaning between replacement intervals, so no attempt should be made to clean it with compressed air.

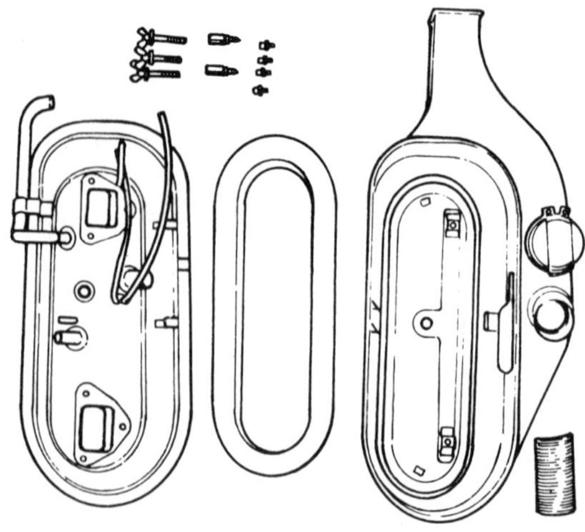

Disassembled view of the air cleaner

### *PCV SYSTEM*

Every 12,000 miles or 1 year, whichever comes first, perform the following checks on the function of the PCV system:

1. Check the ventilation hoses for leaks or clogging, and clean or replace as necessary.
2. Remove the ventilator hose from the PCV valve with the engine idling and place a finger over the valve inlet. If a strong vacuum is felt and a hissing noise is evident, the valve is functional. Otherwise, replace it.

### *EVAPORATIVE EMISSIONS CANISTER*

On 1974 vehicles, check the canister air filter, located under the canister, for contamination. If the filter is dirty, it may be removed and replaced with a clean one as shown, without removing the canister from the vehicle.

A periodic check (every 12,000 miles) should also be made of all hoses and of the filler cap. If there is evidence of leakage, reconnect or replace parts as necessary.

### *BELTS*

At engine tune-up (every 12,000 miles), check the condition of the drive belts and check and adjust belt tension as below:

1. Inspect belts for signs of glazing or cracking. A glazed belt will be perfectly smooth from slippage, while a good belt will have a slight texture of fabric visible. Cracks will usually start at the inner edge of the belt and run outward. Re-

place the belt at the first sign of cracking or if glazing is severe.

2. Belt tension does not refer to play or droop. By placing your thumb midway between two pulleys, it should be possible to depress each belt about .4 in. (10 mm) with about 20 lbs (10 Kg) pressure. The air pump belt runs looser than this. You should be able to depress it about .6 in. (7 mm). If the belt can be depressed more than this, or cannot be depressed this much, adjust the tension as described in Chapter 2. Inadequate tension will result in slippage and wear, while excessive tension will damage bearings and cause belts to fray and crack.

*AIR CONDITIONING.*

When placing the unit in service at the beginning of the summer season, make the following checks:

1. Operate the engine at approximately 1,500 rpm. Locate the sight glass, located on top of the receiver-drier, a small, black cylinder which is in the engine compartment.

2. Have someone turn the blower to high speed and switch the AIR lever to A/C position while you watch the sight glass. The glass should first become clouded with bubbles, and then clear up. Operate the unit for five minutes while watching the glass. If outside temperature is 68° F or above, the glass should be perfectly clear. If there is a continuous stream of bubbles, it indicates that the system has a slight leak and will require additional refrigerant. If the system starts and runs and no bubbles appear, the entire refrigerant charge has been lost. *Stop the system and do not operate it until it has been repaired.*

3. Inspect all lines for signs of oil accumulation, which would indicate leakage. If leaks are indicated, have the leak repaired by a professional mechanic. Do not attempt to tighten fittings or otherwise repair the system unless you have been trained in refrigeration repair as the system contains high pressure. Do not operate the system if it seems to have leaks as this can aggravate possible damage to the system.

4. Check the tension and condition of the compressor drive belt and adjust its tension or replace as necessary.

5. Test the blower to make sure that it operates at all speeds and have it repaired if it does not.

In winter, operate the air conditioner for 10 minutes with the engine at 1,500 rpm once a month to circulate oil to the compressor seal, thus preventing leakage.

*FLUID LEVEL CHECKS*

**Engine Oil**

At every stop for fuel, check the engine oil as follows:

1. Wait until the engine has been turned off for several minutes, so that as much as possible of the oil will have returned to the crankcase. Then, remove the dipstick.

2. Wipe the dipstick clean with a clean rag.

3. Reinsert the dipstick and push it down until it has fully seated.

4. Remove the stick and check the level. If oil has fallen to the lower mark, add 1 quart.

5. If you wish, you may carefully fill the oil pan to the upper mark on the dipstick with less than a full quart. Do not, however, add a full quart when that will overfill the crankcase, as this could cause engine damage. The excess oil will generally be consumed at an excessive rate even if no damage to the engine seals occurs.

**Radiator Coolant**

Datsun recommends checking the radiator coolant every time you stop for gas. If the engine is hot, allow it to cool for several minutes to reduce the pressure in the system. Using a rag, turn the radiator cap ¼ turn to the stop and allow all pressure to escape. Then, remove the cap.

Fill the radiator until the level is within 1 in. (25 mm) of the radiator cap. It is best to add a 50-50 mix of antifreeze and water to avoid diluting the coolant in the system. Use permanent type antifreeze only.

**Brake and Clutch Master Cylinders**

Check the fluid levels in these two units at every gas stop. Add an approved brake fluid which conforms to DOT 3 or 4 standards to bring the reservoirs to the

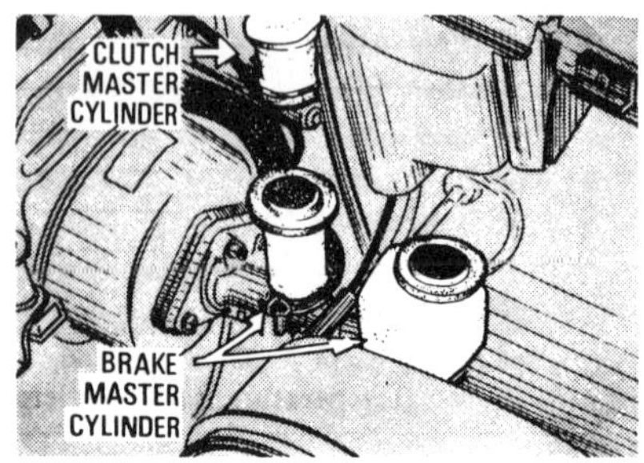


Checking fluid levels in the brake and clutch master cylinders

proper level. Check for signs of leakage from these systems and make repairs or have them made as necessary.

**Transmission and Rear Axle**

At 600 miles and every 3,000 miles thereafter, check the oil in the manual transmission and rear axle. Remove the filler plug, and add oil as necessary to bring the level up to the bottom of the hole. Do not overfill. Use SAE 90 normally, SAE 80 for long periods below freezing, and SAE 140 for temperatures about 104°F.

Checking automatic transmission fluid level

**Automatic Transmission**

At 600 miles and every 3,000 miles thereafter, check the transmission fluid with the engine idling. Use the dipstick precisely as when checking the engine oil. Do not overfill the transmission, as this may cause erratic shifting or damage.

**Battery**

Once a month, remove the battery caps and check the electrolyte levels. If necessary, replace water which has boiled off so that the level is about .2 in.

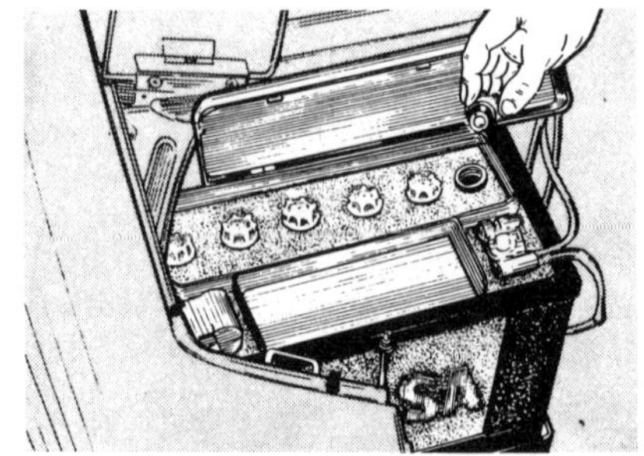

Checking battery electrolyte level

(5 mm) above the plates. Do not overfill. Then, operate the engine for a few minutes to mix electrolyte and water.

At this time it is also a good idea to clean the top of the battery with a clean rag. If necessary, thoroughly clean the battery terminals, and coat them with petroleum jelly. If they are badly corroded, this should include loosening the locknuts, pulling the connections off the battery, and wire brushing all the exposed surfaces. Then, reconnect the terminals, tighten, and apply the petroleum jelly. Check which connection goes to the positive terminal, and which to the negative before disconnecting them. Make sure to install the connections to the right terminals or damage to the alternator may result. Also, make sure that there is good ventilation when connecting or disconnecting the battery wiring, as explosive hydrogen gas is vented by the battery.

Checking carburetor damper oil level

**Carburetor Damper Oil**

Every 3,000 miles, check the level of the carburetor damper oil by removing the oil cap nut. If the oil level is below the lower line, add SAE 20 to restore the proper level. Do not use SAE 30!

## Capacities

| Year | Model | Engine Displacement cu in. (cc) | Engine Crankcase Qts (liters) With Filter | Engine Crankcase Qts (liters) Without Filter | Transmission Pts (liters) Manual | Transmission Pts (liters) Automatic | Drive Axle Pts (liters) | Gasoline Tank Gals (liters) | Cooling System Qts (liters) |
|---|---|---|---|---|---|---|---|---|---|
| 1970–1973 | 240-Z | 146 (2393) | 5 (4.7) | 4.25 (4) | 3⅛ (1.5) | 11¾ (5.5) | 2⅛ (1) | 15⅞ (60) | 10½ (9.9) |
| 1974 | 260-Z | 156.5 (2565) | 5 (4.7) | 4.25 (4) | 3⅛ (1.5) | 11¾ (5.5) | 2⅛ (1) | 15⅞ (60) | 10 (9.4) |

### Steering Gear

Every 30,000 miles, check the fluid level in the steering gear housing, and refill as necessary. Use SAE 90 normally, SAE 80 for long periods below freezing, and SAE 140 for temperatures above 104° F.

### *TIRES AND WHEELS*

Since the air in the tire is in effect a part of the tire's structure, maintenance of the proper pressure is vital to achieving safe handling and maximum tire life. All tires should be inflated to 28 psi when cold or 10–15% higher than that when hot. 32 psi should be used when operating at extreme high speeds (over 100 mph). The tire size for all Datsun 240-Z and 260-Z automobiles is 175-HR-14. All tires should be of the same size and load range. *Belted or bias ply tires must not be used with radials.*

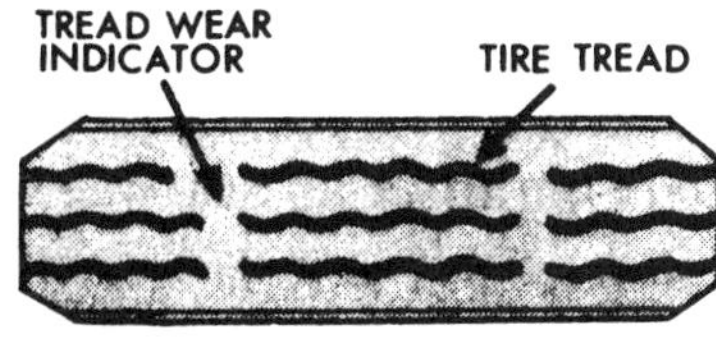

The tread wear indicator

The tires require replacement when the tread wear indicator appears. This indicator is a shallower section of tread and will ordinarily appear as a short bald section running from one side of the tire to the other.

### Tire Rotation

By rotating all the tires every 6,000 miles, the spare tire can be used to increase the life of the other tires and unevenness in wear will have minimal effect. Rotating according to the chart will give maximum possible life and help ensure the stablest possible handling.

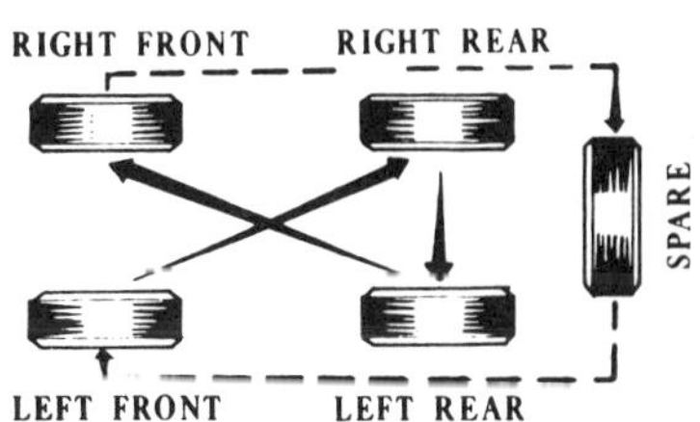

Tire rotation chart

### *FUEL FILTER*

The fuel filter is a replaceable, clear plastic type with a paper element. The filter should be replaced every 12,000 miles unless inspection shows that more frequent replacement is necessary.

The filter is removed by simply disconnecting the inlet and outlet lines. Place a container under the filter to catch fuel draining from the lines. Drainage from the line coming from the fuel tank may be stopped by simply raising the line as far as possible.

Reinstall the filter carefully, ensuring that both lines are forced onto the filter connections as far as they will go and are securely clamped. Then, check the filter for leakage.

### *BATTERY*

At 600 miles, 12,000 miles, and every 12,000 miles thereafter, inspect the battery as described under the "Fluid Level Checks" and then check the specific gravity of the electrolyte in each cell. Gravity should be 1.20–1.26 normally, 1.22–1.28 in frigid climates, and 1.18–1.23 in tropical climates. Correct problems as necessary (see the "Troubleshooting" section).

## Oil Viscosity Chart

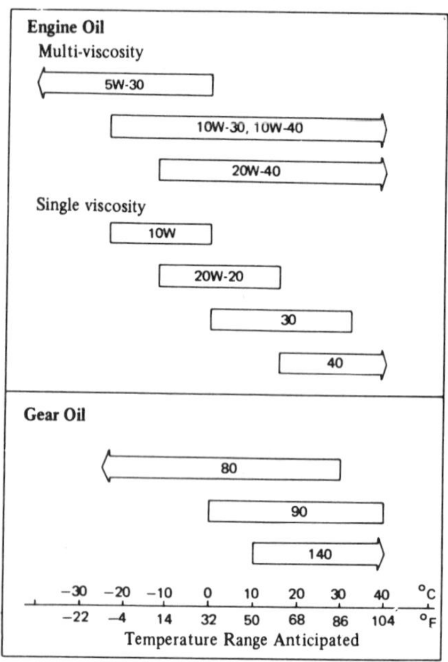


# Lubrication

### *OIL AND FUEL RECOMMENDATIONS*

Datsun recommends the use of high quality oils designated SD or SE. The following chart indicates proper viscosity ranges.

Use a good quality gasoline with a minimum octane rating of 87. This figure represents the average of Research and Motor octanes and compares with the number posted on the pump. If the Research Octane Number is used, the rating should be 91 or higher.

If knocking occurs, try a gasoline of a slightly higher rating until you find a fuel which performs entirely without knock the way you normally drive your car. Knock is extremely damaging and must be avoided.

### *OIL CHANGES*

Change the engine oil at 600 miles and then every 3,000 miles or three months (whichever comes first) thereafter. Change the oil with the engine fully warmed up as this will put as many as possible of the impurities in suspension and bring them out of the crankcase with the oil.

Place a container of adequate size under the crankcase (see the "Capacities" chart) remove the drain plug. Clean the drain plug with a clean rag. Allow the oil to drain as completely as possible. Then, reinstall the drain plug and fill the crankcase to the upper level on the dipstick. Operate the engine until oil pressure has built up, stop it and allow it to sit for several minutes, and then refill the crankcase to the proper level.

### *OIL FILTER CHANGES*

Replace the oil filter at 600 miles and then at every second oil change. To remove the filter, place a container which will hold about two quarts under the filter and unscrew it with a strap wrench.

Thoroughly clean the portion of the block which the oil filter covers when it is installed with a clean rag. Then, thoroughly lubricate the filter gasket with fresh engine oil.

Finally, screw the filter on and tighten it by hand. Start the engine, and operate it at idle until oil pressure has been built up. Then, stop it to allow oil to drain into the crankcase, and refill the crankcase as necessary. Operate the engine and check the filter for leaks.

### *CHASSIS GREASING*

Lubricate the accelerator linkage every 6,000 miles. Lubricate the foot pedal bushings every 12,000 miles.

Every 30,000 miles or 30 months, whichever comes first:

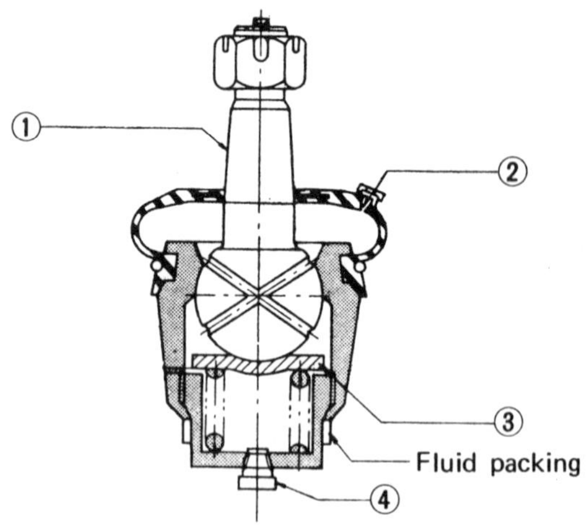


Cross-section of a suspension ball joint

1. Ball stud
2. Grease bleeder
3. Spring seat
4. Plug

## Lubrication

| *Operation* | *Interval* |
|---|---|
| Change engine oil | @ 600 miles, then every 3,000 miles |
| Check and refill auto. transmission fluid | |
| Check and refill carb. damper oil level | Every 3,000 miles |
| Check and refill manual trans. and differential oil levels | |
| Replace oil filter | @ 600 miles, then every 6,000 miles |
| Lubricate accelerator linkage | Every 6,000 miles |
| Grease distributor shaft cam and heel | |
| Lubricate all locks and hinges | |
| Change brake fluid | Every 12,000 miles |
| Lubricate pedal bushings | |
| Change engine coolant | Every 24,000 miles |
| Change manual transmission and differential oil | @ 600 miles, then every 30,000 miles |
| Grease steering and suspension linkage ball joints | Every 30,000 miles |
| Repack wheel bearings | |
| Grease all U-joints and ball splines | |

1. Lubricate the steering and suspension ball joints as follows: Remove the grease plug and install a grease fitting. Install the grease gun connector and *slowly* feed grease into the joint to avoid forcing it out of the joint except at the grease bleeder. Lubricate the joint with multipurpose grease until new grease emerges at the bleeder point.

2. Apply multipurpose grease to the ball splines of the driveshafts and repack the universal joints on the driveshaft and axle shafts. This will require major disassembly operations—see Chapter 7.

*BODY LUBRICATION*

Lubricate all locks and hinges with multipurpose grease every 6,000 miles.

*WHEEL BEARINGS*

Clean and repack wheel bearings every 30,000 miles. See Chapter 9.

## Towing

### Manual Transmission

Tow forward using the hook shown in the illustration. *Do not attempt to tow the vehicle by the front suspension.* Tow the vehicle so as to avoid a sudden impact on the hook.

### Automatic Transmission

If the distance to be traveled is six miles or less, the vehicle may be towed

Towing with manual transmission

with the front wheels off the ground. The speed must not exceed 18.8 mph under these conditions.

If the transmission is not operating properly, greater distance is involved, or higher speeds are required, tow the vehicle with the rear wheels off the ground and the steering wheel secured in a straight-ahead position.

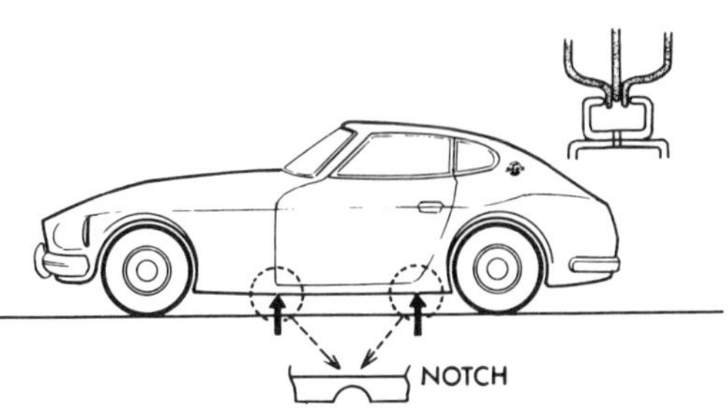

Jacking points when using scissors jack

## Jacking and Hoisting

The vehicle is supplied with a scissors jack for emergency road repairs. The scissors jack may be used to raise the car via the notches on either side at the front and rear of the doors. *Do not attempt to use the jack in any other places.* When using a garage jack, support the car at the center of the front suspension member or at the differential carrier. *Do not attempt to jack the car at the front suspension transverse link.*

When using stands, use the side members at the front and the differential front mounting crossmember at the back for placement points.

Front jacking point—garage jack

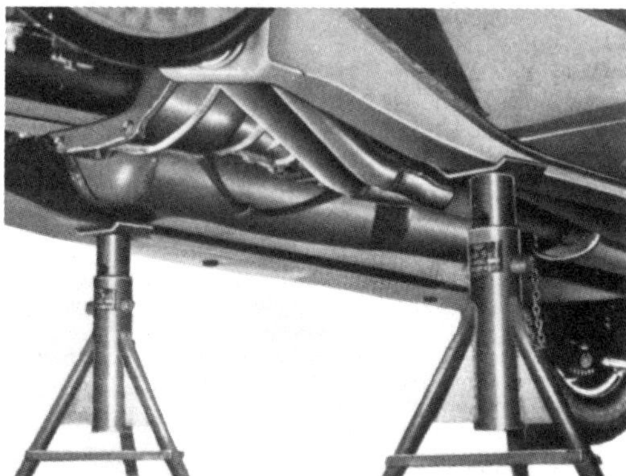

Front support points for axle stands

Rear jacking point—garage jack

Rear support points for axle stands

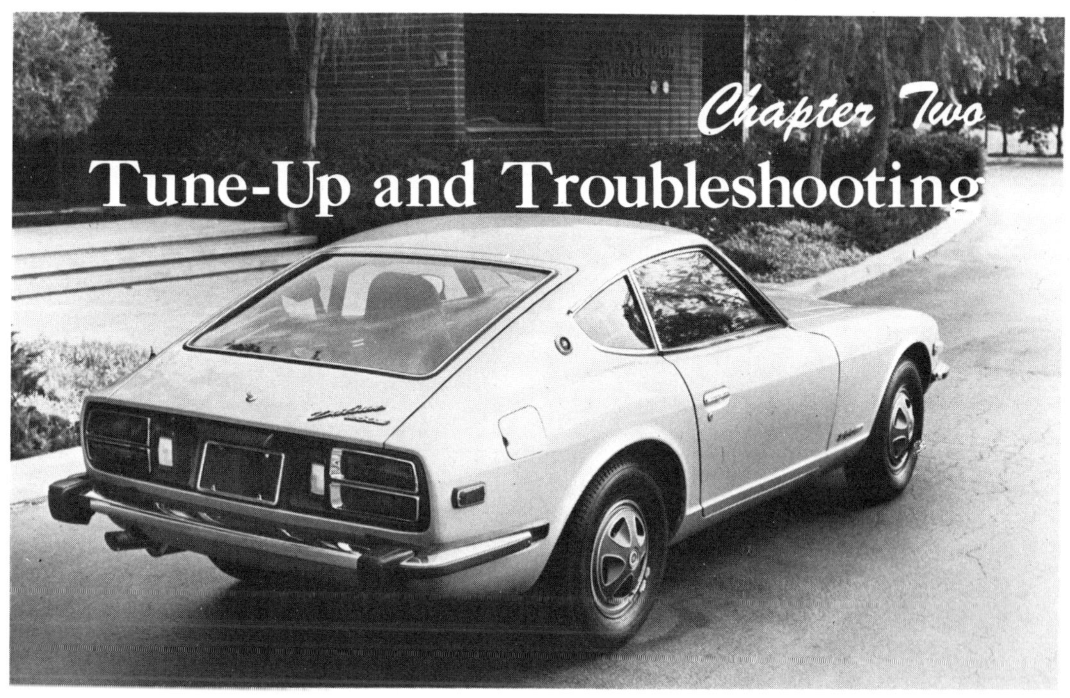


## Tune-Up Procedures

A tune-up is performed periodically (every 12,000 miles on a Datsun) to make a complete check of the operation of the engine and several associated systems, to bring various minor adjustments to the best possible position, and to replace various fast-wearing ignition parts. This section contains all tune-up information that applies specifically to Datsun 240-Z and 260-Z vehicles. A general section (which follows) will provide various kinds of backup information which you will find valuable in tuning either your 240/260-Z or any other car. In addition to the major tune-up at 12,000 miles, valve adjustment is performed every 6,000 miles, and carburetion, timing and dwell, and spark plug checks are made every 3,000 miles.

Since a tune-up is the best way of guaranteeing peak performance and economy from your car, work carefully and slowly and strive for precision. The result will be a smooth sounding and responsive engine that will make you proud of your work.

*SPARK PLUGS*

Remove the spark plugs as follows:

1. Carefully remove the plug wire by pulling on the boot which houses the connector for the plug (pulling farther back will damage the wire).
2. Clean the area surrounding the plug with a rag to avoid having dirt enter the engine while the plug is out.
3. Install the proper socket and remove the plug.

The plugs should be thoroughly cleaned with a wire brush or, if possible, by sand blasting. Then, inspect them carefully to make sure that the electrodes are in good condition and that the insulator is not cracked. Also, make sure that they are of the proper heat range (see chart). File the electrodes flat and carefully adjust the gaps to 0.031–0.035 in. (0.8–0.9 mm).

Where deficiencies are noted or if the

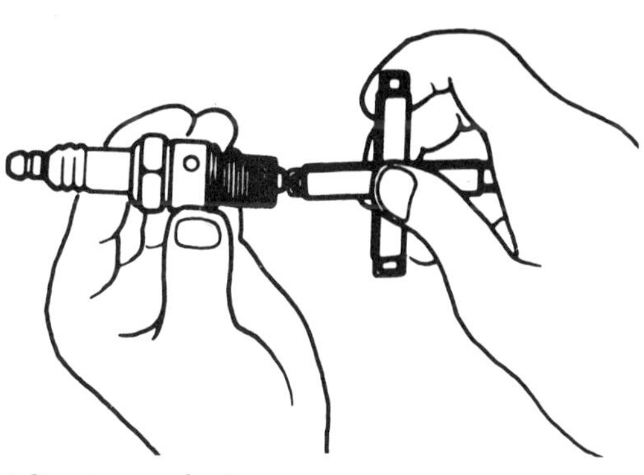

Adjusting spark plug gap

## Tune-Up Specifications

| Year | Engine Displacement cu in. (cc) | Spark Plugs Type | Spark Plugs Gap (in.) (mm) | Distributor Point Dwell (deg) | Distributor Point Gap (in.) (mm) | Ignition Timing (deg) MT | Ignition Timing (deg) AT | Intake Valve Opens (deg) | Fuel Pump Pressure (psi) (kg/cm²) | Compression Pressure (psi) (kg/cm²) | Idle Speed (rpm) MT | Idle Speed (rpm) AT | Valve Clearance (hot) (in.) | Valve Clearance (hot) (mm) |
|---|---|---|---|---|---|---|---|---|---|---|---|---|---|---|
| 1970–71 | 146 (2393) | BP-6E | .031–.035 (.8–.9) | 35–41 | .016–.019 (.4–.5) | 5B@ 750 | TDC@② 600 | 16B | 3.4–4.2 (.24–.30) | 171–185 (12–13) | 750 | 600 | .010 (.25) | .012 (.30) |
| 1972 | 146 (2393) | BP-6ES | .031–.035 (.8–.9) | 35–41 | .016–.019 (.4–.5) | 5B@ 750 | TDC@② 600 | 16B | 3.4–4.2 (.24–.30) | 171–185 (12–13) | 750④ | 600 | .010 (.25) | .012 (.30) |
| 1973 | 146 (2393) | BP-6ES | .031–.035 (.8–.9) | 35–41 | .018–.021 (.45–.55) | 7B@ 750 | 5B@③ 600 | 16B | 3.4–4.2 (.24–.30) | 171–185 (12–13) | 750⑤ | 600⑥ | .010 (.25) | .012 (.30) |
| 1974 | 156 (2565) | BP-6ES | .031–.035 (.8–.9) | —— | .012–.016① (.3–.4) | 8B@ 750 | 8B@③ 600 | 20B | 3.4–4.2 (.24–.30) | 171–185 (12–13) | 750⑤ | 600⑥ | .010 (.25) | .012 (.30) |

① Refers to air gap—electronic ignition
② 10B @ 600 below 30° F
③ 15B @ 600 advance
④ 5–7% CO at idle, air pump disconnected
⑤ 1.0–1.6% CO at idle
⑥ 0.6–1.2 CO in Neutral
—— Not applicable

plugs have been in service for 12,000 miles, replace them. Otherwise, put new gaskets on the old plugs and install them, torquing to 11–15 ft lbs (1.5–2.0 kg-m).

### *BREAKER POINTS AND CONDENSER*

Release the two spring clips, remove the distributor cap, and remove the rotor.

Inspect the breaker points to make sure that they are not excessively pitted improperly aligned, or excessively worn at the rubbing block. If any of these deficiencies are noted, or if they are 12,000 miles old or older, replace them.

Lightly rub the surfaces of the points with a point file to clean them. Do not attempt to remove all roughness.

Apply a small amount of multipurpose grease to the breaker cam and to the heel (leading edge) of the cam follower on the points. If a lubricating wick is used, apply grease to that. Note that only a small amount of grease should be used as too much can get onto the contact surfaces.

To replace the points and condenser, proceed as follows:

1. Disconnect the condenser lead from the outside of the distributor and the primary lead to the points from inside it by loosening the terminal screws and pulling the wires off. Disconnect the primary lead at the contact assembly.
2. Loosen the screw which holds the contact set in place and remove the assembly.

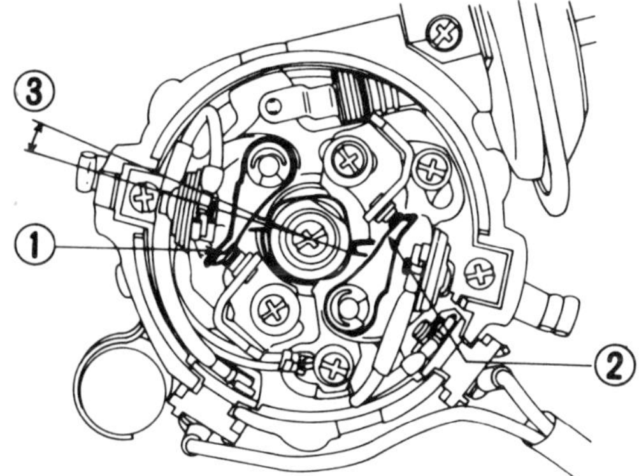


Locations of advanced and retarded point assemblies in dual point distributor

1. Advanced breaker assembly
2. Retarded breaker assembly
3. Phase difference

3. Remove the condenser mounting screw and remove the condenser. On models with an automatic transmission, there are two sets of points and two condensers to replace. Identical procedures apply for replacing both sets of components. In replacing these components, reverse the removal procedure, but leave the mounting screws for the points just slightly loose to permit easy point gap adjustment.

Then, for each set of points which must be adjusted, do the following:

1. Bump the engine over with the starter until the cam follower is on the very tip of the cam.
2. Get a flat feeler gauge within the range shown on the "Tune-Up" chart for point gap and wipe it carefully with a clean rag. Also, wipe the surfaces of the new contacts clean.
3. Insert the gauge straight between the contacts avoiding built up areas, and slide the contact base back and forth on the mounting screw until the gauge can just be inserted straight between the contacts without moving them. There should be a slight drag on the feeler gauge when the contacts are properly adjusted.
4. Tighten the mounting screw, recheck the gap, and readjust as necessary. Reinstall the cap and rotor.

If possible, adjust the dwell, using a dwell meter, as described below.

### *PICK-UP COIL AND AIR GAP*

If the pick-up coil requires replacement, proceed as follows:.

1. Remove the distributor cap and rotor. Remove the two pick-up coil mounting screws and the core screws which hold the primary lead in place.
2. Remove the coil.

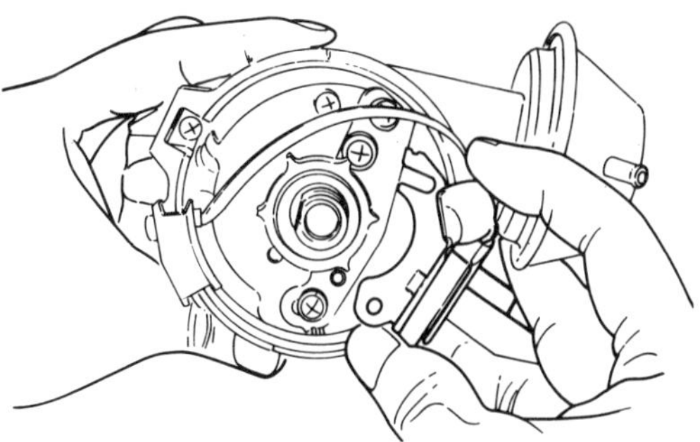

Removing the pick-up coil

To replace the coil, reverse the above procedures, except for leaving the two coil mounting screws slightly loose to facilitate performing the air gap adjustment.

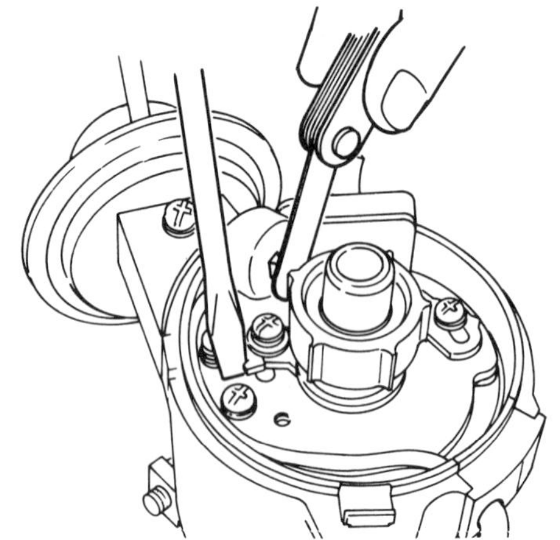

Measuring the air gap

To adjust the air gap during periodic distributor inspection or after pick-up coil replacement, proceed as follows:

1. Slightly loosen the pick-up coil mounting screws.
2. Bump the engine over until one of the reluctor points is directly opposite the coil which requires adjustment.
3. Using a clean feeler gauge of 0.012–0.016 in. (0.3–0.4 mm), position a screwdriver as shown and shift the position of the pick-up coil back and forth until the gauge can just be inserted into the air gap without moving the coil.

   NOTE: *Only a nonmagnetic (brass, paper, etc.) feeler gauge can be used to adjust the reluctor air gap. The pick-up coil may be damaged if a ferrous metal feeler gauge is used.*
4. Tighten the pick-up coil mounting screws and recheck the adjustment, readjusting as necessary. With automatic transmission distributors, repeat the operation for the other pick-up coil.

At the time the air gap is checked, the distributor lubricator should be checked as follows:

1. Remove the rubber cap from the end of the rotor shaft. Add multipurpose grease, as necessary. Replace the cap.

*DWELL ANGLE*

On all distributors with contact points, it is recommended that final gap adjustment be performed by checking the dwell angle with a dwell meter. On distributors with a single set of contact points (used with manual transmissions), operate the engine at idle speed, connect the black lead of the dwell meter to a good ground, and connect the red lead to the distributor side of the ignition coil. Then, read the meter (make sure to read the right scale) and determine whether or not the dwell is in the specified range. If the dwell is not within specification, stop the engine, remove the distributor cap and rotor, and change the point gap slightly. If the dwell is too high, widen the point gap. If the dwell angle is too low, make the point gap slightly narrower. Then, replace the cap and rotor and retest. Repeat the readjustment and testing procedure until the dwell is within specification.

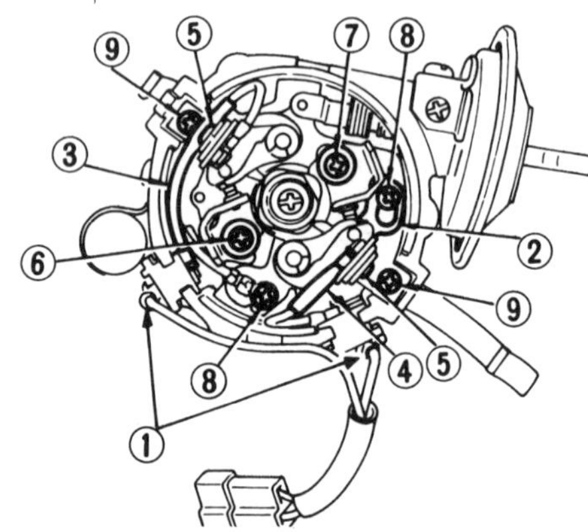


Location of distributor wiring connector and other components

1. Lead wire terminal screws
2. Adjuster plate
3. Primary lead wire (advanced breaker)
4. Primary lead wire (retarded breaker)
5. Primary lead wire screw
6. Mounting screw (advanced breaker)
7. Mounting screw (retarded breaker)
8. Adjuster plate attaching screws
9. Breaker plate mounting screws

Follow the same procedure for each set of contacts with a 1973 dual contact distributor, but hook up the dwell meter as follows:

1. Disconnect the distributor wiring harness from the engine harness. Then, connect a jumper wire between the B (black) terminals of both the engine and distributor wiring harnesses. The dwell meter will now show the dwell for the advance set of contact points.

2. Move the distributor end of the jumper from the black distributor terminal, and connect it to the Y (yellow) terminal of the distributor harness. This will cause the dwell meter to read the dwell of the retard set of points.

When dwell adjustment is complete, remove the jumper and reconnect the harness. On earlier vehicles with automatic transmission, simply disconnect the retard connector (with single lead) at the distributor to get the dwell for advance points, connect it, and disconnect the advance connector to get the dwell for the retard points.

### *IGNITION TIMING*

Ignition timing is adjusted with a timing light which flashes when the ignition points open and the No. 1 spark plug fires. By lining up the pointer or scale on the timing cover on the front of the engine with a scale or line on the crankshaft pulley simultaneous with the flash of the timing light, the position of the crankshaft can be determined.

The distributor is then rotated slowly back and forth until the proper setting in degrees is lined up with the pointer or line.

To time the engine, proceed as follows:

1. Disconnect the No. 1 spark plug wire and connect the heavy lead to the timing light (which is usually equipped with a spring connector designed to fit over the plug and inside the high-tension connection) in series with the No. 1 plug.
2. Connect the red lead to the positive (+) terminal of the battery and the black lead to the negative (−) terminal.
3. On 1973 models with automatic transmission, disconnect the distributor wiring harness and run a jumper wire between the B (black) terminals of the engine and distributor plugs. On 1974 model automatics, disconnect the connector at the water temperature switch. Make sure that *all* wires are out of the way of the engine fan and other rotating parts.
4. Start the engine and operate it at idle speed. If the car has an automatic transmission, securely apply the parking brake and put the transmission in gear.
5. Verify that the idle speed is approximately correct as shown in the "Tune-Up" chart. If not, adjust it until it is correct as described in the carburetor adjustment section of this chapter.
6. Carefully keeping the wires away from all rotating parts, aim the light at the timing marks. Compare the indication with the specified timing (use the *advance* setting on 1973–74 models).

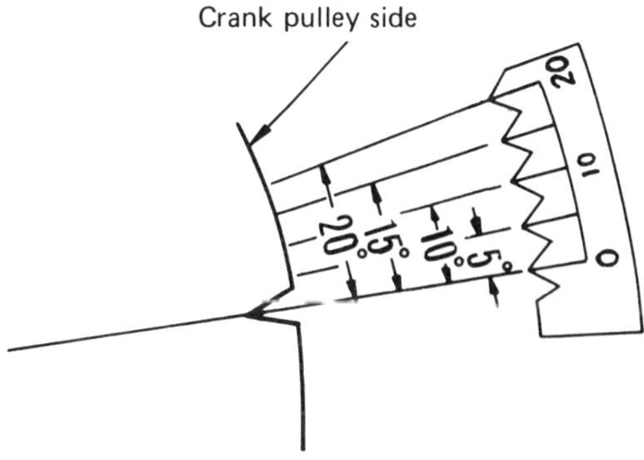


Figure shows the relationship between the crankshaft pulley and timing scale on a 1973 240-Z

7. If the timing is not correct, stop the engine and loosen the nut which holds the distributor clamped in position (it is on the front of the clamp).
8. Then, restart the engine (putting an automatic transmission back in gear).
9. Slowly rotate the distributor back and forth until the timing is correct.
10. Stop the engine and tighten the clamp nut, being careful not to disturb the setting.
11. Recheck the timing and readjust it as necessary.
12. On 1973–74 automatic models, the timing in retard position must be checked. On 1973 models, move the lead over to the Y (yellow) terminal of the distributor plug. On later models,

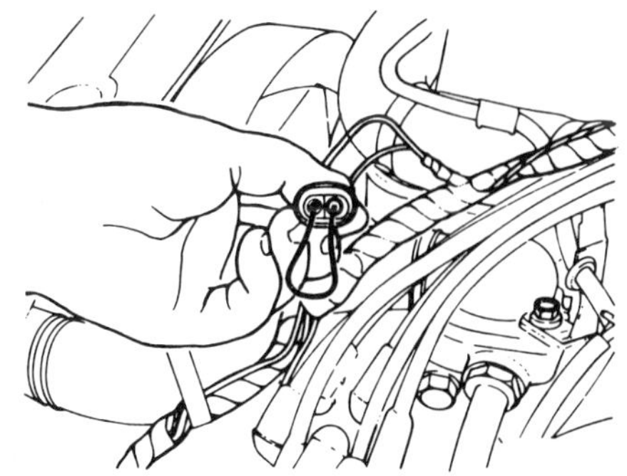

Running a jumper across the terminals of the temperature switch connection run a jumper wire across the two terminals of the connection to the temperature switch.

13. Again check the timing exactly as described above. It should be 10 degrees retarded on 1973 models and 7 degrees retarded on later models. If the timing is incorrect, adjust the phase difference as follows:

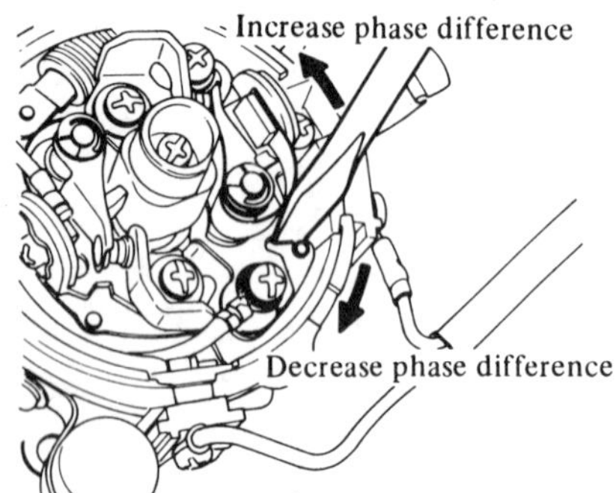

Adjusting the phase difference

a. Loosen the set screws which hold the adjuster plate in position and turn the plate using the notch in the adjuster plate. Timing is retarded by turning the plate counterclockwise. The edge of the distributor is marked in graduations which equal 4 degrees of crankshaft rotation each.

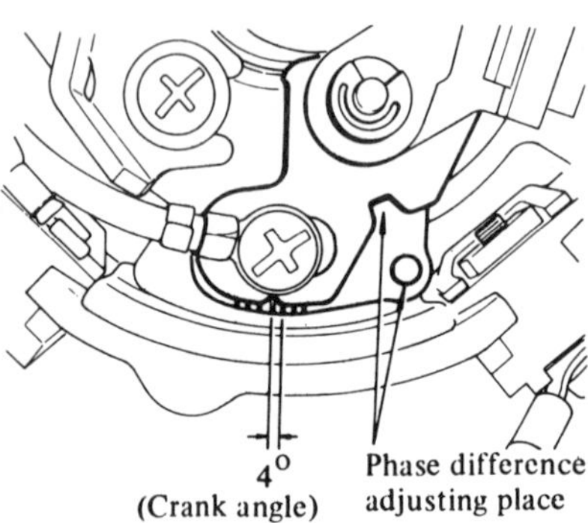

Phase difference adjusting scale

Label arrows "Adjust phase difference here"

b. Recheck the ignition timing. Repeat the adjustment and checks until retard timing is within specification.

c. Make sure to disconnect all jumper wires and securely reconnect all disturbed ignition wiring.

*VALVE LASH*

Valve lash should be adjusted at 600 miles and then every 6,000 miles. Purchase a valve cover gasket and have it on hand before starting work.

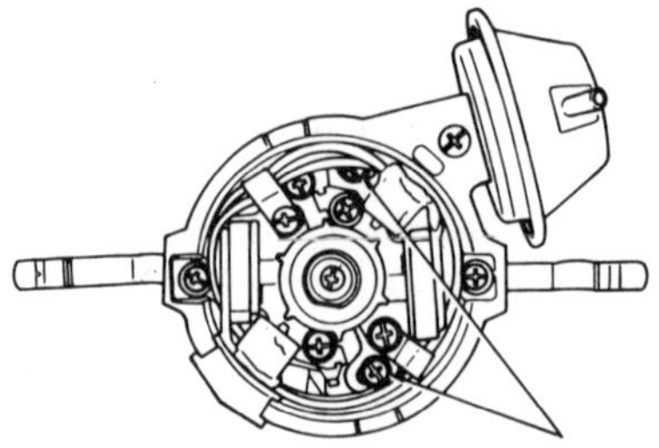
Location of adjuster plate set screws on electronic ignition distributor

Label arrows "Adjuster plate set screws"

The engine must be "overnight" cold before beginning. It must not be operated for about eight hours before adjusting the valves. Then, proceed as follows:

1. Note the locations of all hoses or wires that would interfere with valve cover removal, disconnect them and move them aside. Then, remove the six bolts which hold the valve cover in place.

2. Bump one end of the cover sharply to loosen the gasket and then pull the valve cover off the engine vertically.

3. Crank the engine with the starter until both No. 1 cylinder valves (No. 1 is at the front) are closed (the cams are pointed upward), and the timing mark on the crankshaft pulley is lined up approximately as it would be when the No. 1 spark plug fires.

Adjusting valve clearance

4. Adjust the No. 1 cylinder intake valve to 0.008 in. (0.20 mm). First loosen the pivot locking nut and then insert the feeler gauge between the cam and cam follower. Adjust the pivot screw until there is a slight pull on the gauge when

it is inserted *straight* between the cam and follower. Then, tighten the locking nut, recheck the adjustment, and correct as necessary.

5. Repeat the procedure for the No. 1 cylinder exhaust valve, but use a 0.010 in. (0.25 mm) gauge.

You can differentiate between the intake and exhaust valves by lining them up with the tubes of the intake and exhaust manifolds.

6. Repeat Steps 4 and 5 for the other cylinders, going in the firing order of 1-5-3-6-2-4. Turn the engine ahead ⅓ turn before adjusting the valves for each cylinder so that the cams will point upward.

7. Reinstall the valve cover gasket and hoses, start the engine, and operate it until it is fully warmed up.

8. Repeat the entire valve adjustment procedure using the gauges specified in the "Tune-Up" chart, but do not loosen the locking nuts unless the gauge indicates that adjustment is required.

9. When all valves are at hot specifications, clean all traces of old gasket material from the valve cover and the head. Install the new gasket in the valve cover with sealer and install the valve cover. Tighten the valve cover bolts evenly in several stages going around the cover to ensure a good seal. Reconnect all hoses and wires securely and operate the engine to check for leaks.

### Idle Speed and Mixture Adjustments

1970–72

1. Run the engine until it is at operating temperature. Remove the air cleaner.

2. Adjust the idle speed to 750 rpm. Apply an air flow meter for one or two seconds to one of the carburetor air horns, holding it vertically. Then, check the flow of the other carburetor. Adjust the throttle adjusting screws so that the airflow is equal and the rpm is 750.

3. Disconnect the control vacuum tube from the connector on the manifold and connect the servo diaphragm vac-

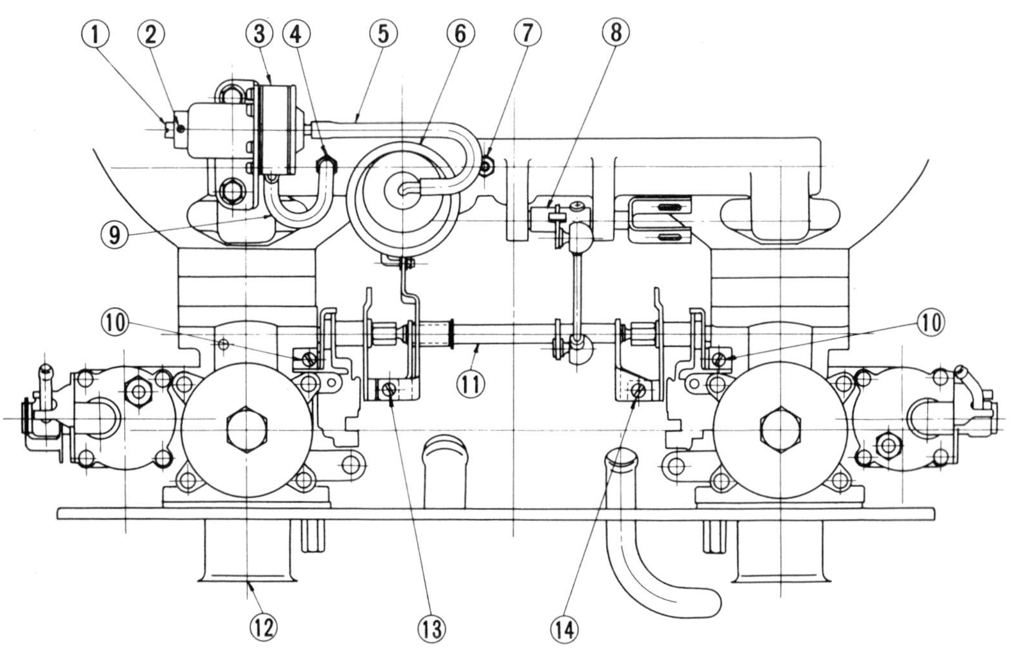


Locations of various throttle linkage and carburetor components on 1972 and earlier models

1. Vacuum adjusting screw
2. Lockscrew
3. Throttle control valve
4. Control valve manifold connection
5. Servo diaphragm vacuum tube
6. Servo diaphragm
7. A. B. valve connector
8. Auxiliary throttle shaft
9. Control valve vacuum tube
10. Throttle adjusting screw
11. Throttle shaft
12. Airhorn
13. Opener adjusting screw
14. Balance screw

uum tube in its place, in order to apply full vacuum to the diaphragm.

4. Adjust the opener adjusting screw to give an rpm of 1,200.

5. Using the flow meter as described above, adjust the balance screw so that the airflow is equal for the carburetors.

6. Disconnect and then reconnect the servo diaphragm vacuum tube where it is connected to the manifold. Check the rpm and flow rates and, if necessary, readjust as in Steps 4 and 5.

7. Return the vacuum hoses to their original positions, disconnect the diaphragm tube from the manifold and reconnect it to the control valve, and then reconnect the control valve hose to the manifold connection.

8. *If a CO meter is available,* adjust CO as follows:

a. Disconnect the air pump belt so that the pump will be inoperative.

Idle mixture adjusting nut—1972 and earlier models

b. Gently tighten the mixture adjusting nuts located under the carburetors until they hit their stops.

c. Turn both nuts equally outward until CO is 5–7%.

d. Reconnect the air pump belt.

### 1973–74

1. Run the engine until it is at operating temperature. Remove the air cleaner.

2. Loosen the throttle adjusting screw all the way. Except on 1974 automatics, loosen the throttle opener adjusting screw all the way.

3. Adjust the idle speed to 750 rpm using the idle speed adjusting screw. On automatic transmission models, securely apply the parking brake and then put the transmission in gear. Then, adjust the idle speed adjusting screw to bring the idle to 600 rpm. Return the selector to "N" position.

4. With 260-Z automatic transmission models, proceed to Step 7 as these cars do not employ a throttle opener control valve.

5. Disconnect the hose which runs between the vacuum control valve and the servo diaphragm. Do the same with the hose running between the control valve and the intake manifold.

6. Connect a longer hose of the same diameter between the servo diaphragm and the open connector on the manifold.

7. On all but 1974 260-Z automatics, adjust the throttle opener adjusting screw for 1,400 rpm. On automatic 260-Zs, do the same with the fast idle adjusting screw.

8. Apply a flow meter briefly to the front carburetor intake. Turn the adjusting screw on the flow meter and align

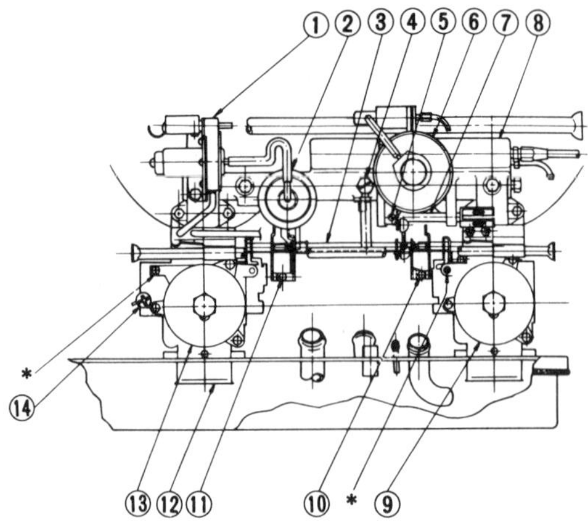


Locations of various throttle linkage components on 1973 and later models

1. Throttle opener control valve
2. Servo diaphragm
3. Throttle shaft
4. Idle speed adjusting screw
5. Fast idle screw
6. E.G.R. valve
7. Auxiliary throttle shaft
8. Balance tube
9. Rear carburetor
10. Balance adjusting screw
11. Throttle opener adjusting screw
12. Airhorn
13. Front carburetor
14. Idle mixture adjusting screw

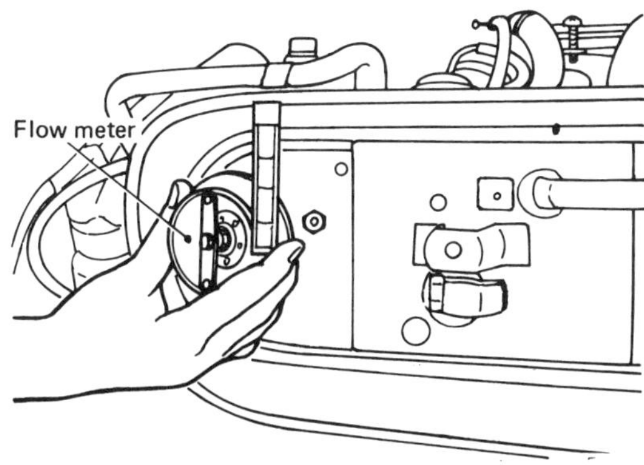


Measuring airflow with flow meter

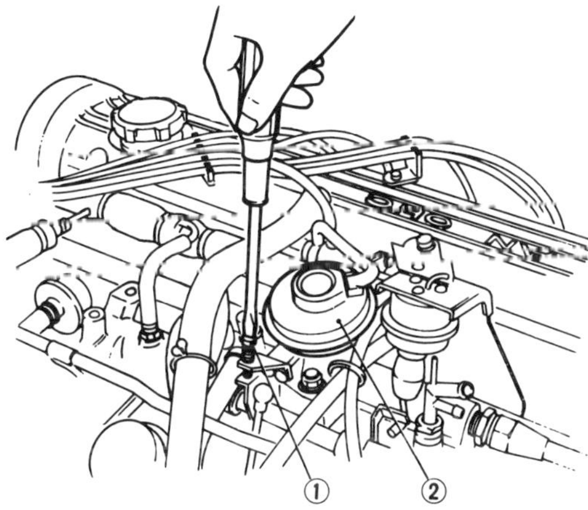


Location of fast idle screw on 1974 automatics

1. Fast idle screw 2. E.G.R. valve

the upper end of the float with the scale. Then, tighten the screw.

9. Apply the meter to the rear carburetor air intake and adjust the balance adjusting screw until the float in the meter is aligned with the scale.

10. Reinstall the air cleaner, connecting the vacuum motor to the temperature sensor with the vacuum hose.

11. Readjust the engine speed to 1,400 rpm as in Step 7.

12. Raise the engine speed briefly to 3,000 rpm. Then, raise it to 1,700 rpm with the throttle opener or fast idle screw (depending on the model as specified above). Finally, gradually lower the speed down to 1,400 rpm.

13. Disconnect the air pump check valve hose and plug the check valve.

14. With a CO meter, adjust the CO to 1.0–1.6% with manual transmission; 0.6–1.2% with automatics (in Neutral). This adjustment is made at the idle mixture adjusting screw.

15. On all cars but 260-Z automatics, disconnect the servo diaphragm vacuum for two to three seconds and then reconnect it. Make sure that the rpm returns to 1,400. If not, readjust it at the throttle opener adjusting screw.

16. On all but 1974 260-Zs, remove the long vacuum hose and reconnect the hoses so that one runs from the manifold to the throttle opener control valve and the other runs from the end of the control valve to the servo. On late model automatics, turn the fast idle screw out until there is a clearance of 0.078 in. (2 mm) between the lever and the tip of the screw.

17. Race the engine several times to verify that the idle speed is correct. Readjust it if necessary.

18. Unplug the check valve and reconnect the hose.

19. Measure the CO percentage and make sure that it is below 2.7%.

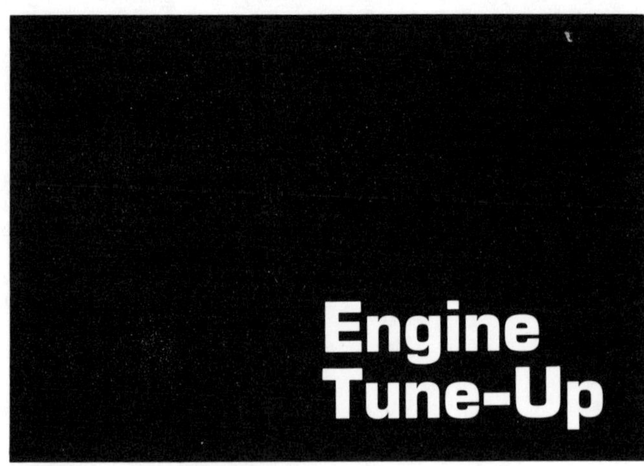


Engine tune-up is a procedure performed to restore engine performance, deteriorated due to normal wear and loss of adjustment. The three major areas considered in a routine tune-up are compression, ignition, and carburetion, although valve adjustment may be included.

A tune-up is performed in three steps: *analysis*, in which it is determined whether normal wear is responsible for performance loss, and which parts require replacement or service; *parts replacement or service*; and *adjustment*, in which engine adjustments are returned to original specifications. Since the advent of emission control equipment, precision adjustment has become increasingly critical, in order to maintain pollutant emission levels.

## Analysis

The procedures below are used to indicate where adjustments, parts service or replacement are necessary within the realm of a normal tune-up. If, following these tests, all systems appear to be functioning properly, proceed to the Troubleshooting Section for further diagnosis.

—Remove all spark plugs, noting the cylinder in which they were installed. Remove the air cleaner, and position the throttle and choke in the full open position. Disconnect the coil high tension lead from the coil and the distributor cap. Insert a compression gauge into the spark plug port of each cylinder, in succession, and crank the engine with the starter to obtain the highest possible reading. Record the readings, and compare the highest to the lowest on the compression pressure limit chart. If the difference exceeds the limits on the chart, or if all readings are excessively low, proceed to a wet compression check (see Troubleshooting Section).

| *Maxi. Press. Lbs. Sq. In.* | *Min. Press. Lbs. Sq. In.* | *Max. Press. Lbs. Sq. In.* | *Min. Press. Lbs. Sq. In.* |
|---|---|---|---|
| 134 | 101 | 188 | 141 |
| 136 | 102 | 190 | 142 |
| 138 | 104 | 192 | 144 |
| 140 | 105 | 194 | 145 |
| 142 | 107 | 196 | 147 |
| 146 | 110 | 198 | 148 |
| 148 | 111 | 200 | 150 |
| 150 | 113 | 202 | 151 |
| 152 | 114 | 204 | 153 |
| 154 | 115 | 206 | 154 |
| 156 | 117 | 208 | 156 |
| 158 | 118 | 210 | 157 |
| 160 | 120 | 212 | 158 |
| 162 | 121 | 214 | 160 |
| 164 | 123 | 216 | 162 |
| 166 | 124 | 218 | 163 |
| 168 | 126 | 220 | 165 |
| 170 | 127 | 222 | 166 |
| 172 | 129 | 224 | 168 |
| 174 | 131 | 226 | 169 |
| 176 | 132 | 228 | 171 |
| 178 | 133 | 230 | 172 |
| 180 | 135 | 232 | 174 |
| 182 | 136 | 234 | 175 |
| 184 | 138 | 236 | 177 |
| 186 | 140 | 238 | 178 |

**Compression pressure limits**
(© Buick Div. G.M. Corp.)

—Evaluate the spark plugs according to the spark plug chart in the Troubleshooting Section, and proceed as indicated in the chart.

—Remove the distributor cap, and inspect it inside and out for cracks and/or carbon tracks, and inside for excessive wear or burning of the rotor contacts. If any of these faults are evident, the cap must be replaced.

—Check the breaker points for burning, pitting or wear, and the contact heel resting on the distributor cam for excessive wear. If defects are noted, replace the entire breaker point set.

—Remove and inspect the rotor. If the contacts are burned or worn, or if the rotor is excessively loose on the distributor shaft (where applicable), the rotor must be replaced.

—Inspect the spark plug leads and the coil high tension lead for cracks or brittleness. If any of the wires appear defective, the entire set should be replaced.

—Check the air filter to ensure that it is functioning properly.

## Parts Replacement and Service

The determination of whether to replace or service parts is at the mechanic's discretion; however, it is suggested that any parts in questionable condition be replaced rather than reused.

—Clean and regap, or replace, the spark plugs as needed. Lightly coat the threads with engine oil and install the plugs. CAUTION: *Do not over-torque taper-seat spark plugs, or plugs being installed in aluminum cylinder heads.*

SPARK PLUG TORQUE

| *Thread size* | *Cast-Iron Heads* | *Aluminum Heads* |
|---|---|---|
| 10 mm. | 14 | 11 |
| 14 mm. | 30 | 27 |
| 18 mm. | 34* | 32 |
| 7/8 in.—18 | 37 | 35 |

* 17 ft. lbs. for tapered plugs using no gaskets.

—If the distributor cap is to be reused, clean the inside with a dry rag, and remove corrosion from the rotor contact points with fine emery cloth. Remove the spark plug wires one by one, and clean the wire ends and the inside of the towers. If the boots are loose, they should be replaced.

If the cap is to be replaced, transfer the wires one by one, cleaning the wire ends and replacing the boots if necessary.

—If the original points are to remain in service, clean them lightly with emery cloth, lubricate the contact heel with grease specifically designed for this purpose. Rotate the crankshaft until the heel rests on a high point of the distributor cam, and adjust the point gap to specifications.

When replacing the points, remove the original points and condenser, and wipe out the inside of the distributor housing with a clean, dry rag. Lightly lubricate the contact heel and pivot point, and install the points and condenser. Rotate the crankshaft until the heel rests on a high point of the distributor cam, and adjust the point gap to specifications. NOTE: *Always replace the condenser when changing the points.*

—If the rotor is to be reused, clean the contacts with solvent. Do not alter the spring tension of the rotor center contact. Install the rotor and the distributor cap.

—Replace the coil high tension lead and/or the spark plug leads as necessary.

—Clean the carburetor using a spray solvent (e.g., Gumout Spray). Remove the varnish from the throttle bores, and clean the linkage. Disconnect and plug the fuel line, and run the engine until it runs out of fuel. Partially fill the float chamber with solvent, and reconnect the fuel line. In extreme cases, the jets can be pressure flushed by inserting a rubber plug into the float vent, running the spray nozzle through it, and spraying the solvent until it squirts out of the venturi fuel dump.

—Clean and tighten all wiring connections in the primary electrical circuit.

### Additional Services

The following services *should* be performed in conjunction with a routine tune-up to ensure efficient performance.

—Inspect the battery and fill to the proper level with distilled water. Remove the cable clamps, clean clamps and posts thoroughly, coat the posts lightly with petroleum jelly, reinstall and tighten.

—Inspect all belts, replace and/or adjust as necessary.

—Test the PCV valve (if so equipped), and clean or replace as indicated. Clean all crankcase ventilation hoses, or replace if cracked or hardened.

—Adjust the valves (if necessary) to manufacturer's specifications.

## Adjustments

—Connect a dwell-tachometer between the distributor primary lead and ground. Remove the distributor cap and rotor (unless equipped with Delco externally adjustable distributor). With the ignition off, crank the engine with a remote starter switch and measure the point dwell angle. Adjust the dwell angle to specifications. NOTE: *Increasing the gap decreases the dwell angle and vice-versa.* Install the rotor and distributor cap.

—Connect a timing light according to the manufacturer's specifications. Identify the proper timing marks with chalk or paint. NOTE: *Luminescent (day-glo) paint is excellent for this purpose.* Start the engine, and run it until it reaches operating temperature. Disconnect and plug any distributor vacuum lines, and adjust idle to the speed required to adjust timing, according to specifications. Loosen the distributor clamp and adjust timing to specifications by rotating the distributor in the engine. NOTE: *To advance timing, rotate distributor opposite normal direction of rotor rotation, and vice-versa.*

—Synchronize the throttles and mixture of multiple carburetors (if so equipped) according to procedures given in the individual car sections.

—Adjust the idle speed, mixture, and idle quality, as specified in the car sections. Final idle adjustments should be made with the air cleaner installed. CAUTION: *Due to strict emission control requirements on 1969 and later models, special test equipment (CO meter, SUN Tester) may be necessary to properly adjust idle mixture to specifications.*

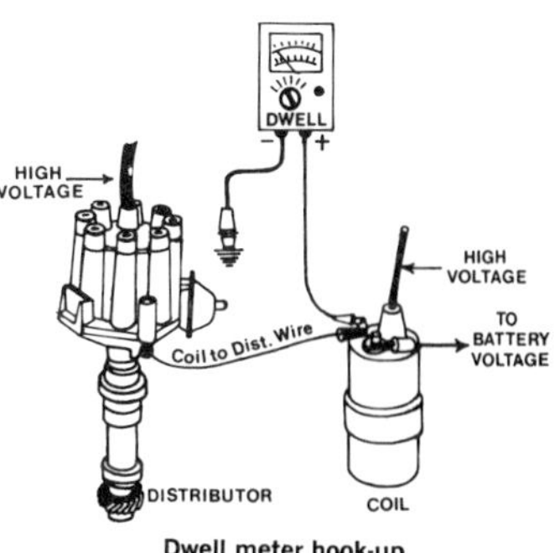

Dwell meter hook-up

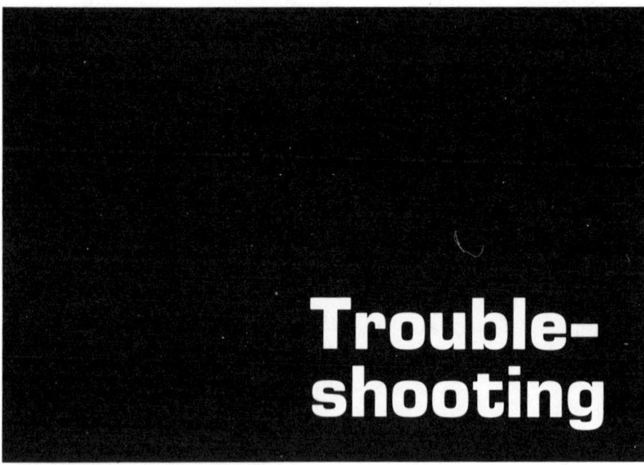


The following section is designed to aid in the rapid diagnosis of engine problems. The systematic format is used to diagnose problems ranging from engine starting difficulties to the need for engine overhaul. It is assumed that the user is equipped with basic hand tools and test equipment (tach-dwell meter, timing light, voltmeter, and ohmmeter).

Troubleshooting is divided into two sections. The first, *General Diagnosis*, is used to locate the problem area. In the second, *Specific Diagnosis*, the problem is systematically evaluated.

## *General Diagnosis*

| *PROBLEM: Symptom* | *Begin diagnosis at Section Two, Number ———* |
|---|---|
| *Engine won't start:* | |
| Starter doesn't turn | 1.1, 2.1 |
| Starter turns, engine doesn't | 2.1 |
| Starter turns engine very slowly | 1.1, 2.4 |
| Starter turns engine normally | 3.1, 4.1 |
| Starter turns engine very quickly | 6.1 |
| Engine fires intermittently | 4.1 |
| Engine fires consistently | 5.1, 6.1 |
| *Engine runs poorly:* | |
| Hard starting | 3.1, 4.1, 5.1, 8.1 |
| Rough idle | 4.1, 5.1, 8.1 |
| Stalling | 3.1, 4.1, 5.1, 8.1 |
| Engine dies at high speeds | 4.1, 5.1 |
| Hesitation (on acceleration from standing stop) | 5.1, 8.1 |
| Poor pickup | 4.1, 5.1, 8.1 |
| Lack of power | 3.1, 4.1, 5.1, 8.1 |
| Backfire through the carburetor | 4.1, 8.1, 9.1 |
| Backfire through the exhaust | 4.1, 8.1, 9.1 |
| Blue exhaust gases | 6.1, 7.1 |
| Black exhaust gases | 5.1 |
| Running on (after the ignition is shut off) | 3.1, 8.1 |
| Susceptible to moisture | 4.1 |
| Engine misfires under load | 4.1, 7.1, 8.4, 9.1 |
| Engine misfires at speed | 4.1, 8.4 |
| Engine misfires at idle | 3.1, 4.1, 5.1, 7.1, 8.4 |

| *PROBLEM: Symptom* | *Probable Cause* |
|---|---|
| *Engine noises:* ① | |
| Metallic grind while starting | Starter drive not engaging completely |
| Constant grind or rumble | *Starter drive not releasing, worn main bearings |
| Constant knock | Worn connecting rod bearings |
| Knock under load | Fuel octane too low, worn connecting rod bearings |
| Double knock | Loose piston pin |
| Metallic tap | *Collapsed or sticky valve lifter, excessive valve clearance, excessive end play in a rotating shaft |
| Scrape | *Fan belt contacting a stationary surface |
| Tick while starting | S.U. electric fuel pump (normal), starter brushes |
| Constant tick | *Generator brushes, shreaded fan belt |
| Squeal | *Improperly tensioned fan belt |
| Hiss or roar | *Steam escaping through a leak in the cooling system or the radiator overflow vent |
| Whistle | *Vacuum leak |
| Wheeze | Loose or cracked spark plug |

①—It is extremely difficult to evaluate vehicle noises. While the above are general definitions of engine noises, those starred (*) should be considered as possibly originating elsewhere in the car. To aid diagnosis, the following list considers other potential sources of these sounds.

Metallic grind:
Throwout bearing; transmission gears, bearings, or synchronizers; differential bearings, gears; something metallic in contact with brake drum or disc.

Metallic tap:
U-joints; fan-to-radiator (or shroud) contact.

Scrape:
Brake shoe or pad dragging; tire to body contact; suspension contacting undercarriage or exhaust; something non-metallic contacting brake shoe or drum.

Tick:
Transmission gears; differential gears; lack of radio suppression; resonant vibration of body panels; windshield wiper motor or transmission; heater motor and blower.

Squeal:
Brake shoe or pad not fully releasing; tires (excessive wear, uneven wear, improper inflation); front or rear wheel alignment (most commonly due to improper toe-in).

Hiss or whistle:
Wind leaks (body or window); heater motor and blower fan.

Roar:
Wheel bearings; wind leaks (body and window).

## Specific Diagnosis

This section is arranged so that following each test, instructions are given to proceed to another, until a problem is diagnosed.

### INDEX

| Group | | Topic |
|---|---|---|
| 1 | * | Battery |
| 2 | * | Cranking system |
| 3 | * | Primary electrical system |
| 4 | * | Secondary electrical system |
| 5 | * | Fuel system |
| 6 | * | Engine compression |
| 7 | ** | Engine vacuum |
| 8 | ** | Secondary electrical system |
| 9 | ** | Valve train |
| 10 | ** | Exhaust system |
| 11 | ** | Cooling system |
| 12 | ** | Engine lubrication |

*—The engine need not be running.
**—The engine must be running.

### SAMPLE SECTION

| *Test and Procedure* | *Results and Indications* | *Proceed to* |
|---|---|---|
| 4.1—Check for spark: Hold each spark plug wire approximately ¼″ from ground with gloves or a heavy, dry rag. Crank the engine and observe the spark. | → If no spark is evident: | 4.2 |
| | → If spark is good in some cases: | 4.3 |
| | → If spark is good in all cases: | 4.6 |

### DIAGNOSIS

| | | |
|---|---|---|
| 1.1—Inspect the battery visually for case condition (corrosion, cracks) and water level. | If case is cracked, replace battery: | 1.4 |
| | If the case is intact, remove corrosion with a solution of baking soda and water (CAUTION: *do not get the solution into the battery*), and fill with water: | 1.2 |
| 1.2—Check the battery cable connections: Insert a screwdriver between the battery post and the cable clamp. Turn the headlights on high beam, and observe them as the screwdriver is gently twisted to ensure good metal to metal contact. | If the lights brighten, remove and clean the clamp and post; coat the post with petroleum jelly, install and tighten the clamp: | 1.4 |
| | If no improvement is noted: | 1.3 |
| 1.3—Test the state of charge of the battery using an individual cell tester or hydrometer. | If indicated, charge the battery. NOTE: *If no obvious reason exists for the low state of charge (i.e., battery age, prolonged storage), the charging system should be tested:* | 1.4 |

Testing battery cable connections using a screwdriver

| *Spec. Grav. Reading* | *Charged Condition* |
|---|---|
| 1.260-1.280 | Fully Charged |
| 1.230-1.250 | Three Quarter Charged |
| 1.200-1.220 | One Half Charged |
| 1.170-1.190 | One Quarter Charged |
| 1.140-1.160 | Just About Flat |
| 1.110-1.130 | All The Way Down |

State of battery charge

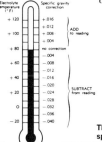

The effect of temperature on the specific gravity of battery electrolyte

| *Test and Procedure* | *Results and Indications* | *Proceed to* |
|---|---|---|
| 1.4—Visually inspect battery cables for cracking, bad connection to ground, or bad connection to starter. | If necessary, tighten connections or replace the cables: | 2.1 |

**Tests in Group 2 are performed with coil high tension lead disconnected to prevent accidental starting.**

| *Test and Procedure* | *Results and Indications* | *Proceed to* |
|---|---|---|
| 2.1—Test the starter motor and solenoid: Connect a jumper from the battery post of the solenoid (or relay) to the starter post of the solenoid (or relay). | If starter turns the engine normally: | 2.2 |
| | If the starter buzzes, or turns the engine very slowly: | 2.4 |
| | If no response, replace the solenoid (or relay). | 3.1 |
| | If the starter turns, but the engine doesn't, ensure that the flywheel ring gear is intact. If the gear is undamaged, replace the starter drive. | 3.1 |
| 2.2—Determine whether ignition override switches are functioning properly (clutch start switch, neutral safety switch), by connecting a jumper across the switch(es), and turning the ignition switch to "start". | If starter operates, adjust or replace switch: | 3.1 |
| | If the starter doesn't operate: | 2.3 |
| 2.3—Check the ignition switch "start" position: Connect a 12V test lamp between the starter post of the solenoid (or relay) and ground. Turn the ignition switch to the "start" position, and jiggle the key. | If the lamp doesn't light when the switch is turned, check the ignition switch for loose connections, cracked insulation, or broken wires. Repair or replace as necessary: | 3.1 |
| | If the lamp flickers when the key is jiggled, replace the ignition switch. | 3.3 |

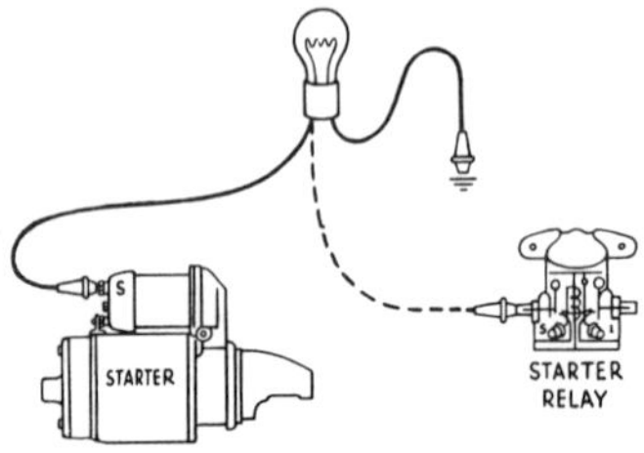

**Checking the ignition switch "start" position**

| *Test and Procedure* | *Results and Indications* | *Proceed to* |
|---|---|---|
| 2.4—Remove and bench test the starter, according to specifications in the car section. | If the starter does not meet specifications, repair or replace as needed: | 3.1 |
| | If the starter is operating properly: | 2.5 |
| 2.5—Determine whether the engine can turn freely: Remove the spark plugs, and check for water in the cylinders. Check for water on the dipstick, or oil in the radiator. Attempt to turn the engine using an 18″ flex drive and socket on the crankshaft pulley nut or bolt. | If the engine will turn freely only with the spark plugs out, and hydrostatic lock (water in the cylinders) is ruled out, check valve timing: | 9.2 |
| | If engine will not turn freely, and it is known that the clutch and transmission are free, the engine must be disassembled for further evaluation: | Next Chapter |

| *Tests and Procedures* | *Results and Indications* | *Proceed to* |
|---|---|---|
| 3.1—Check the ignition switch "on" position: Connect a jumper wire between the distributor side of the coil and ground, and a 12V test lamp between the switch side of the coil and ground. Remove the high tension lead from the coil. Turn the ignition switch on and jiggle the key. | If the lamp lights: | 3.2 |
| | If the lamp flickers when the key is jiggled, replace the ignition switch: | 3.3 |
| | If the lamp doesn't light, check for loose or open connections. If none are found, remove the ignition switch and check for continuity. If the switch is faulty, replace it: | 3.3 |

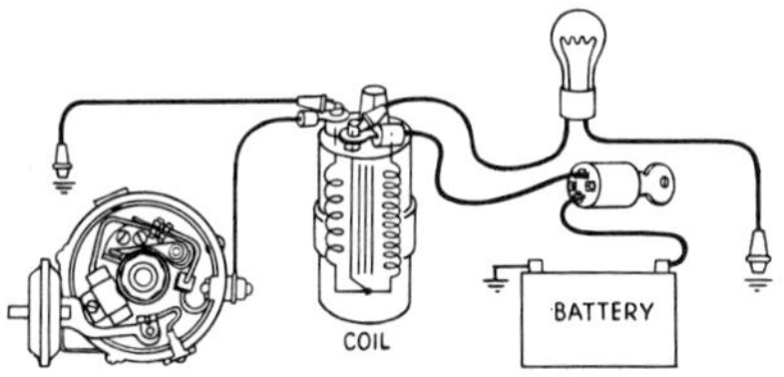

COIL
BATTERY

Checking the ignition switch "on" position

| | | |
|---|---|---|
| 3.2—Check the ballast resistor or resistance wire for an open circuit, using an ohmmeter. | Replace the resistor or the resistance wire if the resistance is zero. | 3.3 |
| 3.3—Visually inspect the breaker points for burning, pitting, or excessive wear. Gray coloring of the point contact surfaces is normal. Rotate the crankshaft until the contact heel rests on a high point of the distributor cam, and adjust the point gap to specifications. | If the breaker points are intact, clean the contact surfaces with fine emery cloth, and adjust the point gap to specifications. If pitted or worn, replace the points and condenser, and adjust the gap to specifications: NOTE: *Always lubricate the distributor cam according to manufacturer's recommendations when servicing the breaker points.* | 3.4 |
| 3.4—Connect a dwell meter between the distributor primary lead and ground. Crank the engine and observe the point dwell angle. | If necessary, adjust the point dwell angle: NOTE: *Increasing the point gap decreases the dwell angle, and vice-versa.* | 3.6 |
| | If dwell meter shows little or no reading: | 3.5 |

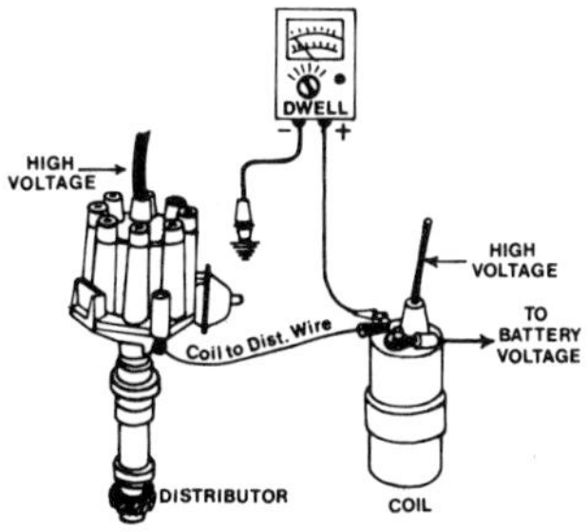

DWELL
HIGH VOLTAGE
HIGH VOLTAGE
TO BATTERY VOLTAGE
Coil to Dist. Wire
DISTRIBUTOR
COIL

Dwell meter hook-up

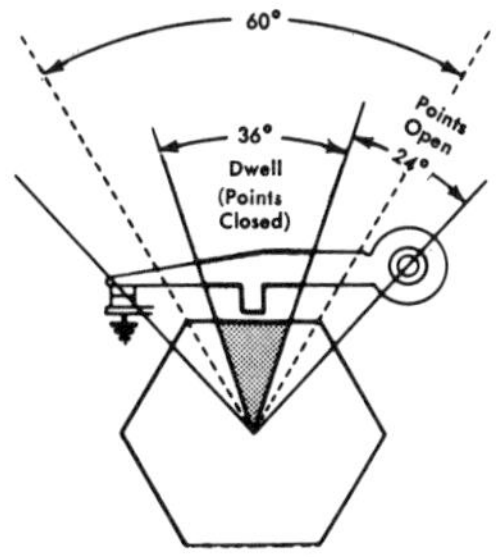

60°
36° Dwell (Points Closed)
Points Open 24°

Dwell angle

| | | |
|---|---|---|
| 3.5—Check the condenser for short: Connect an ohmmeter across the condenser body and the pigtail lead. | If any reading other than infinite resistance is noted, replace the condenser: | 3.6 |

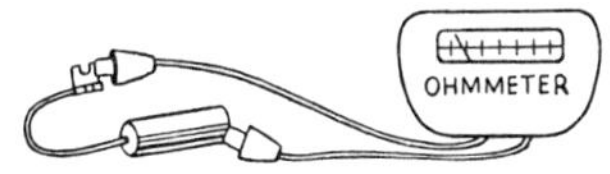

OHMMETER

Checking the condenser for short

| *Test and Procedure* | *Results and Indications* | *Proceed to* |
|---|---|---|
| 3.6—Test the coil primary resistance: Connect an ohmmeter across the coil primary terminals, and read the resistance on the low scale. Note whether an external ballast resistor or resistance wire is utilized.<br><br>Testing the coil primary resistance | Coils utilizing ballast resistors or resistance wires should have approximately 1.0Ω resistance; coils with internal resistors should have approximately 4.0Ω resistance. If values far from the above are noted, replace the coil: | 4.1 |
| 4.1—Check for spark: Hold each spark plug wire approximately ¼″ from ground with gloves or a heavy, dry rag. Crank the engine, and observe the spark. | If no spark is evident: | 4.2 |
| | If spark is good in some cylinders: | 4.3 |
| | If spark is good in all cylinders: | 4.6 |
| 4.2—Check for spark at the coil high tension lead: Remove the coil high tension lead from the distributor and position it approximately ¼″ from ground. Crank the engine and observe spark.<br>CAUTION: *This test should not be performed on cars equipped with transistorized ignition.* | If the spark is good and consistent: | 4.3 |
| | If the spark is good but intermittent, test the primary electrical system starting at 3.3: | 3.3 |
| | If the spark is weak or non-existent, replace the coil high tension lead, clean and tighten all connections and retest. If no improvement is noted: | 4.4 |
| 4.3—Visually inspect the distributor cap and rotor for burned or corroded contacts, cracks, carbon tracks, or moisture. Also check the fit of the rotor on the distributor shaft (where applicable). | If moisture is present, dry thoroughly, and retest per 4.1: | 4.1 |
| | If burned or excessively corroded contacts, cracks, or carbon tracks are noted, replace the defective part(s) and retest per 4.1: | 4.1 |
| | If the rotor and cap appear intact, or are only slightly corroded, clean the contacts thoroughly (including the cap towers and spark plug wire ends) and retest per 4.1: | |
| | If the spark is good in all cases: | 4.6 |
| | If the spark is poor in all cases: | 4.5 |
| 4.4—Check the coil secondary resistance: Connect an ohmmeter across the distributor side of the coil and the coil tower. Read the resistance on the high scale of the ohmmeter.<br><br>Testing the coil secondary resistance | The resistance of a satisfactory coil should be between 4KΩ and 10KΩ. If the resistance is considerably higher (i.e., 40KΩ) replace the coil, and retest per 4.1: NOTE: *This does not apply to high performance coils.* | 4.1 |

| *Test and Procedure* | *Results and Indications* | *Proceed to* |
|---|---|---|
| 4.5—Visually inspect the spark plug wires for cracking or brittleness. Ensure that no two wires are positioned so as to cause induction firing (adjacent and parallel). Remove each wire, one by one, and check resistance with an ohmmeter. | Replace any cracked or brittle wires. If any of the wires are defective, replace the entire set. Replace any wires with excessive resistance (over 8000Ω per foot for suppression wire), and separate any wires that might cause induction firing. | 4.6 |
| 4.6—Remove the spark plugs, noting the cylinders from which they were removed, and evaluate according to the chart below. | See below. | See below. |

| *Condition* | *Cause* | *Remedy* | *Proceed to* |
|---|---|---|---|
| Electrodes eroded, light brown deposits. | Normal wear. Normal wear is indicated by approximately .001″ wear per 1000 miles. | Clean and regap the spark plug if wear is not excessive: Replace the spark plug if excessively worn: | 4.7 |
| Carbon fouling (black, dry, fluffy deposits). | If present on one or two plugs: | | |
| | Faulty high tension lead(s). | Test the high tension leads: | 4.5 |
| | Burnt or sticking valve(s). | Check the valve train: (Clean and regap the plugs in either case.) | 9.1 |
| | If present on most or all plugs: Overly rich fuel mixture, due to restricted air filter, improper carburetor adjustment, improper choke or heat riser adjustment or operation. | Check the fuel system: | 5.1 |
| Oil fouling (wet black deposits) | Worn engine components. NOTE: *Oil fouling may occur in new or recently rebuilt engines until broken in.* | Check engine vacuum and compression: | 6.1 |
| | | Replace with new spark plug | |
| Lead fouling (gray, black, tan, or yellow deposits, which appear glazed or cinder-like). | Combustion by-products. | Clean and regap the plugs: (Use plugs of a different heat range if the problem recurs.) | 4.7 |

| Condition | Cause | Remedy | Proceed to |
|---|---|---|---|
| Gap bridging (deposits lodged between the electrodes). | Incomplete combustion, or transfer of deposits from the combustion chamber. | Replace the spark plugs: | 4.7 |
| Overheating (burnt electrodes, and extremely white insulator with small black spots). | Ignition timing advanced too far. | Adjust timing to specifications: | 8.2 |
| | Overly lean fuel mixture. | Check the fuel system: | 5.1 |
| | Spark plugs not seated properly. | Clean spark plug seat and install a new gasket washer: (Replace the spark plugs in all cases.) | 4.7 |
| Fused spot deposits on the insulator. | Combustion chamber blow-by. | Clean and regap the spark plugs: | 4.7 |
| Pre-ignition (melted or severely burned electrodes, blistered or cracked insulators, or metallic deposits on the insulator). | Incorrect spark plug heat range. | Replace with plugs of the proper heat range: | 4.7 |
| | Ignition timing advanced too far. | Adjust timing to specifications: | 8.2 |
| | Spark plugs not being cooled efficiently. | Clean the spark plug seat, and check the cooling system: | 11.1 |
| | Fuel mixture too lean. | Check the fuel system: | 5.1 |
| | Poor compression. | Check compression: | 6.1 |
| | Fuel grade too low. | Use higher octane fuel: | 4.7 |

| Test and Procedure | Results and Indications | Proceed to |
|---|---|---|
| 4.7—Determine the static ignition timing: Using the flywheel or crankshaft pulley timing marks as a guide, locate top dead center on the *compression* stroke of the No. 1 cylinder. Remove the distributor cap. | Adjust the distributor so that the rotor points toward the No. 1 tower in the distributor cap, and the points are just opening: | 4.8 |
| 4.8—Check coil polarity: Connect a voltmeter negative lead to the coil high tension lead, and the positive lead to ground (NOTE: *reverse the hook-up for positive ground cars*). Crank the engine momentarily. (Checking coil polarity) | If the voltmeter reads up-scale, the polarity is correct: | 5.1 |
| | If the voltmeter reads down-scale, reverse the coil polarity (switch the primary leads): | 5.1 |

| *Test and Procedure* | *Results and Indications* | *Proceed to* |
|---|---|---|
| 5.1—Determine that the air filter is functioning efficiently: Hold paper elements up to a strong light, and attempt to see light through the filter. | Clean permanent air filters in gasoline (or manufacturer's recommendation), and allow to dry. Replace paper elements through which light cannot be seen: | 5.2 |
| 5.2—Determine whether a flooding condition exists: Flooding is identified by a strong gasoline odor, and excessive gasoline present in the throttle bore(s) of the carburetor. | If flooding is not evident: | 5.3 |
| | If flooding is evident, permit the gasoline to dry for a few moments and restart. If flooding doesn't recur: | 5.6 |
| | If flooding is persistant: | 5.5 |
| 5.3—Check that fuel is reaching the carburetor: Detach the fuel line at the carburetor inlet. Hold the end of the line in a cup (not styrofoam), and crank the engine. | If fuel flows smoothly: | 5.6 |
| | If fuel doesn't flow (NOTE: *Make sure that there is fuel in the tank*), or flows erratically: | 5.4 |
| 5.4—Test the fuel pump: Disconnect all fuel lines from the fuel pump. Hold a finger over the input fitting, crank the engine (with electric pump, turn the ignition or pump on); and feel for suction. | If suction is evident, blow out the fuel line to the tank with low pressure compressed air until bubbling is heard from the fuel filler neck. Also blow out the carburetor fuel line (both ends disconnected): | 5.6 |
| | If no suction is evident, replace or repair the fuel pump: | 5.6 |
| | NOTE: *Repeated oil fouling of the spark plugs, or a no-start condition, could be the result of a ruptured vacuum booster pump diaphragm, through which oil or gasoline is being drawn into the intake manifold (where applicable).* | |
| 5.5—Check the needle and seat: Tap the carburetor in the area of the needle and seat. | If flooding stops, a gasoline additive (e.g., Gumout) will often cure the problem: | 5.6 |
| | If flooding continues, check the fuel pump for excessive pressure at the carburetor (according to specifications). If the pressure is normal, the needle and seat must be removed and checked, and/or the float level adjusted: | 5.6 |
| 5.6—Test the accelerator pump by looking into the throttle bores while operating the throttle. | If the accelerator pump appears to be operating normally: | 5.7 |
| | If the accelerator pump is not operating, the pump must be reconditioned. Where possible, service the pump with the carburetor(s) installed on the engine. If necessary, remove the carburetor. Prior to removal: | 5.7 |
| 5.7—Determine whether the carburetor main fuel system is functioning: Spray a commercial starting fluid into the carburetor while attempting to start the engine. | If the engine starts, runs for a few seconds, and dies: | 5.8 |
| | If the engine doesn't start: | 6.1 |

| *Test and Procedures* | *Results and Indications* | *Proceed to* |
|---|---|---|
| 5.8—Uncommon fuel system malfunctions: See below: | If the problem is solved: | 6.1 |
| | If the problem remains, remove and recondition the carburetor. | |

| *Condition* | *Indication* | *Test* | *Usual Weather Conditions* | *Remedy* |
|---|---|---|---|---|
| Vapor lock | Car will not restart shortly after running. | Cool the components of the fuel system until the engine starts. | Hot to very hot | Ensure that the exhaust manifold heat control valve is operating. Check with the vehicle manufacturer for the recommended solution to vapor lock on the model in question. |
| Carburetor icing | Car will not idle, stalls at low speeds. | Visually inspect the throttle plate area of the throttle bores for frost. | High humidity, 32-40° F. | Ensure that the exhaust manifold heat control valve is operating, and that the intake manifold heat riser is not blocked. |
| Water in the fuel | Engine sputters and stalls; may not start. | Pump a small amount of fuel into a glass jar. Allow to stand, and inspect for droplets or a layer of water. | High humidity, extreme temperature changes. | For droplets, use one or two cans of commercial gas dryer (Dry Gas) For a layer of water, the tank must be drained, and the fuel lines blown out with compressed air. |

| *Test and Procedure* | *Results and Indications* | *Proceed to* |
|---|---|---|
| 6.1—Test engine compression: Remove all spark plugs. Insert a compression gauge into a spark plug port, crank the engine to obtain the maximum reading, and record. | If compression is within limits on all cylinders: | 7.1 |
| | If gauge reading is extremely low on all cylinders: | 6.2 |
| | If gauge reading is low on one or two cylinders: (If gauge readings are identical and low on two or more adjacent cylinders, the head gasket must be replaced.) | 6.2 |

Testing compression
(© Chevrolet Div. G.M. Corp.)

| *Maxi. Press. Lbs. Sq. In.* | *Min. Press. Lbs. Sq. In.* | *Maxi. Press. Lbs. Sq. In.* | *Min. Press. Lbs. Sq. In.* | *Max. Press. Lbs. Sq. In.* | *Min. Press. Lbs. Sq. In.* | *Max. Press. Lbs. Sq. In.* | *Min. Press. Lbs. Sq. In.* |
|---|---|---|---|---|---|---|---|
| 134 | 101 | 162 | 121 | 188 | 141 | 214 | 160 |
| 136 | 102 | 164 | 123 | 190 | 142 | 216 | 162 |
| 138 | 104 | 166 | 124 | 192 | 144 | 218 | 163 |
| 140 | 105 | 168 | 126 | 194 | 145 | 220 | 165 |
| 142 | 107 | 170 | 127 | 196 | 147 | 222 | 166 |
| 146 | 110 | 172 | 129 | 198 | 148 | 224 | 168 |
| 148 | 111 | 174 | 131 | 200 | 150 | 226 | 169 |
| 150 | 113 | 176 | 132 | 202 | 151 | 228 | 171 |
| 152 | 114 | 178 | 133 | 204 | 153 | 230 | 172 |
| 154 | 115 | 180 | 135 | 206 | 154 | 232 | 174 |
| 156 | 117 | 182 | 136 | 208 | 156 | 234 | 175 |
| 158 | 118 | 184 | 138 | 210 | 157 | 236 | 177 |
| 160 | 120 | 186 | 140 | 212 | 158 | 238 | 178 |

Compression pressure limits
(© Buick Div. G.M. Corp.)

| *Test and Procedure* | *Results and Indications* | *Proceed to* |
|---|---|---|
| 6.2—Test engine compression (wet): Squirt approximately 30 cc. of engine oil into each cylinder, and retest per 6.1. | If the readings improve, worn or cracked rings or broken pistons are indicated:<br>If the readings do not improve, burned or excessively carboned valves or a jumped timing chain are indicated:<br>NOTE: *A jumped timing chain is often indicated by difficult cranking.* | Next Chapter<br><br>7.1 |
| 7.1—Perform a vacuum check of the engine: Attach a vacuum gauge to the intake manifold beyond the throttle plate. Start the engine, and observe the action of the needle over the range of engine speeds. | See below. | See below |

| *Reading* | *Indications* | *Proceed to* |
|---|---|---|
|  Steady, from 17-22 in. Hg. | Normal. | 8.1 |
|  Low and steady. | Late ignition or valve timing, or low compression: | 6.1 |
|  Very low | Vacuum leak: | 7.2 |
|  Needle fluctuates as engine speed increases. | Ignition miss, blown cylinder head gasket, leaking valve or weak valve spring: | 6.1, 8.3 |
|  Gradual drop in reading at idle. | Excessive back pressure in the exhaust system: | 10.1 |
|  Intermittent fluctuation at idle. | Ignition miss, sticking valve: | 8.3, 9.1 |
|  Drifting needle. | Improper idle mixture adjustment, carburetors not synchronized (where applicable), or minor intake leak. Synchronize the carburetors, adjust the idle, and retest. If the condition persists: | 7.2 |
|  High and steady. | Early ignition timing: | 8.2 |

| *Test and Procedure* | *Results and Indications* | *Proceed to* |
|---|---|---|
| 7.2—Attach a vacuum gauge per 7.1, and test for an intake manifold leak. Squirt a small amount of oil around the intake manifold gaskets, carburetor gaskets, plugs and fittings. Observe the action of the vacuum gauge. | If the reading improves, replace the indicated gasket, or seal the indicated fitting or plug:<br>If the reading remains low: | 8.1<br>7.3 |
| 7.3—Test all vacuum hoses and accessories for leaks as described in 7.2. Also check the carburetor body (dashpots, automatic choke mechanism, throttle shafts) for leaks in the same manner. | If the reading improves, service or replace the offending part(s):<br>If the reading remains low: | 8.1<br>6.1 |
| 8.1—Check the point dwell angle: Connect a dwell meter between the distributor primary wire and ground. Start the engine, and observe the dwell angle from idle to 3000 rpm. | If necessary, adjust the dwell angle. NOTE: *Increasing the point gap reduces the dwell angle and vice-versa.* If the dwell angle moves outside specifications as engine speed increases, the distributor should be removed and checked for cam accuracy, shaft endplay and concentricity, bushing wear, and adequate point arm tension (NOTE: *Most of these items may be checked with the distributor installed in the engine, using an oscilloscope*): | 8.2 |
| 8.2—Connect a timing light (per manufacturer's recommendation) and check the dynamic ignition timing. Disconnect and plug the vacuum hose(s) to the distributor if specified, start the engine, and observe the timing marks at the specified engine speed. | If the timing is not correct, adjust to specifications by rotating the distributor in the engine: (Advance timing by rotating distributor opposite normal direction of rotor rotation, retard timing by rotating distributor in same direction as rotor rotation.) | 8.3 |
| 8.3—Check the operation of the distributor advance mechanism(s): To test the mechanical advance, disconnect all but the mechanical advance, and observe the timing marks with a timing light as the engine speed is increased from idle. If the mark moves smoothly, without hesitation, it may be assumed that the mechanical advance is functioning properly. To test vacuum advance and/or retard systems, alternately crimp and release the vacuum line, and observe the timing mark for movement. If movement is noted, the system is operating. | If the systems are functioning:<br>If the systems are not functioning, remove the distributor, and test on a distributor tester: | 8.4<br>8.4 |
| 8.4—Locate an ignition miss: With the engine running, remove each spark plug wire, one by one, until one is found that doesn't cause the engine to roughen and slow down. | When the missing cylinder is identified: | 4.1 |

| *Test and Procedure* | *Results and Indications* | *Proceed to* |
|---|---|---|
| 9.1—Evaluate the valve train: Remove the valve cover, and ensure that the valves are adjusted to specifications. A mechanic's stethoscope may be used to aid in the diagnosis of the valve train. By pushing the probe on or near push rods or rockers, valve noise often can be isolated. A timing light also may be used to diagnose valve problems. Connect the light according to manufacturer's recommendations, and start the engine. Vary the firing moment of the light by increasing the engine speed (and therefore the ignition advance), and moving the trigger from cylinder to cylinder. Observe the movement of each valve. | See below | See below |

| *Observation* | *Probable Cause* | *Remedy* | *Proceed to* |
|---|---|---|---|
| Metallic tap heard through the stethoscope. | Sticking hydraulic lifter or excessive valve clearance. | Adjust valve. If tap persists, remove and replace the lifter: | 10.1 |
| Metallic tap through the stethoscope, able to push the rocker arm (lifter side) down by hand. | Collapsed valve lifter. | Remove and replace the lifter: | 10.1 |
| Erratic, irregular motion of the valve stem.* | Sticking valve, burned valve. | Recondition the valve and/or valve guide: | Next Chapter |
| Eccentric motion of the pushrod at the rocker arm.* | Bent pushrod. | Replace the pushrod: | 10.1 |
| Valve retainer bounces as the valve closes.* | Weak valve spring or damper. | Remove and test the spring and damper. Replace if necessary: | 10.1 |

*—When observed with a timing light.

| *Test and Procedure* | *Results and Indications* | *Proceed to* |
|---|---|---|
| 9.2—Check the valve timing: Locate top dead center of the No. 1 piston, and install a degree wheel or tape on the crankshaft pulley or damper with zero corresponding to an index mark on the engine. Rotate the crankshaft in its direction of rotation, and observe the opening of the No. 1 cylinder intake valve. The opening should correspond with the correct mark on the degree wheel according to specifications. | If the timing is not correct, the timing cover must be removed for further investigation: | |

| *Test and Procedure* | *Results and Indications* | *Proceed to* |
|---|---|---|
| 10.1—Determine whether the exhaust manifold heat control valve is operating: Operate the valve by hand to determine whether it is free to move. If the valve is free, run the engine to operating temperature and observe the action of the valve, to ensure that it is opening. | If the valve sticks, spray it with a suitable solvent, open and close the valve to free it, and retest.<br>If the valve functions properly: | <br>10.2 |
| | If the valve does not free, or does not operate, replace the valve: | 10.2 |
| 10.2—Ensure that there are no exhaust restrictions: Visually inspect the exhaust system for kinks, dents, or crushing. Also note that gasses are flowing freely from the tailpipe at all engine speeds, indicating no restriction in the muffler or resonator. | Replace any damaged portion of the system: | 11.1 |
| 11.1—Visually inspect the fan belt for glazing, cracks, and fraying, and replace if necessary. Tighten the belt so that the longest span has approximately ½" play at its midpoint under thumb pressure. | Replace or tighten the fan belt as necessary: | 11.2 |

**Checking the fan belt tension**
(© Nissan Motor Co. Ltd.)

| *Test and Procedure* | *Results and Indications* | *Proceed to* |
|---|---|---|
| 11.2—Check the fluid level of the cooling system. | If full or slightly low, fill as necessary: | 11.5 |
| | If extremely low: | 11.3 |
| 11.3—Visually inspect the external portions of the cooling system (radiator, radiator hoses, thermostat elbow, water pump seals, heater hoses, etc.) for leaks. If none are found, pressurize the cooling system to 14-15 psi. | If cooling system holds the pressure: | 11.5 |
| | If cooling system loses pressure rapidly, reinspect external parts of the system for leaks under pressure. If none are found, check dipstick for coolant in crankcase. If no coolant is present, but pressure loss continues: | 11.4 |
| | If coolant is evident in crankcase, remove cylinder head(s), and check gasket(s). If gaskets are intact, block and cylinder head(s) should be checked for cracks or holes.<br>If the gasket(s) is blown, replace, and purge the crankcase of coolant: | <br>12.6 |
| | NOTE: *Occasionally, due to atmospheric and driving conditions, condensation of water can occur in the crankcase. This causes the oil to appear milky white. To remedy, run the engine until hot, and change the oil and oil filter.* | |

| *Test and Procedure* | *Results and Indication* | *Proceed to* |
|---|---|---|
| 11.4—Check for combustion leaks into the cooling system: Pressurize the cooling system as above. Start the engine, and observe the pressure gauge. If the needle fluctuates, remove each spark plug wire, one by one, noting which cylinder(s) reduce or eliminate the fluctuation.<br>Radiator pressure tester (© American Motors Corp.) | Cylinders which reduce or eliminate the fluctuation, when the spark plug wire is removed, are leaking into the cooling system. Replace the head gasket on the affected cylinder bank(s). | |
| 11.5—Check the radiator pressure cap: Attach a radiator pressure tester to the radiator cap (wet the seal prior to installation). Quickly pump up the pressure, noting the point at which the cap releases.<br>Testing the radiator pressure cap (© American Motors Corp.) | If the cap releases within ± 1 psi of the specified rating, it is operating properly: | 11.6 |
| | If the cap releases at more than ± 1 psi of the specified rating, it should be replaced: | 11.6 |
| 11.6—Test the thermostat: Start the engine cold, remove the radiator cap, and insert a thermometer into the radiator. Allow the engine to idle. After a short while, there will be a sudden, rapid increase in coolant temperature. The temperature at which this sharp rise stops is the thermostat opening temperature. | If the thermostat opens at or about the specified temperature: | 11.7 |
| | If the temperature doesn't increase:<br>(If the temperature increases slowly and gradually, replace the thermostat.) | 11.7 |
| 11.7—Check the water pump: Remove the thermostat elbow and the thermostat, disconnect the coil high tension lead (to prevent starting), and crank the engine momentarily. | If coolant flows, replace the thermostat and retest per 11.6: | 11.6 |
| | If coolant doesn't flow, reverse flush the cooling system to alleviate any blockage that might exist. If system is not blocked, and coolant will not flow, recondition the water pump. | — |
| 12.1—Check the oil pressure gauge or warning light: If the gauge shows low pressure, or the light is on, for no obvious reason, remove the oil pressure sender. Install an accurate oil pressure gauge and run the engine momentarily. | If oil pressure builds normally, run engine for a few moments to determine that it is functioning normally, and replace the sender. | — |
| | If the pressure remains low: | 12.2 |
| | If the pressure surges: | 12.3 |
| | If the oil pressure is zero: | 12.3 |

| *Test and Procedure* | *Results and Indications* | *Proceed to* |
|---|---|---|
| 12.2—Visually inspect the oil: If the oil is watery or very thin, milky, or foamy, replace the oil and oil filter. | If the oil is normal: | 12.3 |
| | If after replacing oil the pressure remains low: | 12.3 |
| | If after replacing oil the pressure becomes normal: | — |
| 12.3—Inspect the oil pressure relief valve and spring, to ensure that it is not sticking or stuck. Remove and thoroughly clean the valve, spring, and the valve body. 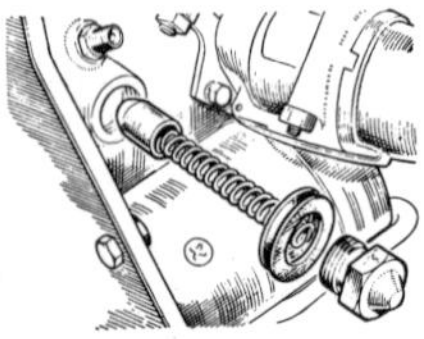<br>Oil pressure relief valve<br>(© British Leyland Motors) | If the oil pressure improves: | — |
| | If no improvement is noted: | 12.4 |
| 12.4—Check to ensure that the oil pump is not cavitating (sucking air instead of oil): See that the crankcase is neither over nor underfull, and that the pickup in the sump is in the proper position and free from sludge. | Fill or drain the crankcase to the proper capacity, and clean the pickup screen in solvent if necessary. If no improvement is noted: | 12.5 |
| 12.5—Inspect the oil pump drive and the oil pump: | If the pump drive or the oil pump appear to be defective, service as necessary and retest per 12.1: | 12.1 |
| | If the pump drive and pump appear to be operating normally, the engine should be disassembled to determine where blockage exists: | Next Chapter |
| 12.6—Purge the engine of ethylene glycol coolant: Completely drain the crankcase and the oil filter. Obtain a commercial butyl cellosolve base solvent, designated for this purpose, and follow the instructions precisely. Following this, install a new oil filter and refill the crankcase with the proper weight oil. The next oil and filter change should follow shortly thereafter (1000 miles). | | |

## Engine Electrical

*DISTRIBUTOR*

**Removal and Installation**

1. Pull off the spring clamps and remove the distributor cap. Pull the cap and wires out of the way.
2. On 1972 and earlier distributors, loosen the terminal screw and disconnect the primary lead. On later distributors, disconnect the plug which connects the engine and distributor wiring harnesses.
3. Carefully mark:
   a. The relationship between the distributor body and the engine.
   b. The position of the contact on the rotor and the edge of the distributor body.
4. Remove the hold-down bolt.
5. Carefully pull the distributor assembly out of the engine.
6. In reinstalling the distributor, first line up the distributor body with the engine and then carefully start the assembly down into the block.
7. Line up the mark on the edge of the distributor and the rotor contact. Carefully push the assembly down into the block until resistance is felt. If the distributor shaft is properly timed, the distributor will drop down until the flange which the mounting bolt passes through will be in contact with the top of the block and the shaft will be in a fixed position. If the shaft is not properly timed (engine turned while the distributor was out), it will be possible to turn the shaft, and the distributor flange will not fit against the block. If the shaft is not timed, carefully place very slight downward pressure on the distributor body while turning the shaft very slowly. When timing is correct, the shaft will lock and the distributor will move down into its normal position. The shaft is designed so that only the proper position will allow this.

## Firing Order

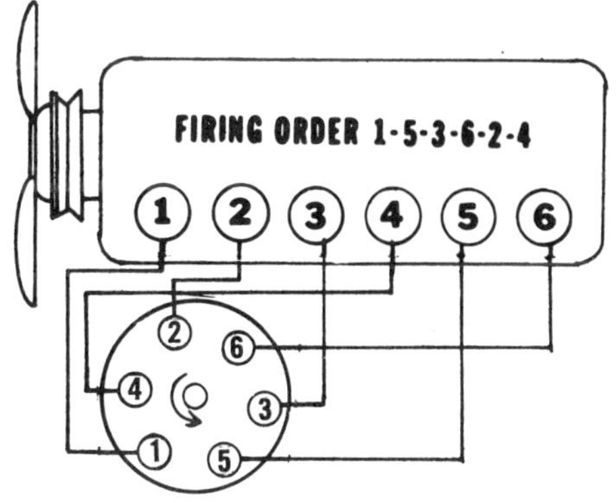


Firing order

8. When the shaft and distributor body are properly in place, loosely install the mounting bolt and reconnect the primary wiring.

9. Install the cap, and time the distributor as described in Chapter 2.

The firing order for all Datsun 240-Z and 260-Z engines is: 1-5-6-3-2-4. The No. 1 cylinder is the one closest to the fan.

## *ALTERNATOR*

### Alternator Precautions

1. When connecting jumper cables, make sure that there is good ventilation and verify that you are connecting positive (+) to positive (+) and negative (−) to negative (−) or the alternator will be damaged.

2. In all alternator and regulator testing procedures, double-check that you are making all the right connections according to the wiring diagrams, using the specified resistors where necessary.

3. On 1972 and earlier regulators, disconnect the regulator while removing the cover or adjusting the voltage screw and then reconnect it to measure voltage. Also, make sure to replace the cover and check regulator operation when adjustment is complete.

### Removal and Installation

1. Disconnect the negative (−) battery terminal. *Failure to do this will damage the electrical system.*

2. Disconnect the plug connecting alternator to the wiring harness. Disconnect the two lead wires.

3. Remove the alternator adjusting bolt, move the alternator toward the crankshaft pulley and remove the belt from the alternator pulley.

4. Remove the nut at the rear end of the lower mounting bolt and then slide the bolt out the front while supporting the alternator.

5. Pull the alternator out of the engine compartment.

To install the alternator:

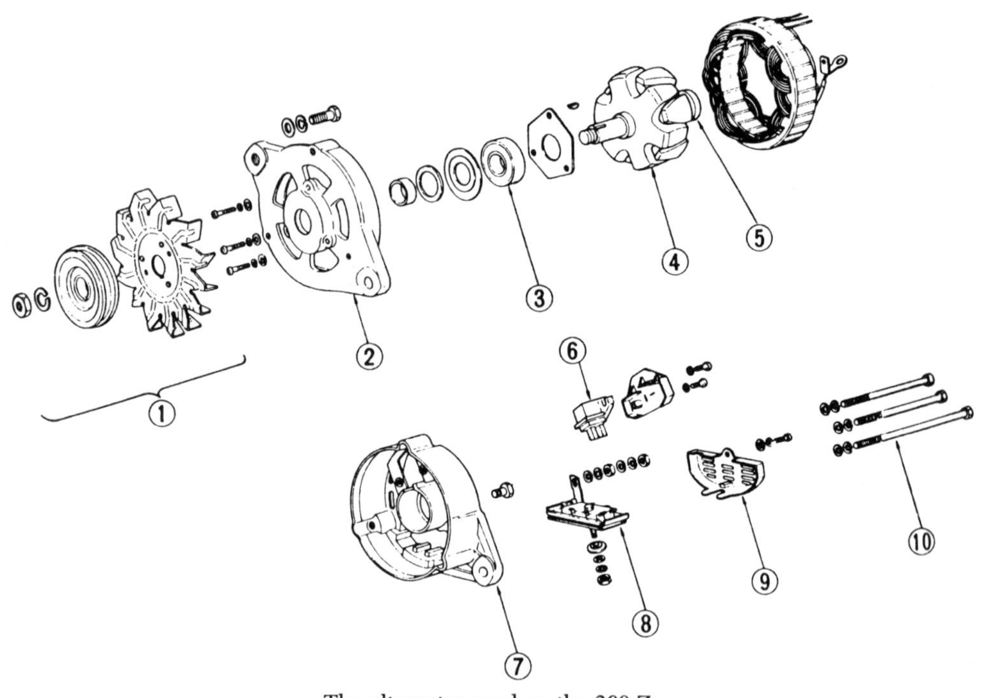


The alternator used on the 260-Z

1. Pulley assembly
2. Front cover
3. Front bearing
4. Rotor
5. Rear bearing
6. Brush assembly
7. Rear cover
8. Diode (and plate) assembly
9. Diode cover
10. Through-bolts

1. Put the alternator in position, lining up the two hinges with the bolt hole. Insert the bolt through the hinges and bolt hole from the front.
2. Install the nut at the rear of the mounting bolt.
3. Tilt the alternator until the adjusting bolt can be installed and install it.
4. Install and tension the V-belt as described in Chapter 1.
5. Connect the plug connecting the alternator to the wiring harness and the two lead wires.
6. Connect the negative battery cable.

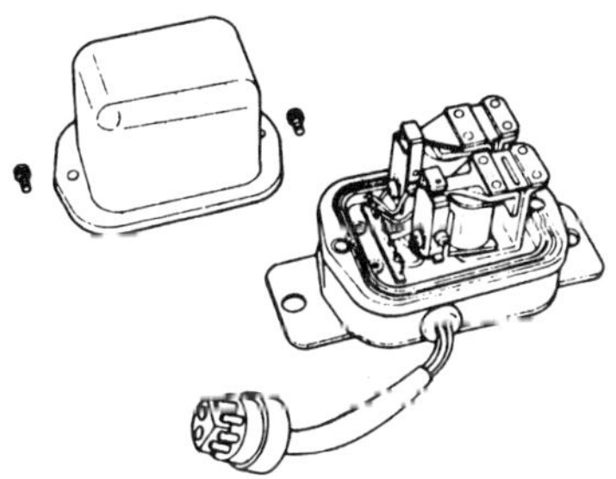
The regulator used on the 260-Z

*REGULATOR*

**Removal and Installation**

Disconnect the battery negative (−) cable. Then, unplug the connection between the regulator and wiring harness. Finally, remove the two mounting bolts and remove the regulator. To replace the regulator, reverse the removal procedures, but make sure to leave the battery disconnected until the last step.

**Voltage Adjustment**

1. Using an ammeter rated at 10 amps, a 30-volt voltmeter, and a resistor rated at

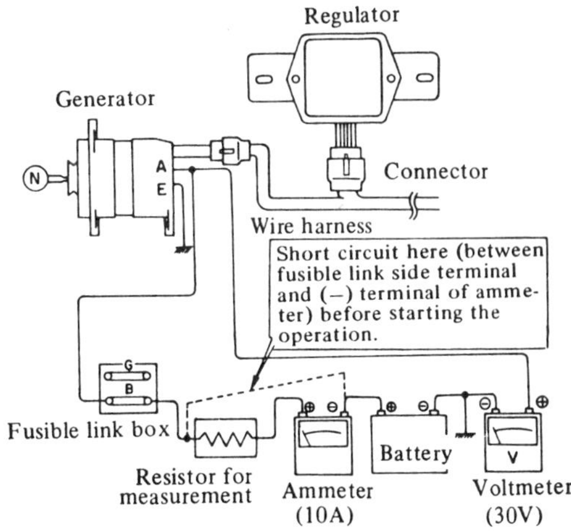

Hookup for voltage adjustment

.25 ohms, connect up a test circuit as shown in the illustrations. On 1972 and earlier models, the regulator must be disconnected and held with the connector plug downward.

2. MAKE SURE TO SHORT CIRCUIT BETWEEN THE FUSE BOX SIDE OF THE RESISTOR AND THE NEGATIVE TERMINAL OF THE AMMETER EVERY TIME THE ENGINE IS STARTED. Then, disconnect the short circuit wire during testing.
3. Turn off all accessories. Operate the engine at 2,500 rpm for several minutes.
4. Make sure that the ammeter reading is below 5 amps. If not, the battery must be charged or another battery substituted so that the test may be made with the amperage within this range. Stop the engine.
5. Wait several minutes, then start the engine and slowly increase rpm to 2,500 rpm.
6. Compare the reading with the chart,

| Temperature °C (°F) | Voltage V |
|---|---|
| −10 (14) | 14.75 to 15.25 |
| 0 (32) | 14.60 to 15.10 |
| 10 (50) | 14.45 to 14.95 |
| 20 (68) | 14.30 to 14.80 |
| 30 (86) | 14.15 to 14.65 |
| 40 (104) | 14.00 to 14.50 |

Temperature/Voltage chart for 1972–75 models

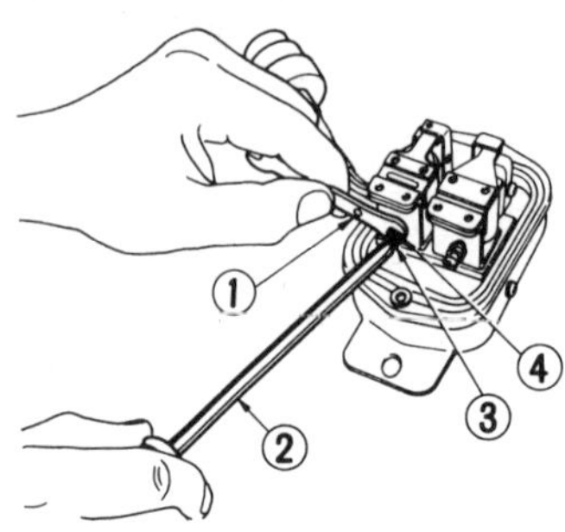

Adjusting regulated voltage

1. Wrench
2. Phillips screwdriver
3. Adjusting screw
4. Locknut

allowing for the temperature around the regulator.

7. If the voltage is not within the specified range, adjust it as follows:

a. Stop the engine, remove the cover, and on 1972 and earlier regulators, disconnect the regulator connector.

b. Loosen the locknut and adjust the voltage screw inward to increase, or outward to decrease voltage.

c. Start the engine (and reconnect connector on earlier models) and check the voltage. Repeat the adjustment process until voltage is correct, taking readings within the first minute of operation and disconnecting the connector on 1972 and earlier regulators while adjusting.

8. When adjustment is complete, tighten the locknut, replace the regulator cover, remount the regulator (on 1972 and earlier models) and remove all meters and test wiring. If the voltage cannot be brought within specifications, replace the regulator or have it repaired.

## *STARTER*

### Removal and Installation

1. Disconnect the negative battery cable.

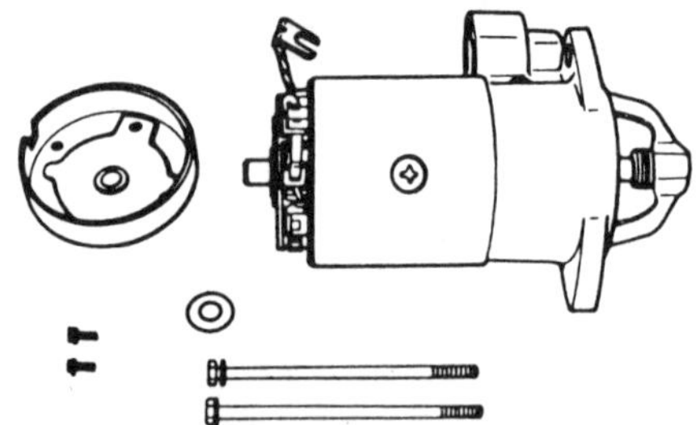
Parts of the brush cover

2. Disconnect the black wire with a yellow tracer and black battery cable from the terminals on the solenoid.

3. Remove the two bolts which secure the starter to the flywheel housing and pull the starter forward and out. To reinstall, reverse the removal procedure.

### Starter Overhaul

#### Brush Replacement

1. Loosen the locknut and remove the connection which goes to the "M" terminal of the solenoid.

2. Remove the brush cover through-bolts, and remove the cover.

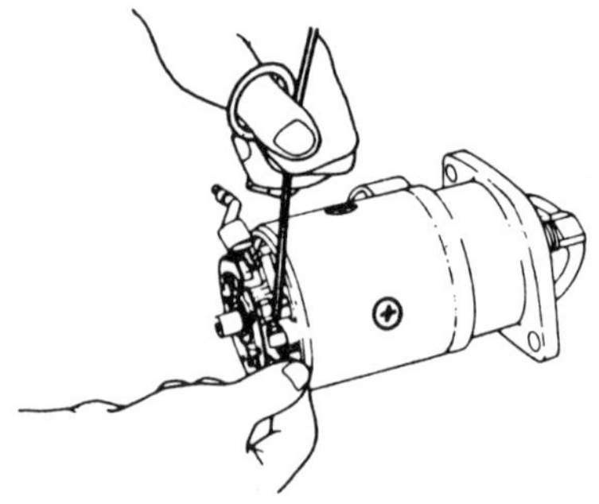
Lifting the brushes to clear the commutator

3. Lift the brushes free of the commutator and remove the brush holder.

4. Unsolder the electrical connections.

5. Remove the brushes going toward the center of the brush holder.

To reinstall the brushes:

1. Insert the brushes from the center of the holder.

2. Solder the connections.

3. Raise the brushes far enough to permit installing the brush holder over the commutator and install the holder.

4. Install the brush cover.

5. Remake the connection to the "M" terminal of the solenoid.

#### Drive Replacement

1. Loosen the locknut and remove the connection going to the "M" terminal of the solenoid. Remove the securing screws and remove the solenoid.

2. Remove the brush cover through-bolts and remove the cover assembly.

3. Lift the brushes to free them from the commutator and remove the brush holder.

4. Tap the yoke assembly lightly with

## Alternator and Regulator Specifications

| | ALTERNATOR | | | REGULATOR | | | | | | |
|---|---|---|---|---|---|---|---|---|---|---|
| | | | | | Field Relay | | | Regulator | | |
| Year | Part No. or Manu-facturer | Field Current @ 12 V | Out-put (amps) | Part No. or Manu-facturer | Air Gap in. (mm) | Point Gap in. (mm) | Volts to Close | Air Gap in. (mm) | Point Gap in. (mm) | Volts @ 68° F |
| 1970–72 | Hitachi LT145-35 | — | 45 | TL1Z-37 | .0315–.0394 (.8–1.0) | .0157–.0236 (.4–.6) | 8–10① | .0236–.0394 (.6–1.0) | .0118–.0157 (.3–.4) | 14.3–15.3 |
| 1973 | Hitachi L150-10 | — | 50 | TL1Z-57 | .0315–.0394 (.8–1.0) | .0157–.0236 (.4–.6) | 4.2–5.2② | .0236–.0394 (.6–1.0) | .0118–.0157 (.3–.4) | 14.3–15.3 |
| 1974 | Hitachi L150-10 | — | 50 | TL1Z-79 | .0315–.0394 (.8–1.0) | .0157–.0236 (.4–.6) | 4.2–5.2② | .024–.039 (.6–1.0) | .012–.016 (.3–.4) | 14.3–15.3 |

① At terminal A
② At terminal N

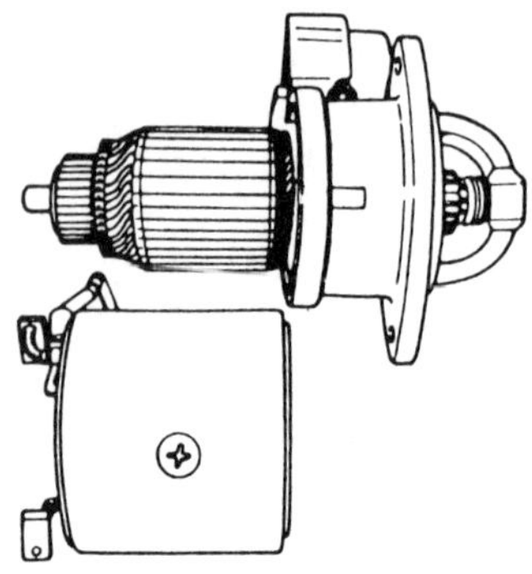

Removing the yoke assembly

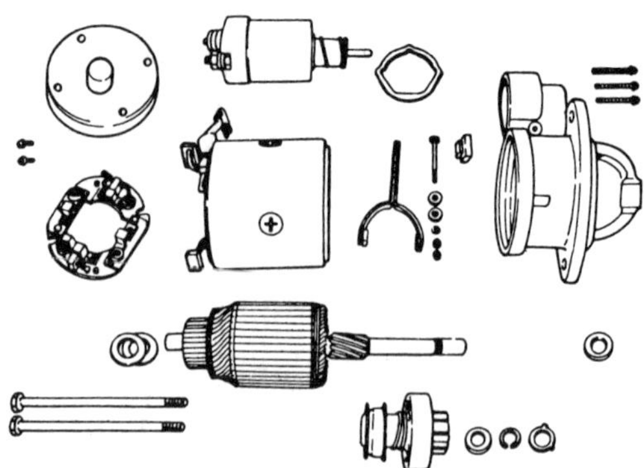

Disassembled view of the starter parts

a wooden hammer and remove it from the field and case.

5. Remove the nut and bolt which serve as a pin for the shift lever, carefully retaining the associated washers.

6. Remove the armature assembly and shift lever.

7. Push the stop ring (located at the end of the armature shaft) toward the clutch and remove the snap-ring. Remove the stop ring.

8. Remove the clutch assembly from the armature shaft.

To install the drive:

1. Install the clutch assembly onto the armature shaft.

2. Put the stop ring on and hold it toward the clutch while installing the snap-ring.

3. Install the armature assembly and shift lever into the yoke.

4. Install the washers, nut and bolt which serve as a shift lever pivot pin.

5. Install the field back onto the yoke assembly.

6. Lift the brushes and install the brush holder. Install the brush cover and through-bolts.

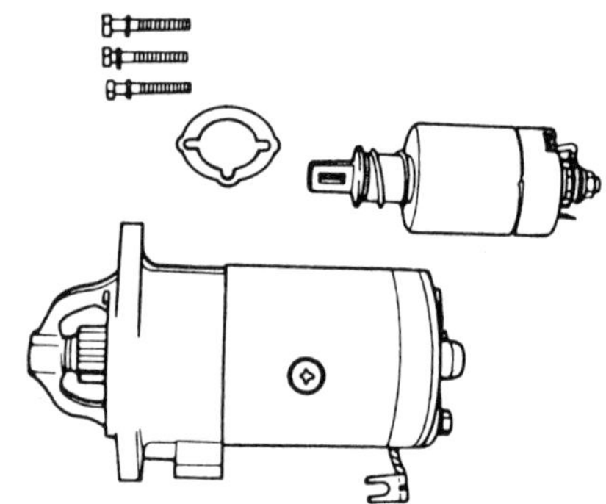

The solenoid and associated parts disassembled from the starter

7. Reinstall the solenoid with the securing screws and reconnect the wire to the "M" terminal of the solenoid.

### Solenoid Replacement

1. Loosen the locknut and remove the connection going to the "M" terminal of the solenoid.

## Battery and Starter Specifications

| | | *BATTERY* | | | *STARTER* | | | | | | |
|---|---|---|---|---|---|---|---|---|---|---|---|
| | | | | | *Lock Test* | | | *No-Load Test* | | | |
| *Year* | *Engine Displacement cu in. (cc)* | *Ampere Hour Capacity* | *Volts* | *Terminal Grounded* | *Amps* | *Volts* | *Torque ft lbs (kg)* | *Amps* | *Volts* | *RPM* | *Brush Spring Tension lbs (kg)* |
| 1970–72 | 146 (2393) | 60 | 12 | Neg | 460 | 6 | 10.1 (1.4) | 60 | 12 | 5000 | 1.76 (0.8) |
| 1973–74 | 146 (2393), 156 (2565) | 60 | 12 | Neg | 460① | 6② | 10.1 (1.4) | 60 | 12 | 5000③ | 3.53 (1.6) |

① Automatic—500 amps
② Automatic—5 volts
③ Automatic—6000 rpm

2. Remove the three securing screws and remove the solenoid.

To install, reverse the removal procedures.

## BATTERY

### Removal and Installation

1. Disconnect both battery terminals by loosening locknuts, slightly prying apart the connectors, and pulling them off.
2. Remove the clamp nuts and remove the battery clamps.
3. Remove the battery.

To install the battery:

1. Put the battery in position.
2. Install the clamps. Install the clamp nuts securely (looseness of the battery mounts can cause battery damage).
3. Clean the battery terminals and cable connections with a wire brush. Install and tighten the connections, and apply grease to protect them from dirt and corrosion.

# Engine Mechanical

## *DESIGN*

The L26 engine displaces 156.5 cubic inches (2565 cc) with a bore and stroke of 3.27 in. (83 mm) x 3.11 in. (79 mm). The L24 engine displaces 146.0 cubic inches (2393 cc) with bore and stroke of 3.27 in. (83 mm) x 2.90 in. (74 mm). Except for the change in the stroke of the piston, the engines are alike but use different valve seats.

The block is a single casting, providing seven main bearing supports for quiet and durable operation. The block is especially rigid due to the existence of a deep skirt around the crankshaft. Minimal weight is assured through the use of an overhead cam which eliminates the need for a tappet chamber. The main oil gallery runs parallel to the cylinder bores and an oil hole connects each main bearing with the gallery.

The crankshaft, made of forged steel, is precision balanced and fully counterweighted.

The pistons are of cast aluminum and are of the slipper skirt type with struts. The piston pin is a hollow steel fabrication, and is press fitted into the connecting rod.

The connecting rods are of forged steel and are pressure lubricated via oil passages drilled between the connecting rod and main bearing journals.

The cylinder head is of an aluminum alloy which is chosen partially for its excellent heat transfer. Replaceable valve seats are used in both engines. While

Cutaway of the 2400 cc engine

intake seats are aluminum and exhaust seats are iron in the L24 engine, the L26 engine employs brass and steel seats, respectively. The seats are hot press fitted. The heads also include five alloy brackets for support of the camshaft bearings.

The camshaft is of cast iron alloy and features five bearings. It is lubricated via holes through the support brackets which intersect with the main oil gallery for the head. The camshaft is driven via a double row roller chain. The chain tensioner is controlled through both spring and oil pressure.

The valve actuating mechanism consists of inner and outer springs and pivot type rocker arms which are driven directly off the camshaft. The elimination of pushrods substantially reduces valve train mass for stress-free operation at high rpm and long service life.

The intake manifold is cast aluminum while the exhaust manifold is of cast iron and is ram-tuned for minimum backpressure.

## *ENGINE REMOVAL AND INSTALLATION*

The instructions below provide for removal of the engine and transmission as a unit, as this makes the operation easier and faster, and transmission removal is easier after the engine is out.

All operations involving hoisting the engine-transmission unit should be done with extreme care and should be carefully planned beforehand. Read the procedure through before beginning. It is best to use fender covers so that the fenders will not be damaged during removal or installation.

1. Disconnect the battery cables.
2. Mark the location of each hood hinge on the hood to facilitate reinstallation.
3. Carefully support the hood so that its weight will not be resting on the hinge bolts. Then, remove the bolts.
4. Remove the hood with the help of an assistant.
5. Remove the air cleaner.
6. Drain the radiator and crankcase.
7. Disconnect both radiator hoses at the radiator. Remove the radiator mounting bolts and pull the radiator and shroud up and out of the engine compartment.
8. On automatic transmission models, remove the splash board, disconnect both oil cooler hoses at the cooler under the radiator, and disconnect the vacuum modulator hose from the manifold.

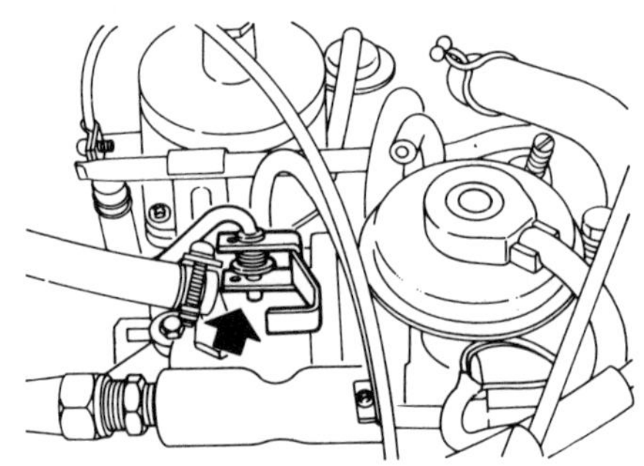

Disconnecting the accelerator linkage

9. Disconnect the accelerator linkage (see the illustration).
10. Disconnect the:
    a. battery ground cable at the engine;
    b. starter wiring;
    c. coil-to-distributor high-tension cable;
    d. primary wire to the distributor at the connection;

## General Engine Specifications

| *Year* | *Engine Displacement cu in. (cc)* | *Carburetor Type* | *Horsepower @ rpm (Gross)* | *Horsepower @ rpm (Net)* | *Bore x Stroke (in.) (mm)* | *Compression Ratio* | *Oil Pressure @ rpm (psi) (kg cm²)* |
|---|---|---|---|---|---|---|---|
| 1970–73 | 146 (2393) | Twin SU | 151 @ 5600 | 147.7 @ 4400 | 3.27 (83) x 2.90 (74) | 8.8 : 1 | 50–57 (3.5–4.0) @ 2000 |
| 1974 | 156 (2565) | Twin SU | 162 @ 5600 | 152 @ 4400 | 3.27 (83) x 3.11 (79) | 8.8 : 1 | 50–57 (3.5–4.0) @ 2000 |

## Valve Specifications

| Year | Engine Displacement cu in. (cc) | Seat Angle (deg) | Face Angle (deg) | Lift Intake in. (mm) | Lift Exhaust in. (mm) | Spring Test Pressure lbs @ in. (kg @ mm) | Spring Installed Height in. (mm) | Stem To Guide① Clearance in. (mm) Intake | Stem To Guide① Clearance in. (mm) Exhaust | Stem Diameter in. (mm) Intake | Stem Diameter in. (mm) Exhaust |
|---|---|---|---|---|---|---|---|---|---|---|---|
| 1970–72 | 146 (2393) | 45 | — | .413 (10.5) | .413 (10.5) | 108 @ 1.61② (49 @ 29.5) | 1.575③ (40.0) | .0008–.0021 (.020–.053) | .0016–.0029 (.040–.073) | .3136–.3142 (7.965–7.980) | .3128–.3134 (7.945–7.960) |
| 1973 | 146 (2393) | 45 | — | .433 (11) | .433 (11) | 108 @ 1.61② (49 @ 29.5) | 1.575③ (40.0) | .0008–.0021 (.020–.053) | .0016–.0029 (.040–.073) | .3114–.3138 (7.970–7.985) | .3128–.3134 (7.945–7.960) |
| 1974 | 156 (2565) | 45 | — | .433 (11) | .433 (11) | 108 @ 1.61② (49 @ 29.5) | 1.575③ (40.0) | .0005–.0021 (.020–.053) | .0016–.0029 (.040–.073) | .3100 (8.0) | .3100 (8.0) |

① Guides are replaceable
② Inner spring—56.2 @ 0.965 (25.5 @ 24.5)
③ Inner spring—1.380 (35.0)

## Crankshaft and Connecting Rod Specifications

All measurements are given in inches (mm)

| | | Crankshaft | | | | Connecting Rod | | |
|---|---|---|---|---|---|---|---|---|
| *Year* | *Engine Displace-ment cu in. (cc)* | *Main Brg Journal Dia* | *Main Brg Oil Clearance* | *Shaft End-Play* | *Thrust on No.* | *Journal Diameter* | *Oil Clearance* | *Side Clearance* |
| 1970–72 | 146 (2393) | 2.1631–2.1636 (54.924–54.945) | .0008–.0028 (.020–.072) | .0020–.0071 (.05–.18) | center | 1.9670–1.9675 (49.961–49.974) | .0006–.0022 (.014–.066) | .0079–.0118 (.20–.30) |
| 1973 | 146 (2393) | 2.1631–2.1636 (54.942–54.955) | .0008–.0028 (.020–.072) | .0020–.0071 (.05–.18) | center | 1.9670–1.9675 (49.961–49.974) | .0010–.0022 (.025–.055) | .0079–.0118 (.20–.30) |
| 1974 | 156 (2565) | 2.1631–2.1636 (54.942–54.955) | .0008–.0028 (.020–.072) | .0020–.0071 (.05–.18) | center | 1.9670–1.9675 (49.961–49.974) | .0010–.0022 (.025–.055) | .0079–.0118 (.20–.30) |

## Piston and Ring Specifications

All measurements in inches (mm)

| Year | Engine Displacement cu in. (cc) | Piston Clearance | Ring Gap | | | Ring Side Clearance | | |
|---|---|---|---|---|---|---|---|---|
| | | | Top Compression | Bottom Compression | Oil Control | Top Compression | Bottom Compression | Oil Control |
| 1970–72 | 146 (2393) | .0010–.0018 (.025–.045) | .0091–.0150 (.23–.38) | .0059–.0118 (.15–.30) | .0059–.0118 (.15–.30) | .0018–.0031 (.045–.080) | .0012–.0025 (.030–.063) | .0010–.0025 (.025–.063) |
| 1973 | 146 (2393) | .0010–.0018 (.025–.045) | .0091–.0150 (.23–.38) | .0059–.0118 (.15–.30) | .0059–.0118 (.15–.30) | .0018–.0031 (.045–.080) | .0012–.0028 (.030–.070) | 0 |
| 1974 | 156 (2565) | .0010–.0018 (.025–.045) | .0091–.0150 (.23–.38) | .0059–.0118 (.15–.30) | .0059–.0118 (.15–.30) | .0018–.0031 (.045–.080) | .0012–.0028 (.030–.070) | 0 |

## Torque Specifications

All readings in ft lbs (kg-m)

| *Year* | *Engine Displace-ment cu in. (cc)* | *Cylinder Head Bolts* | *Rod Bearing Bolts* | *Main Bearing Bolts* | *Crankshaft Pulley Bolt* | *Flywheel To Crankshaft Bolts* | *Manifold①* | | *Camshaft Sprocket Bolt* |
|---|---|---|---|---|---|---|---|---|---|
| | | | | | | | *Intake* | *Exhaust* | |
| 1970–72 | 146 (2393) | 47 (6.5) | 19.5–23.9 (2.7–3.3) | 33–40 (4.5–5.5) | 115–130 (16–18) | 101 (14) | 5.8–8.7 (0.8–1.2) | | 36–43 (5–6) |
| 1973 | 146 (2393) | 47–61 (6.5–8.5) | 33–40 (4.5–5.5) | 33–40 (4.5–5.5) | 87–116 (12–16) | 101–116 (14–16) | 5.8–8.7 (0.8–1.2) | | 86–116 (12–16) |
| 1974 | 156 (2565) | 54–61 (7.5–8.5) | 27–31 (3.7–4.3) | 33–40 (4.5–5.5) | 94–108 (13–15) | 94–108 (13–15) | 5.8–8.7 (0.8–1.2) | | 94–108 (13–15) |

① Intake and exhaust manifolds mounted with common studs

e. wire to the temperature senders;

f. wire to the water temperature switch at the connector;

g. alternator wires;

h. choke heat wires (1974) or linkage;

i. throttle solenoid wire (manual transmission) and throttle linkage;

j. EGR solenoid wire at the connector (1973–74);

k. wire to the vacuum solenoid (manual transmission);

l. fuel line(s) (two for 1974 models);

m. heater hoses;

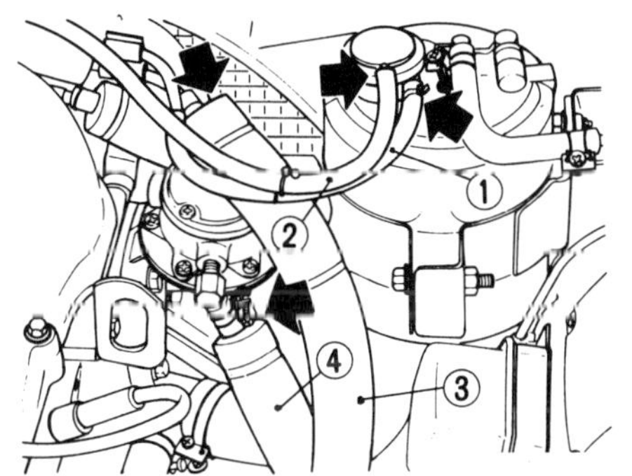

Remove: canister purge hose (1), vacuum signal hose (2), fuel return hose (3), and fuel charge hose (4)

n. vacuum line to the brake cylinder at the manifold;

o. wires for the back-up lights, neutral safety switch, and top detecting switch;

p. inhibitor switch and kick-down solenoid wires (automatic only).

11. Remove the clutch master cylinder and return spring (manual transmission only).

12. Disconnect the speedometer cable where it enters the rear extension housing of the transmission.

13. Disconnect the transmission control linkage.

14. Remove the shift lever (manual transmission) or disconnect the range selector (automatic transmission).

15. Disconnect the exhaust tube at the manifold.

16. Mark the companion flange and driveshaft for installation in the same place and disconnect the shaft at the rear by removing the four bolts. Remove the shaft from the rear of the transmission and seal the opening.

17. Support the transmission carefully to remove all weight from the rear mounts. Remove the bolts which secure the rear mounts to the body.

18. Connect an adequate cable or chain between the two lifting hooks on the engine. Hook the cable or chain to a hoist and apply just enough lift to take all weight off the front mounts.

19. Remove the bolts which attach the engine support to the front mounting insulators.

20. Working carefully to avoid damaging engine or body parts, tilt the engine, lowering the transmission jack as necessary, until it can be pulled up and out of the engine compartment, front first. The engine should be mounted on a secure stand as soon as possible.

When reinstalling the engine, first carefully inspect the engine mounts. If any part of the mount is damaged or if the bonded surface is deteriorated or separated, replace the mount.

The front mounts are identical, but are installed in different positions on the right and left. The rear mount must also be installed in the proper direction. See the illustrations.

In all other respects engine installation is accomplished in the reverse of removal. If possible, tighten the mounting nuts with a torque wrench to specifications. Make sure that all engine mounts are properly assembled and tight before removing support.

## *CYLINDER HEAD*

### Removal and Installation

1. Drain the coolant and disconnect the negative battery cable.

2. Remove the upper radiator hose, water outlet elbow, and thermostat. Remove heater hoses.

3. Disconnect all high-tension cables from the spark plugs. Remove the spark plugs.

4. Disconnect both fuel lines. Remove the fuel pump.

5. Disconnect all vacuum hoses and remove the air cleaner.

6. Disconnect water, air, vacuum, and fuel hoses or lines from the carburetors. Remove both carburetors from the manifold.

7. Disconnect and remove EGR con-

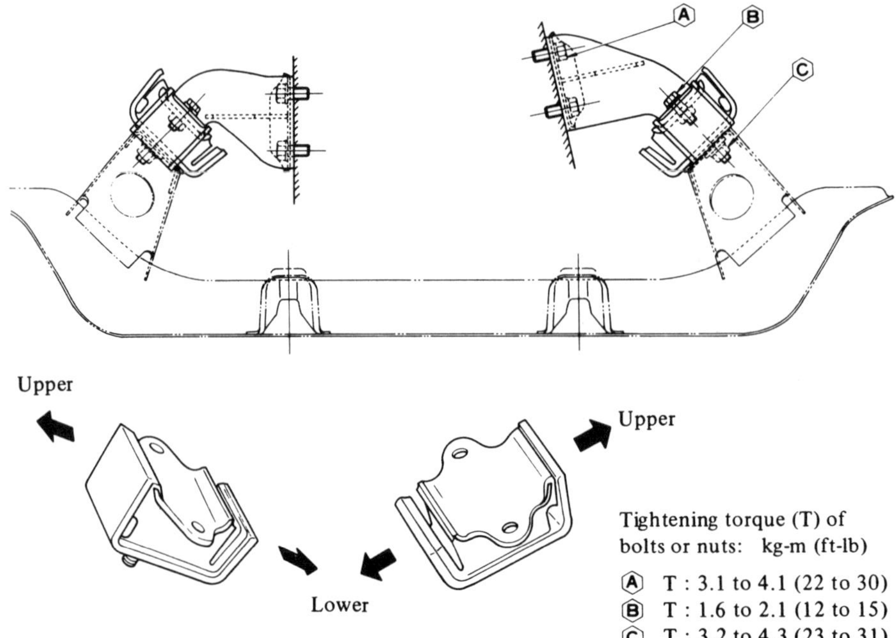


Position and torque of front mounts

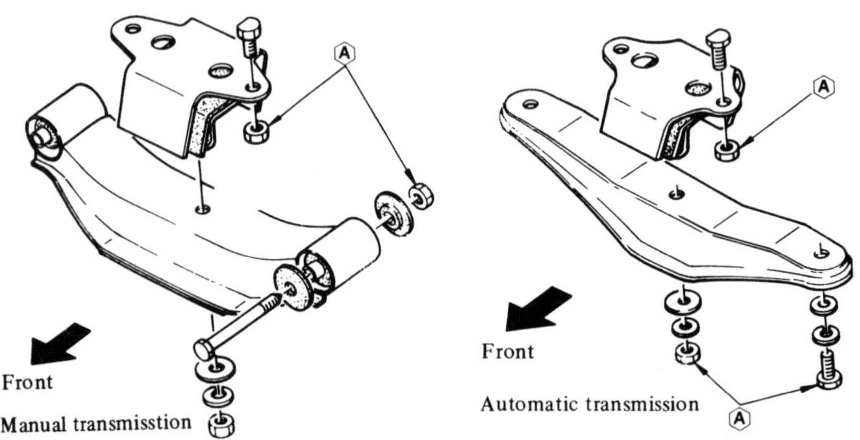


Position and torque of rear mounts

trol tube, then remove the EGR valve on 1973–74 models.

8. Disconnect coolant piping and the exhaust gas inlet tube from the intake manifold.

9. Remove the camshaft cover.

10. Remove the air conditioner fast idle mechanism and bracket, if so equipped.

11. Remove the coolant tube from the balance tube of the manifold, then remove the balance tube.

12. Remove the exhaust heat shield plate.

13. Remove the intake and exhaust manifolds.

14. Disconnect the temperature sender on the head.

15. Mark the relationships between the camshaft and camshaft sprocket and

between the sprocket and the timing chain.

16. Remove the camshaft sprocket and use a special wooden wedge or other means to retain the chain's position on the sprocket to avoid disturbing the timing.

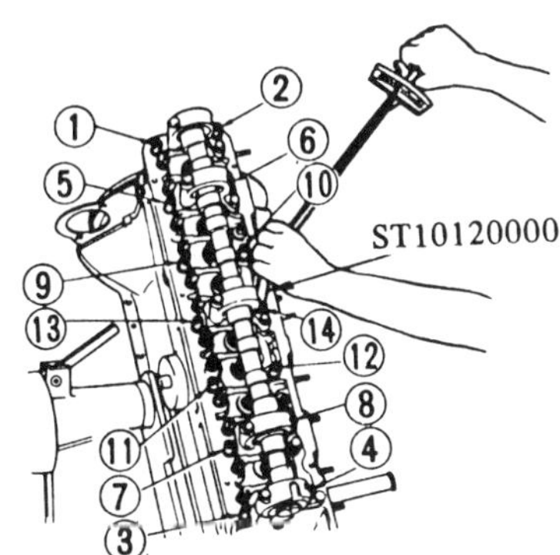


Loosen the head bolts in the numbered sequence

17. Remove the valve train oiling pipe.

18. Loosen the head bolts in sequence, as shown, with a special allen wrench. Mark each bolt for installation in the same position as two different sizes of bolts are used.

19. Lift the head off the engine.

To install the cylinder head:

1. Make checks of cylinder head condition, inspect for warpage, etc., as described in the cylinder head overhaul section.

2. Install a new head gasket and put the head in position on the block.

3. Install head bolts in original locations hand tight.

| O | O | O | O | O | O | O |
|---|---|---|---|---|---|---|
| 12 | 8 | 4 | 2 | 6 | 10 | 14 |
| 11 | 7 | 3 | 1 | 5 | 9 | 13 |
| O | O | O | O | O | O | O |

Head bolt tightening sequence

4. Torque all bolts, in sequence shown to 29 ft lbs (4.0 kg-m).

5. Torque all bolts, in sequence, to 43 ft lbs (6.0 kg-m).

6. Torque all bolts to the specified torque, in sequence.

7. Reinstall the camshaft sprocket in the original position and torque the mounting bolt. If the position of the sprocket has been disturbed, correct the the timing as described under "Timing Chain Removal and Installation."

8. Adjust the valves as described in Chapter 2.

9. See the "Cylinder Head Removal and Installation" procedures for reinstallation of all cylinder head auxiliary parts, coolant, etc.

10. Operate the engine until it is at normal operating temperature, remove the camshaft cover, retorque the head bolts and adjust the valves hot, as described in Chapter 2.

11. Reinstall the camshaft cover, etc. Retorque the head bolts and readjust the valves after 600 miles of operation.

### Valve Guide Removal and Installation

1. Measure the clearance between each valve guide and the valve stem with a micrometer and telescope hole gauge. Measure the valve stem diameter at top, center, and bottom; determine the highest reading. Then, with the hole gauge, measure the bore of the valve guide at the center. Subtract the highest stem diameter from the guide bore, and check to see if the stem-to-guide clearance is within specifications. If this procedure cannot be performed, install the valve in its normal closed position in the head and move it back-and-forth parallel with the position of the rocker arm. If the tip deflects 0.0079 in. (.0.1 mm) or more, stem-to-guide clearance is excessive.

2. Remove guides that are excessively worn with a press and drift pin. This requires about two tons pressure. This procedure is easier to perform if the cylinder head is heated before attempting it. Press toward the camshaft cover.

3. Allow the head to cool to room temperature, as necessary, and ream the guide hole to 0.4794–0.4802 in. (12.185–12.196 mm).

4. Heat the cylinder head to 302–392° F (150–200° C). Press 0.008 in. (0.2 mm) oversize guides into the head. Interference fit of the guide should be 0.0011–0.0019 in. (0.027–0.049 mm).

5. Ream the bore of the new guides to 0.3150–0.3157 in. (8.000–8.018 mm).

6. Correct the valve seat surface as described under "Valve Seat Removal and Installation" if a new seat is not required.

### Valve Seat Removal and Installation

1. Check the valve seat inserts for pitting where the valve contacts them and recut the seat, or replace it as necessary.

2. Bore the old seat until it collapses, setting the machine depth stop so boring cannot affect the bottom of the insert recess.

3. Select a standard or 0.197 in. (0.5 mm) oversize seat as determined by measuring the cylinder head recess. Machine the recess to the proper size concentric with the valve guide center, according to a measurement of the outside diameter of the seat, and the following charts. Do this at room temperature.

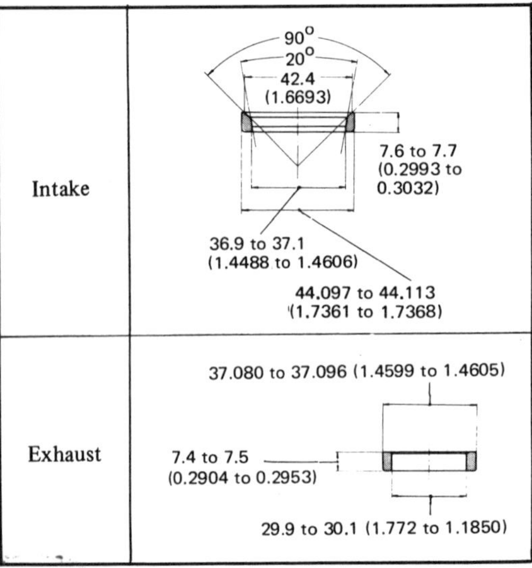


Valve seat dimensions for 1973 engines (in. in parentheses)

## Valve Seat Interference Fit—in. (mm)

| *Year* | *Intake* | *Exhaust* |
|---|---|---|
| 1970–73 | 0.0031–0.0043 (0.08–0.11) | 0.0024–0.0039 (0.06–0.10) |
| 1974 | 0.0032–0.0044 (0.081–0.113) | 0.0025–0.0038 (0.064–0.096) |

## Cylinder Head Recess Diameter—in. (mm)

| *Year-Type* | *Intake* | *Exhaust* |
|---|---|---|
| 1970–72 | 1.791–1.7918 (45.5–45.57) | 1.476–1.4768 (37.5–37.52) |
| 1973 | | |
| Standard | 1.732–1.734 (43.987–44.003) | 1.456–1.458 (36.980–37.036) |
| Service | 1.749–1.751 (44.433–44.487) | 1.476–1.478 (37.480–37.536) |
| 1974 | | |
| Standard | 1.7323–1.7329 (44.0–44.016) | 1.4567–1.4573 (37.0–37.016) |
| Service | 1.7520–1.7526 (44.5–44.516) | 1.4764–1.4770 (37.5–37.516) |

4. Heat the cylinder head to 302–392° F (150–200° C).

5. Press the insert in and make sure that it seats properly in the recess.

6. Cut the seat to the dimensions shown in the correct illustration.

7. Put a small amount of fine grinding compound onto the valve seat face, put

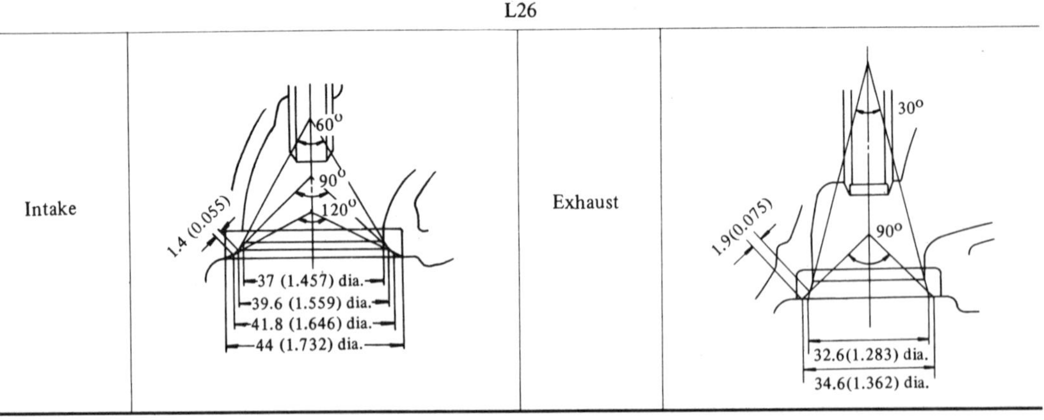


Valve seat dimensions for the 2600 cc engine (in. in parentheses)

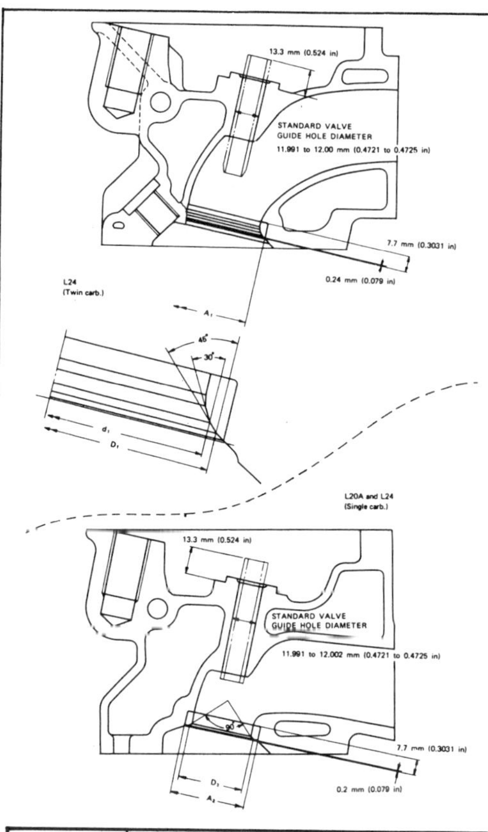


| | L20A and L24 (Single carb.) | L24 (Twin carb.) |
|---|---|---|
| A1 mm (in) dia. | 41.000 to 41.016 (1.6140 to 1.6148) | 44.000 to 44.016 (1.7323 to 1.7329) |
| D1 mm (in) dia. | 37.6 to 37.8 (1.480 to 1.488) | 41.6 to 41.8 (1.638 to 1.646) |
| d1 mm (in) dia. | 35.6 (1.402) | 39.6 (1.559) |
| A2 mm (in) dia. | 37.000 to 37.016 (1.4567 to 1.4573) | 37.000 to 37.016 (1.4567 to 1.4573) |
| D2 mm (in) dia. | 32.4 to 32.6 (1.276 to 1.283) | 32.4 to 32.6 (1.276 to 1.283) |

Valve seat dimensions for 1972 and earlier engines

the valve into the guide, and lap until the proper seal is obtained. Remove the valve and clean the valve and seat.

### Overhaul

Inspect the cylinder head for cracks and other flaws. Measure the head on the cylinder block mating surface to check for warpage, employing a straightedge and feeler gauge. If warpage exceeds 0.0039 in. (0.1 mm) or there is other damage, repair or replace the head as required. See the "Engine Rebuilding" section for additional information.

## *VALVE ROCKERS*

### Removal and Installation

1. Remove the valve rocker spring.
2. Loosen the rocker pivot locknut, loosen the adjustment as far as possible, depress the valve spring and remove the rocker.

To install the rocker, reverse the above procedures.

### Inspection

Inspect the pivot head and cam and pivot contact surfaces for damage or excessive wear. If wear is excessive, the faulty parts should be replaced. Whenever the pivot is defective, replace the rocker arm also.

## *INTAKE AND EXHAUST MANIFOLDS*

### Removal and Installation

1. Disconnect air and vacuum hoses from the air cleaner. Disconnect the hose linking the balance tube and temperature sensor at the balance tube end.
2. Remove the air cleaner.
3. Disconnect water, air, vacuum, and fuel hoses to both carburetors (drain enough coolant from the bottom of the radiator to perform this without losing the coolant).
4. Remove the carburetors from the manifold.
5. On 1973 and later models, disconnect the EGR control tube between the balance tube and exhaust manifold. Remove the EGR valve.
6. Disconnect the rear coolant inlet pipe and the exhaust gas inlet tube at the manifold.
7. Remove the air conditioner fast idle mechanism and bracket from the intake manifold.
8. Remove the securing nut and disconnect the coolant tube from the balance tube.
9. Remove the exhaust manifold heat shield.
10. Remove the intake and exhaust manifolds.

To install the manifolds, reverse the

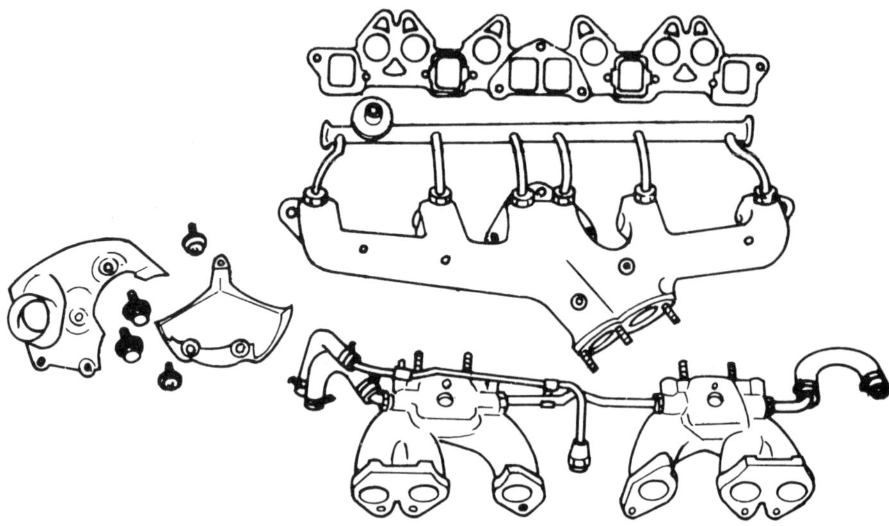

Intake and exhaust manifolds

above procedures. Use a new gasket, clean both sealing surfaces and torque the bolts in several stages, working from the center outward.

### *TIMING GEAR COVER*

#### Removal and Installation

1. Drain the radiator, disconnect both hoses and remove the radiator and shroud.
2. Remove the fan and fan pulley.
3. Remove the air pump drive belt, air pump, and adjusting link.
4. Loosen the adjusting bolt for the air conditioner idler pulley and remove the belt.
5. When air conditioner equipped, remove the two lower bolts for the air conditioner compressor. Then, remove the two upper bolts while supporting the compressor, and remove the assembly. Remove the mounting bracket.

NOTE: *Support the compressor in such a way that stress will not be placed on the refrigerant hoses.*

6. Remove the crank pulley with a puller.
7. Remove the water pump.
8. Drain the engine oil and remove the oil pan, as described in the "Engine Lubrication" section.
9. Unbolt and remove the distributor. Remove the oil pump as described in the "Engine Lubrication" section.
10. Unbolt and remove the front cover.

To install the front cover:

1. Replace the seal, as described below.
2. Reverse the removal procedures, paying particular attention to the timing of the oil pump (see "Oil Pump Removal and Installation").

#### Timing Gear Cover Oil Seal Replacement

Press the old seal out the back of the cover. Press the new seal in and coat the sealing lip with lithium grease.

### *TIMING CHAIN AND TENSIONER, AND TIMING GEAR*

#### Removal and Installation

1. Remove the timing chain cover and, if necessary, the camshaft cover.
2. Remove the camshaft sprocket.
3. Remove the chain and tensioner.
4. Remove the oil slinger and distrib-

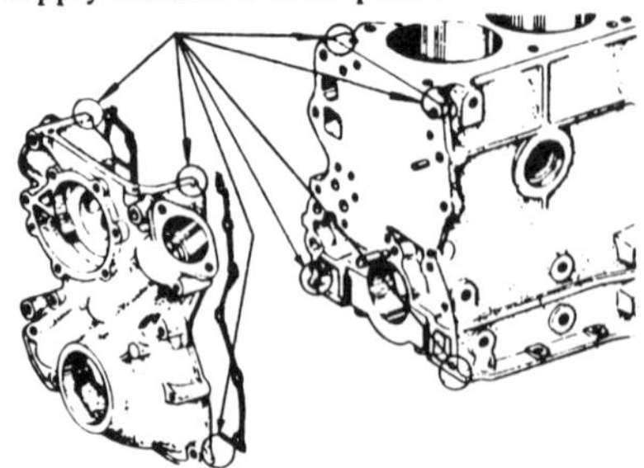
Apply sealant at these points.

Apply sealant to the timing cover at points shown

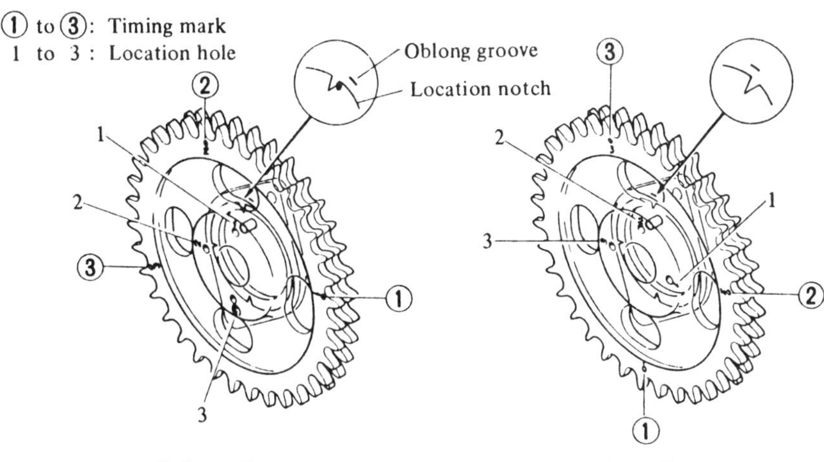

Adjusting camshaft sprocket location

utor drive gear from the crankshaft. Remove the timing gear

To install the timing gear, chain, and tensioner:

1. Install the timing gear onto the crankshaft. Install the distributor drive gear and oil slinger. Install the camshaft sprocket.

2. Make sure that the crankshaft and camshaft keys both point upward. Avoid damage due to contact between the valves and the pistons.

3. Install the timing chain, aligning its mating marks with those on the two sprockets on the right-side. There are 42 links between the two marks on the chain.

4. The camshaft sprocket is adjusted at the factory for hole No. 1. If chain wear is great enough, it may be necessary to use No. 2 or No. 3 hole to get the proper valve timing. If the camshaft location hole is to the left of the groove in the locating plate, use hole No. 2 or No. 3 as required.

5. Install the chain guide onto the block. Install the chain tensioner.

6. Adjust the tension by adjusting the chain tensioner spindle protrusion to zero.

7. Install the front and camshaft covers, and other parts.

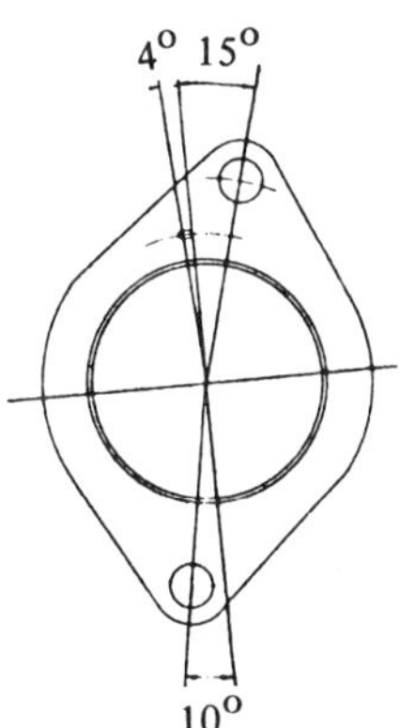

The camshaft locating plate

## *CAMSHAFT*

### Removal and Installation

1. Remove the cylinder head.
2. For each valve rocker:
   a. Remove the valve rocker spring;
   b. Loosen the rocker pivot locknut, loosen the adjustment as far as possible, depress the valve spring, and remove the rocker.
3. Remove the camshaft locating plate.
4. Pull the camshaft slowly out toward the front of the head, being especially careful to avoid damaging the lobes and bearings.

To install the camshaft:

1. Carefully reposition the camshaft in the head.
2. Install the camshaft locating plate with the groove in the upward position.
3. Install the cylinder head.
4. Install the camshaft drive sprocket in the same position.
5. Install the valve rockers.

NOTE: *The camshaft may be removed with the head in place, if you wish. First, remove the radiator and the hood. Then follow all instructions, including preliminary cylinder head removal procedures. Be especially careful not to disturb the timing.*

### *PISTONS AND CONNECTING RODS*

**Removal and Installation**

1. Pistons and upper rods are removed by pushing the the piston carefully out the top of the block. Mark all connecting rods so that they can be replaced in the same direction and in conjunction with the same piston.

During installation:

1. The "F" mark on the side of the piston must face the front of the engine.
2. The connecting rod oil hole must face the right-side of the engine.
3. Locate the compression rings so that the gaps are 180° apart, and equidistant from pin direction and thrust direction.

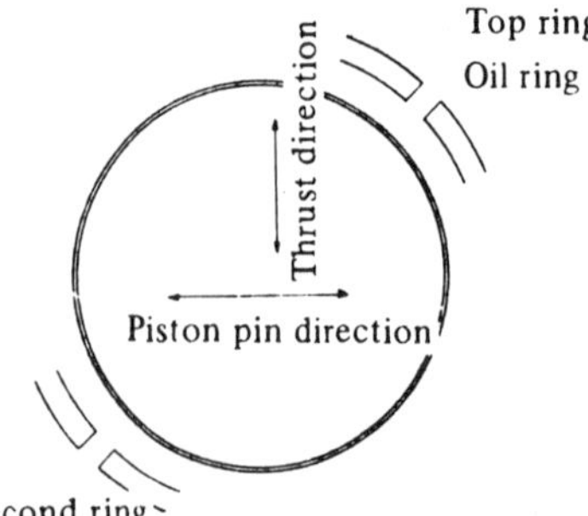

Locate the rings as shown

4. Thoroughly lubricate all surfaces with clean engine oil.
5. Fit a ring compressor around the piston, insert the rod into the block from the top and then slide each piston in with the ring compressor held tightly against the top of the block.
6. When installing connecting rod caps, make sure that the cylinder numbers on the rods and rod caps face in the same direction.

## Engine Lubrication

### *OIL PAN*

**Removal and Installation**

1. If the engine is in the vehicle, attach a lift, support the engine, and remove the engine mounting bolts as described in "Engine Removal and Installation".
2. Raise the engine just slightly, watching to make sure that no hoses or wires are damaged.
3. Drain the engine oil.
4. Remove the oil pan bolts and slide the pan out to the rear.

To install the pan:

1. Use a new gasket, coated on both sides with sealer.
2. Torque the pan bolts evenly and in stages.
3. Reinstall engine mounting bolts as described under "Engine Removal and Installation", using the specified torque and maintaining support until all mounts are secure.
4. Refill the oil pan to the specified level.

### *REAR MAIN OIL SEAL*

**Replacement**

1. Remove the engine from the vehicle. Separate the transmission from the engine.
2. Remove the flywheel and end plate.
3. Remove the rear main bearing cap using a puller. Remove old side seals.
4. Remove the rear main seal.

To reinstall the seal:

1. Apply sealant to each side of the rear main bearing cap and each corner of the block.

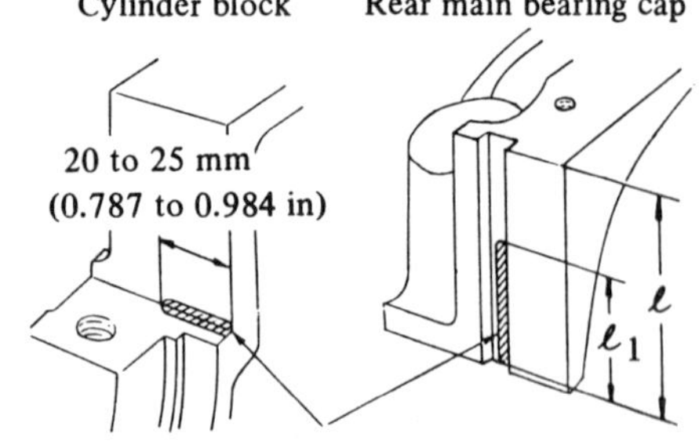

Apply sealant to points shown

2. Put the cap in position, and install and torque cap bolts.
3. Apply sealant, and drive new side oil seals in.
4. Apply lithium grease to the sealing lip of the seal, and install it with a drift.
5. Install the rear end plate and fly-

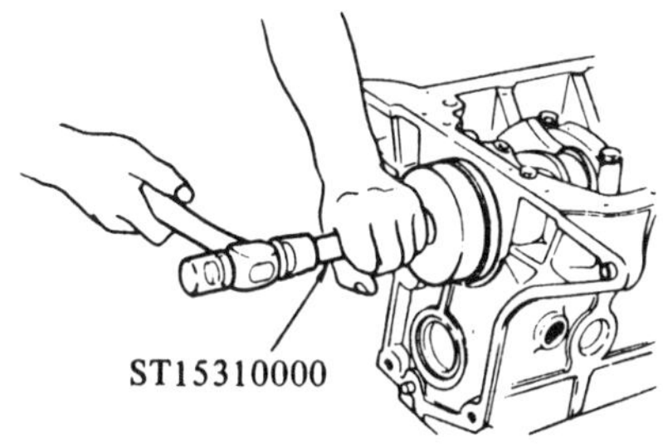


Installing the rear main oil seal

wheel, torquing flywheel mounting bolts to specification.

6. Remount the transmission onto the engine, and reinstall the engine.

### *OIL PUMP*

#### Removal and Installation

1. Turn the engine over until the No. 1 cylinder is at TDC on the compression stroke.

2. Drain the oil pan. Remove the splash shield.

3. Remove high-tension wires, and unbolt and remove the distributor.

4. Remove the four pump bolts, and pull the oil pump out.

To install:

1. Replace the oil pump gasket.

2. Align the drive pump hole and spindle mark by turning the spindle. Then, turn the spindle one gear tooth to the right.

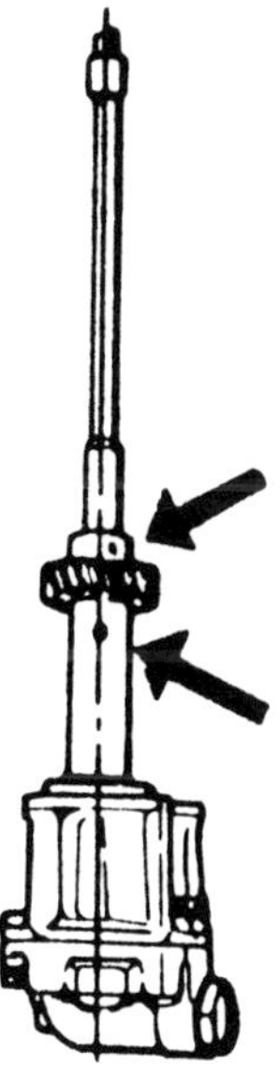

Lining up marks on oil pump and distributor drive spindle

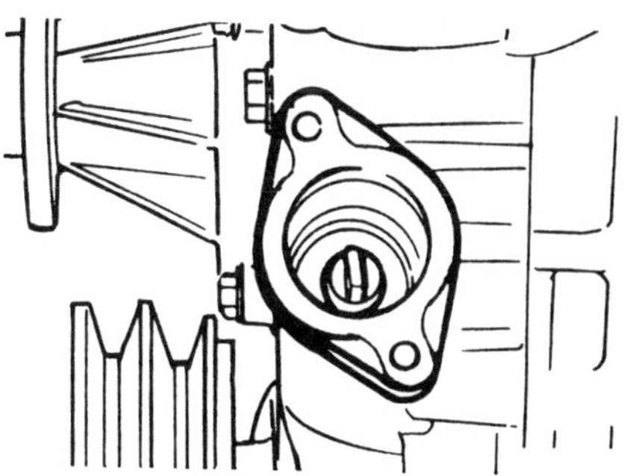

Proper alignment of distributor drive spindle

3. Install the pump with the mounting bolts, torquing them to 8.0–10.8 ft lbs (1.1–1.5 kg-m).

4. The projection on top of the spindle should now be at the 11:25 o'clock position, with the smaller half of the spindle facing forward.

5. Reinstall the splash shield.

6. Refill the oil pan to the specified level.

7. Reinstall the distributor, carefully rotating the rotor back-and-forth until the bottom of the distributor shaft engages the projection on top of the oil pump spindle. Install mounting bolts.

## Engine Cooling

### *RADIATOR*

#### Removal and Installation

1. Drain the radiator coolant by opening the drain cock at the bottom. Removal of the pressure cap will speed the process.

2. Disconnect the upper and lower hoses at the radiator.

3. On air conditioned models, unbolt the lower radiator shroud and remove it from underneath.

4. On automatic transmission equipped cars, disconnect both transmission cooler lines and cap them.

5. Remove the radiator mounting bolts and remove it (and shroud) by pulling it upward and out of the compartment.

To install the radiator, reverse these procedures. Refill both radiator and transmission to the specified levels. Operate the engine and continue filling radiator to the proper level until all air bubbles are expelled.

*WATER PUMP*

**Removal and Installation**

1. Drain the radiator coolant through the lower drain cock.
2. Remove the fan shroud mounting bolts and remove the shroud.
3. Loosen and then remove the fan belt.
4. Remove the fan and pulley from the water pump hub.
5. Remove the pump and gasket.

To install, first clean all traces of old gasket material from both surfaces and install a new gasket coated with sealer.

Then, reverse the removal procedure. Finally, refill the radiator with the engine idling to remove all air bubbles.

*THERMOSTAT*

**Removal and Installation**

1. Drain the radiator coolant through the lower drain cock.
2. Disconnect the upper radiator hose at the water outlet.
3. Loosen the mounting bolts and remove the water outlet, gasket, and thermostat.

To install the thermostat, reverse the above procedures. Install the thermostat with the wax pellet downward and use a new water outlet gasket coated with sealer.

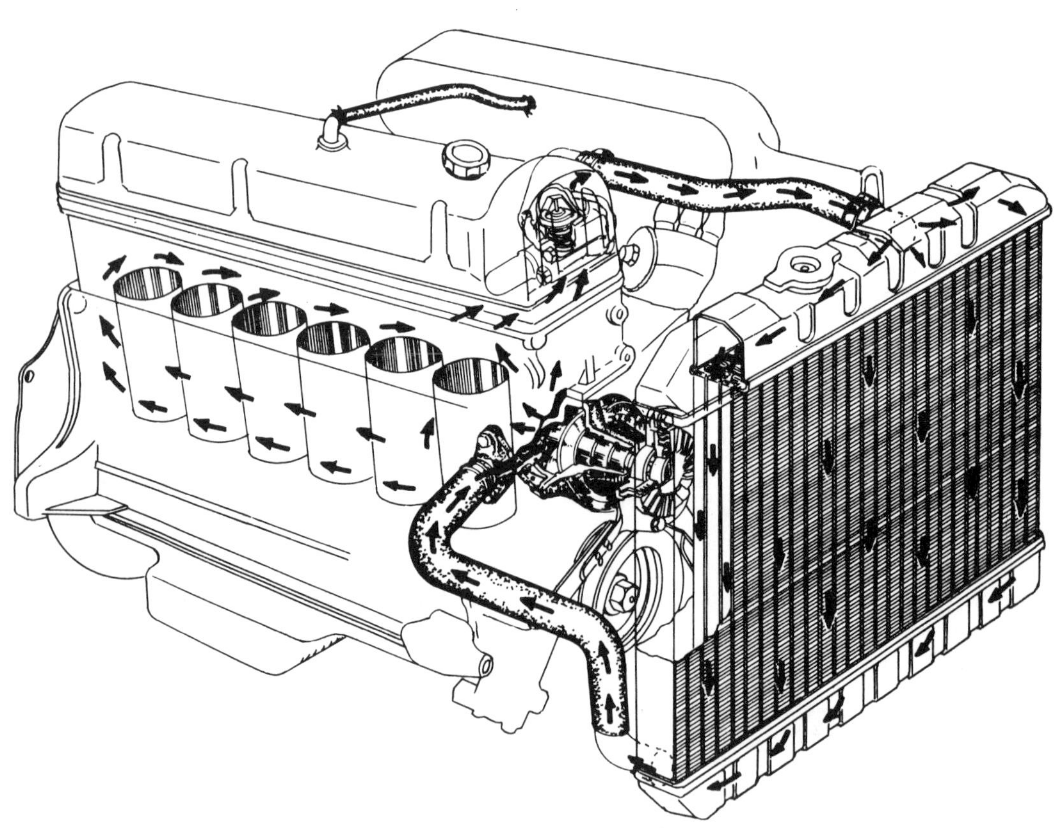

Cooling system flow diagram—260-Z

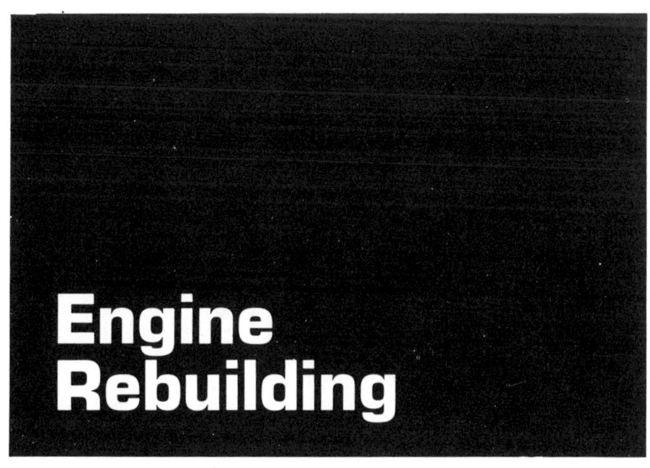

# Engine Rebuilding

This section describes, in detail, the procedures involved in rebuilding a typical engine. The procedures specifically refer to an inline engine, however, they are basically identical to those used in rebuilding engines of nearly all design and configurations. Procedures for servicing atypical engines (i.e., horizontally opposed) are described in the appropriate section, although in most cases, cylinder head reconditioning procedures described in this chapter will apply.

The section is divided into two sections. The first, Cylinder Head Reconditioning, assumes that the cylinder head is removed from the engine, all manifolds are removed, and the cylinder head is on a workbench. The camshaft should be removed from overhead cam cylinder heads. The second section, Cylinder Block Reconditioning, covers the block, pistons, connecting rods and crankshaft. It is assumed that the engine is mounted on a work stand, and the cylinder head and all accessories are removed.

Procedures are identified as follows:

*Unmarked*—Basic procedures that must be performed in order to successfully complete the rebuilding process.

*Starred* (*)—Procedures that should be performed to ensure maximum performance and engine life.

*Double starred* (**)—Procedures that may be performed to increase engine performance and reliability. These procedures are usually reserved for extremely heavy-duty or competition usage.

In many cases, a choice of methods is also provided. Methods are identified in the same manner as procedures. The choice of method for a procedure is at the discretion of the user.

The tools required for the basic rebuilding procedure should, with minor exceptions, be those

TORQUE (ft. lbs.)*

U.S.

| Bolt Diameter (inches) | Bolt Grade (SAE) 1 and 2 | 5 | 6 | 8 | Wrench Size (inches) Bolt | Nut |
|---|---|---|---|---|---|---|
| 1/4 | 5 | 7 | 10 | 10.5 | 3/8 | 7/16 |
| 5/16 | 9 | 14 | 19 | 22 | 1/2 | 9/16 |
| 3/8 | 15 | 25 | 34 | 37 | 9/16 | 5/8 |
| 7/16 | 24 | 40 | 55 | 60 | 5/8 | 3/4 |
| 1/2 | 37 | 60 | 85 | 92 | 3/4 | 13/16 |
| 9/16 | 53 | 88 | 120 | 132 | 7/8 | 7/8 |
| 5/8 | 74 | 120 | 167 | 180 | 15/16 | 1 |
| 3/4 | 120 | 200 | 280 | 296 | 1-1/8 | 1-1/8 |
| 7/8 | 190 | 302 | 440 | 473 | 1-5/16 | 1-5/16 |
| 1 | 282 | 466 | 660 | 714 | 1-1/2 | 1-1/2 |

Metric

| Bolt Diameter (mm) | Bolt Grade 5D | 8G | 10K | 12K | Wrench Size (mm) Bolt and Nut |
|---|---|---|---|---|---|
| 6 | 5 | 6 | 8 | 10 | 10 |
| 8 | 10 | 16 | 22 | 27 | 14 |
| 10 | 19 | 31 | 40 | 49 | 17 |
| 12 | 34 | 54 | 70 | 86 | 19 |
| 14 | 55 | 89 | 117 | 137 | 22 |
| 16 | 83 | 132 | 175 | 208 | 24 |
| 18 | 111 | 182 | 236 | 283 | 27 |
| 22 | 182 | 284 | 394 | 464 | 32 |
| 24 | 261 | 419 | 570 | 689 | 36 |

*—Torque values are for lightly oiled bolts. CAUTION: Bolts threaded into aluminum require much less torque.

General Torque Specifications

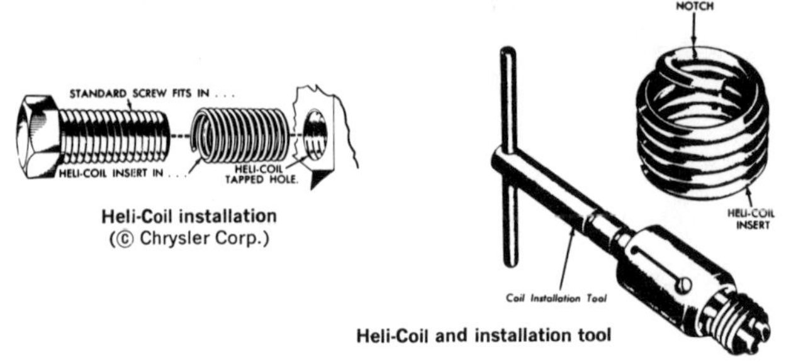


Heli-Coil installation
(© Chrysler Corp.)

Heli-Coil and installation tool

| *Heli-Coil Insert* | | | *Drill* | *Tap* | *Insert. Tool* | *Extracting Tool* |
|---|---|---|---|---|---|---|
| *Thread Size* | *Part No.* | *Insert Length (In.)* | *Size* | *Part No.* | *Part No.* | *Part No.* |
| 1/2 -20 | 1185-4 | 3/8 | 17/64(.266) | 4 CPB | 528-4N | 1227-6 |
| 5/16-18 | 1185-5 | 15/32 | Q(.332) | 5 CPB | 528-5N | 1227-6 |
| 3/8 -16 | 1185-6 | 9/16 | X(.397) | 6 CPB | 528-6N | 1227-6 |
| 7/16-14 | 1185-7 | 21/32 | 29/64(.453) | 7 CPB | 528-7N | 1227-16 |
| 1/2 -13 | 1185-8 | 3/4 | 33/64(.516) | 8 CPB | 528-8N | 1227-16 |

Heli-Coil Specifications

included in a mechanic's tool kit. An accurate torque wrench, and a dial indicator (reading in thousandths) mounted on a universal base should be available. Bolts and nuts with no torque specification should be tightened according to size (see chart). Special tools, where required, all are readily available from the major tool suppliers (i.e., Craftsman, Snap-On, K-D). The services of a competent automotive machine shop must also be readily available.

When assembling the engine, any parts that will be in frictional contact must be pre-lubricated, to provide protection on initial start-up. Vortex Pre-Lube, STP, or any product specifically formulated for this purpose may be used. NOTE: *Do not use engine oil.* Where semi-permanent (locked but removable) installation of bolts or nuts is desired, threads should be cleaned and coated with Loctite. Studs may be permanently installed using Loctite Stud and Bearing Mount.

Aluminum has become increasingly popular for use in engines, due to its low weight and excellent heat transfer characteristics. The following precautions must be observed when handling aluminum engine parts:

—Never hot-tank aluminum parts.

—Remove all aluminum parts (identification tags, etc.) from engine parts before hot-tanking (otherwise they will be removed during the process).

—Always coat threads lightly with engine oil or anti-seize compounds before installation, to prevent seizure.

—Never over-torque bolts or spark plugs in aluminum threads. Should stripping occur, threads can be restored according to the following procedure, using Heli-Coil thread inserts:

Tap drill the hole with the stripped threads to the specified size (see chart). Using the specified tap (NOTE: *Heli-Coil tap sizes refer to the size thread being replaced, rather than the actual tap size*), tap the hole for the Heli-Coil. Place the insert on the proper installation tool (see chart). Apply pressure on the insert while winding it clockwise into the hole, until the top of the insert is one turn below the surface. Remove the installation tool, and break the installation tang from the bottom of the insert by moving it up and down. If the Heli-Coil must be removed, tap the removal tool firmly into the hole, so that it engages the top thread, and turn the tool counter-clockwise to extract the insert.

Snapped bolts or studs may be removed, using a stud extractor (unthreaded) or Vise-Grip pliers (threaded). Penetrating oil (e.g., Liquid Wrench) will often aid in breaking frozen threads. In cases where the stud or bolt is flush with, or below the surface, proceed as follows:

Drill a hole in the broken stud or bolt, approximately ½ its diameter. Select a screw extractor (e.g., Easy-Out) of the proper size, and tap it into the stud or bolt. Turn the extractor counter-clockwise to remove the stud or bolt.

Magnaflux and Zyglo are inspection techniques used to locate material flaws, such as stress cracks. Magnafluxing coats the part with fine magnetic particles, and subjects the part to a magnetic field. Cracks cause breaks

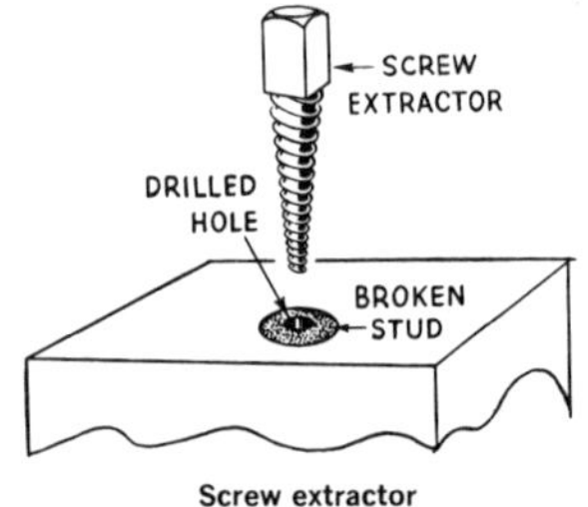


Screw extractor

in the magnetic field, which are outlined by the particles. Since Magnaflux is a magnetic process, it is applicable only to ferrous materials. The Zyglo process coats the material with a fluorescent dye penetrant, and then subjects it to blacklight inspection, under which cracks glow bright-

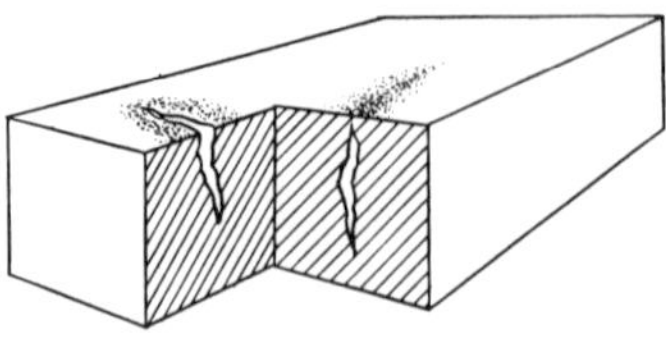

Magnaflux indication of cracks

ly. Parts made of any material may be tested using Zyglo. While Magnaflux and Zyglo are excellent for general inspection, and locating hidden defects, specific checks of suspected cracks may be made at lower cost and more readily using spot check dye. The dye is sprayed onto the suspected area, wiped off, and the area is then sprayed with a developer. Cracks then will show up brightly. Spot check dyes will only indicate surface cracks; therefore, structural cracks below the surface may escape detection. When questionable, the part should be tested using Magnaflux or Zyglo.

## CYLINDER HEAD RECONDITIONING

| *Procedure* | *Method* |
|---|---|
| Identify the valves:  Valve identification (© SAAB) | Invert the cylinder head, and number the valve faces front to rear, using a permanent felt-tip marker. |
| Remove the rocker arms: | Remove the rocker arms with shaft(s) or balls and nuts. Wire the sets of rockers, balls and nuts together, and identify according to the corresponding valve. |
| Remove the valves and springs: | Using an appropriate valve spring compressor (depending on the configuration of the cylinder head), compress the valve springs. Lift out the keepers with needlenose pliers, release the compressor, and remove the valve, spring, and spring retainer. |
| Check the valve stem-to-guide clearance:  Checking the valve stem-to-guide clearance (© American Motors Corp.) | Clean the valve stem with lacquer thinner or a similar solvent to remove all gum and varnish. Clean the valve guides using solvent and an expanding wire-type valve guide cleaner. Mount a dial indicator so that the stem is at 90° to the valve stem, as close to the valve guide as possible. Move the valve off its seat, and measure the valve guide-to-stem clearance by moving the stem back and forth to actuate the dial indicator. Measure the valve stems using a micrometer, and compare to specifications, to determine whether stem or guide wear is responsible for excessive clearance. |
| De-carbon the cylinder head and valves: 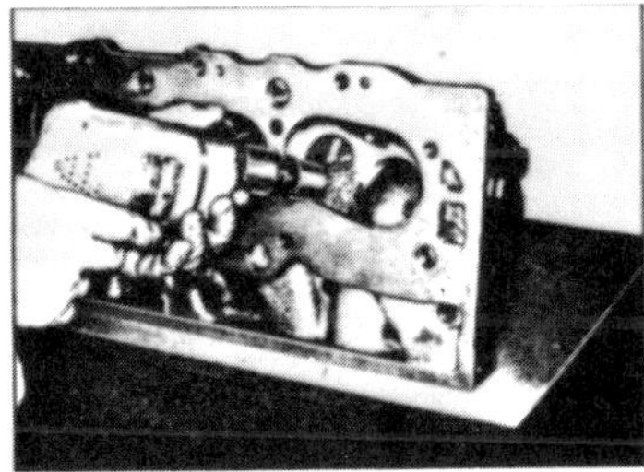 Removing carbon from the cylinder head (© Chevrolet Div. G.M. Corp.) | Chip carbon away from the valve heads, combustion chambers, and ports, using a chisel made of hardwood. Remove the remaining deposits with a stiff wire brush. NOTE: *Ensure that the deposits are actually removed, rather than burnished.* |

| *Procedure* | *Method* |
|---|---|
| Hot-tank the cylinder head: | Have the cylinder head hot-tanked to remove grease, corrosion, and scale from the water passages. NOTE: *In the case of overhead cam cylinder heads, consult the operator to determine whether the camshaft bearings will be damaged by the caustic solution.* |
| Degrease the remaining cylinder head parts: | Using solvent (i.e., Gunk), clean the rockers, rocker shaft(s) (where applicable), rocker balls and nuts, springs, spring retainers, and keepers. Do not remove the protective coating from the springs. |
| Check the cylinder head for warpage: 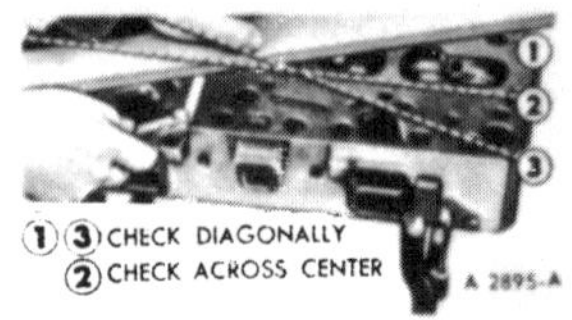  **Checking the cylinder head for warpage** (© Ford Motor Co.) | Place a straight-edge across the gasket surface of the cylinder head. Using feeler gauges, determine the clearance at the center of the straight-edge. Measure across both diagonals, along the longitudinal centerline, and across the cylinder head at several points. If warpage exceeds .003″ in a 6″ span, or .006″ over the total length, the cylinder head must be resurfaced. NOTE: *If warpage exceeds the manufacturers maximum tolerance for material removal, the cylinder head must be replaced.* When milling the cylinder heads of V-type engines, the intake manifold mounting position is altered, and must be corrected by milling the manifold flange a proportionate amount. |
| ** Porting and gasket matching:  **Marking the cylinder head for gasket matching** (© Petersen Publishing Co.)  **Port configuration before and after gasket matching** (© Petersen Publishing Co.) | 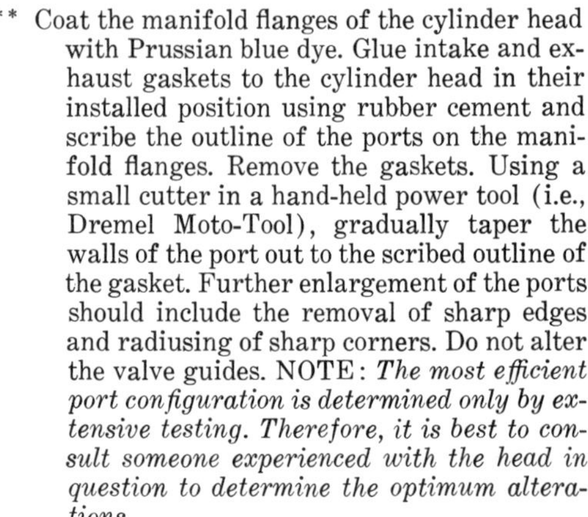 ** Coat the manifold flanges of the cylinder head with Prussian blue dye. Glue intake and exhaust gaskets to the cylinder head in their installed position using rubber cement and scribe the outline of the ports on the manifold flanges. Remove the gaskets. Using a small cutter in a hand-held power tool (i.e., Dremel Moto-Tool), gradually taper the walls of the port out to the scribed outline of the gasket. Further enlargement of the ports should include the removal of sharp edges and radiusing of sharp corners. Do not alter the valve guides. NOTE: *The most efficient port configuration is determined only by extensive testing. Therefore, it is best to consult someone experienced with the head in question to determine the optimum alterations.* |

| *Procedure* | *Method* |
|---|---|

** Polish the ports:

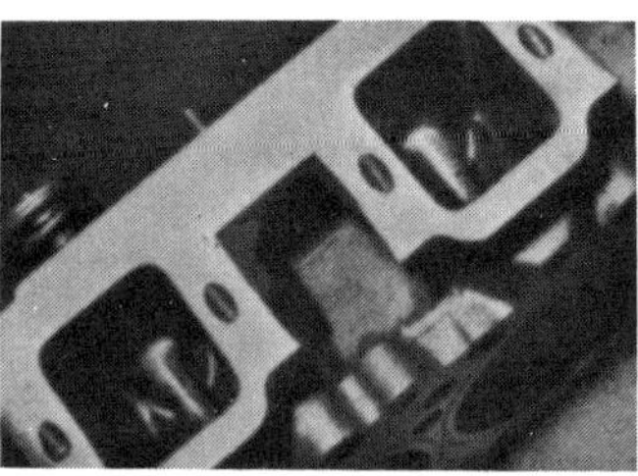

**Relieved and polished ports**
(© Petersen Publishing Co.)

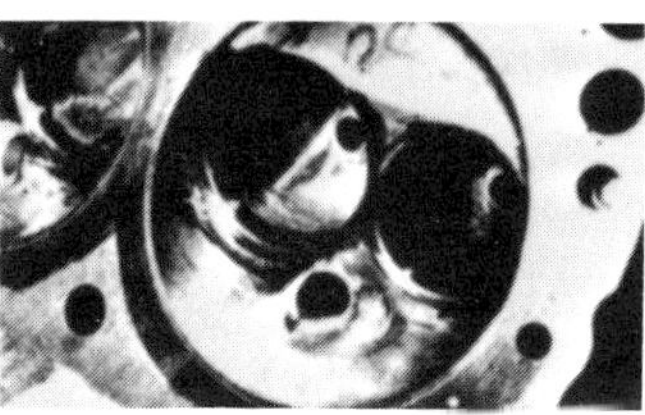

**Polished combustion chamber**
(© Petersen Publishing Co.)

** Using a grinding stone with the above mentioned tool, polish the walls of the intake and exhaust ports, and combustion chamber. Use progressively finer stones until all surface imperfections are removed. NOTE: *Through testing, it has been determined that a smooth surface is more effective than a mirror polished surface in intake ports, and vice-versa in exhaust ports.*

---

* Knurling the valve guides:

**Cut-away view of a knurled valve guide**
(© Petersen Publishing Co.)

* Valve guides which are not excessively worn or distorted may, in some cases, be knurled rather than replaced. Knurling is a process in which metal is displaced and raised, thereby reducing clearance. Knurling also provides excellent oil control. The possibility of knurling rather than replacing valve guides should be discussed with a machinist.

---

Replacing the valve guides: NOTE: *Valve guides should only be replaced if damaged or if an oversize valve stem is not available.*

B
A

A-VALVE GUIDE I.D.
B-SLIGHTLY SMALLER THAN VALVE GUIDE O.D.

**Valve guide removal tool**

WASHERS
B A

A-VALVE GUIDE I.D.
B-LARGER THAN THE VALVE GUIDE O.D.

**Valve guide installation tool (with washers used during installation)**

Depending on the type of cylinder head, valve guides may be pressed, hammered, or shrunk in. In cases where the guides are shrunk into the head, replacement should be left to an equipped machine shop. In other cases, the guides are replaced as follows: Press or tap the valve guides out of the head using a stepped drift (see illustration). Determine the height above the boss that the guide must extend, and obtain a stack of washers, their I.D. similar to the guide's O.D., of that height. Place the stack of washers on the guide, and insert the guide into the boss. NOTE: *Valve guides are often tapered or beveled for installation.* Using the stepped installation tool (see illustration), press or tap the guides into position. Ream the guides according to the size of the valve stem.

| *Procedure* | *Method* |
|---|---|
| Replacing valve seat inserts: | Replacement of valve seat inserts which are worn beyond resurfacing or broken, if feasible, must be done by a machine shop. |
| Resurfacing (grinding) the valve face:<br>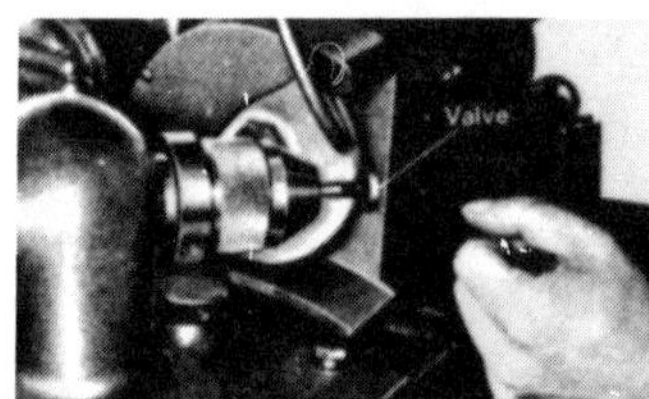<br><br>**Grinding a valve**<br>(© Subaru)<br>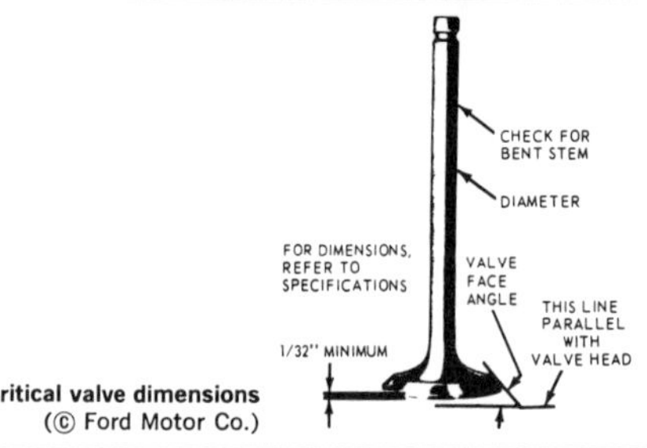<br><br>**Critical valve dimensions**<br>(© Ford Motor Co.) | Using a valve grinder, resurface the valves according to specifications. CAUTION: *Valve face angle is not always identical to valve seat angle.* A minimum margin of 1/32" should remain after grinding the valve. The valve stem tip should also be squared and resurfaced, by placing the stem in the V-block of the grinder, and turning it while pressing lightly against the grinding wheel. |
| Resurfacing the valve seats using reamers:<br><br>**Reaming the valve seat**<br>(© S.p.A. Fiat)<br>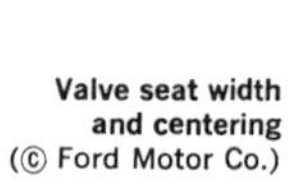<br>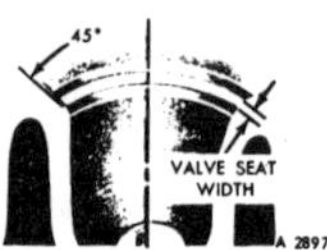<br><br>**Valve seat width and centering**<br>(© Ford Motor Co.) | Select a reamer of the correct seat angle, slightly larger than the diameter of the valve seat, and assemble it with a pilot of the correct size. Install the pilot into the valve guide, and using steady pressure, turn the reamer clockwise. CAUTION: *Do not turn the reamer counter-clockwise.* Remove only as much material as necessary to clean the seat. Check the concentricity of the seat (see below). If the dye method is not used, coat the valve face with Prussian blue dye, install and rotate it on the valve seat. Using the dye marked area as a centering guide, center and narrow the valve seat to specifications with correction cutters. NOTE: *When no specifications are available, minimum seat width for exhaust valves should be 5/64", intake valves 1/16".* After making correction cuts, check the position of the valve seat on the valve face using Prussian blue dye. |
| * Resurfacing the valve seats using a grinder:<br>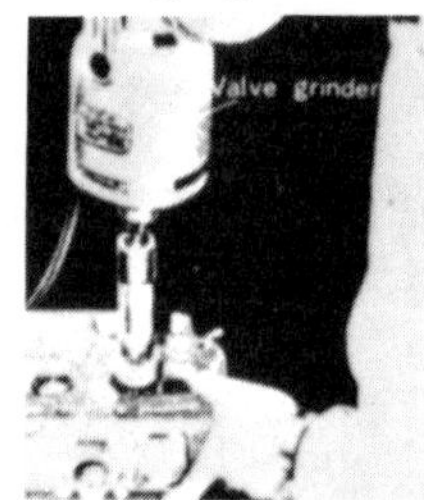<br><br>**Grinding a valve seat**<br>(© Subaru) | Select a pilot of the correct size, and a coarse stone of the correct seat angle. Lubricate the pilot if necessary, and install the tool in the valve guide. Move the stone on and off the seat at approximately two cycles per second, until all flaws are removed from the seat. Install a fine stone, and finish the seat. Center and narrow the seat using correction stones, as described above. |

| *Procedure* | *Method* |
|---|---|

Checking the valve seat concentricity:

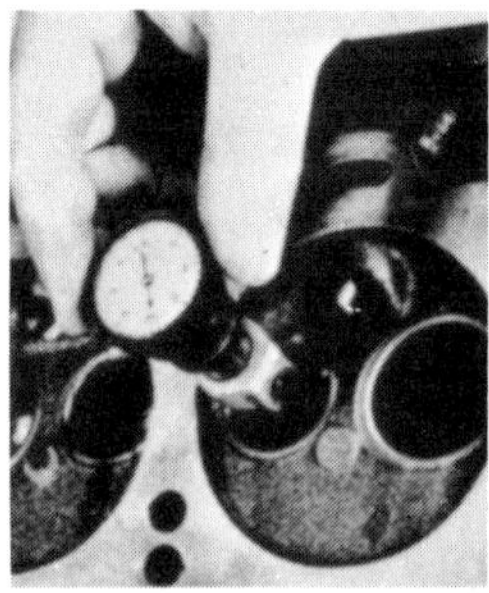

Checking the valve seat concentricity using a dial gauge (© American Motors Corp.)

Coat the valve face with Prussian blue dye, install the valve, and rotate it on the valve seat. If the entire seat becomes coated, and the valve is known to be concentric, the seat is concentric.

* Install the dial gauge pilot into the guide, and rest the arm on the valve seat. Zero the gauge, and rotate the arm around the seat. Run-out should not exceed .002″.

---

* Lapping the valves: NOTE: *Valve lapping is done to ensure efficient sealing of resurfaced valves and seats. Valve lapping alone is not recommended for use as a resurfacing procedure.*

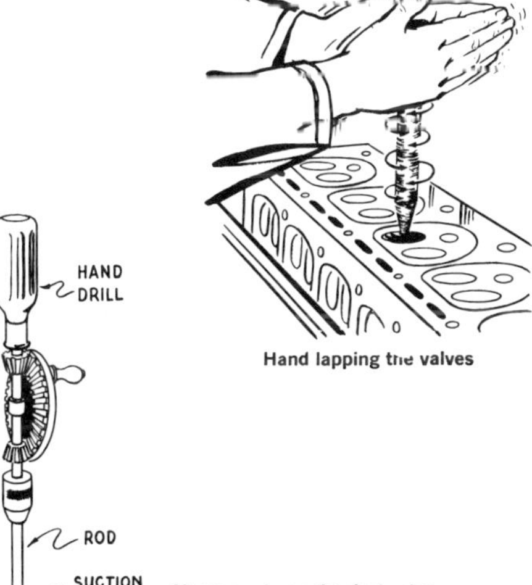


Hand lapping the valves

Home made mechanical valve lapping tool

* Invert the cylinder head, lightly lubricate the valve stems, and install the valves in the head as numbered. Coat valve seats with fine grinding compound, and attach the lapping tool suction cup to a valve head (NOTE: *Moisten the suction cup*). Rotate the tool between the palms, changing position and lifting the tool often to prevent grooving. Lap the valve until a smooth, polished seat is evident. Remove the valve and tool, and rinse away all traces of grinding compound.

** Fasten a suction cup to a piece of drill rod, and mount the rod in a hand drill. Proceed as above, using the hand drill as a lapping tool. CAUTION: *Due to the higher speeds involved when using the hand drill, care must be exercised to avoid grooving the seat.* Lift the tool and change direction of rotation often.

---

Check the valve springs:

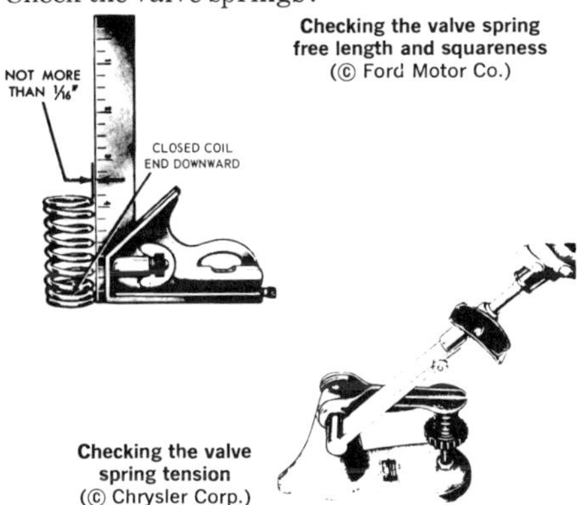


Checking the valve spring free length and squareness (© Ford Motor Co.)

Checking the valve spring tension (© Chrysler Corp.)

Place the spring on a flat surface next to a square. Measure the height of the spring, and rotate it against the edge of the square to measure distortion. If spring height varies (by comparison) by more than 1/16″ or if distortion exceeds 1/16″, replace the spring.

** In addition to evaluating the spring as above, test the spring pressure at the installed and compressed (installed height minus valve lift) height using a valve spring tester. Springs used on small displacement engines (up to 3 liters) should be ± 1 lb. of all other springs in either position. A tolerance of ± 5 lbs. is permissible on larger engines.

| *Procedure* | *Method* |
| --- | --- |
| * Install valve stem seals: 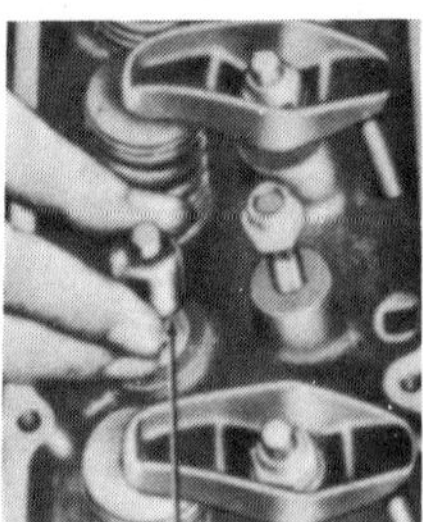  **Valve stem seal installation** (© Ford Motor Co.) | * Due to the pressure differential that exists at the ends of the intake valve guides (atmospheric pressure above, manifold vacuum below), oil is drawn through the valve guides into the intake port. This has been alleviated somewhat since the addition of positive crankcase ventilation, which lowers the pressure above the guides. Several types of valve stem seals are available to reduce blow-by. Certain seals simply slip over the stem and guide boss, while others require that the boss be machined. Recently, Teflon guide seals have become popular. Consult a parts supplier or machinist concerning availability and suggested usages. NOTE: *When installing seals, ensure that a small amount of oil is able to pass the seal to lubricate the valve guides; otherwise, excessive wear may result.* |
| Install the valves: | Lubricate the valve stems, and install the valves in the cylinder head as numbered. Lubricate and position the seals (if used, see above) and the valve springs. Install the spring retainers, compress the springs, and insert the keys using needlenose pliers or a tool designed for this purpose. NOTE: *Retain the keys with wheel bearing grease during installation.* |
| Checking valve spring installed height: 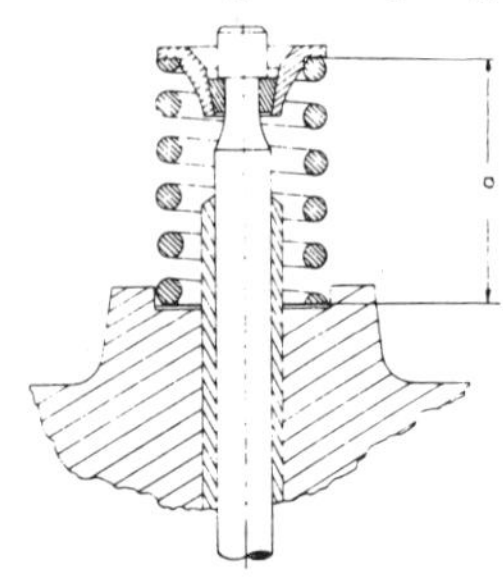 **Valve spring installed height dimension** (© Porsche) 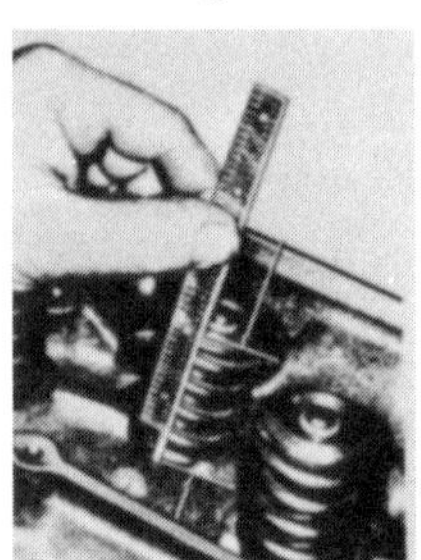 **Measuring valve spring installed height** (© Petersen Publishing Co.) | Measure the distance between the spring pad and the lower edge of the spring retainer, and compare to specifications. If the installed height is incorrect, add shim washers between the spring pad and the spring. CAUTION: *Use only washers designed for this purpose.* |
| ** CC'ing the combustion chambers: | ** Invert the cylinder head and place a bead of sealer around a combustion chamber. Install an apparatus designed for this purpose (burette mounted on a clear plate; see illustration) over the combustion chamber, and fill with the specified fluid to an even mark on the burette. Record the burette reading, and fill the combustion chamber with fluid. (NOTE: *A hole drilled in the plate will permit air to escape*). Subtract the burette reading, with the combustion chamber filled, from the previous reading, to determine combustion chamber volume in cc's. Duplicate this procedure in all combustion |

| *Procedure* | *Method* |
|---|---|
|  CC'ing the combustion chamber (© Petersen Publishing Co.) | chambers on the cylinder head, and compare the readings. The volume of all combustion chambers should be made equal to that of the largest. Combustion chamber volume may be increased in two ways. When only a small change is required (usually), a small cutter or coarse stone may be used to remove material from the combustion chamber. NOTE: *Check volume frequently.* Remove material over a wide area, so as not to change the configuration of the combustion chamber. When a larger change is required, the valve seat may be sunk (lowered into the head). NOTE: *When altering valve seat, remember to compensate for the change in spring installed height.* |
| Inspect the rocker arms, balls, studs, and nuts (where applicable):   Stress cracks in rocker nuts (© Ford Motor Co.) | Visually inspect the rocker arms, balls, studs, and nuts for cracks, galling, burning, scoring, or wear. If all parts are intact, liberally lubricate the rocker arms and balls, and install them on the cylinder head. If wear is noted on a rocker arm at the point of valve contact, grind it smooth and square, removing as little material as possible. Replace the rocker arm if excessively worn. If a rocker stud shows signs of wear, it must be replaced (see below). If a rocker nut shows stress cracks, replace it. If an exhaust ball is galled or burned, substitute the intake ball from the same cylinder (if it is intact), and install a new intake ball. NOTE: *Avoid using new rocker balls on exhaust valves.* |
| Replacing rocker studs:  Reaming the stud bore for oversize rocker studs (© Buick Div. G.M. Corp.) 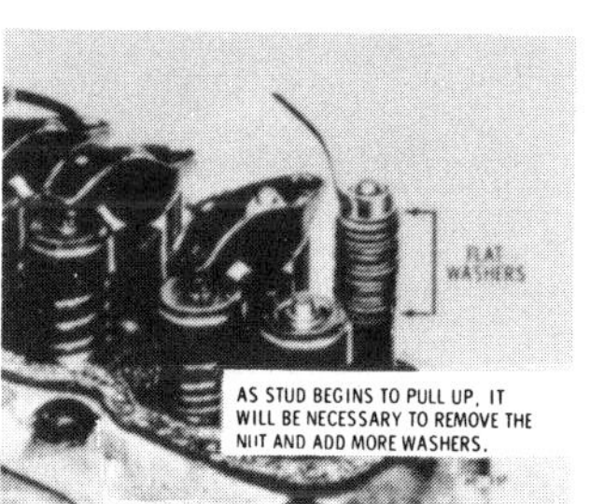  Extracting a pressed in rocker stud (© Buick Div. G.M. Corp.) | In order to remove a threaded stud, lock two nuts on the stud, and unscrew the stud using the lower nut. Coat the lower threads of the new stud with Loctite, and install.<br>Two alternative methods are available for replacing pressed in studs. Remove the damaged stud using a stack of washers and a nut (see illustration). In the first, the boss is reamed .005-.006″ oversize, and an oversize stud pressed in. Control the stud extension over the boss using washers, in the same manner as valve guides. Before installing the stud, coat it with white lead and grease. To retain the stud more positively, drill a hole through the stud and boss, and install a roll pin. In the second method, the boss is tapped, and a threaded stud installed. Retain the stud using Loctite Stud and Bearing Mount. |

| *Procedure* | *Method* |
|---|---|

Inspect the rocker shaft(s) and rocker arms (where applicable):

Disassembled rocker shaft parts arranged for inspection
(© American Motors Corp.)

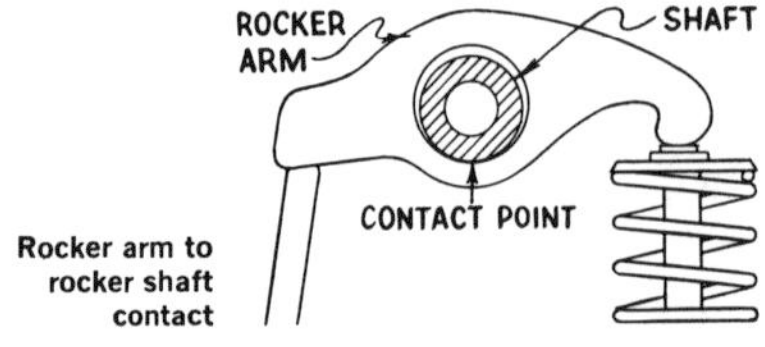


Rocker arm to rocker shaft contact

Remove rocker arms, springs and washers from rocker shaft. NOTE: *Lay out parts in the order they are removed.* Inspect rocker arms for pitting or wear on the valve contact point, or excessive bushing wear. Bushings need only be replaced if wear is excessive, because the rocker arm normally contacts the shaft at one point only. Grind the valve contact point of rocker arm smooth if necessary, removing as little material as possible. If excessive material must be removed to smooth and square the arm, it should be replaced. Clean out all oil holes and passages in rocker shaft. If shaft is grooved or worn, replace it. Lubricate and assemble the rocker shaft.

---

Inspect the camshaft bushings and the camshaft (overhead cam engines):

See next section.

---

Inspect the pushrods:

Remove the pushrods, and, if hollow, clean out the oil passages using fine wire. Roll each pushrod over a piece of clean glass. If a distinct clicking sound is heard as the pushrod rolls, the rod is bent, and must be replaced.

* The length of all pushrods must be equal. Measure the length of the pushrods, compare to specifications, and replace as necessary.

---

Inspect the valve lifters:

Checking the lifter face
(© American Motors Corp.)

Remove lifters from their bores, and remove gum and varnish, using solvent. Clean walls of lifter bores. Check lifters for concave wear as illustrated. If face is worn concave, replace lifter, and carefully inspect the camshaft. Lightly lubricate lifter and insert it into its bore. If play is excessive, an oversize lifter must be installed (where possible). Consult a machinist concerning feasibility. If play is satisfactory, remove, lubricate, and reinstall the lifter.

---

* Testing hydraulic lifter leak down:

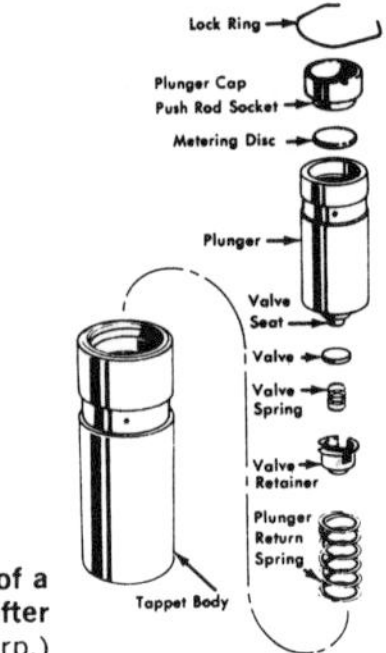


Exploded view of a typical hydraulic lifter
(© American Motors Corp.)

Submerge lifter in a container of kerosene. Chuck a used pushrod or its equivalent into a drill press. Position container of kerosene so pushrod acts on the lifter plunger. Pump lifter with the drill press, until resistance increases. Pump several more times to bleed any air out of lifter. Apply very firm, constant pressure to the lifter, and observe rate at which fluid bieeds out of lifter. If the fluid bleeds very quickly (less than 15 seconds), lifter is defective. If the time exceeds 60 seconds, lifter is sticking. In either case, recondition or replace lifter. If lifter is operating properly (leak down time 15-60 seconds), lubricate and install it.

## CYLINDER BLOCK RECONDITIONING

| *Procedure* | *Method* |
|---|---|
| Checking the main bearing clearance:  Plastigage installed on main bearing journal (© Chevrolet Div. G.M. Corp.)  Measuring Plastigage to determine main bearing clearance (© Chevrolet Div. G.M. Corp.) 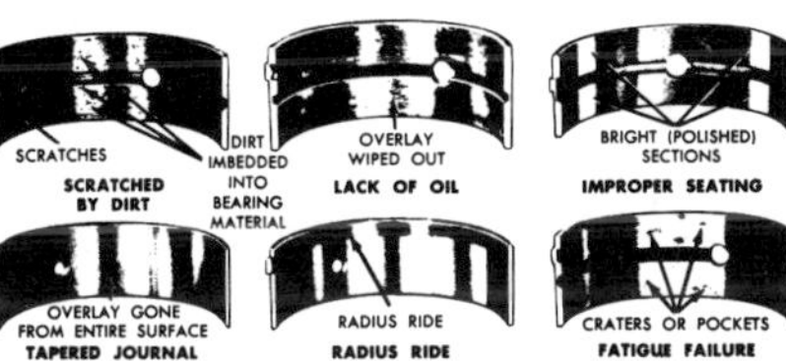  Causes of bearing failure (© Ford Motor Co.) | Invert engine, and remove cap from the bearing to be checked. Using a clean, dry rag, thoroughly clean all oil from crankshaft journal and bearing insert. NOTE: *Plastigage is soluble in oil; therefore, oil on the journal or bearing could result in erroneous readings.* Place a piece of Plastigage along the full length of journal, reinstall cap, and torque to specifications. Remove bearing cap, and determine bearing clearance by comparing width of Plastigage to the scale on Plastigage envelope. Journal taper is determined by comparing width of the Plastigage strip near its ends. Rotate crankshaft 90° and retest, to determine journal eccentricity. NOTE: *Do not rotate crankshaft with Plastigage installed.* If bearing insert and journal appear intact, and are within tolerances, no further main bearing service is required. If bearing or journal appear defective, cause of failure should be determined before replacement.<br><br>* Remove crankshaft from block (see below). Measure the main bearing journals at each end twice (90° apart) using a micrometer, to determine diameter, journal taper and eccentricity. If journals are within tolerances, reinstall bearing caps at their specified torque. Using a telescope gauge and micrometer, measure bearing I.D. parallel to piston axis and at 30° on each side of piston axis. Subtract journal O.D. from bearing I.D. to determine oil clearance. If crankshaft journals appear defective, or do not meet tolerances, there is no need to measure bearings; for the crankshaft will require grinding and/or undersize bearings will be required. If bearing appears defective, cause for failure should be determined prior to replacement. |
| Checking the connecting rod bearing clearance:  Plastigage installed on connecting rod bearing journal (© Chevrolet Div. G.M. Corp.) | Connecting rod bearing clearance is checked in the same manner as main bearing clearance, using Plastigage. Before removing the crankshaft, connecting rod side clearance also should be measured and recorded.<br><br>* Checking connecting rod bearing clearance, using a micrometer, is identical to checking main bearing clearance. If no other service |

| *Procedure* | *Method* |
|---|---|
| <br>Measuring Plastigage to determine connecting rod bearing clearance<br>(© Chevrolet Div. G.M. Corp.) | is required, the piston and rod assemblies need not be removed. |
| Removing the crankshaft:<br><br>Connecting rod matching marks<br>(© Ford Motor Co.) | Using a punch, mark the corresponding main bearing caps and saddles according to position (i.e., one punch on the front main cap and saddle, two on the second, three on the third, etc.). Using number stamps, identify the corresponding connecting rods and caps, according to cylinder (if no numbers are present). Remove the main and connecting rod caps, and place sleeves of plastic tubing over the connecting rod bolts, to protect the journals as the crankshaft is removed. Lift the crankshaft out of the block. |
| Remove the ridge from the top of the cylinder:<br>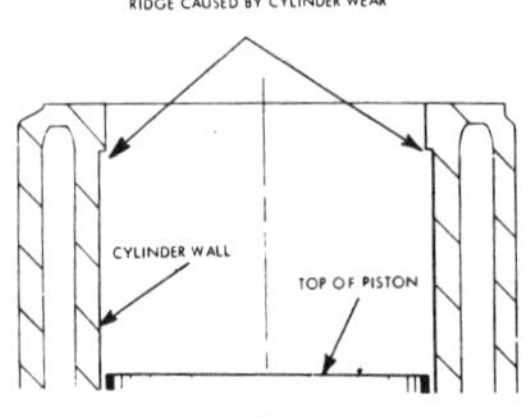<br><br>Cylinder bore ridge<br>(© Pontiac Div. G.M. Corp.) | In order to facilitate removal of the piston and connecting rod, the ridge at the top of the cylinder (unworn area; see illustration) must be removed. Place the piston at the bottom of the bore, and cover it with a rag. Cut the ridge away using a ridge reamer, exercising extreme care to avoid cutting too deeply. Remove the rag, and remove cuttings that remain on the piston. CAUTION: *If the ridge is not removed, and new rings are installed, damage to rings will result.* |
| Removing the piston and connecting rod:<br><br>Removing the piston<br>(© SAAB) | Invert the engine, and push the pistons and connecting rods out of the cylinders. If necessary, tap the connecting rod boss with a wooden hammer handle, to force the piston out. CAUTION: *Do not attempt to force the piston past the cylinder ridge* (see above). |

| *Procedure* | *Method* |
|---|---|
| Service the crankshaft: | Ensure that all oil holes and passages in the crankshaft are open and free of sludge. If necessary, have the crankshaft ground to the largest possible undersize. |
| | ** Have the crankshaft Magnafluxed, to locate stress cracks. Consult a machinist concerning additional service procedures, such as surface hardening (e.g., nitriding, Tuftriding) to improve wear characteristics, cross drilling and chamfering the oil holes to improve lubrication, and balancing. |
| Removing freeze plugs: | Drill a hole in the center of the freeze plugs, and pry them out using a screwdriver or drift. |
| Remove the oil gallery plugs: | Threaded plugs should be removed using an appropriate (usually square) wrench. To remove soft, pressed in plugs, drill a hole in the plug, and thread in a sheet metal screw. Pull the plug out by the screw using pliers |
| Hot tank the block: | Have the block hot-tanked to remove grease, corrosion, and scale from the water jackets. NOTE: *Consult the operator to determine whether the camshaft bearings will be damaged during the hot-tank process.* |
| Check the block for cracks: | Visually inspect the block for cracks or chips. The most common locations are as follows:<br>Adjacent to freeze plugs.<br>Between the cylinders and water jackets.<br>Adjacent to the main bearing saddles.<br>At the extreme bottom of the cylinders.<br>Check only suspected cracks using spot check dye (see introduction). If a crack is located, consult a machinist concerning possible repairs. |
| | ** Magnaflux the block to locate hidden cracks. If cracks are located, consult a machinist about feasibility of repair. |
| Install the oil gallery plugs and freeze plugs: | Coat freeze plugs with sealer and tap into position using a piece of pipe, slightly smaller than the plug, as a driver. To ensure retention, stake the edges of the plugs. Coat threaded oil gallery plugs with sealer and install. Drive replacement soft plugs into block using a large drift as a driver. |
| | * Rather than reinstalling lead plugs, drill and tap the holes, and install threaded plugs. |

| *Procedure* | *Method* |
| --- | --- |

Check the bore diameter and surface:

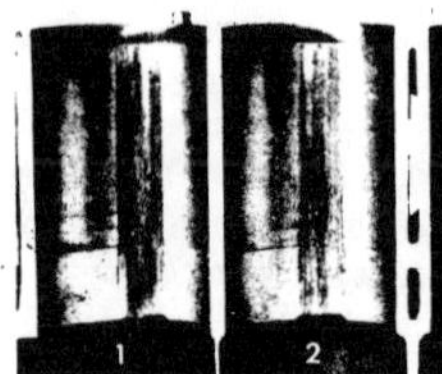


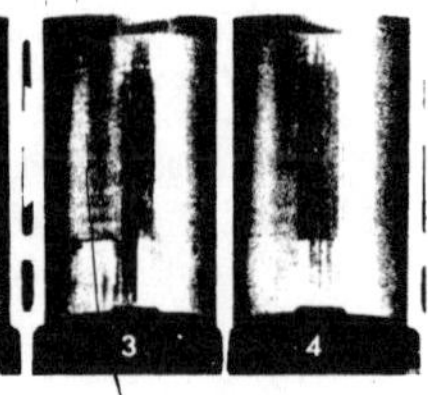


1, 2, 3 Piston skirt seizure resulted in this pattern. Engine must be rebored

4. Piston skirt and oil ring seizure caused this damage. Engine must be rebored

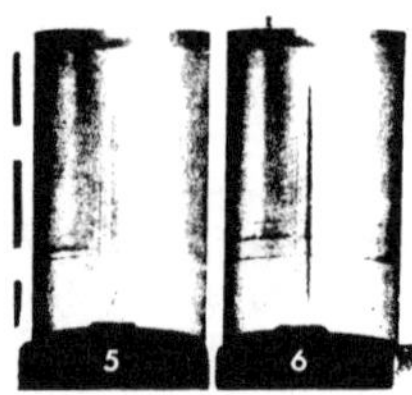

5, 6 Score marks caused by a split piston skirt. Damage is not serious enough to warrant reboring

7. Ring seized longitudinally, causing a score mark 1 3/16" wide, on the land side of the piston groove. The honing pattern is destroyed and the cylinder must be rebored

8. Result of oil ring seizure. Engine must be rebored

9. Oil ring seizure here was not serious enough to warrant reboring. The honing marks are still visible

**Cylinder wall damage**
(© Daimler-Benz A.G.)

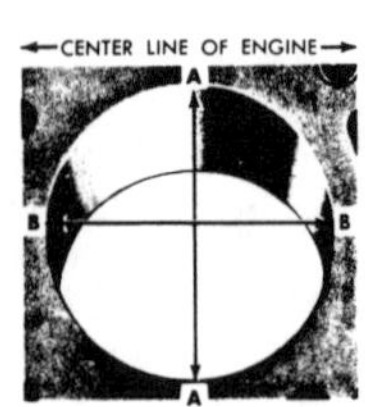


A AT RIGHT ANGLE TO CENTER LINE OF ENGINE
B PARALLEL TO CENTER LINE OF ENGINE

**Cylinder bore measuring positions**
(© Ford Motor Co.)

**Measuring the cylinder bore with a telescope gauge**
(© Buick Div. G.M. Corp.)

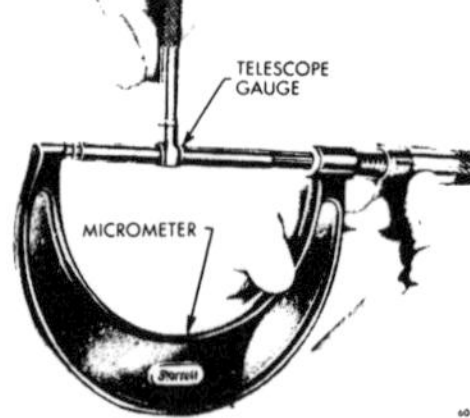


**Determining the cylinder bore by measuring the telescope gauge with a micrometer**
(© Buick Div. G.M. Corp.)

**Measuring the cylinder bore with a dial gauge**
(© Chevrolet Div. G.M. Corp.)

Visually inspect the cylinder bores for roughness, scoring, or scuffing. If evident, the cylinder bore must be bored or honed oversize to eliminate imperfections, and the smallest possible oversize piston used. The new pistons should be given to the machinist with the block, so that the cylinders can be bored or honed exactly to the piston size (plus clearance). If no flaws are evident, measure the bore diameter using a telescope gauge and micrometer, or dial gauge, parallel and perpendicular to the engine centerline, at the top (below the ridge) and bottom of the bore. Subtract the bottom measurements from the top to determine taper, and the parallel to the centerline measurements from the perpendicular measurements to determine eccentricity. If the measurements are not within specifications, the cylinder must be bored or honed, and an oversize piston installed. If the measurements are within specifications the cylinder may be used as is, with only finish honing (see below). NOTE: *Prior to submitting the block for boring, perform the following operation(s).*

| *Procedure* | *Method* |
|---|---|
| Check the block deck for warpage: | Using a straightedge and feeler gauges, check the block deck for warpage in the same manner that the cylinder head is checked (see Cylinder Head Reconditioning). If warpage exceeds specifications, have the deck resurfaced. NOTE: *In certain cases a specification for total material removal (Cylinder head and block deck) is provided. This specification must not be exceeded.* |
| * Check the deck height: | The deck height is the distance from the crankshaft centerline to the block deck. To measure, invert the engine, and install the crankshaft, retaining it with the center main cap. Measure the distance from the crankshaft journal to the block deck, parallel to the cylinder centerline. Measure the diameter of the end (front and rear) main journals, parallel to the centerline of the cylinders, divide the diameter in half, and subtract it from the previous measurement. The results of the front and rear measurements should be identical. If the difference exceeds .005", the deck height should be corrected. NOTE: *Block deck height and warpage should be corrected concurrently.* |
| Check the cylinder block bearing alignment: 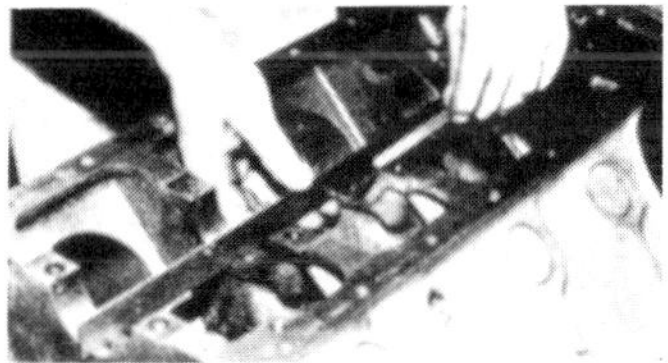 Checking main bearing saddle alignment (© Petersen Publishing Co.) | Remove the upper bearing inserts. Place a straightedge in the bearing saddles along the centerline of the crankshaft. If clearance exists between the straightedge and the center saddle, the block must be alignbored. |
| Clean and inspect the pistons and connecting rods: 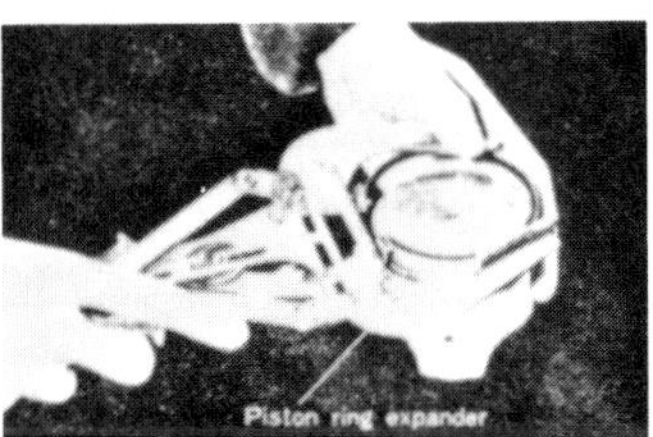  Removing the piston rings (© Subaru) | Using a ring expander, remove the rings from the piston. Remove the retaining rings (if so equipped) and remove piston pin. NOTE: *If the piston pin must be pressed out, determine the proper method and use the proper tools; otherwise the piston will distort.* Clean the ring grooves using an appropriate tool, exercising care to avoid cutting too deeply. Thoroughly clean all carbon and varnish from the piston with solvent. CAUTION: *Do not use a wire brush or caustic solvent on pistons.* Inspect the pistons for scuffing, scoring, cracks, pitting, or excessive ring groove wear. If wear is evident, the piston must be replaced. Check the connecting rod length by measuring the rod from the inside of the large end to the inside of the small end using calipers (see |

| Procedure | Method |
|---|---|
|   Cleaning the piston ring grooves (© Ford Motor Co.) 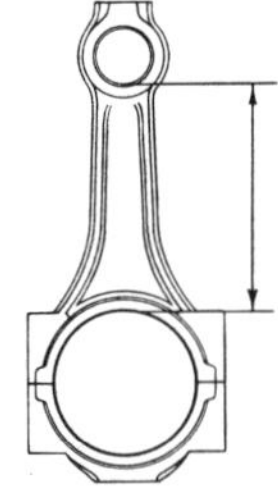 Connecting rod length checking dimension | illustration). All connecting rods should be equal length. Replace any rod that differs from the others in the engine.<br><br>* Have the connecting rod alignment checked in an alignment fixture by a machinist. Replace any twisted or bent rods.<br><br>* Magnaflux the connecting rods to locate stress cracks. If cracks are found, replace the connecting rod. |
| Fit the pistons to the cylinders: 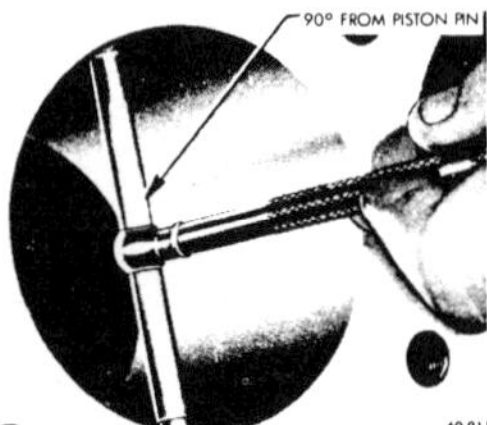  Measuring the cylinder with a telescope gauge for piston fitting (© Buick Div. G.M. Corp.)   Measuring the piston for fitting (© Buick Div. G.M. Corp.) | Using a telescope gauge and micrometer, or a dial gauge, measure the cylinder bore diameter perpendicular to the piston pin, 2½″ below the deck. Measure the piston perpendicular to its pin on the skirt. The difference between the two measurements is the piston clearance. If the clearance is within specifications or slightly below (after boring or honing), finish honing is all that is required. If the clearance is excessive, try to obtain a slightly larger piston to bring clearance within specifications. Where this is not possible, obtain the first oversize piston, and hone (or if necessary, bore) the cylinder to size. |
| Assemble the pistons and connecting rods: 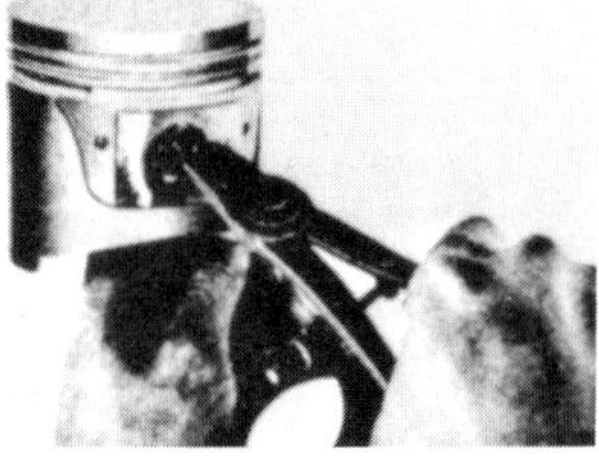 Installing piston pin lock rings (© Nissan Motor Co., Ltd.) | Inspect piston pin, connecting rod small end bushing, and piston bore for galling, scoring, or excessive wear. If evident, replace defective part(s). Measure the I.D. of the piston boss and connecting rod small end, and the O.D. of the piston pin. If within specifications, assemble piston pin and rod. CAUTION: *If piston pin must be pressed in, determine the proper method and use the proper tools; otherwise the piston will distort.* Install the lock rings; ensure that they seat properly. If the parts are not within specifications, determine the service method for the type of engine. In some cases, piston and pin are serviced as an assembly when either is defective. Others specify reaming the piston and connecting rods for an oversize pin. If the connecting rod bushing is worn, it may in many cases be replaced. Reaming the piston and replacing the rod bushing are machine shop operations. |

| *Procedure* | *Method* |
|---|---|
| Clean and inspect the camshaft: 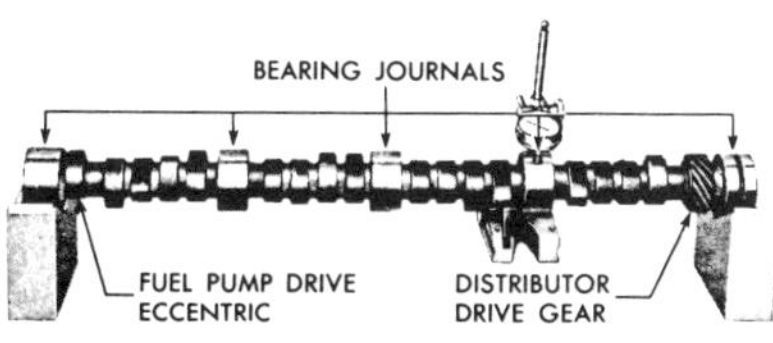  **Checking the camshaft for straightness** (© Chevrolet Motor Div. G.M. Corp.) | Degrease the camshaft, using solvent, and clean out all oil holes. Visually inspect cam lobes and bearing journals for excessive wear. If a lobe is questionable, check all lobes as indicated below. If a journal or lobe is worn, the camshaft must be reground or replaced. NOTE: *If a journal is worn, there is a good chance that the bushings are worn.* If lobes and journals appear intact, place the front and rear journals in V-blocks, and rest a dial indicator on the center journal. Rotate the camshaft to check straightness. If deviation exceeds .001″, replace the camshaft. |
| 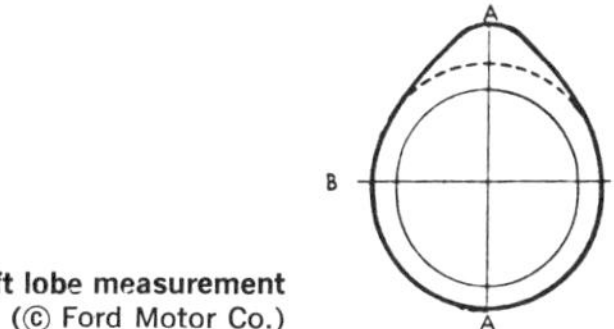  **Camshaft lobe measurement** (© Ford Motor Co.) | * Check the camshaft lobes with a micrometer, by measuring the lobes from the nose to base and again at 90° (see illustration). The lift is determined by subtracting the second measurement from the first. If all exhaust lobes and all intake lobes are not identical, the camshaft must be reground or replaced. |
| Replace the camshaft bearings: 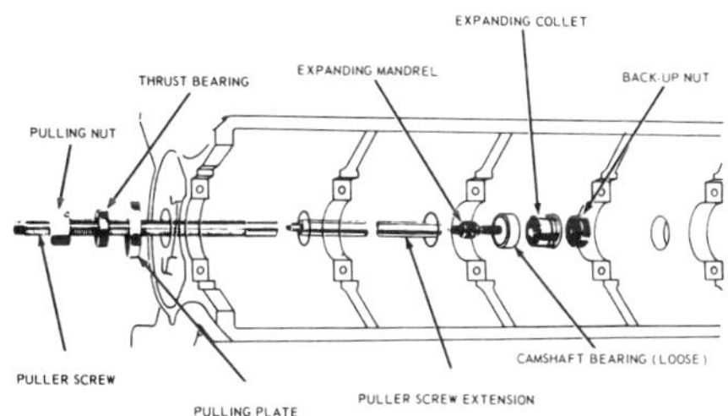  **Camshaft removal and installation tool (typical)** (© Ford Motor Co.) | If excessive wear is indicated, or if the engine is being completely rebuilt, camshaft bearings should be replaced as follows: Drive the camshaft rear plug from the block. Assemble the removal puller with its shoulder on the bearing to be removed. Gradually tighten the puller nut until bearing is removed. Remove remaining bearings, leaving the front and rear for last. To remove front and rear bearings, reverse position of the tool, so as to pull the bearings in toward the center of the block. Leave the tool in this position, pilot the new front and rear bearings on the installer, and pull them into position. Return the tool to its original position and pull remaining bearings into position. NOTE: *Ensure that oil holes align when installing bearings.* Replace camshaft rear plug, and stake it into position to aid retention. |
| Finish hone the cylinders: 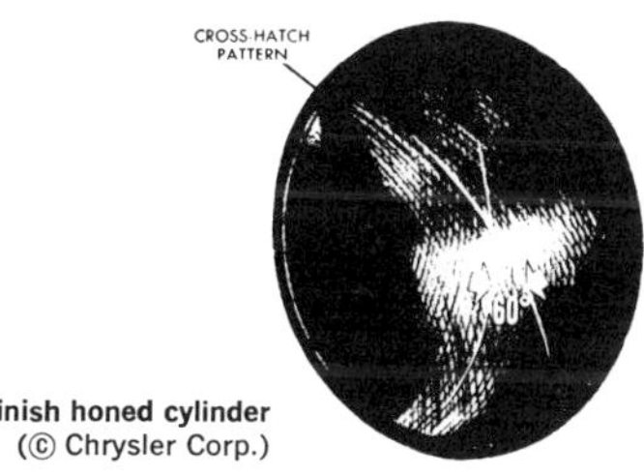  **Finish honed cylinder** (© Chrysler Corp.) | Chuck a flexible drive hone into a power drill, and insert it into the cylinder. Start the hone, and move it up and down in the cylinder at a rate which will produce approximately a 60° cross-hatch pattern (see illustration). NOTE: *Do not extend the hone below the cylinder bore.* After developing the pattern, remove the hone and recheck piston fit. Wash the cylinders with a detergent and water solution to remove abrasive dust, dry, and wipe several times with a rag soaked in engine oil. |

| Procedure | Method |
| --- | --- |
| Check piston ring end-gap: 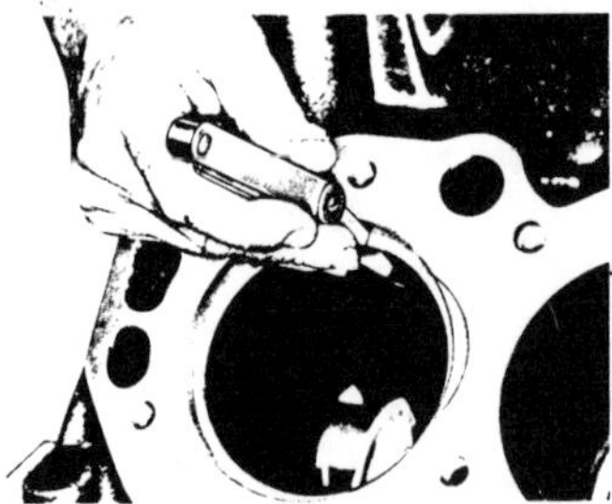 Checking ring end-gap (© Chevrolet Motor Div. G.M. Corp.) | Compress the piston rings to be used in a cylinder, one at a time, into that cylinder, and press them approximately 1″ below the deck with an inverted piston. Using feeler gauges, measure the ring end-gap, and compare to specifications. Pull the ring out of the cylinder and file the ends with a fine file to obtain proper clearance. CAUTION: *If inadequate ring end-gap is utilized, ring breakage will result.* |
| Install the piston rings: 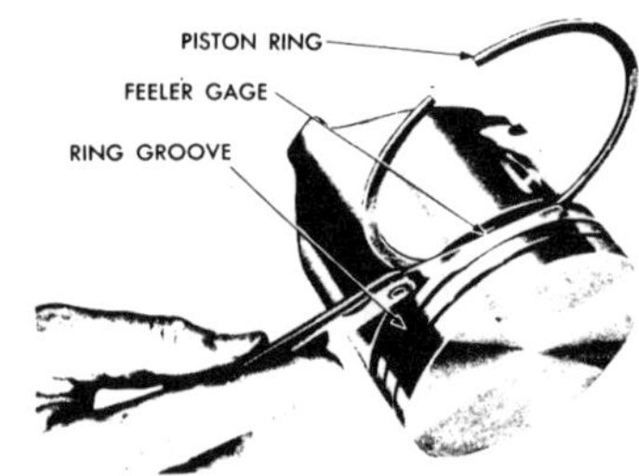  Checking ring side clearance (© Chrysler Corp.) 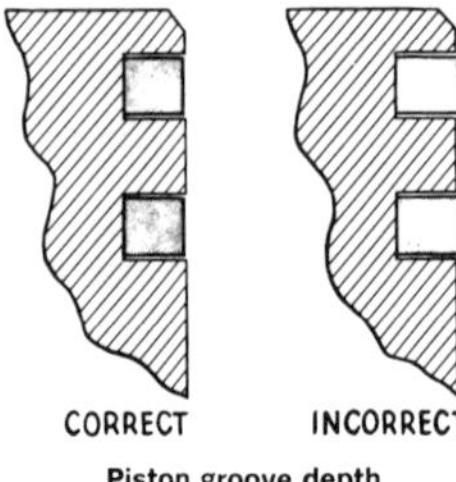  Piston groove depth 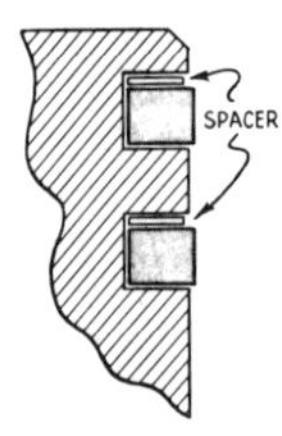  Correct ring spacer installation | Inspect the ring grooves in the piston for excessive wear or taper. If necessary, recut the groove(s) for use with an overwidth ring or a standard ring and spacer. If the groove is worn uniformly, overwidth rings, or standard rings and spacers may be installed without recutting. Roll the outside of the ring around the groove to check for burrs or deposits. If any are found, remove with a fine file. Hold the ring in the groove, and measure side clearance. If necessary, correct as indicated above. NOTE: *Always install any additional spacers above the piston ring.* The ring groove must be deep enough to allow the ring to seat below the lands (see illustration). In many cases, a "go-no-go" depth gauge will be provided with the piston rings. Shallow grooves may be corrected by recutting, while deep grooves require some type of filler or expander behind the piston. Consult the piston ring supplier concerning the suggested method. Install the rings on the piston, lowest ring first, using a ring expander. NOTE: *Position the ring markings as specified by the manufacturer (see car section).* |
| Install the camshaft: | Liberally lubricate the camshaft lobes and journals, and slide the camshaft into the block. CAUTION: *Exercise extreme care to avoid damaging the bearings when inserting the camshaft.* Install and tighten the camshaft thrust plate retaining bolts. |
| Check camshaft end-play: 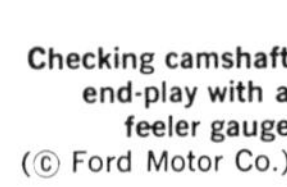  Checking camshaft end-play with a feeler gauge (© Ford Motor Co.) | Using feeler gauges, determine whether the clearance between the camshaft boss (or gear) and backing plate is within specifications. Install shims behind the thrust plate, or reposition the camshaft gear and retest end-play. |

| *Procedure* | *Method* |
|---|---|
| Checking camshaft end-play with a dial indicator | * Mount a dial indicator stand so that the stem of the dial indicator rests on the nose of the camshaft, parallel to the camshaft axis. Push the camshaft as far in as possible and zero the gauge. Move the camshaft outward to determine the amount of camshaft end-play. If the end-play is not within tolerance, install shims behind the thrust plate, or reposition the camshaft gear and retest. |
| Install the rear main seal (where applicable): <br> Seating the rear main seal (© Buick Div. G.M. Corp.) | Position the block with the bearing saddles facing upward. Lay the rear main seal in its groove and press it lightly into its seat. Place a piece of pipe the same diameter as the crankshaft journal into the saddle, and firmly seat the seal. Hold the pipe in position, and trim the ends of the seal flush if required. |
| Install the crankshaft: | Thoroughly clean the main bearing saddles and caps. Place the upper halves of the bearing inserts on the saddles and press into position. NOTE: *Ensure that the oil holes align.* Press the corresponding bearing inserts into the main bearing caps. Lubricate the upper main bearings, and lay the crankshaft in position. Place a strip of Plastigage on each of the crankshaft journals, install the main caps, and torque to specifications. Remove the main caps, and compare the Plastigage to the scale on the Plastigage envelope. If clearances are within tolerances, remove the Plastigage, turn the crankshaft 90°, wipe off all oil and retest. If all clearances are correct, remove all Plastigage, thoroughly |

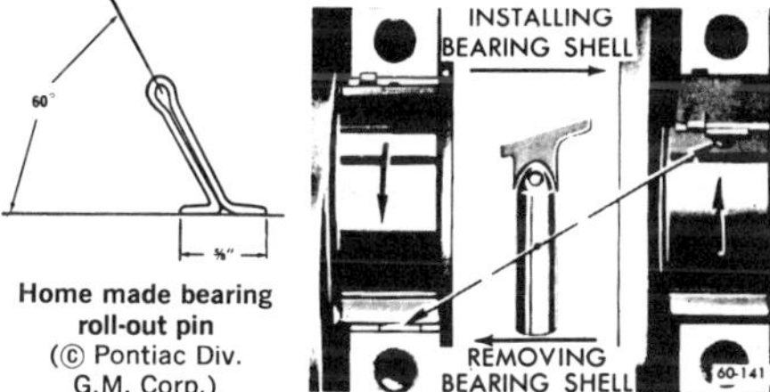


Home made bearing roll-out pin (© Pontiac Div. G.M. Corp.)

Removal and installation of upper bearing insert using a roll-out pin (© Buick Div. G.M. Corp.)

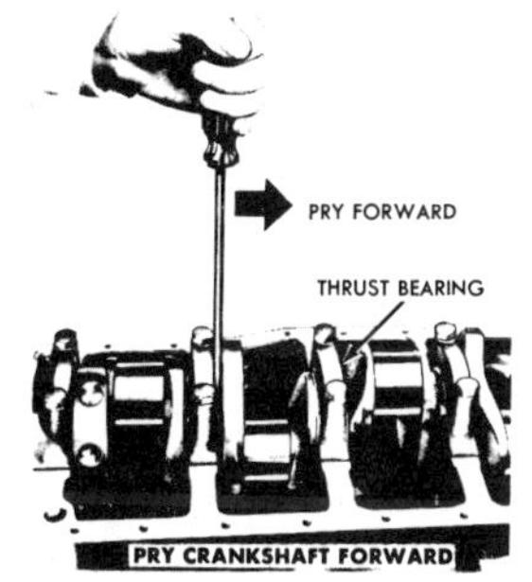


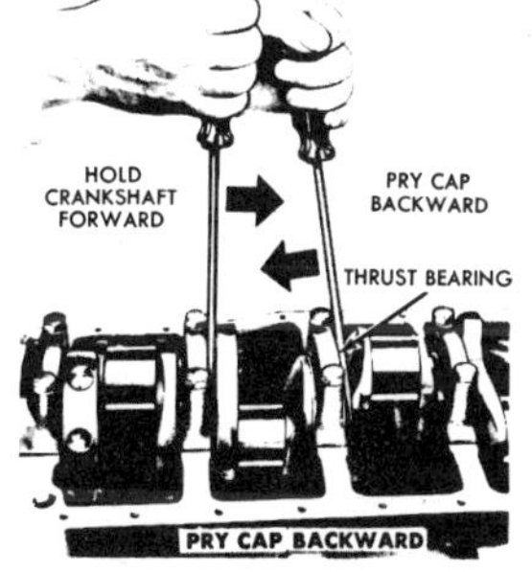


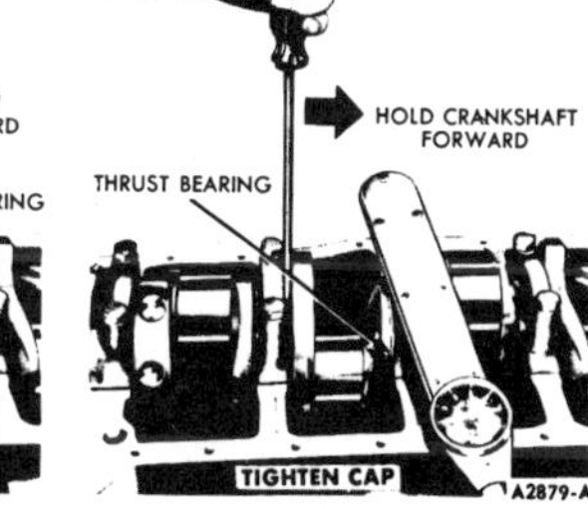


Aligning the thrust bearing (© Ford Motor Co.)

| *Procedure* | *Method* |
| --- | --- |
| | lubricate the main caps and bearing journals, and install the main caps. If clearances are not within tolerance, the upper bearing inserts may be removed, without removing the crankshaft, using a bearing roll out pin (see illustration). Roll in a bearing that will provide proper clearance, and retest. Torque all main caps, excluding the thrust bearing cap, to specifications. Tighten the thrust bearing cap finger tight. To properly align the thrust bearing, pry the crankshaft the extent of its axial travel several times, the last movement held toward the front of the engine, and torque the thrust bearing cap to specifications. Determine the crankshaft end-play (see below), and bring within tolerance with thrust washers. |
| Measure crankshaft end-play:<br><br>Checking crankshaft end-play with a dial indicator (© Ford Motor Co.)<br><br>Checking crankshaft end-play with a feeler gauge (© Chevrolet Div. (G.M. Corp.) | Mount a dial indicator stand on the front of the block, with the dial indicator stem resting on the nose of the crankshaft, parallel to the crankshaft axis. Pry the crankshaft the extent of its travel rearward, and zero the indicator. Pry the crankshaft forward and record crankshaft end-play. NOTE: *Crankshaft end-play also may be measured at the thrust bearing, using feeler gauges* (see illustration). |
| Install the pistons: | Press the upper connecting rod bearing halves into the connecting rods, and the lower halves into the connecting rod caps. Position the piston ring gaps according to specifications (see car section), and lubricate the pistons. Install a ring compresser on a piston, and press two long (8″) pieces of plastic tubing over the rod bolts. Using the plastic tubes as a guide, press the pistons into the bores and onto the crankshaft with a wooden hammer handle. After seating the rod on the crankshaft journal, remove the tubes and install the cap finger tight. Install the remaining pistons in the same man- |

| *Procedure* | *Method* |
|---|---|
|   **Tubing used as guide when installing a piston** (© Oldsmobile Div. G.M. Corp.) 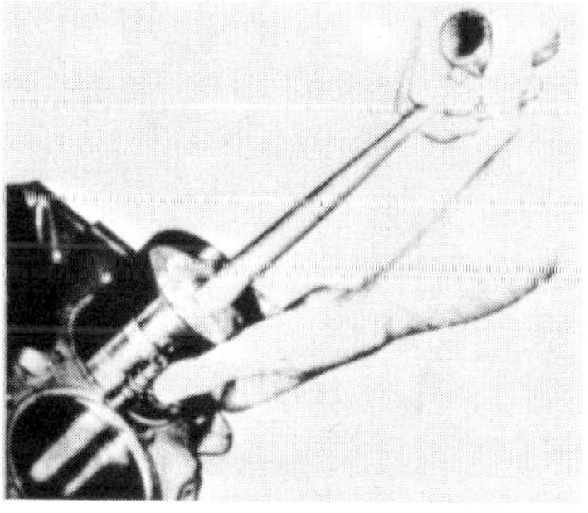 **Installing a piston** (© Chevrolet Div. G.M. Corp.) | ner. Invert the engine and check the bearing clearance at two points (90° apart) on each journal with Plastigage. NOTE: *Do not turn the crankshaft with Plastigage installed.* If clearance is within tolerances, remove *all* Plastigage, thoroughly lubricate the journals, and torque the rod caps to specifications. If clearance is not within specifications, install different thickness bearing inserts and recheck. CAUTION: *Never shim or file the connecting rods or caps.* Always install plastic tube sleeves over the rod bolts when the caps are not installed, to protect the crankshaft journals. |
| Check connecting rod side clearance: 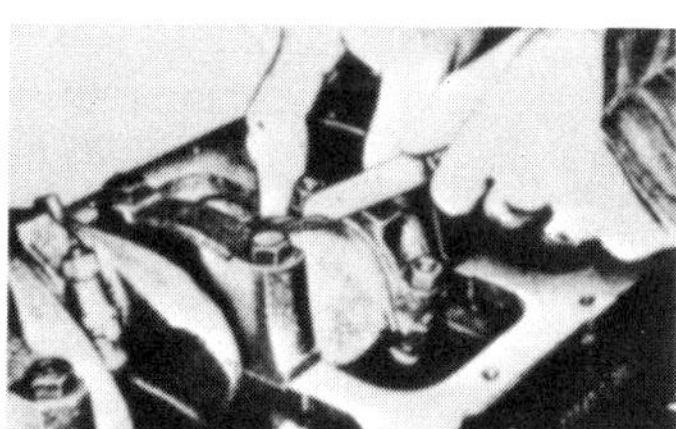 **Checking connecting rod side clearance** (© Chevrolet Div. G.M. Corp.) | Determine the clearance between the sides of the connecting rods and the crankshaft, using feeler gauges. If clearance is below the minimum tolerance, the rod may be machined to provide adequate clearance. If clearance is excessive, substitute an unworn rod, and recheck. If clearance is still outside specifications, the crankshaft must be welded and reground, or replaced. |
| Inspect the timing chain: | Visually inspect the timing chain for broken or loose links, and replace the chain if any are found. If the chain will flex sideways, it must be replaced. Install the timing chain as specified. NOTE: *If the original timing chain is to be reused, install it in its original position.* |

| *Procedure* | *Method* |
|---|---|
| Check timing gear backlash and runout: | Mount a dial indicator with its stem resting on a tooth of the camshaft gear (as illustrated). Rotate the gear until all slack is removed, and zero the indicator. Rotate the gear in the opposite direction until slack is removed, and record gear backlash. Mount the indicator with its stem resting on the edge of the camshaft gear, parallel to the axis of the camshaft. Zero the indicator, and turn the camshaft gear one full turn, recording the runout. If either backlash or runout exceed specifications, replace the worn gear(s). |

Checking camshaft gear backlash
(© Chevrolet Div. G.M. Corp.)

Checking camshaft gear runout
(© Chevrolet Div. G.M. Corp.)

## Completing the Rebuilding Process

Following the above procedures, complete the rebuilding process as follows:

Fill the oil pump with oil, to prevent cavitating (sucking air) on initial engine start up. Install the oil pump and the pickup tube on the engine. Coat the oil pan gasket as necessary, and install the gasket and the oil pan. Mount the flywheel and the crankshaft vibrational damper or pulley on the crankshaft. NOTE: *Always use new bolts when installing the flywheel.* Inspect the clutch shaft pilot bushing in the crankshaft. If the bushing is excessively worn, remove it with an expanding puller and a slide hammer, and tap a new bushing into place.

Position the engine, cylinder head side up. Lubricate the lifters, and install them into their bores. Install the cylinder head, and torque it as specified in the car section. Insert the pushrods (where applicable), and install the rocker shaft(s) (if so equipped) or position the rocker arms on the pushrods. If solid lifters are utilized, adjust the valves to the "cold" specifications.

Mount the intake and exhaust manifolds, the carburetor(s), the distributor and spark plugs. Adjust the point gap and the static ignition timing. Mount all accessories and install the engine in the car. Fill the radiator with coolant, and the crankcase with high quality engine oil.

## Break-in Procedure

Start the engine, and allow it to run at low speed for a few minutes, while checking for leaks. Stop the engine, check the oil level, and fill as necessary. Restart the engine, and fill the cooling system to capacity. Check the point dwell angle and adjust the ignition timing and the valves. Run the engine at low to medium speed (800-2500 rpm) for approximately ½ hour, and retorque the cylinder head bolts. Road test the car, and check again for leaks.

Follow the manufacturer's recommended engine break-in procedure and maintenance schedule for new engines.

# Chapter Four
# Emission Controls and Fuel System

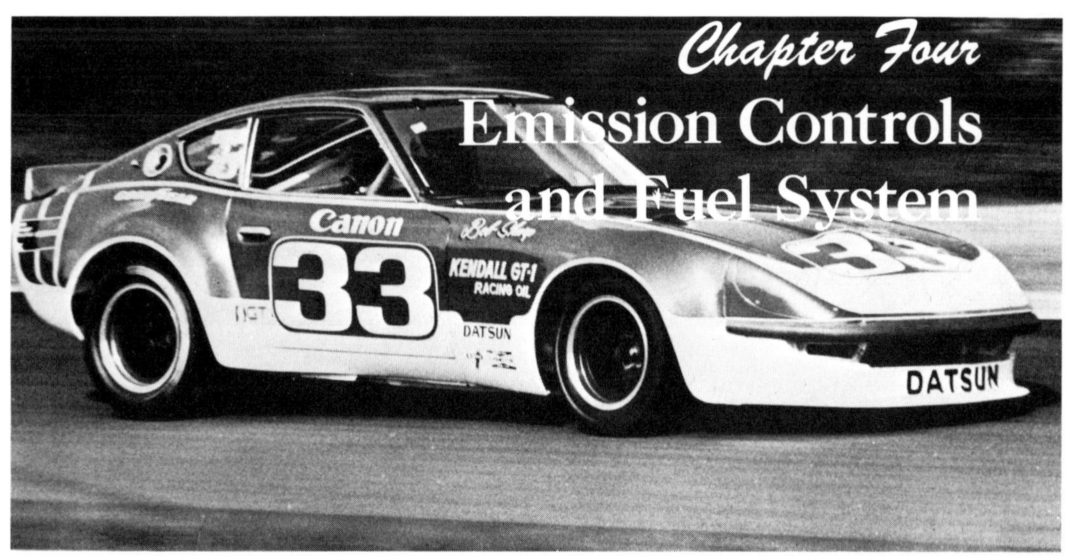


## Emission Controls

*CRANKCASE VENTILATION SYSTEM*

A closed, positive crankcase ventilation system is employed on all Datsun 240-Z and 260-Z vehicles. This system cycles incompletely burned fuel which works its way past the piston rings back into the intake manifold for reburning with the fuel/air mixture. The oil filler cap is sealed and air is drawn from the top of the crankcase into the intake manifold through a valve with a variable orifice.

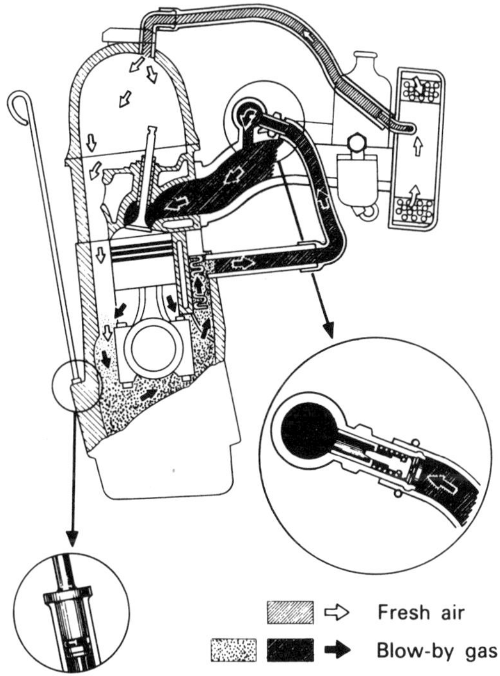


The closed positive crankcase ventilation system

This valve (commonly known as the PCV valve) employs spring pressure and a sliding plunger to regulate the flow of air into the manifold according to the amount of manifold vacuum. When the carburetor throttles are open fairly wide, this valve opens to maximize the flow. However, at idle speed, when manifold vacuum is at maximum, the PCV valve throttles the flow in order not to unnecessarily affect the small volume of mixture passing to the engine.

A ventilating line connects the valve cover with the air cleaner. During most driving conditions, manifold vacuum is high and all of the vapor from the crankcase, plus a small amount of excess air, is drawn into the manifold via the PCV. However, at full-throttle, the increase in the volume of blow-by and the decrease in manifold vacuum make the flow via the PCV inadequate. Under these conditions excess vapors are drawn into the air cleaner and pass through the carburetors and into the engine.

**Service Checks**

After every 12,000 miles or every year, perform the following services:

1. Check the condition of the hoses and the connectors to ensure that there is no leakage. Replace parts if necessary.
2. Disconnect the hoses and blow them clean with compressed air. Where extreme clogging is encountered, replace the hose.
3. Check the PCV valve as follows:
   a. Start the engine and allow it to idle. Then, disconnect the ventilating hose from the PCV valve, allowing air to be drawn into the manifold through the valve. The flow of air should produce an audible "hiss" and it should be possible to feel a strong vacuum when placing a finger over the valve inlet. If the valve is clogged, replace it as it is not serviceable.

*EVAPORATIVE EMISSION CONTROL SYSTEM*

The Evaporative Emission Control System employs:

1. A sealed filler cap.
2. A vapor-liquid separator and vent line.
3. A flow guide valve (240-Z).

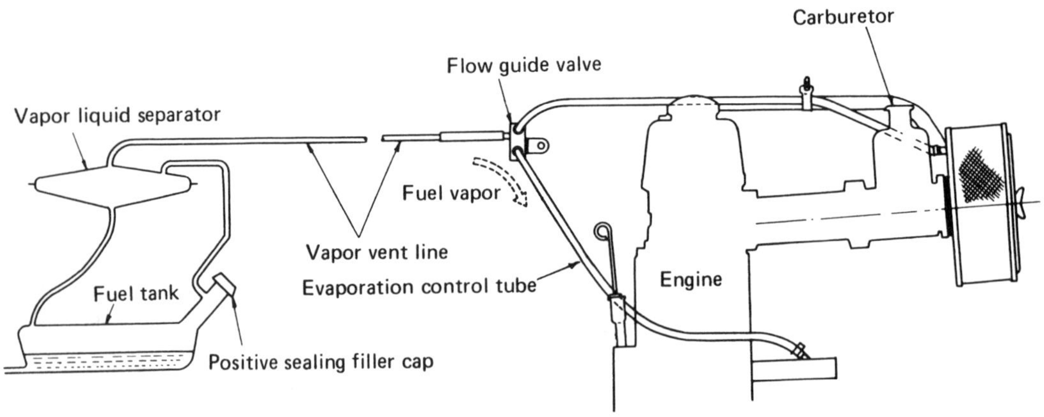


Evaporative emission control system (1970–73)

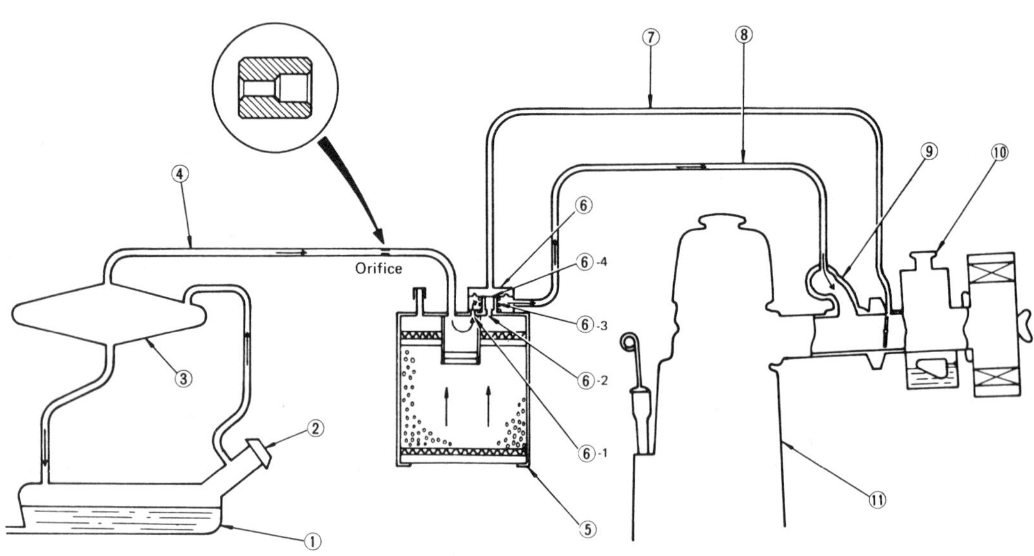


Evaporative emission control system (1974–75)

1. Fuel tank
2. Positive sealing filler cap
3. Vapor liquid separator
4. Vapor vent line
5. Carbon canister
6. Purge control valve
6-1. Small orifice
6-2. Large orifice
6-3. Diaphragm spring
6-4. Diaphragm
7. Vacuum signal line
8. Canister purge line
9. Balance tube
10. Carburetor
11. Engine

4. An evaporation control tube (240-Z).

5. A carbon storage canister (260-Z).

The sealed filler cap allows vacuum (created as the fuel pump empties the tank) to draw air into the tank to replace the used fuel. This avoids damaging the tank or starving the fuel system. It will not, however, allow fuel vapor to escape.

The vapor-liquid separator allows a vent line to collect the vapor formed in the gas tank and store it in the crankcase or in a carbon canister, but prohibits liquid fuel from passing into the vent line.

The flow guide valve allows vapor sorted in the crankcase to be drawn into the intake manifold when the engine is operated, while shunting fuel vapor to the crankcase and closing off the line to the manifold when the engine is stopped.

The evaporation control tube carries the fuel vapor into the crankcase when the engine is stopped.

The carbon canister stores the fuel vapor from the tank when the engine is not running. When the engine starts, vacuum carried by a vacuum signal line opens a purge valve on the top of the canister. Air is then drawn through a filter on the bottom of the canister, through the charcoal, a nozzle in the purge valve, and into the manifold.

## Checking Fuel Tank, Filler Cap, and Vent Line

1. Periodically inspect all hoses and the fuel tank filler cap for poor connections, cracks, or other deficiencies, and replace parts as necessary. When inspecting the filler cap, pull the pressure relief valve outward to check for free, smooth operation. Check that it seals ef-

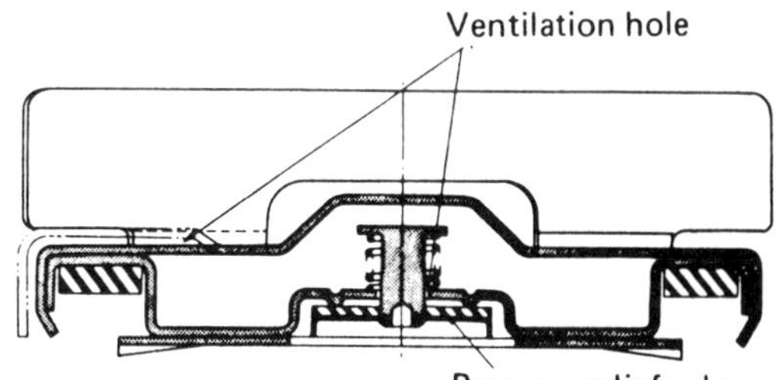

Fuel filler cap

fectively. Replace defective parts as necessary.

2. Disconnect the vapor vent line at the canister or flow guide valve. Install a "T," connecting a source of air pressure and a pressure gauge which reads in inches of water.

3. Slowly apply pressure until the pressure gauge reads 14.5 inches. Close off the air supply, and wait 2½ minutes.

4. Check the reading on the gauge. It should not have dropped below 13.5 inches.

5. Remove the filler cap. The pressure should drop to zero in a few seconds. If not, the vent line is clogged.

## Checking the Carbon Canister Purge Valve

1. Disconnect the rubber hose which runs between the manifold and canister at the T-connector.

2. Blow into the open end of the hose and listen for leaks.

3. If there are leaks, remove the top cover of the purge valve and check for a dislocated or cracked diaphragm. Replace parts as necessary.

4. At this time the filter on the bottom of the canister should be inspected. If the filter is clogged, replace it. Inspec-

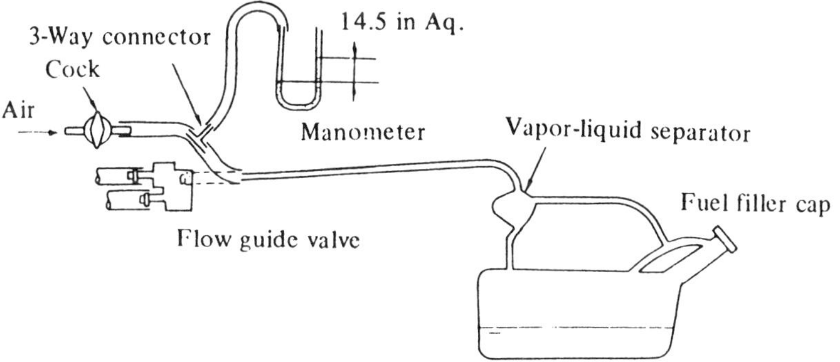

Gauge hook-up for checking evaporative emission control system

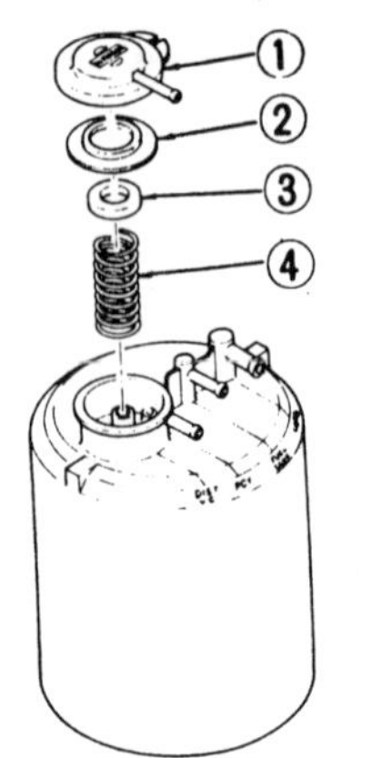


Exploded view of the carbon canister purge valve

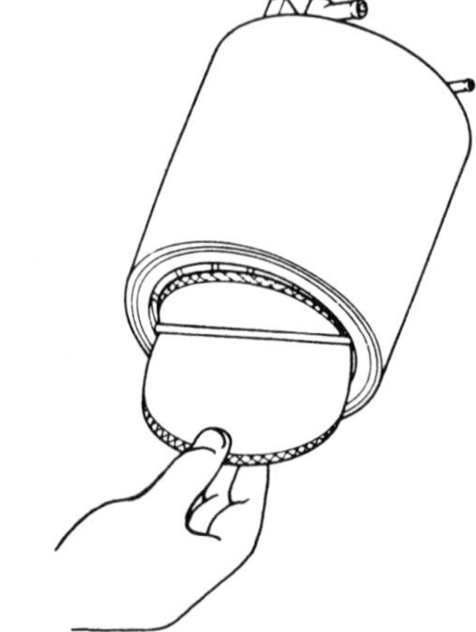

Replacing the canister filter

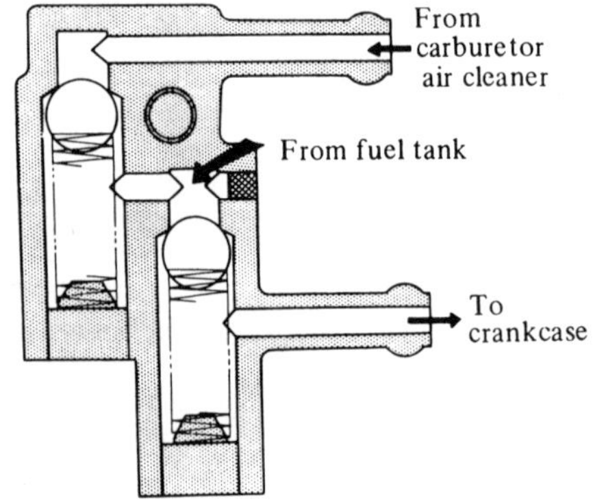


The flow guide valve

tion and replacement can be accomplished without removing the canister.

### Checking the Flow Guide Valve

1. Disconnect all hoses to the valve.
2. Force low pressure air into the fuel tank vent connection. Air should emerge from the crankcase side.
3. Force air into the air cleaner connection. Air should emerge from the fuel tank and/or crankcase vent connection.
4. Force air into the crankcase vent line connection. There should be no leakage.
5. If the valve fails any of these tests, replace it.

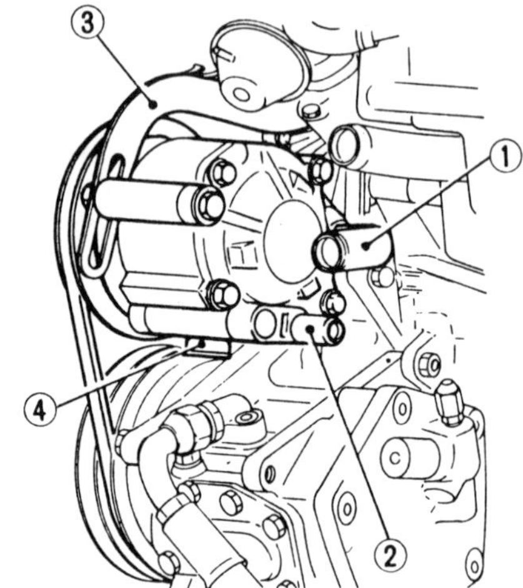

Rear view of the air pump

1. Inlet port
2. Outlet port
3. Belt adjusting bar
4. Relief valve

### *AIR INJECTION REACTOR*

A positive displacement air pump is provided to inject fresh air into the exhaust ports to accelerate combustion in the manifold. The system includes:

1. An antibackfire valve. When the throttle is suddenly closed, this valve diverts the air pump discharge into the intake manifold in order to promote combustion in the combustion chambers and minimize combustion in the exhaust manifold.
2. A check valve. This device prevents exhaust gases from traveling back into the air pump when exhaust pressure exceeds air pump discharge pressure.
3. An air pump relief valve. This valve controls the air pump discharge pressure in order to protect the pump from excessive pressure and control exhaust temperature and pump power requirements.

### Testing the Air Pump and Valves

1. Operate the engine until it reaches operating temperature.
2. Inspect all hoses and connections, replace any damaged hoses or clamps, and retighten connections as necessary.

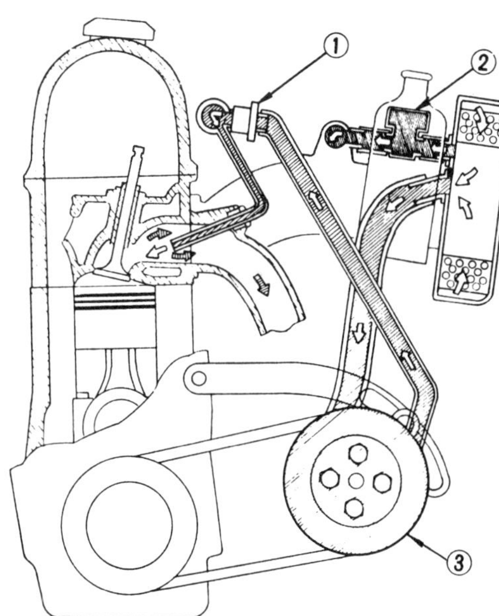

The air injection system

1. Check valve 2. Antibackfire valve 3. Air pump

3. Check the air pump belt tension and adjust as necessary.

4. Disconnect the air supply hose at the check valve.

5. Insert the open end of a special Air Pump Test Gauge Adapter into the air supply hose and clamp it securely. This adapter is required because it provides a relief port of critical size.

6. Operate the engine at 1,500 rpm and read the test gauge. The pressure should be 0.63 in. Hg (16 mm) or more.

7. With the engine still at 1,500 rpm, close the relief port in the gauge adapter and listen for leaks. If there is any leakage from the relief valve, it is faulty.

8. If the system fails the pressure test, the pump must be replaced unless the problem is in the relief valve.

9. Stop the engine. Inspect the check valve plate position. The plate should be lightly in contact with the seat away from the air manifold.

10. Insert a small screwdriver into the valve connection, depress the valve plate, and release it. It should return to the seat freely.

11. Start the engine and slowly bring its speed to 1,500 rpm. There should be no leakage of exhaust gas from the check valve although a slight fluttering at idle is normal.

12. If the check valve fails any of the tests, replace it.

13. Reconnect the air supply hose and remove the air cleaner cover.

14. Lightly position a finger over the inlet hole for the antibackfire valve (see the illustration). Do not shut the hole off entirely.

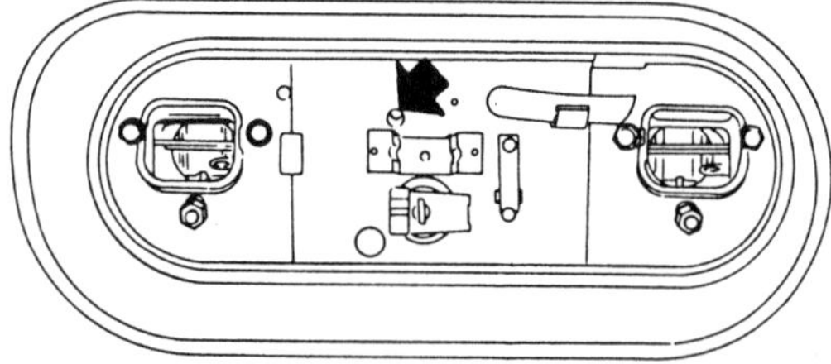
The antibackfire valve air inlet hole

15. Raise the engine rpm to between 3,000 and 3,500, and then suddenly release the linkage. There should be a sudden flow of air during deceleration. If there is no airflow or if airflow exists under other than deceleration conditions, replace the valve.

### Air Pump Removal and Installation

1. Disconnect all hoses from the housing.

2. Remove the bolt used to position the pump on the belt adjusting bar. Remove the bolt which secures the pump to the mounting bracket.

3. Remove the belt, and remove the pump.

To install the pump:

1. Put the pump and belt into position. Install the pump mounting bolt.

2. Install the bolt which positions the pump loosely on the adjusting bar. Adjust the belt tension to specifications and tighten the nut.

3. Reinstall all hoses.

### Antibackfire Valve Replacement

No special instructions are required except that the valve *must* be replaced with its diaphragm chamber upward. Never attempt to disassemble and repair the valve.

### Check Valve Removal and Installation

1. Disconnect the air supply hose.

2. While removing the valve, put opposing pressure on the flange of the air manifold with a wrench.

To install the valve:

1. Reverse the removal procedure, again putting pressure in opposition to installation torque on the air manifold flange. Never attempt to disassemble and repair the valve.

## *THROTTLE OPENER*

### Adjustment

1. Bring the engine to operating temperature.
2. Disconnect the vacuum hose at point "A." Connect a vacuum gauge which gives quick response where the hose was removed.
3. On 1973 and later models, disconnect the throttle opener solenoid harness.
4. Rev the engine to approximately 3,000 rpm and release the throttle. Note the reading on the pressure gauge between the time that the throttle actuator begins to work and the time that the throttle reaches normal idle position. The reading should be constant between these two points.

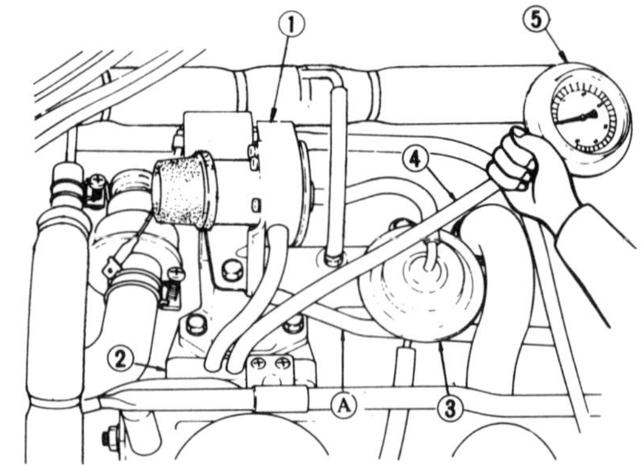

Connecting the vacuum gauge to the manifold

1. Throttle opener control valve
2. Intake manifold
3. Servo diaphragm
4. Vacuum gauge hose
5. Vacuum gauge

5. Compare the reading with the appropriate chart, using the altitude or barometric pressure.
6. Loosen the vacuum adjusting screw locknut and adjust the pressure as necessary. If the pressure is too low, adjust the

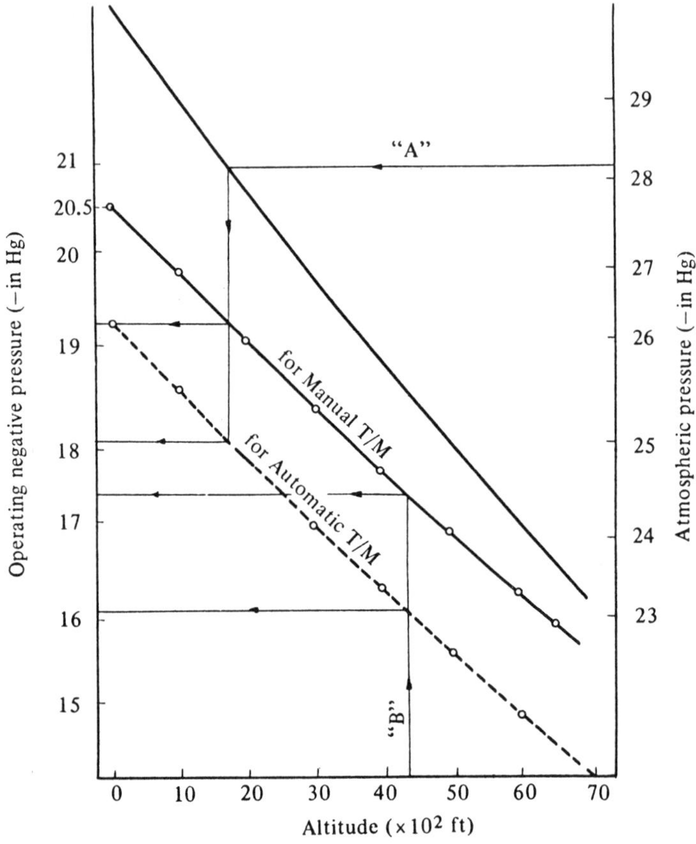

Operating pressure of the throttle opener—1972 and earlier

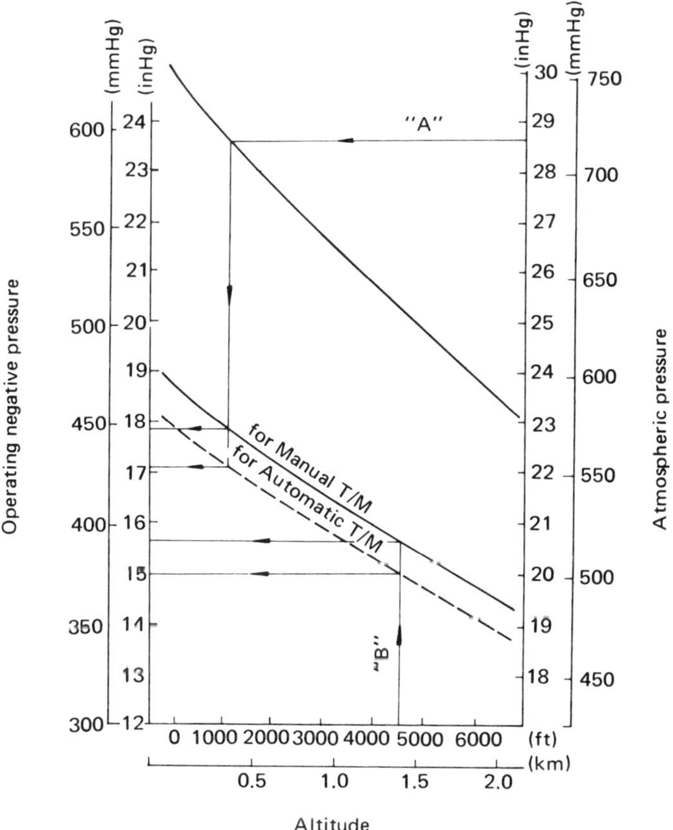

Operating pressure of the throttle opener—1973 and later

screw clockwise. If it is too high, turn the screw counterclockwise.

7. Tighten the locknut and recheck the adjustment.

8. If the throttle actuator holds the throttle open all the time (engine does not drop to idle speed), it will be necessary to rig the gauge so that it can be read with the car decelerating from about 50 mph in High gear. Adjust the screw as necessary on the basis of this test.

### *EXHAUST GAS RECIRCULATION SYSTEM*

The exhaust gas recirculation system reduces peak combustion temperatures by recirculating a very small portion of cooled exhaust gases to the intake manifold to slow combustion. The system incorporates carburetor vacuum control to eliminate recirculation at idle speed and at full-throttle. A thermostatically-operated solenoid also interrupts vacuum to the valve when the passenger compartment temperature is below freezing.

#### Inspection

1. Check the solenoid operation. Temperature must be above 55° F (13° C) and engine hot. Raise the engine rpm from idle to about 3,000 and check to see that the diaphragm and shaft move upward as the speed is increased.

2. On 240-Z models, disconnect the solenoid harness and jumper the harness connection directly to the battery positive terminal. On 260-Z models, engine must be below 77° F (25° C). Repeat the increase in engine rpm and check to see that the EGR valve does not open.

3. Rewire the solenoid and then push the bottom dish of the EGR valve upward. The engine should idle roughly and lose speed.

4. Remove the EGR vacuum tube at the carburetor and inspect it. If it is deformed, replace it. Reconnect the tube, torquing to 3.0 ft lbs (0.4 kg-m).

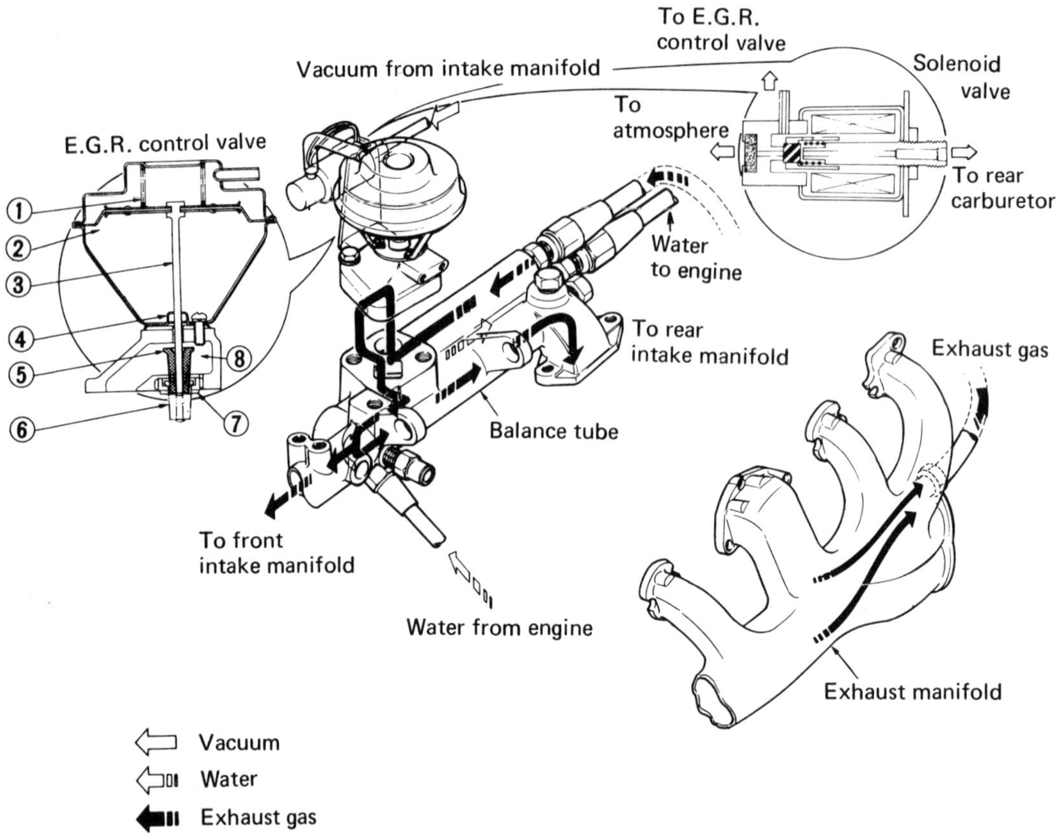

To E.G.R.
control valve
Vacuum from intake manifold
Solenoid
valve
To
atmosphere
To rear
carburetor
E.G.R. control valve
Water
to engine
To rear
intake manifold
Exhaust gas
Balance tube
To front
intake manifold
Water from engine
Exhaust manifold

Vacuum
Water
Exhaust gas

The Exhaust Gas Recirculation system

1. Diaphragm spring
2. Diaphragm
3. Valve shaft
4. Seal
5. Valve (open)
6. Valve (closed)
7. Valve seat
8. Valve chamber

5. Remove the EGR valve (see the following procedure).

6. Apply a vacuum of 6 in. Hg (152 mm). The valve should open all the way.

7. Pinch the vacuum hose and check that the valve remains closed for 30 seconds or more.

8. Inspect the valve for damage or a wrinkled diaphragm. Check the seat for accumulation of carbon and clean with a soft wire brush, if necessary.

9. Make sure that the seat is tight. Replace the valve if there are any abnormalities.

10. Inspect the valve mounting flange and adjusting screw block for carbon accumulation. If the balance tube passages are clogged or dirty, remove and clean it.

### EGR Valve and Balance Tube Removal and Installation

1. Disconnect the vacuum line at the solenoid.

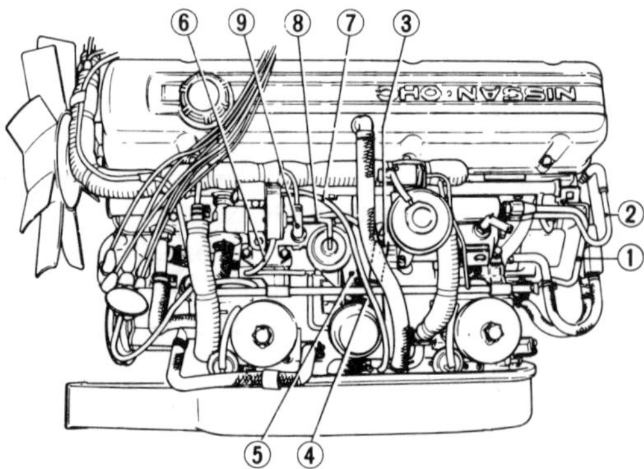


Disconnecting related plumbing

1. Exhaust gas return tube
2. Water outlet tube
3. ISS hose
4. Crankcase ventilation hose
5. Antibackfire valve hose
6. Throttle opener vacuum signal hose
7. Throttle opener hose (throttle opener to air cleaner)
8. Throttle opener hose (throttle opener to servo diaphragm)
9. Canister purge hose

2. Remove the two valve mounting bolts and remove the valve.

3. Disconnect:

a. The fuel hose to the rear carburetor;

b. The hose between the air cleaner and rocker cover;

c. The hose between the anti-backfire valve and balance tube;

d. The vacuum lines between the balance tube and air cleaner, intake manifold and throttle opener valve, and throttle opener valve and air cleaner.

4. Remove the throttle opener valve and servo.

5. Disconnect the water tube between the thermostat housing and balance tube.

6. Remove the exhaust gas return tube and water outlet hose.

7. Disconnect the throttle linkage at the joint.

8. Remove the four mounting bolts and pull the balance tube off the engine. Disconnect the hose which runs between the idle screw block and air/fuel by-pass tube.

To install, reverse the removal procedures exactly.

### *AUTOMATIC TEMPERATURE CONTROL AIR CLEANER*

This system is designed to stabilize the temperature of air going to the carburetors in order to permit smooth operation with leaner fuel/air mixtures. It incorporates a temperature sensor which feeds a vacuum motor varying amounts of vacuum according to the temperature of the air in the air cleaner. The vacuum motor controls an air door which in turn controls the amount of air to pass over the exhaust manifold on its way to the air cleaner.

#### A.T.C. System Test

1. Allow the engine to cool until the engine compartment is below 86° F (30° C). Make sure that the air door is open.

2. Start the engine and operate it at idle. If the air door closes right away, it and the vacuum motor are in good condition.

3. Watch the air door to ensure that it opens gradually. In hot weather, it will eventually open all the way while in cold weather, it will open only slightly.

4. If there is doubt about the operation of the system, tape a small thermometer to the inside of the air cleaner cover, as close as possible to the sensor. Then operate the engine until the thermometer has had a chance to reach a stable reading. Finally, open the air cleaner and read the thermometer. It should read between 100–130° F (38–55° C).

5. If the system is faulty, the vacuum motor may be tested by removing its vacuum supply hose from the temperature sensor and connecting it directly to

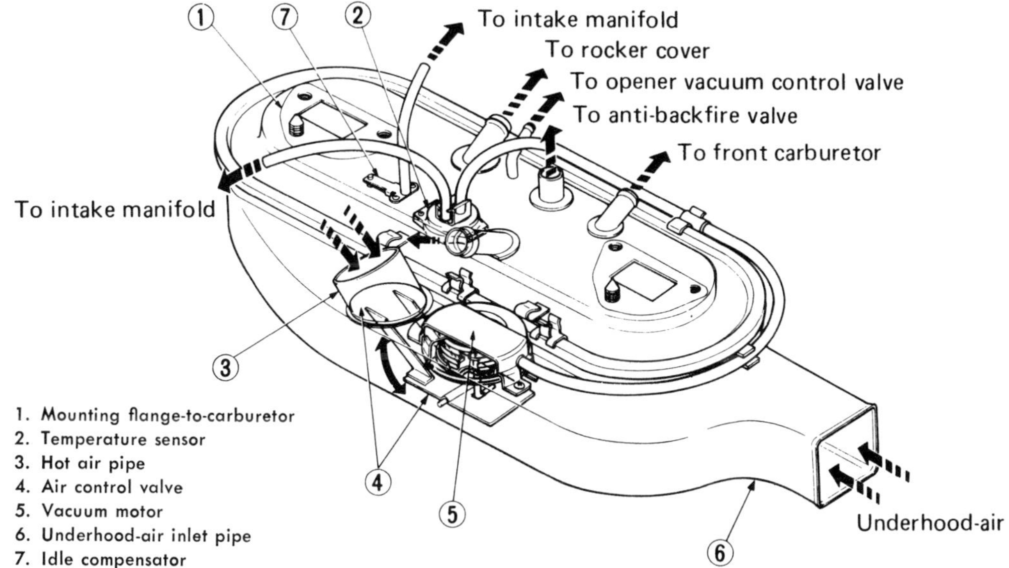


The ATC air cleaner

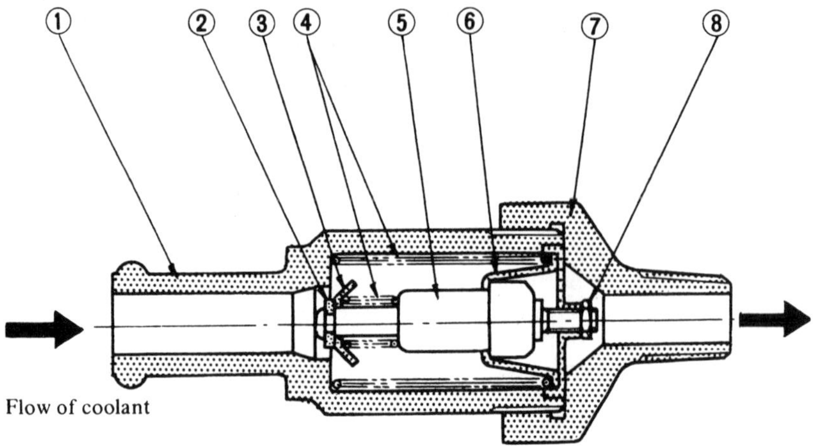


The manifold heat control thermostat

1. Case
2. E-ring
3. Valve
4. Spring
5. Pellet
6. Supporting case
7. Adjusting nut
8. Case cover

the manifold. If the valve closes with the engine operating at idle speed, the problem must be in the temperature sensor or the hoses.

*MANIFOLD HEAT CONTROL THERMOSTAT*

This device is installed on 1972 and earlier vehicles to heat the manifold during engine warmup. Engine coolant passes through passages in the manifold until a temperature of about 150° F exists. At this point, the thermostat closes off the flow of coolant through the manifold.

To test the thermostat, remove it and attach a length of rubber hose to the inlet end. Then immerse the thermostat in water heated to 175° F. After the thermostat has had a minute or so to reach the temperature of the water, force air at low pressure into the hose. If bubbles come out the other end of the thermostat, replace it.

## Fuel System

*MECHANICAL FUEL PUMP*

**Removal and Installation**

1. Disconnect the inlet and outlet lines from the pump.
2. Remove the mounting bolts.

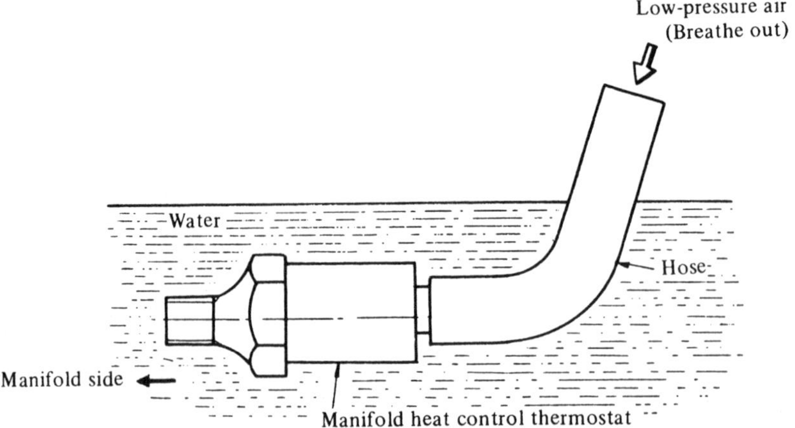


Checking the manifold heat control thermostat

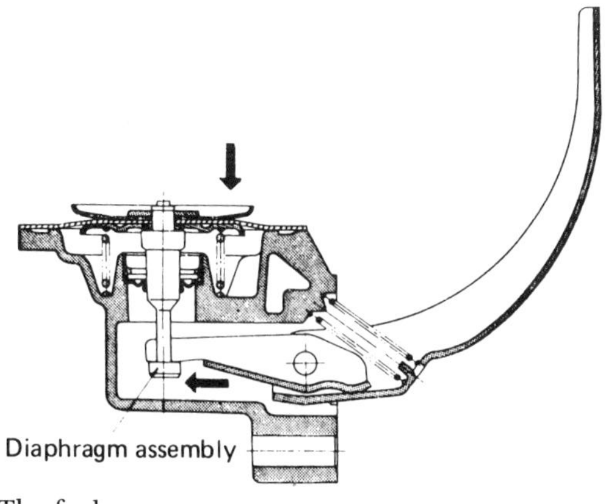

The fuel pump

3. Remove the pump and discard the gasket.
4. Lubricate the rocker arm, rocker arm pin, and lever pin of the pump.
5. Put a new gasket in position and bolt the pump in place.
6. Connect the fuel lines.

### Fuel Pump Test

1. Disconnect the line from the fuel pump to the carburetor at the pump.
2. Tee in a pressure gauge going as close to the carburetor as possible.
3. Start the engine and operate it at various speeds. The fuel pump pressure should be 3.4–4.25 psi (0.24–0.30 kg/cm $^2$).

Pressure below these specifications indicates excessive wear, while high pressures indicate a faulty spring or diaphragm. In either case, the pump requires removal and disassembly for replacement of faulty parts. If the pump passes the pressure test, but if there is still a question that its performance may not be adequate, proceed with the capacity test below.

1. Disconnect the pressure gauge from the tee, and position a large container under the open end.
2. Start the engine and operate it at 1,000 rpm for 15 seconds. The pump should deliver at least 0.42 qts (400 cc) of fuel in this time.

Failure of this test indicates a faulty pump or clogged suction line.

## *ELECTRIC FUEL PUMP*

### Location and Type

The electric fuel pump used on 260-Z models is a transistorized plunger type which force feeds the conventional mechanical fuel pump in order to minimize

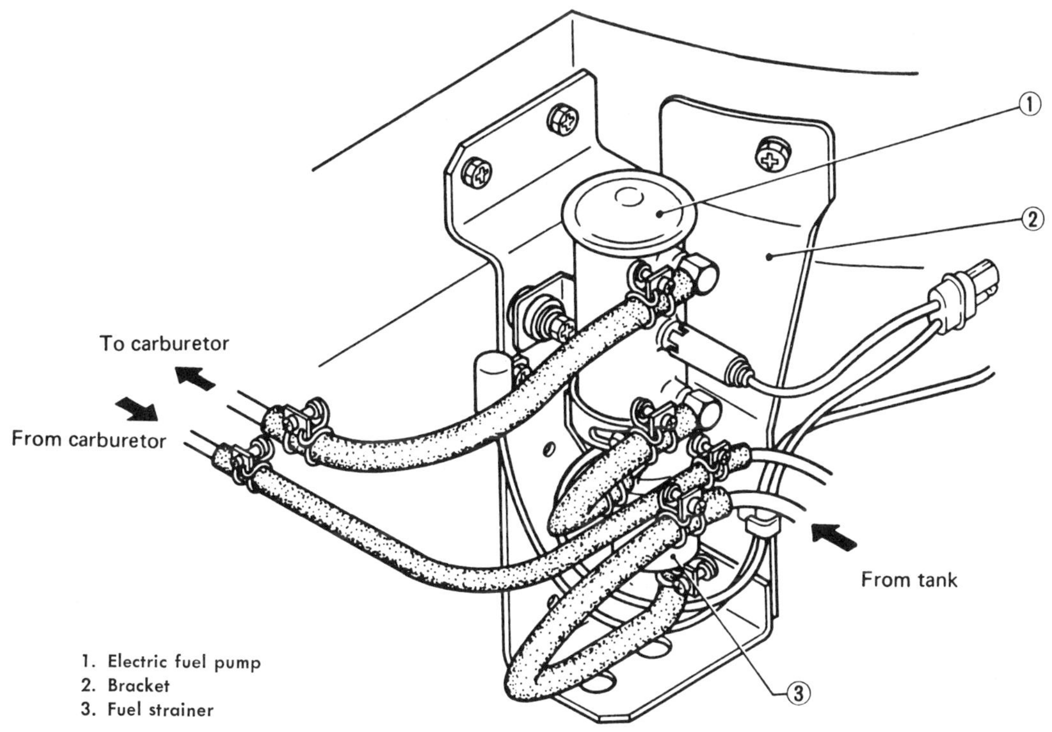

The electric fuel pump and strainer

the chances of vapor lock or other fuel deficiency problems. The pump is located in the corner where the differential mounting member intersects the side member.

**Removal and Installation**

1. Remove the inlet hose at the fuel strainer. Remove the outlet hose at the pump and drain the remaining fuel into a suitable container.
2. Disconnect both electrical connections at the pump.
3. Remove the mounting bolts, and remove the pump from the bracket.

To install, reverse the removal procedures.

**Electric Fuel Pump Test**

1. Disconnect the pump discharge hose and replace it with a hose of equal inside diameter.
2. Place a large container under the hose outlet. Start the engine and idle it for at least 7–8 seconds in order to run the pump.
3. Check the volume of fuel discharged. It should be at least 0.73 qts. (700 cc).
4. If there is doubt about pump discharge pressure, a pressure gauge may be connected to the pump and the pump operated as in Step 2. The discharge pressure must not exceed 4.6 psi (0.42 kg/cm $^2$).

*CARBURETORS*

**Removal and Installation**

1. Remove the three thumbscrews and detach the air cleaner cover.
2. Disconnect all hoses between air cleaner and other components.
3. Remove the six screws retaining the air cleaner flange to the carburetors and remove it.
4. Remove the fuel and ISS hoses from both carburetors. Remove the by-pass hose from the front carburetor.
5. Remove the distributor and canister vacuum hose from the front carburetor.
6. Remove the EGR vacuum hose from the rear carburetor (on 1973 and later models).
7. Remove the coolant inlet hose from the front carburetor and the outlet hose from the rear carburetor.
8. Disconnect the throttle linkage and, on earlier models, the choke linkage.
9. Remove the attaching nuts and remove the carburetors.
10. To separate the two carburetors, disconnect and remove the air by-pass and coolant hoses.
11. Reverse the removal procedures to install.

**Float Level Adjustment**

1974

1. Remove the carburetor from the intake manifold. Remove the seven attaching screws and remove the float chamber cover.
2. Turn the carburetor upside down to check the position of the float lever. Both floats should touch the inner wall of the carburetor.

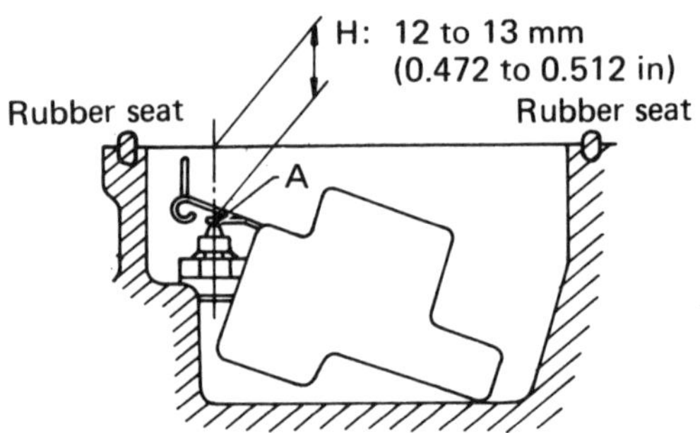


Measuring dimension "H"

3. Measure dimension "H" between the end face of the float chamber and the float lever tongue which contacts the needle valve (point "A"). It should be 0.472–0.512 in. (12–13 mm).

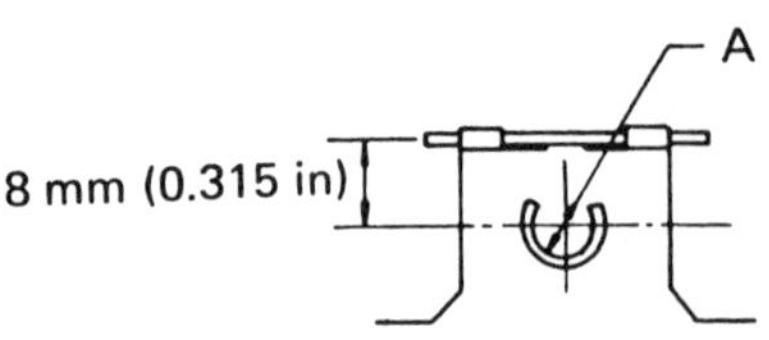


The location of point "A"

4. If necessary, bend the float lever near the float to bring the dimension to within specifications.
5. Turn the carburetor right side up. Measure the gap ("G") between the

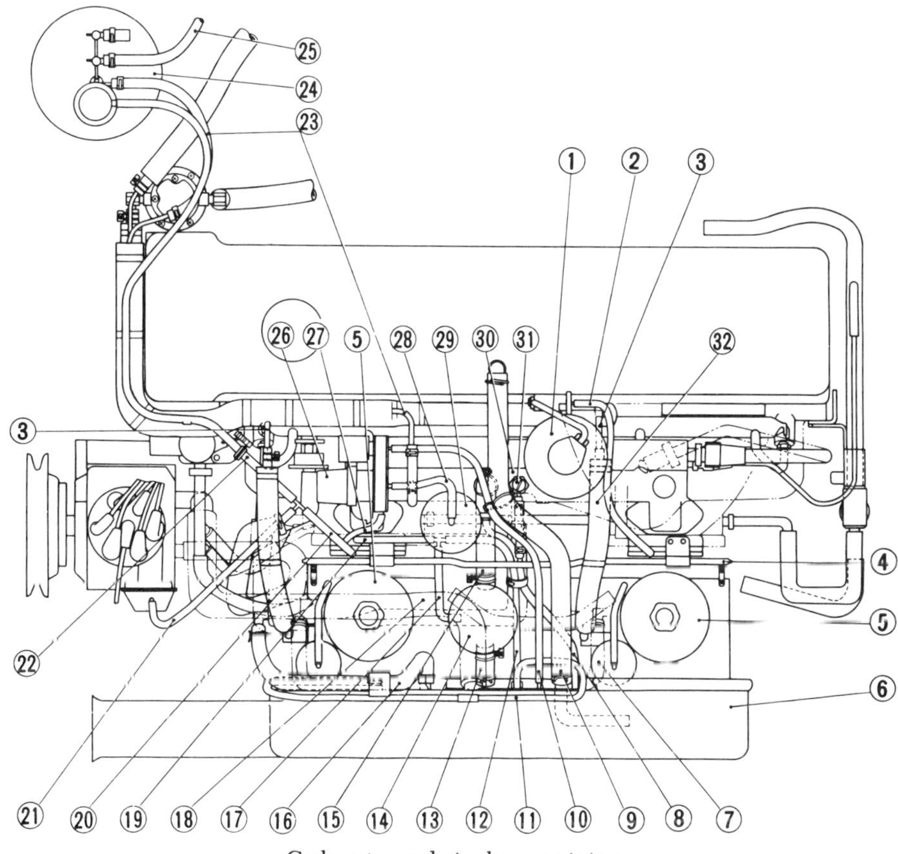


Carburetor and air cleaner piping

1. E.G.R. control valve
2. E.G.R. vacuum signal hose
3. Fuel inlet hose
4. I.S.S. tube
5. Carburetor
6. Air cleaner
7. Air by-pass hose
8. Idle compensator hose
9. Crankcase ventilation hose
10. Throttle opener hose (from throttle opener solenoid to air cleaner)
11. Temp. sensor hose (from temp. sensor to vacuum motor)
12. Temp. sensor hose (from temp. sensor to intake manifold)
13. A. B. valve hose (from air cleaner to A. B. valve)
14. Antibackfire (A B.) valve
15. A. B. valve hose (from A. B. valve to balance tube)
16. Air by-pass hose (from air cleaner to front carburetor)
17. A. B. valve vacuum signal hose
18. Air pump inlet hose
19. A. B. valve and temp. sensor vacuum signal hose
20. Distributor and canister vacuum signal hose
21. Distributor vacuum signal hose
22. Canister vacuum signal hose
23. Canister purge hose
24. Carbon canister
25. Vapor vent hose
26. Throttle opener control valve
27. Throttle opener vacuum signal hose
28. Throttle opener servo diaphragm hose
29. Throttle opener servo diaphragm
30. Balance tube
31. Idle speed adjusting screw
32. Heat shield material

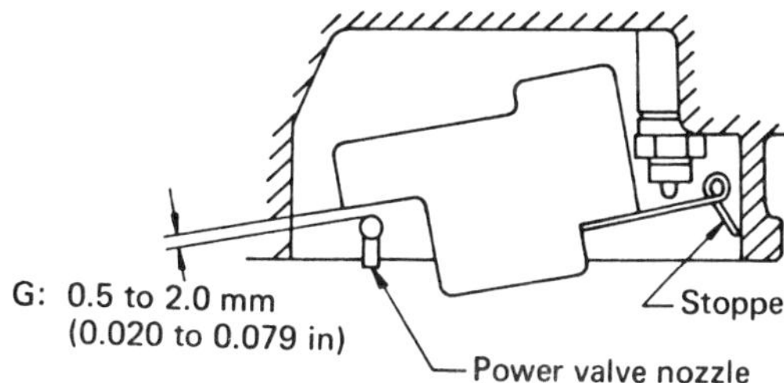


The location of dimension "G"

power valve nozzle and float. It should be 0.020–0.079 in. (0.5–2.0 mm).

6. Adjust the gap, as necessary, by bending the stop as required. Then, recheck dimension "H."

7. Install the float chamber cover and install the carburetor on the engine.

8. When the engine is operating, the fuel level should be even with the center line of the float level window.

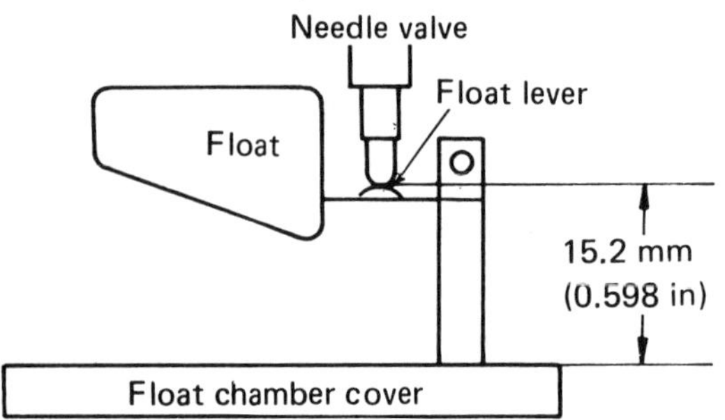


Where to check float level height—1973 models

### 1973

1. Remove the carburetor from the engine. Remove the float chamber cover.
2. Measure the distance between the portion of the float lever which contacts the needle valve and the float chamber cover. It should be 0.598 in. (15.2 mm).
3. If necessary, bend the float lever to adjust the dimension. Recheck to make sure that the dimension is to specification.
4. Install the float chamber cover and reinstall the carburetor on the engine.
5. Check float level by operating the engine and checking that the fuel level is in the center of the float level window.

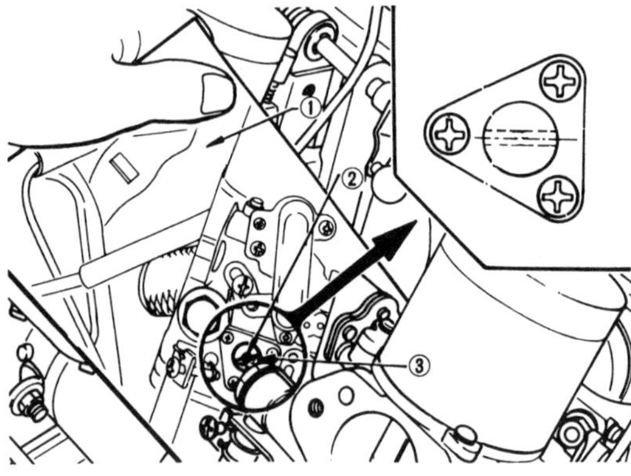

Checking float level

1. Mirror 2. Float level point 3. Float level window

### 1970–72

1. Remove the four float chamber cover screws and remove the cover.
2. Place the cover on a flat surface with the float upward.
3. Lift the float up until the needle valve is open and then lower it just until the needle valve contacts the seat.
4. See the illustration and measure the distance between fuel level and the top of the float chamber. It should be 0.5512–0.5906 in. (14–15 mm).
5. If necessary, correct the dimension by bending the float lever.
6. Replace the float chamber cover.

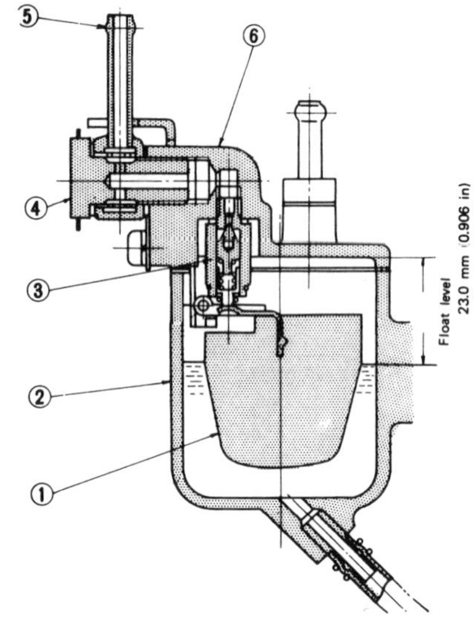


Adjustment of float level—1972 and earlier models

1. Float
2. Float chamber
3. Needle valve
4. Filter bolt
5. Nipple
6. Float chamber cover

## Fast Idle Adjustment

### 1973–74

1. Place the fast idle screw on the first step of the fast idle cam.

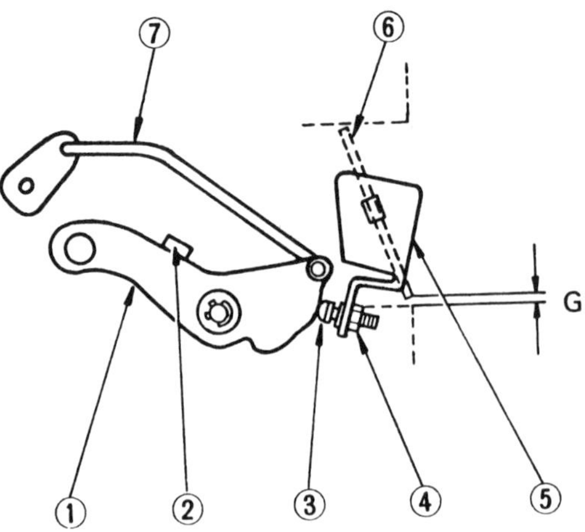


Adjusting the fast idle opening—260-Z

1. Choke lever
2. Choke lever stopper
3. Fast idle screw
4. Locknut
5. Fast idle lever
6. Throttle valve
7. Connecting rod

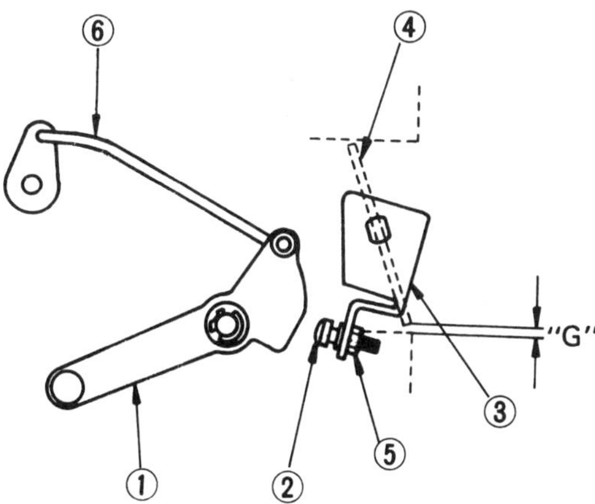


Adjusting fast idle opening—1973 models

1. Choke lever
2. Fast idle screw
3. Fast idle lever
4. Throttle valve
5. Locknut
6. Connecting rod

2. Adjust the screw so that the clearance between the throttle valve and the lower throttle bore is 0.023–0.025 in. (0.59–0.64 mm).

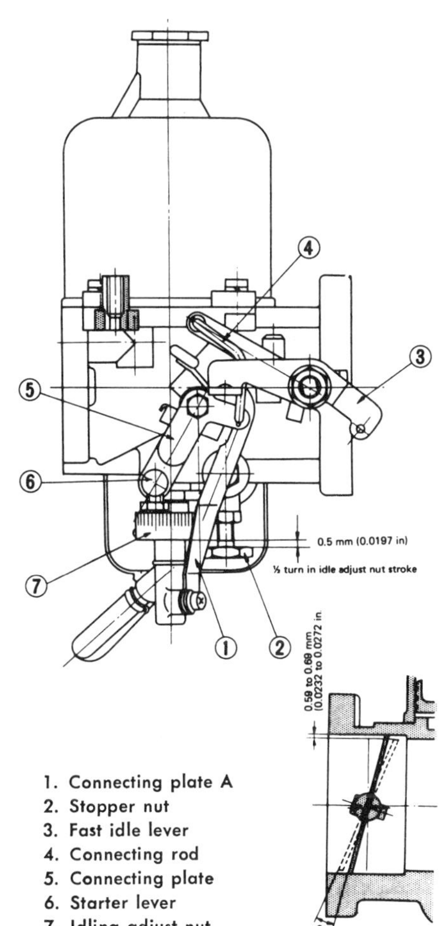


1. Connecting plate A
2. Stopper nut
3. Fast idle lever
4. Connecting rod
5. Connecting plate
6. Starter lever
7. Idling adjust nut

Adjusting fast idle opening—1970–72

1970–72

1. Measure the clearance between the throttle valve and bore when the choke lever is out all the way. The clearance should be 0.232–0.271 in. (0.59–0.69 mm).

2. Correct the clearance by bending the connecting rod. Making the rod longer increases the clearance.

### Choke Piston Adjustment

1974

1. Close the choke valve all the way.

2. Hold the valve shut by stretching a rubber band between the lever connected to the choke wire and the carburetor.

3. Using a pair of pliers, gently grip the diaphragm rod and pull it all the way out.

4. Hold the rod in this position and check the gap between the choke valve and carburetor body. The gap should be 0.0925 in. (2.35 mm).

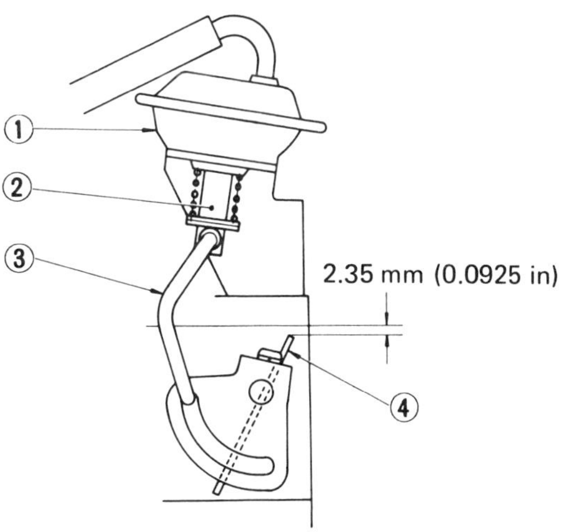


Adjusting the 260-Z choke piston

1. Choke piston
2. Diaphragm rod
3. Choke piston rod
4. Choke valve

5. Bend the choke piston rod as necessary to secure the proper adjustment.

### Suction Piston and Chamber Inspection

1. Remove the air cleaner and the oil cap nut.

2. Gradually raise the suction piston with a suitable probe on 1973 and later models. On 1972 and earlier carburetors, the piston should be raised so that the

Location of the suction piston lifter

lifter is well beyond the point where the lifter head contacts the suction piston.

3. Release the piston. The piston should drop smoothly and a sucking sound should be audible.

4. Install the oil cap nut. Raise the suction with your finger, going in through the throttle bore, and then let it drop. The piston should resist rising due to damper operation and it should return to the bottom of its travel smoothly. Otherwise, the piston and chamber require cleaning.

### Overhaul

1973–74

On 1973 and later models the factory does not recommend overhaul, except as described below, because of the extreme precision with which carburetors are calibrated at the factory.

### Float Chamber

1974

1. Remove the seven mounting screws which secure the float chamber cover and remove it.
2. Do not attempt to remove the float and needle valve parts.
3. Adjust the float (see "Float Level Adjustment"), and reassemble.

1973

1. Loosen the six mounting screws and remove the float chamber cover.
2. Remove the clip and remove the needle valve parts. Do not touch the needle jet setting nut or bend the float stopper.
3. Reassemble parts of the needle valve. Adjust the float level as described above.
4. Install the float chamber cover.

### Power Valve

1973–74

If the carbon monoxide (CO) emissions in the exhaust are abnormally high and there is no obvious reason, check the power valve. Remove the three mounting screws and remove the valve from the carburetor. Remove the other three screws and disassemble the valve. Carefully inspect the diaphragm and replace it if necessary. Reassemble and install the valve.

### Overhaul

1970–72

To disassemble the carburetors:

1. Remove screws and suction chamber.
2. Remove suction spring, nylon packing, and suction piston from chamber. Be extremely careful not to bend the jet needle.
3. Do not remove the jet needle from the suction piston unless it must be replaced. To remove, loosen jet needle setscrew. Hold the needle with pliers at a point no more than 0.10 in. from the

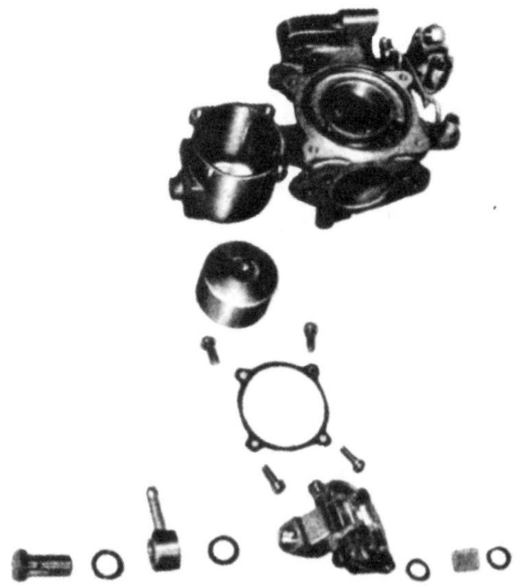
The float bowl assembly

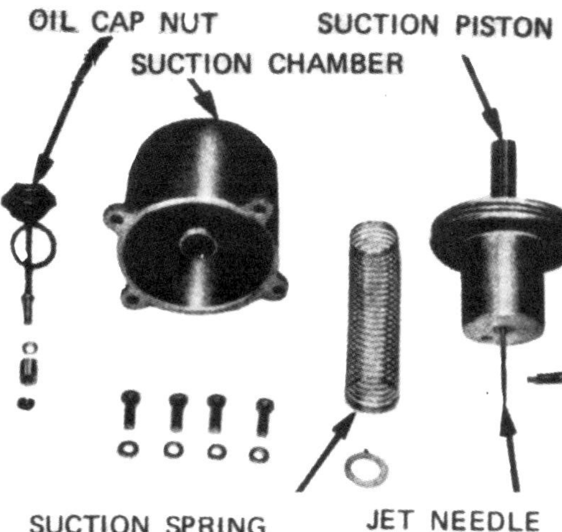

The suction chamber assembly

piston. Remove needle by pulling and turning slowly. Replace the needle with the shoulder portion flush with the piston surface. Check this with a straightedge. Tighten the setscrew.

4. Clean all parts of suction chamber assembly with a safe solvent. Reassemble, using all new parts supplied in overhaul kit. Do not lubricate piston.

5. To dismantle nozzle assembly, remove 4 mm screw and remove connecting plate from nozzle head by pulling lightly on starter (choke) lever. Remove fuel line and nozzle. Be careful not to bend jet needle if suction chamber assembly is mounted on carburetor. Remove idle (mixture) adjusting nut and spring. Do not remove nozzle sleeve unless absolutely necessary. Special care is required to replace this part. Remove nozzle sleeve setscrew and nozzle sleeve.

6. Clean all parts of nozzle assembly with a safe solvent. Be very careful of nozzle. Do not pass anything through nozzle for cleaning purposes.

7. The jet needle must now be carefully centered in the nozzle, unless the nozzle sleeve and setscrew were not disturbed. Even so, it is a good idea to check this. To center the jet needle, insert nozzle sleeve into carburetor body with setscrew loose. Carefully install the suction piston assembly without the plunger rod. Insert the nozzle without spring and mixture adjusting nut until the nozzle contacts the nozzle sleeve. Position the nozzle sleeve so that the jet needle is centered inside the sleeve and does not contact the sleeve. Test centering by raising and releasing suction piston. It should drop smoothly, making a metallic sound when it hits the stop.

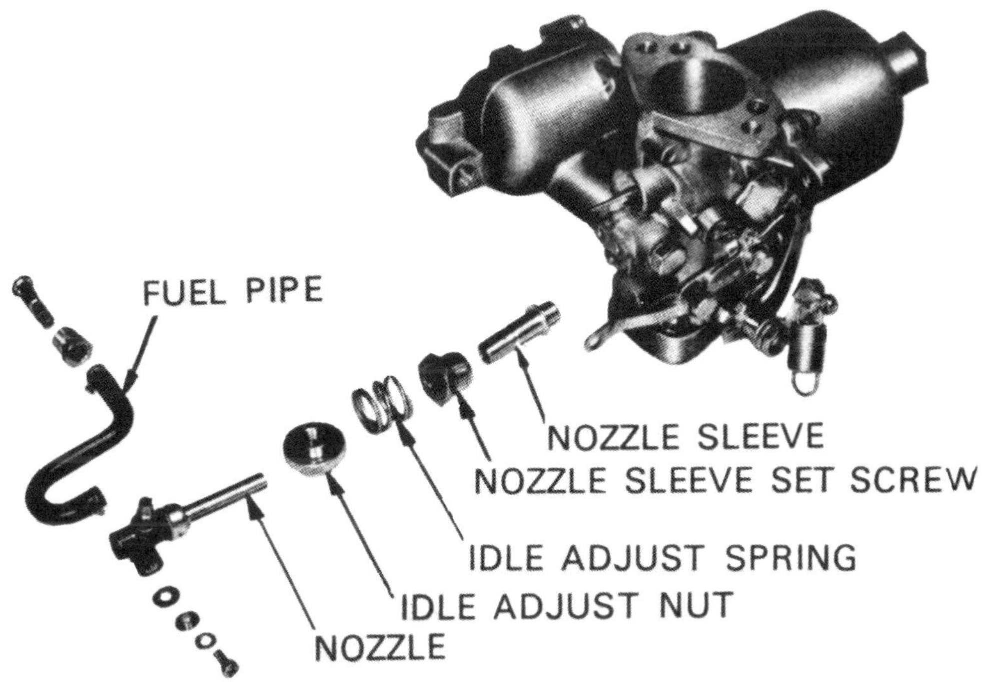

The nozzle assembly

Tighten the nozzle sleeve setscrew when the needle is centered.

8. Reassemble nozzle assembly. Replace fuel line. Replace damper plunger rod.

9. Pull starter lever slightly, replace connecting plate and 4 mm screw.

10. Carburetor synchronization and mixture adjustments must be performed after reinstalling carburetors.

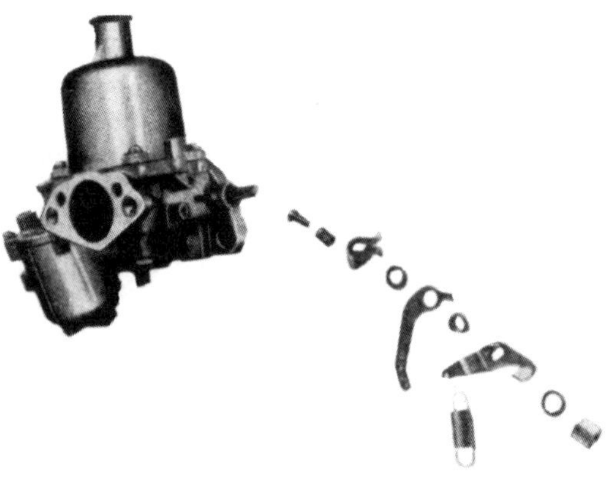

Throttle linkage—exploded view

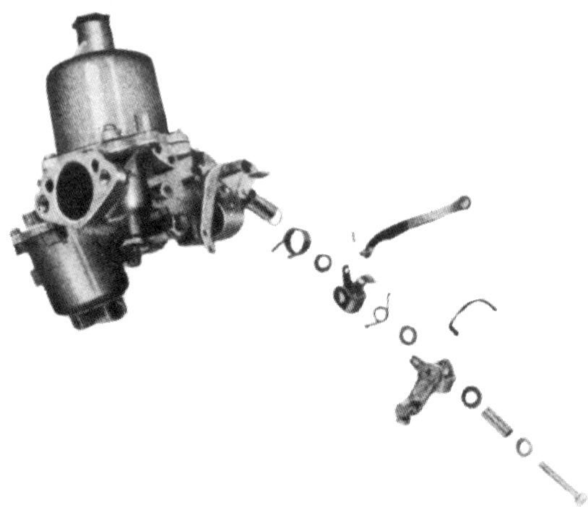

Choke linkage—exploded view

## Carburetor Specifications

in. (mm)

| Engine and Year | Make and Type | Bore Dia | Venturi Dia | Fuel Pressure psi (kg/cm²) | Needle Valve Dia | Nozzle No. | Power Jet No. | Jet Needle No. | Suction Spring No. | Suction Hole Dia | Fast Idle Throttle Opening | Damper Plunger Dia |
|---|---|---|---|---|---|---|---|---|---|---|---|---|
| L24 1970–72 | Hitachi HJG46W-3A | 1.811 (46) | 1.339 (34) | 3.4 (.24) | .0787 (2.0) | A | — | N-27 | 23 | — | — | — |
| L24 1973 | Hitachi HMB46W-1 | 1.811 (46) | 1.654 (42) | 3.4 (.24) | — | — | 40 | N-62 | 50 | .295 (7.5) | .0232–.0252 (.59–.64) | .349 (8.86) |
| L26 1974 | Hitachi HMB46W-4 | 1.811 (46) | 1.654 (42) | 4.6 (.32) | — | — | 40 | — | 50 | .295 (7.5) | .0232–.0252 (.59–.64) | .349 (8.86) |

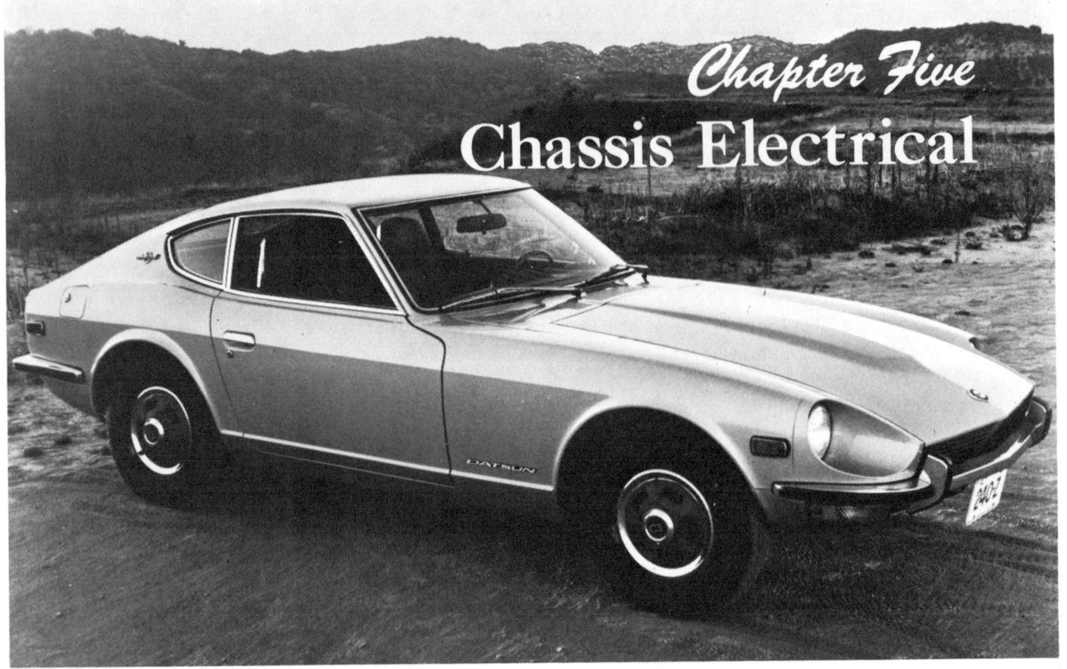


# Chapter Five
# Chassis Electrical

## Heater

*BLOWER (WITHOUT A/C)*

**Removal and Installation**

1. Disconnect the negative battery cable.
2. Remove the clamp at the air intake duct so as to disconnect the air intake box control cable.
3. Disconnect blower and resistor wires at the connectors.
4. Remove the retaining screws and remove the blower unit.
5. The motor and fan may be separated from the blower unit by removing the three mounting screws. Be careful to retain the washers and spacers.
6. Reassembly is accomplished in reverse order. When reassembling the control cable for the air intake door, set the AIR lever in the OFF position and position the wire in the clamp so that the door will just be closed.

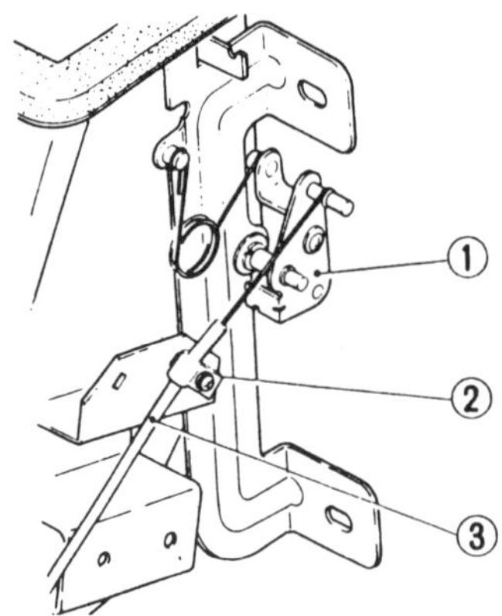


Disconnecting the intake door control cable

1. Lever 2. Clamp 3. Cable

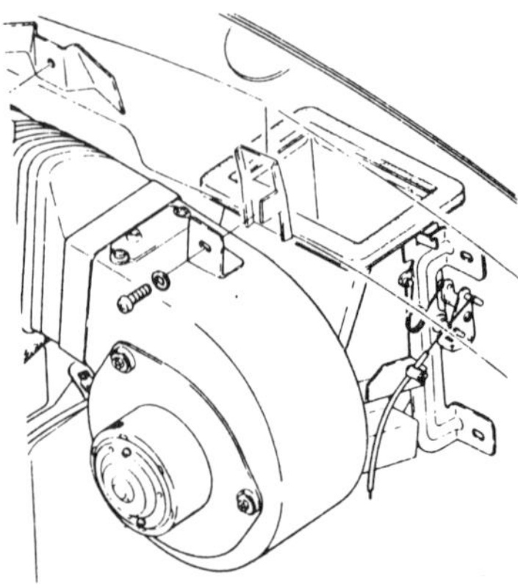

Removing the blower housing

*BLOWER (WITH A/C)*

1. Disconnect the battery negative cable. Disconnect the vacuum hose at the intake door actuator.
2. Remove the defroster duct which is located near the passenger seat.
3. Disconnect the connectors at the blower motor and at the resistor.

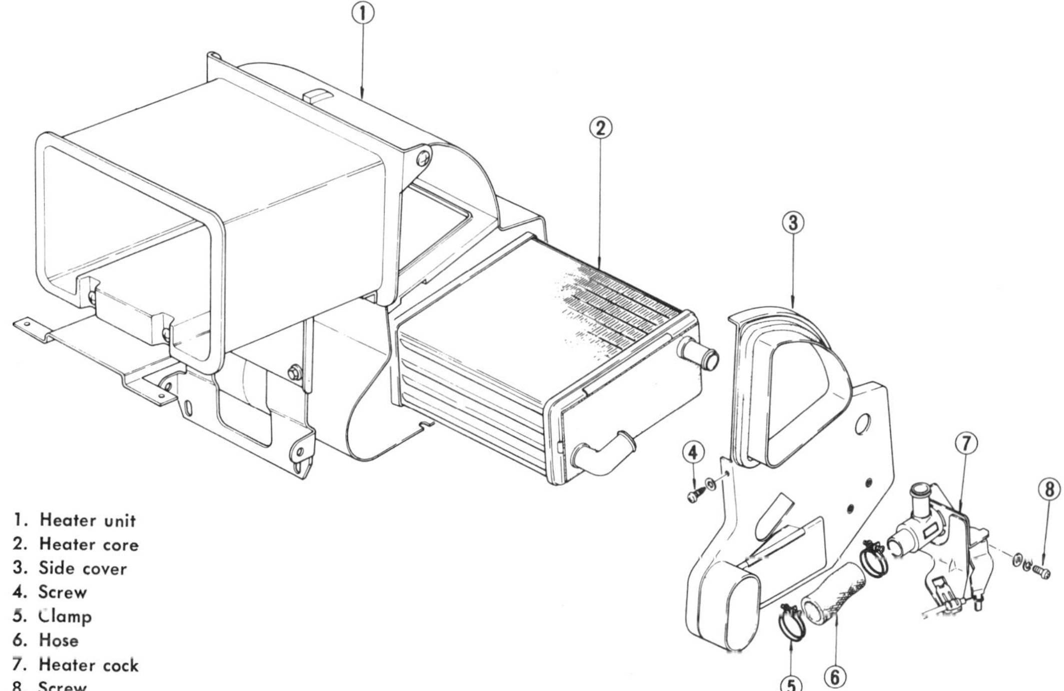


Removal of the heater core and water valve

Removing the blower housing (with A/C)

4. Remove the three housing mounting bolts and remove the housing.

5. The motor may be removed by removing the three bolts and pulling it out. Be careful to retain the three washers and three spacers.

6. Installation is the reverse of removal.

## *HEATER CORE*

### Removal and Installation

1. Disconnect the battery negative cable and drain the radiator.

2. Disconnect the two heater hoses where they connect with the inlet and outlet connections on the heater core inside the engine compartment.

3. Remove the glove box.

4. Remove the blower housing as described above.

5. On cars with A/C, loosen the clamps and remove the two hoses from the vacuum water valve.

6. Disconnect the vacuum hose. Remove the vacuum water valve mounting screws and remove it from the heater unit.

7. Remove the control cable from the remaining water valve. Remove the heater door control cable at the heater door. Remove the snap-ring and disconnect the heater door rod at the door.

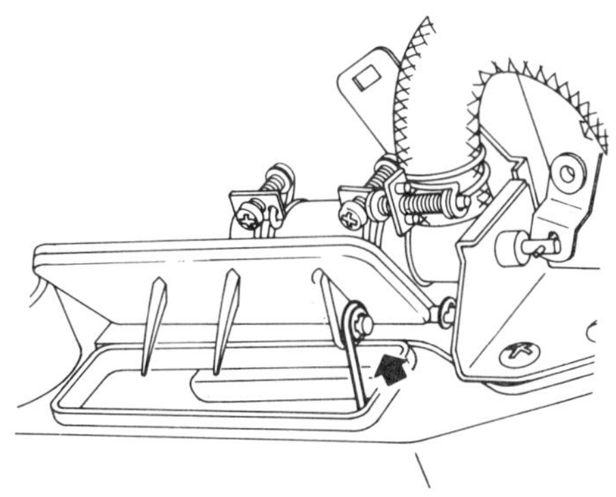

Disconnecting the heater door rod

8. Remove the two water valve mounting screws, the two heater core cover mounting screws, and remove the valve and core. *Keep the heater door open during removal to avoid damaging the core.*

9. Loosen the hose clamps and remove the valve from the core.

10. Installation is accomplished in reverse. Make sure to adjust the heater door and heater valve control cables so that the door and valve will be fully closed when the control levers are in the OFF and COLD positions.

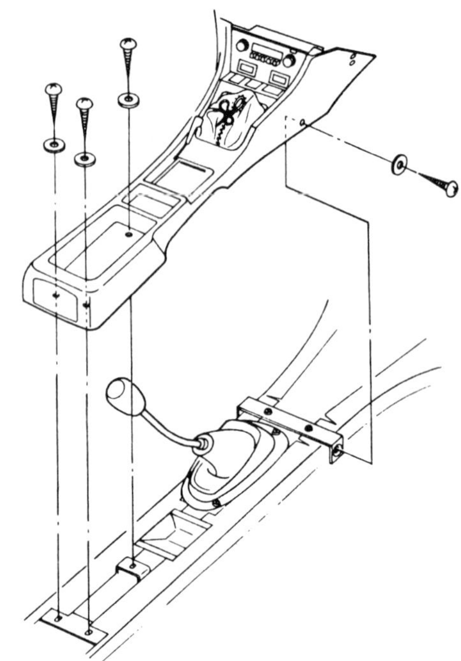

Console removal

# Radio

## Removal and Installation

260-Z

1. Remove the five screws holding the floor console in place. Remove the choke control wire from the console. Disconnect the wiring harness and remove the console.
2. Disconnect the radio power and antenna switch wires at the connectors. Remove the feeder cable.
3. Pull off the two knobs and remove the nuts which retain the escutcheon.

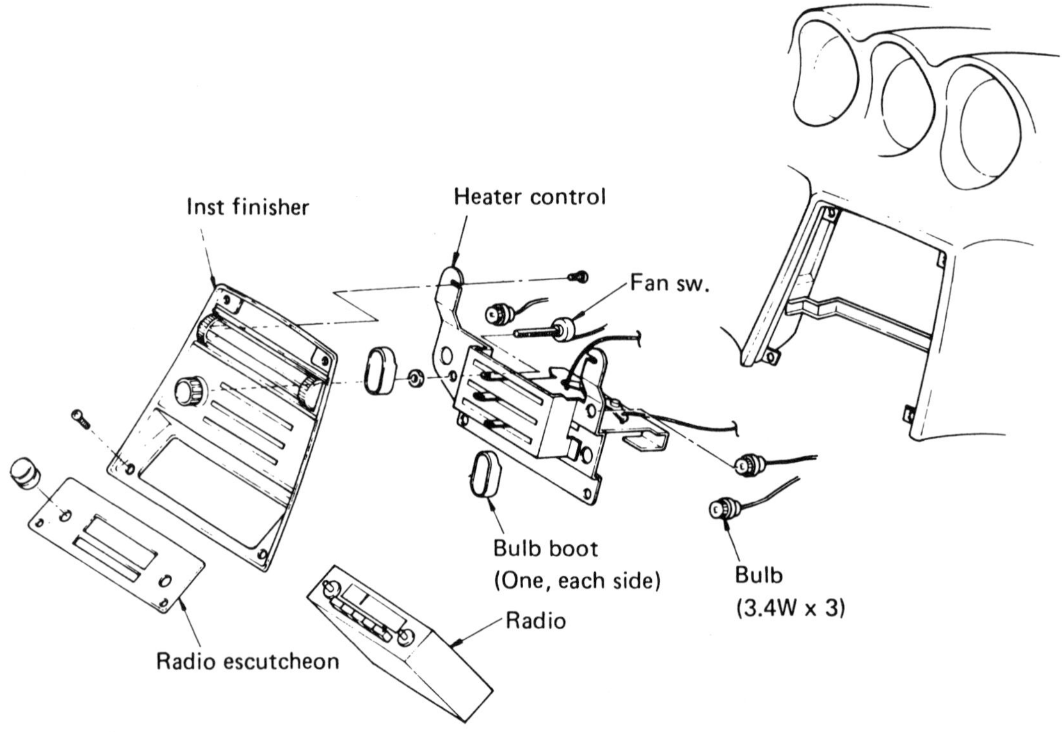


Removing the radio

4. Remove the screws which hold the radio to the console box and remove it.
5. To install the radio, reverse Steps 2 through 4 and reinstall the console.

240-Z

1. Remove the four mounting screws for the instrument console finish panel, and remove it.
2. Pull off the two knobs and remove the retaining nuts. Disconnect the power and antenna switch wires at the connectors.
3. Remove the radio.
4. Install the radio in reverse of the above.

## Windshield Wipers

*BLADE AND ARM*

### Replacement

1. Raise the wiper blade off the glass, unscrew the set nut on the arm, and pull the arm off the pivot.
2. To install, reverse the above procedure, pushing each blade onto the pivot so that the limits of movement will be as shown in the illustration.

*MOTOR AND LINKAGE*

### Removal and Installation

1. Remove the wiper arms as described above.
2. Disconnect the wiper motor connector from under the hood.

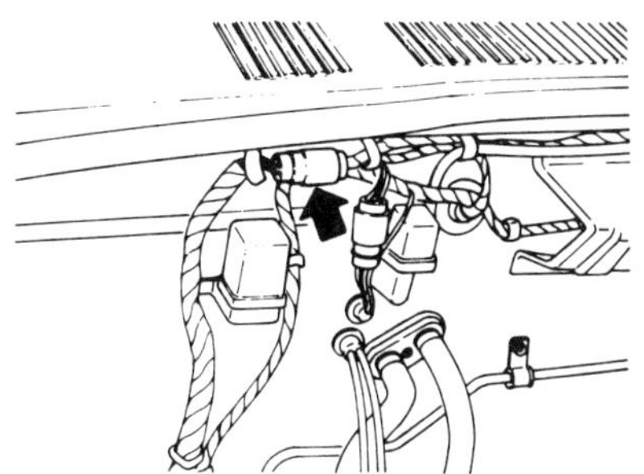

Arrow shows the wiper motor connector

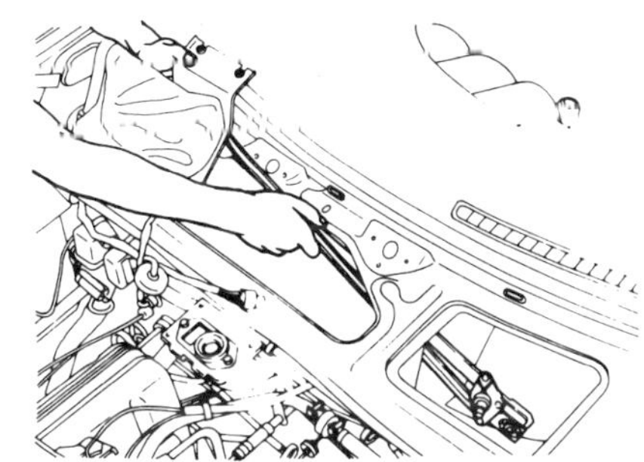

Removing the wiper linkage

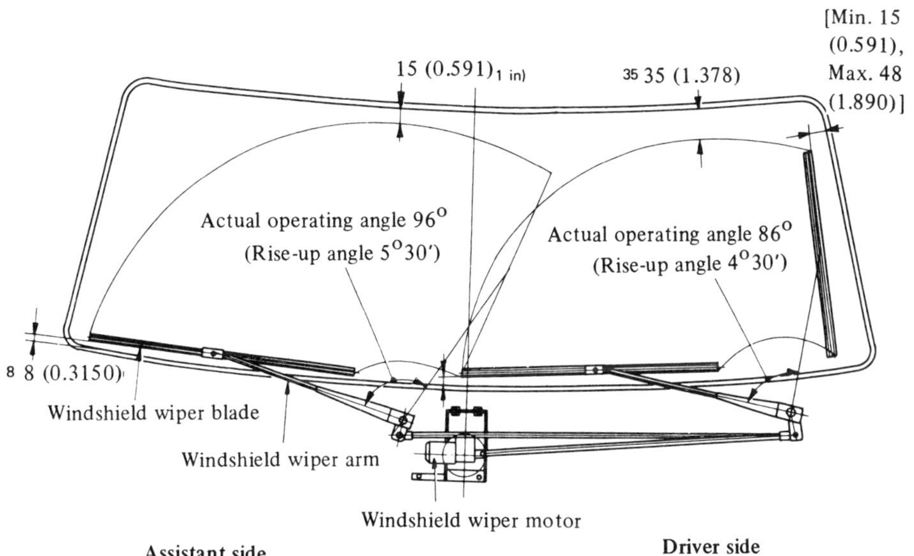


Wiper motor and linkage

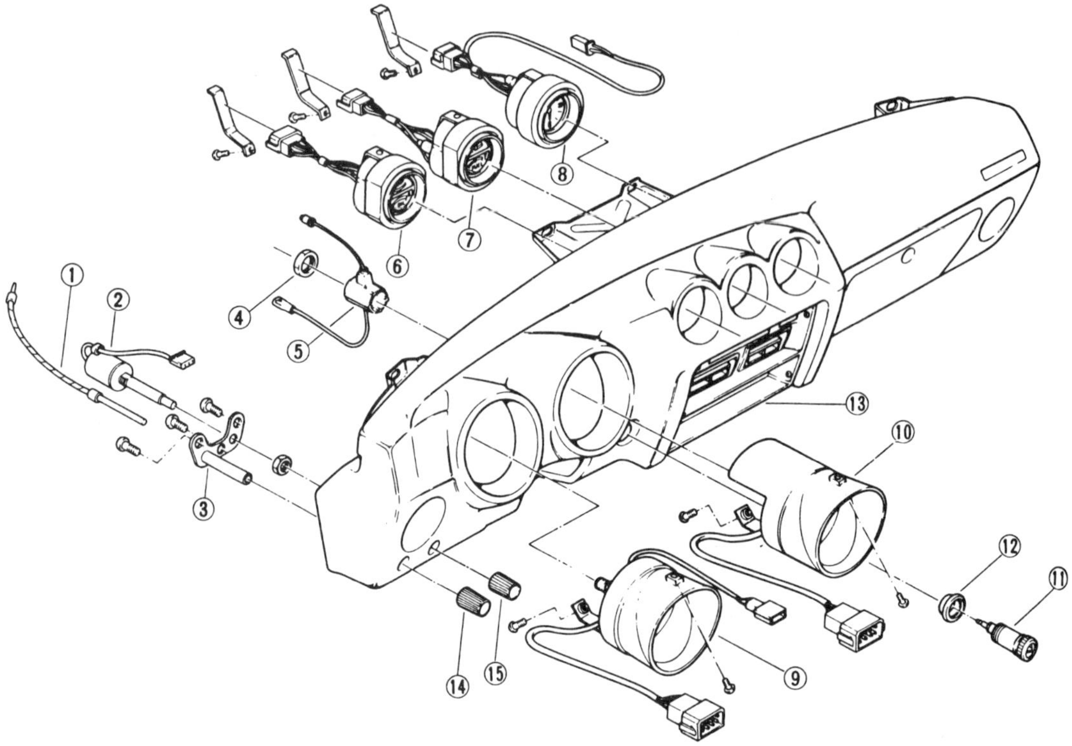

Locations of meters and gauges

1. Trip meter reset knob
2. Resistor (illumination control)
3. Bracket
4. Cigarette lighter retaining nut
5. Cigarette lighter housing
6. Oil-temp gauge
7. Amp-fuel gauge
8. Clock
9. Speedometer
10. Tachometer
11. Cigarette lighter
12. Escutcheon
13. Instrument finish panel
14. Knob (trip meter reset)
15. Knob (resistor)

3. Remove the cowl retaining screws and remove the cowl.
4. Remove the wiper motor bracket retaining screws and remove the bracket.
5. If only the motor is to be removed, disconnect the linkage from the motor and remove the motor.
6. If the motor and linkage are to be removed, remove the screws which retain each pivot and remove the linkage.
7. Install in the reverse order.

# Gauges

## Tachometer Removal and Installation

260-Z

1. Remove the screw, located just above the tachometer face, which retains the tach at the top.
2. From under the instrument panel, remove the screw which holds the tach to the instrument panel bracket.
3. Pull the tach out, disconnect the instrument harness connector, and fully remove the tach.
4. Reverse the procedure to install.

## Speedometer Removal and Installation

260-Z

1. Remove the tachometer, as described above.

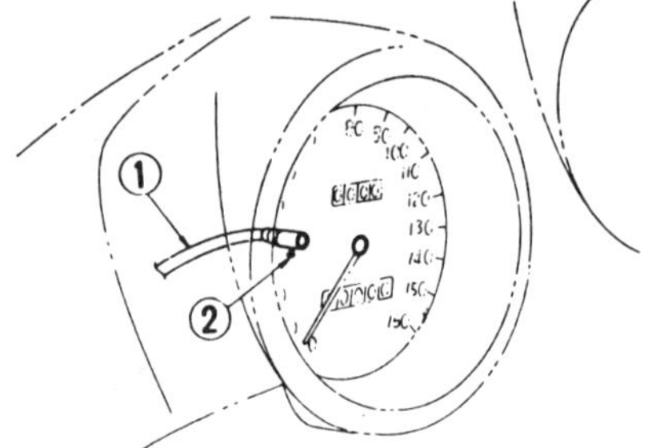

Removing the reset cable

1. Trip meter reset cable 2. Retaining screw

2. Disconnect the speedometer cable at the junction screw on speedometer back.

3. Disconnect the trip meter reset cable, going in through the tachometer opening.

4. Disconnect the two retaining screws for the speedometer in the same way as the two tachometer retaining screws were removed. Disconnect the resistor lead wire from the connector while under the instrument panel.

5. Pull speedometer out slightly, disconnect the instrument harness connector and remove the speedometer.

6. To reinstall, first install the speedometer in the reverse of the above, then install the tach, reversing the tachometer removal procedures.

### Speedometer or Tachometer Removal and Installation

240-Z

1. Remove the heater air duct which passes behind the instruments.

2. Remove the wing nuts and washers which retain the instrument to be removed from behind.

3. Pull the instrument down slightly, remove wires and, in the case of the speedometer, the cable. Remove the instrument.

4. To install, reverse the removal procedure.

### Temp-Oil and Amp-Fuel Gauges

260-Z

1. Remove the four retaining screws for the instrument finish panel (located under the three small gauges), and pull it out slightly. Disconnect the two connectors and remove the finish panel.

2. Remove the two screws which retain the three-way duct to the instrument panel and the four screws which retain it to the bracket.

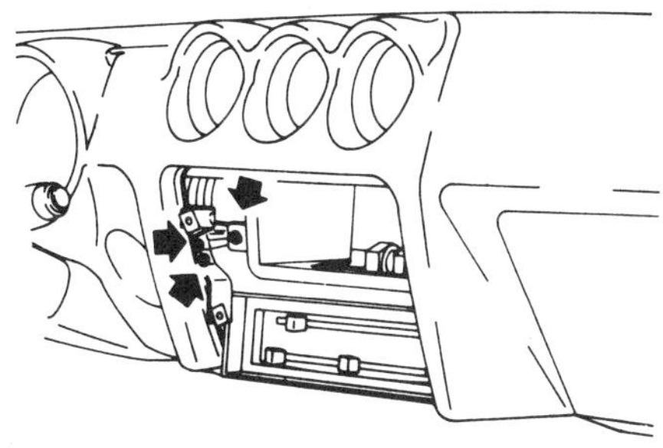

Removing the three-way duct retaining screws

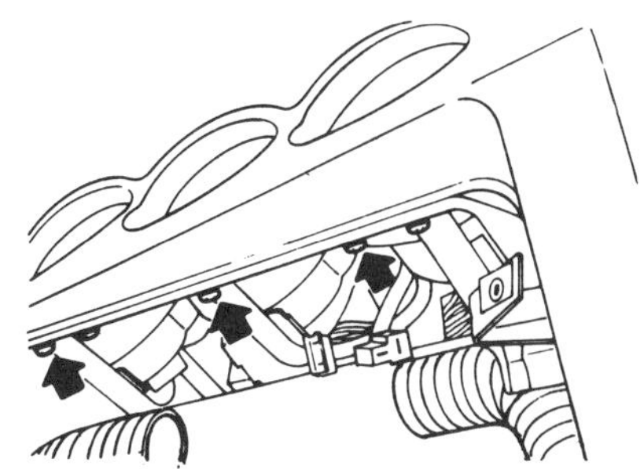

Removing the gauge retaining screws

3. Disconnect the duct hoses and remove the duct.

4. Remove the screw(s) retaining the gauge or gauges to be removed from the instrument panel.

5. Pull the gauge to the rear, disconnect the connector(s), and remove the gauge.

6. Install reversing the above procedures.

240-Z

1. Remove the instrument panel finish panel.

2. Go in where the panel was with a pair of pliers and carefully loosen the hex-head screws on the back of the instrument to be removed.

Removing mounting screws for the temperature/oil pressure gauge

3. Pull the gauge to the rear, disconnect the connector(s), and remove it.

4. Reverse the procedure to install.

## 260-Z Seatbelt Interlock System

This system is designed to prevent the engine from starting unless all persons in the car have seat belts on. If either seat is unoccupied, a sensor in the seat by-passes the belt switch for that seat. If system failure prevents the car from starting, it can be started by turning the ignition switch on, depressing the button in the engine compartment, and then turning the key to the start position. In addition, whenever a seat is occupied and the belt is not connected, a warning light and buzzer will be activated.

The system should be checked out using a special factory Interlock Checker. However, once the cause of trouble has been located, an individual component can be replaced using the following procedures.

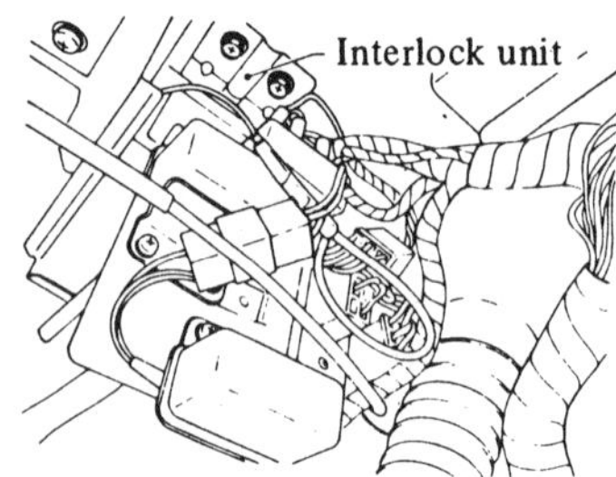


Location of the interlock unit

*INTERLOCK UNIT*

**Removal and Installation**

The interlock unit is located behind the relay bracket, under the dash.

1. Disconnect the interlock relay lead wires at the connectors.
2. Remove the three relay bracket retaining screws and remove the relay bracket and relays.
3. Remove the two screws which hold the interlock unit to the dash side panel and remove the unit.
4. To install, reverse these procedures.

*SEAT BELT SWITCH AND FASTENER*

**Removal and Installation**

1. Slide the seat all the way forward.
2. Remove the belt fastener securing bolt.
3. Disconnect the belt switch lead wire at the connector. Remove the fastener.
4. Install in reverse sequence.

*SEAT SWITCH*

**Removal and Installation**

1. Remove the four seat mounting bolts.
2. Lift the seat and disconnect the seat switch wires at the connector.
3. Remove the seat from the car.
4. Install a new seat in reverse order, as the seat switch is integral with the seat assembly.

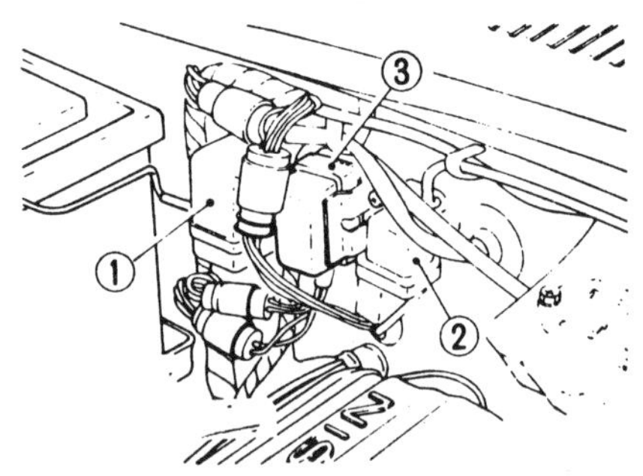


Location of the seat belt warning relay and interlock relay

1. Fusible link box
2. Seat belt warning relay
3. Interlock relay

*INTERLOCK RELAY*

**Removal and Installation**

1. Open the hood. Disconnect the relay lead wires at the connector.
2. Remove the two screws which attach the relay to the front of the dash panel and remove the relay.
3. Install in reverse order.

*SEAT BELT WARNING RELAY (AUTOMATIC TRANSMISSION ONLY)*

See the procedures for removal of the Interlock Relay. This relay is retained by the same screws which retain the interlock relay, although wiring is separate.

*EMERGENCY SWITCH*

This switch is located on the right-side of the engine compartment, except when the car is equipped with air conditioning. In this case it is located on the vacuum tank retainer. Simply disconnect the wires and remove the retaining screws to remove it. Reverse the procedure to install.

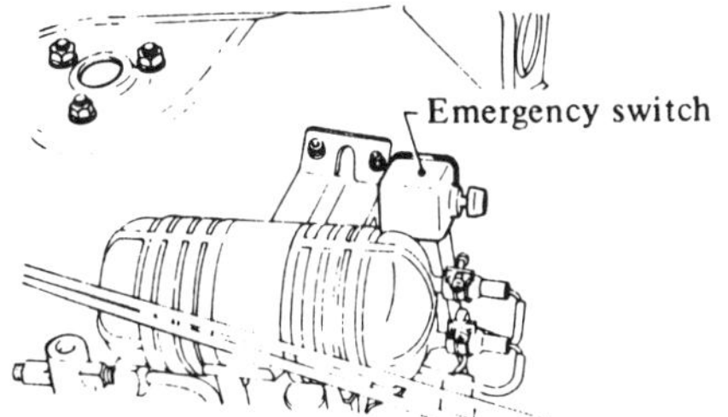


Location of emergency switch

*WARNING BUZZER*

**Removal and Installation**

1. Disconnect the negative battery cable. Remove the speedometer as described above.
2. Going in through the speedometer hole, disconnect the lead wires for the buzzer at the connector.
3. Remove the retaining screw and remove the buzzer, gaining access the same way.
4. Install by reversing the above procedures.

*WARNING LAMP BULB*

**Removal and Installation**

1. Remove the heater control knobs and the four screws retaining the finish panel to the instrument panel.
2. Pull the finish panel out slightly and disconnect the map lamp and seat belt lamp connector. Remove the finish panel.
3. Twist the socket mounted at the rear of the seat belt warning lamp and remove it. The bulb may now be removed and replaced.
4. Install the socket and then replace the finish panel in reverse of the above.

## Lighting

*HEADLAMP*

**Removal and Installation**

1. Disconnect the headlamp connector behind the front fender panel.
2. Go in through the wheel opening

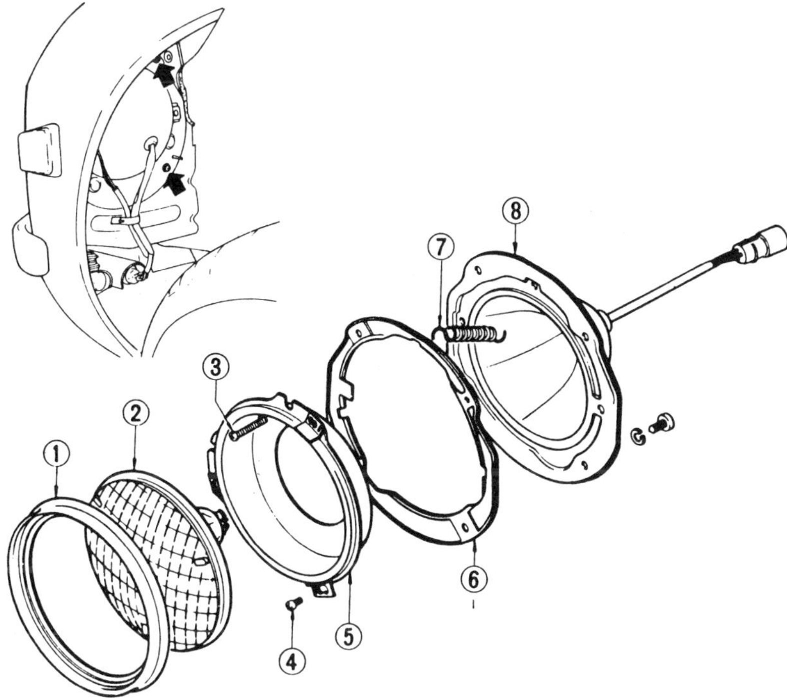


The parts of the headlamp

1. Retaining ring
2. Sealed beam
3. Adjust screw
4. Retaining screw
5. Sub-body
6. Packing sheet
7. Extension spring
8. Housing

and remove the four headlamp housing retaining screws.

3. Pull the headlamp assembly out.

4. Loosen the retaining ring screws, rotate the ring, and remove it.

5. Disconnect the connector and remove the sealed beam unit.

To install:

1. Connect the wiring connector to the new sealed beam unit, and position it so that the three location tabs fit the hollows in the mounting ring. The letters on the sealed beam must be in an upright position.

2. Install the retaining ring and new lamp by positioning the ring and rotating it in the reverse of removal. Tighten the ring retaining screws.

3. Install the housing to the fender panel with the four screws and connect the wiring connector.

4. Aim the new headlamp.

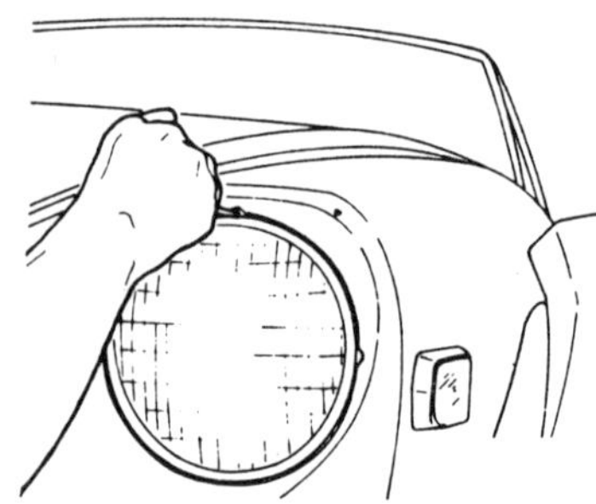

Headlamp aiming adjustment

### Headlight Adjustment

The headlight aiming screws are accessible by going through the cutting hole of the headlight case. The vertical screw is located on top, while the horizontal screw is to the side.

## Light Bulb Specifications

*260-Z, 1974*

| | *Wattage or Candle Power* | *SAE Trade Number* |
|---|---|---|
| Headlamp | 50/40 | 6012 |
| Front Combination | | |
| Park/Turn Signal | 23/8 | 1034 |
| Side Marker | 8 | 67 |
| Rear Combination | | |
| Stop/Tail | 23/8 | 1034 |
| Tail | 8 | 67 |
| Turn | 23 | 1073 |
| Back-up | 23 | 1073 |

*240-Z, 1972–73*

| | *Wattage or Candle Power* | *SAE Trade Number* |
|---|---|---|
| Headlamp | 50/40 | 612 |
| Front Park/ Turn Signal | 32/3 cp | 1034 |
| Side Marker | 4 cp | 67 |
| Rear Combination | | |
| Stop/Tail | 32/3 cp | 1034 |
| Turn | 32 | 1073 |
| Back-up | 32 | 1073 |

*240-Z, 1970–71*

| | *Wattage or Candle Power* | *SAE Trade Number* |
|---|---|---|
| Headlamp | 50/40 | 612 |
| Front Park/ Turn Signal | 23/7 cp | — |
| Side Marker | 7.5 | — |
| Rear Combination | | |
| Tail | 7 | — |
| Stop | 23 | — |
| Turn | 23 | — |
| Back-up | 23 | — |

*FUSIBLE LINKS*

On the 260-Z, the fusible link box is located on the firewall on the right-side of the engine compartment. These links protect the alternator and starter.

On the 240-Z, the links are located at the starter motor and alternator.

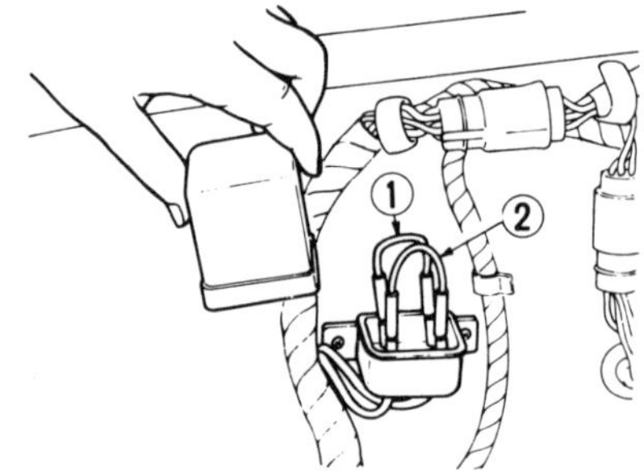


Fusible links—black (1) and green (2)—used in the 260-Z

*FUSES AND FLASHERS*

Flashers are located at the left-side trim panel under the instrument panel.

On 260-Z models, the fuse block is located at the right-side trim panel under the instrument panel.

On 240-Z models, the fuse block is in the console under the ash tray.

# Wiring Diagrams

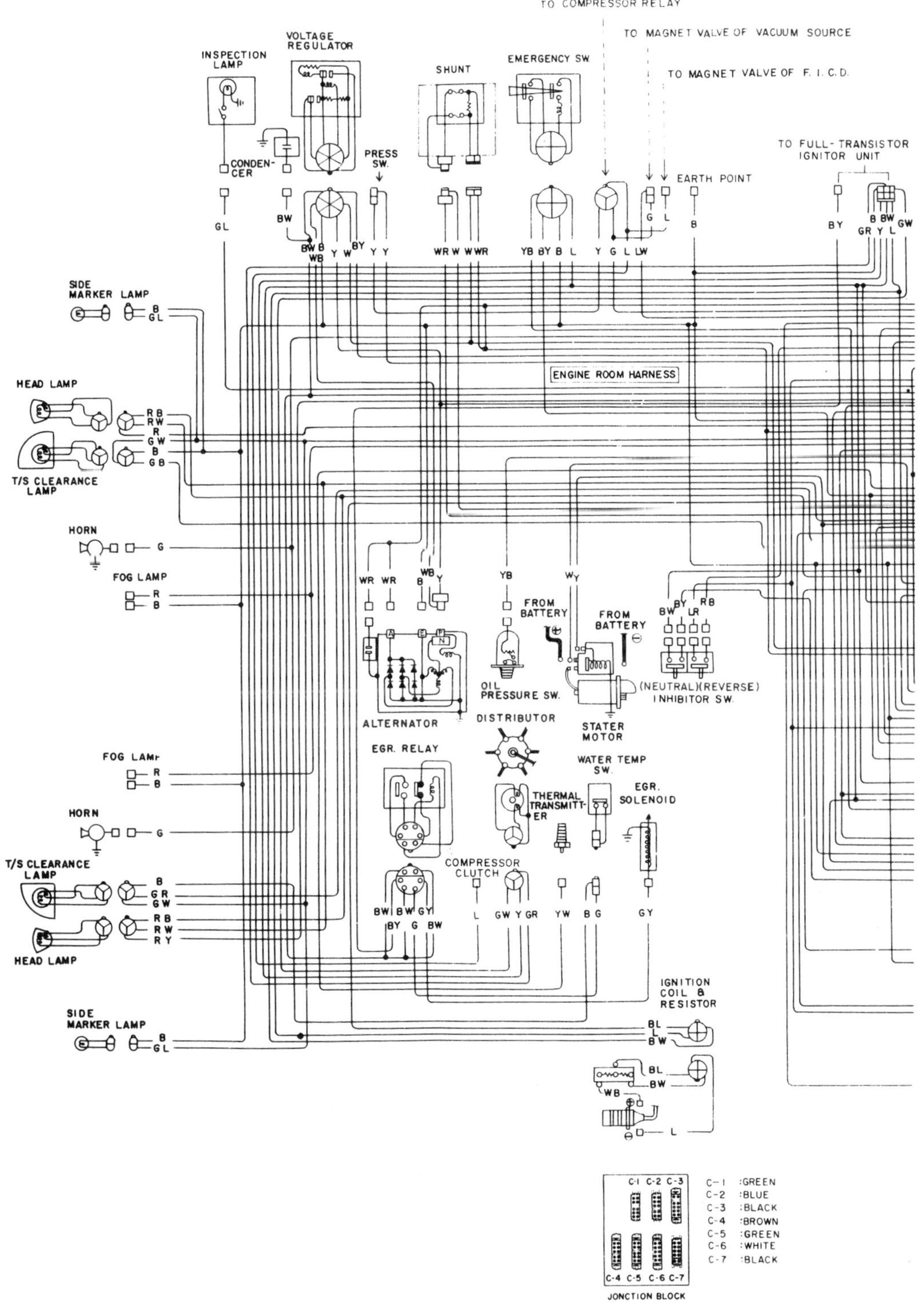


260-Z, manual transmission

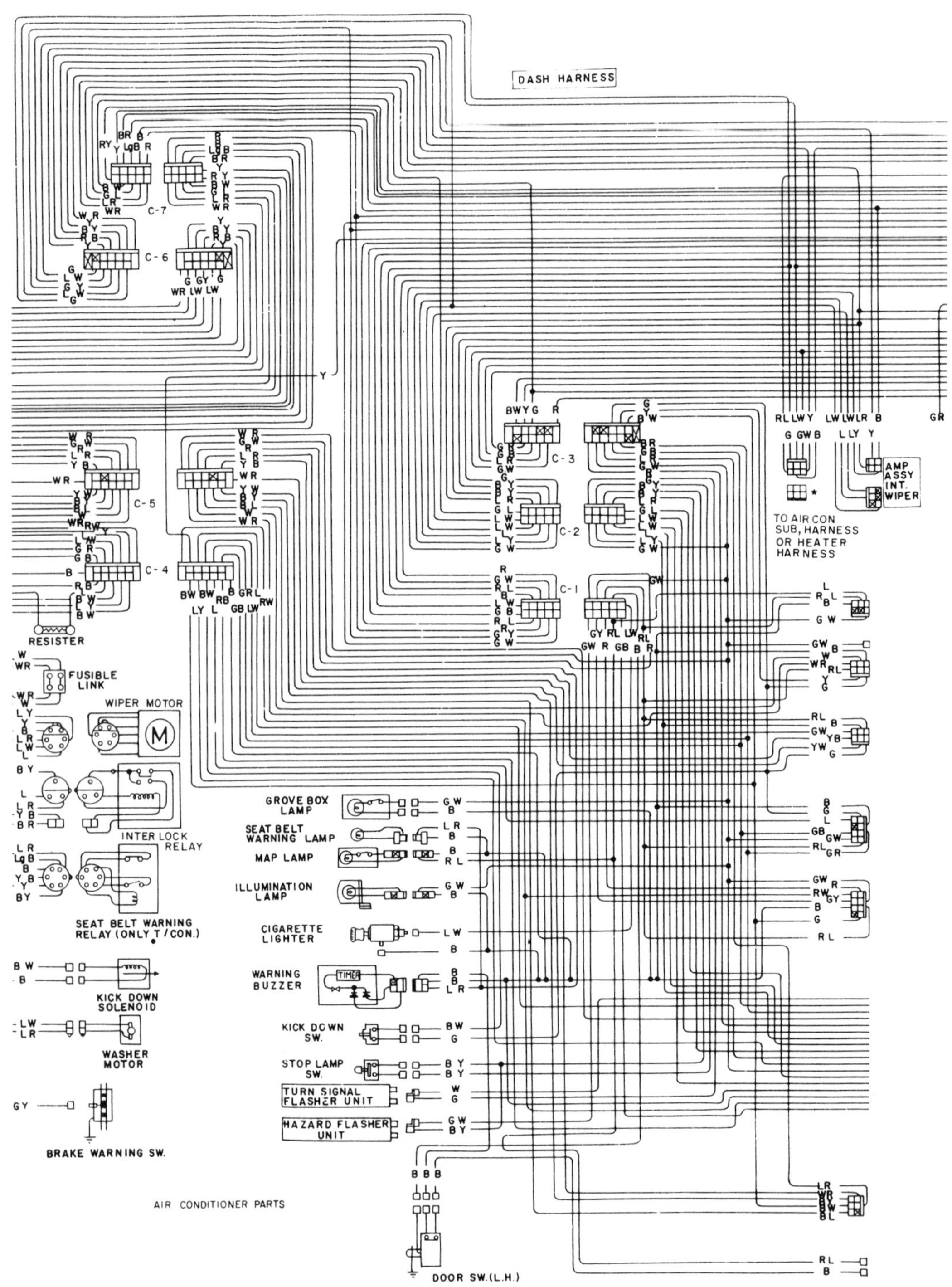


260-Z, manual transmission

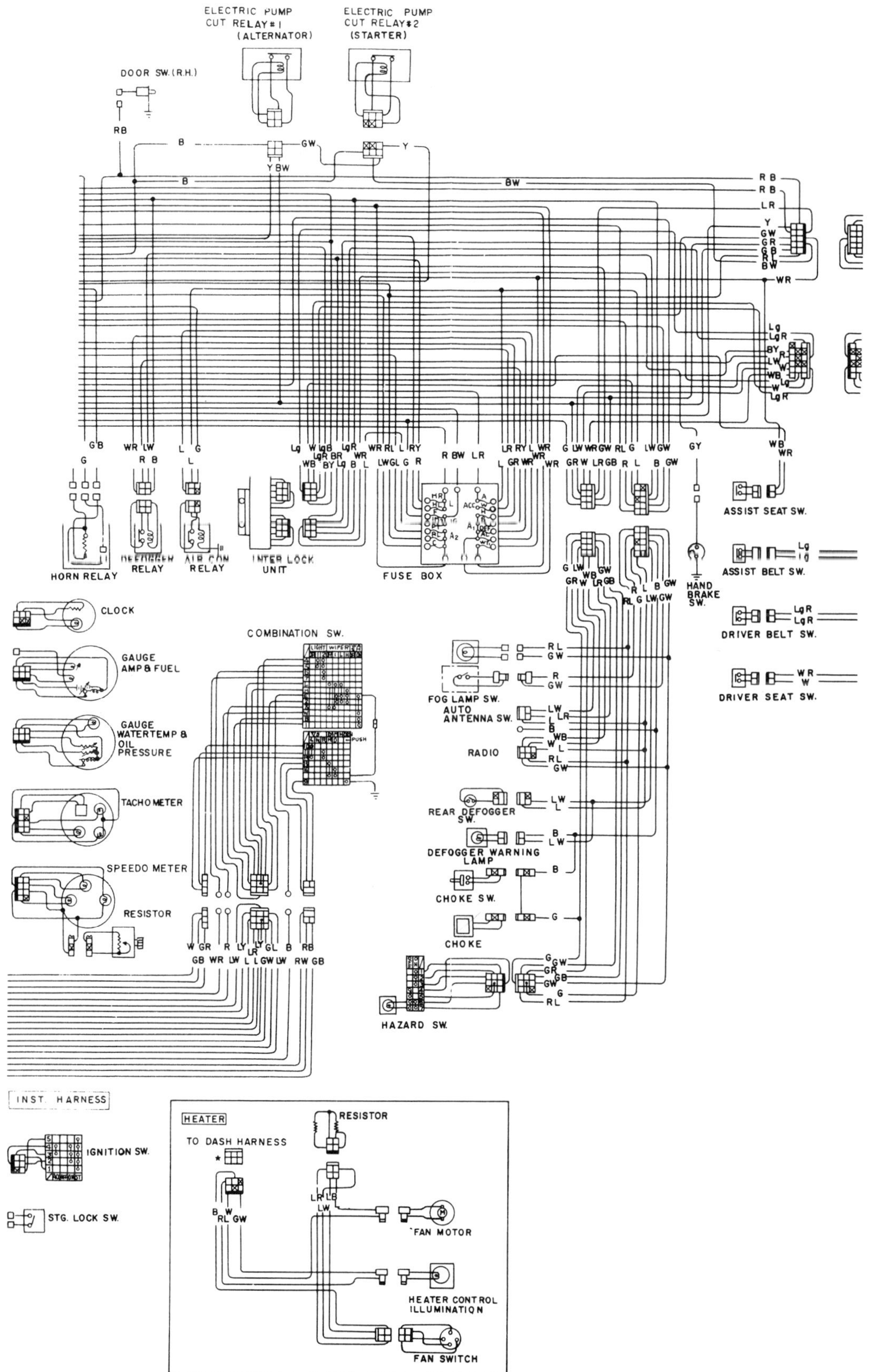


260-Z, manual transmission

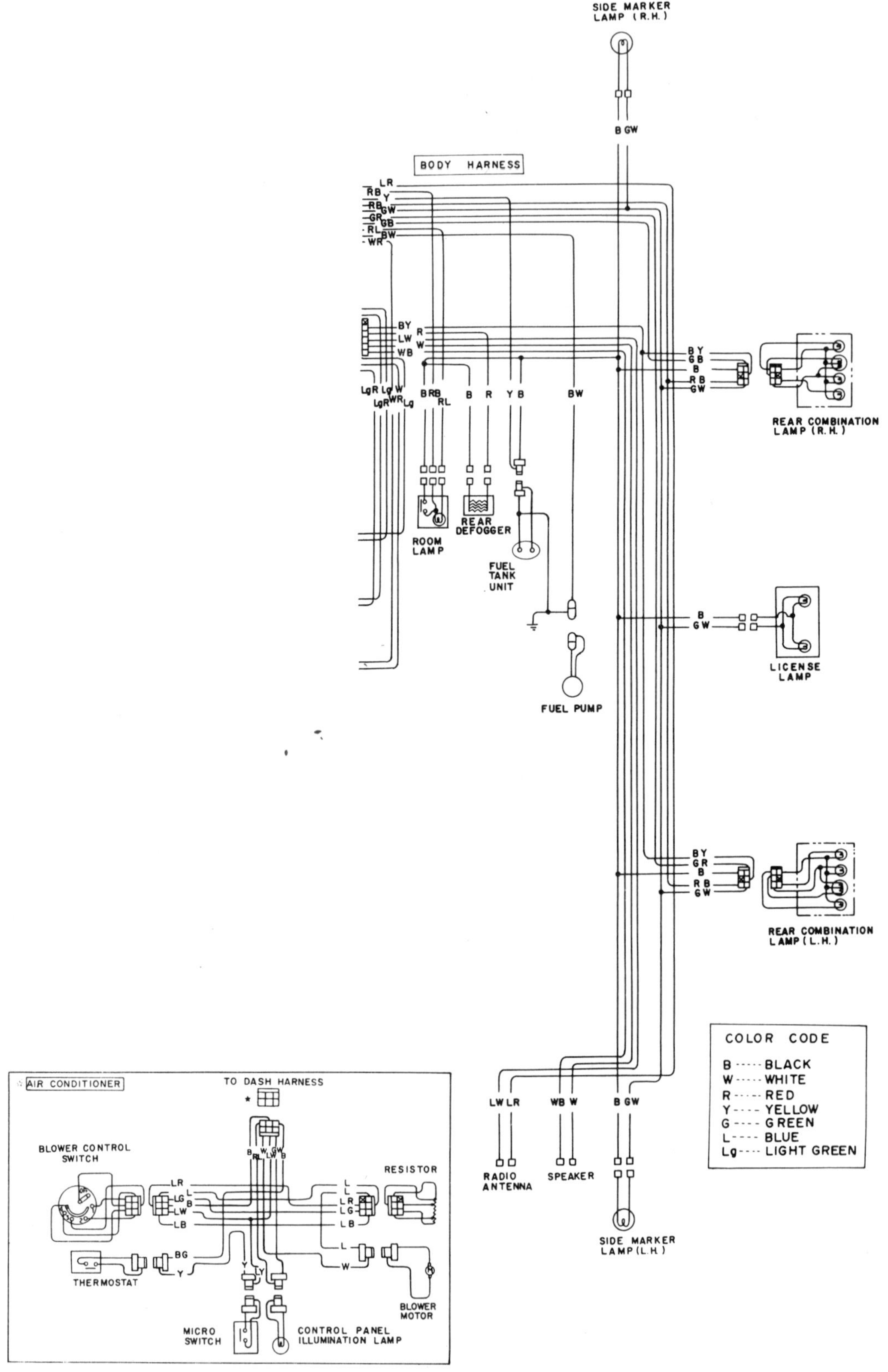


260-Z, manual transmission

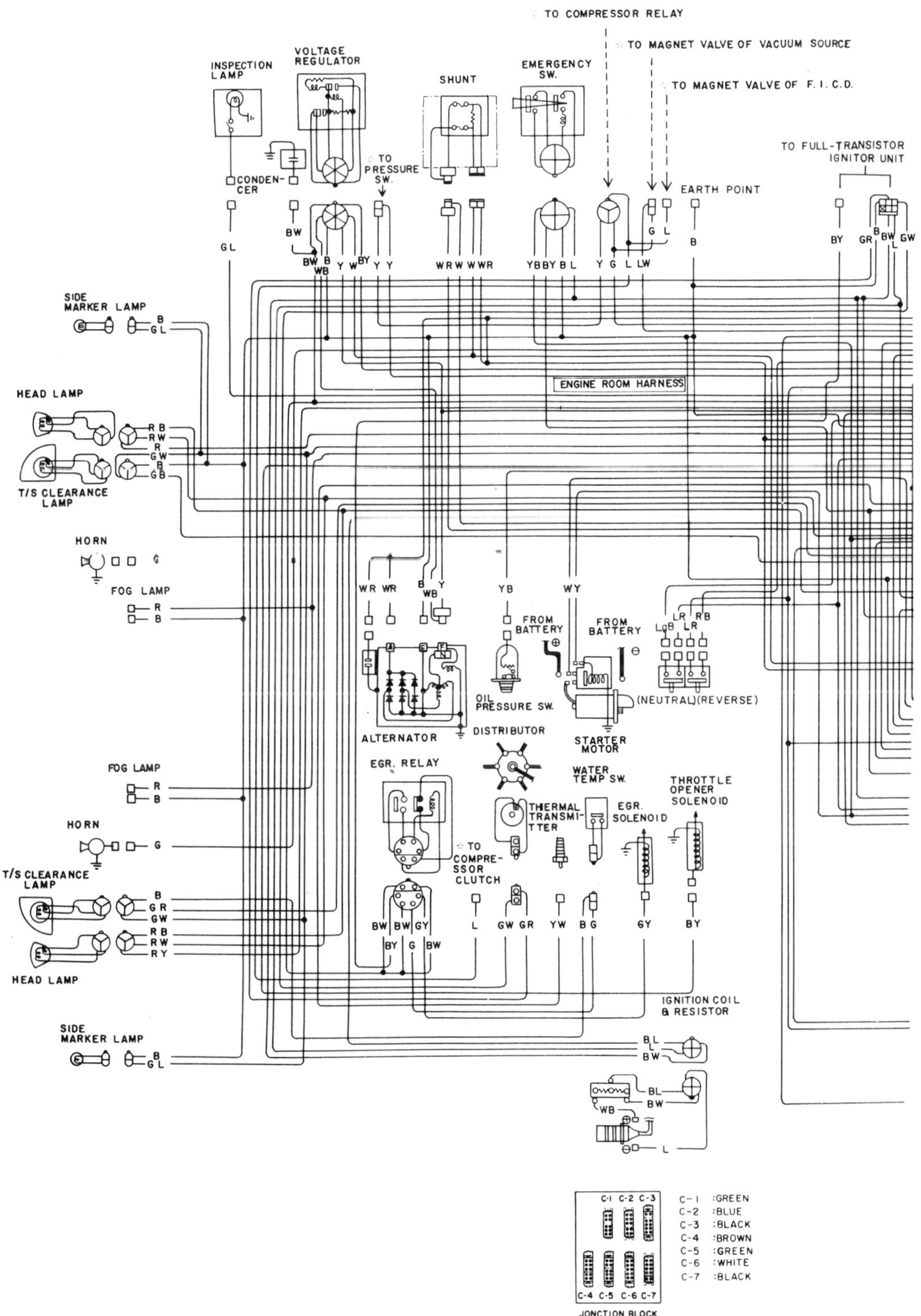


260-Z, automatic transmission

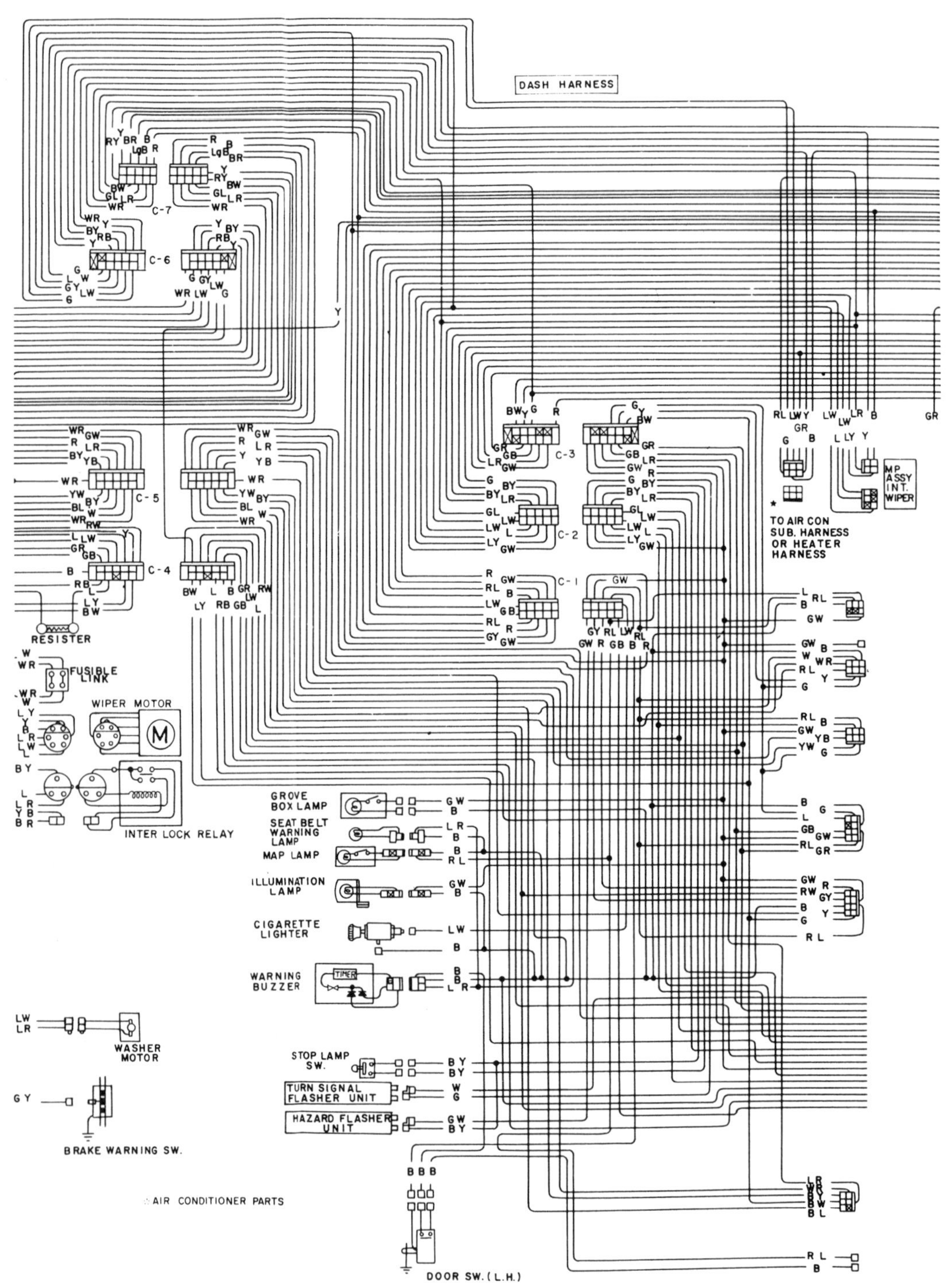


260-Z, automatic transmission

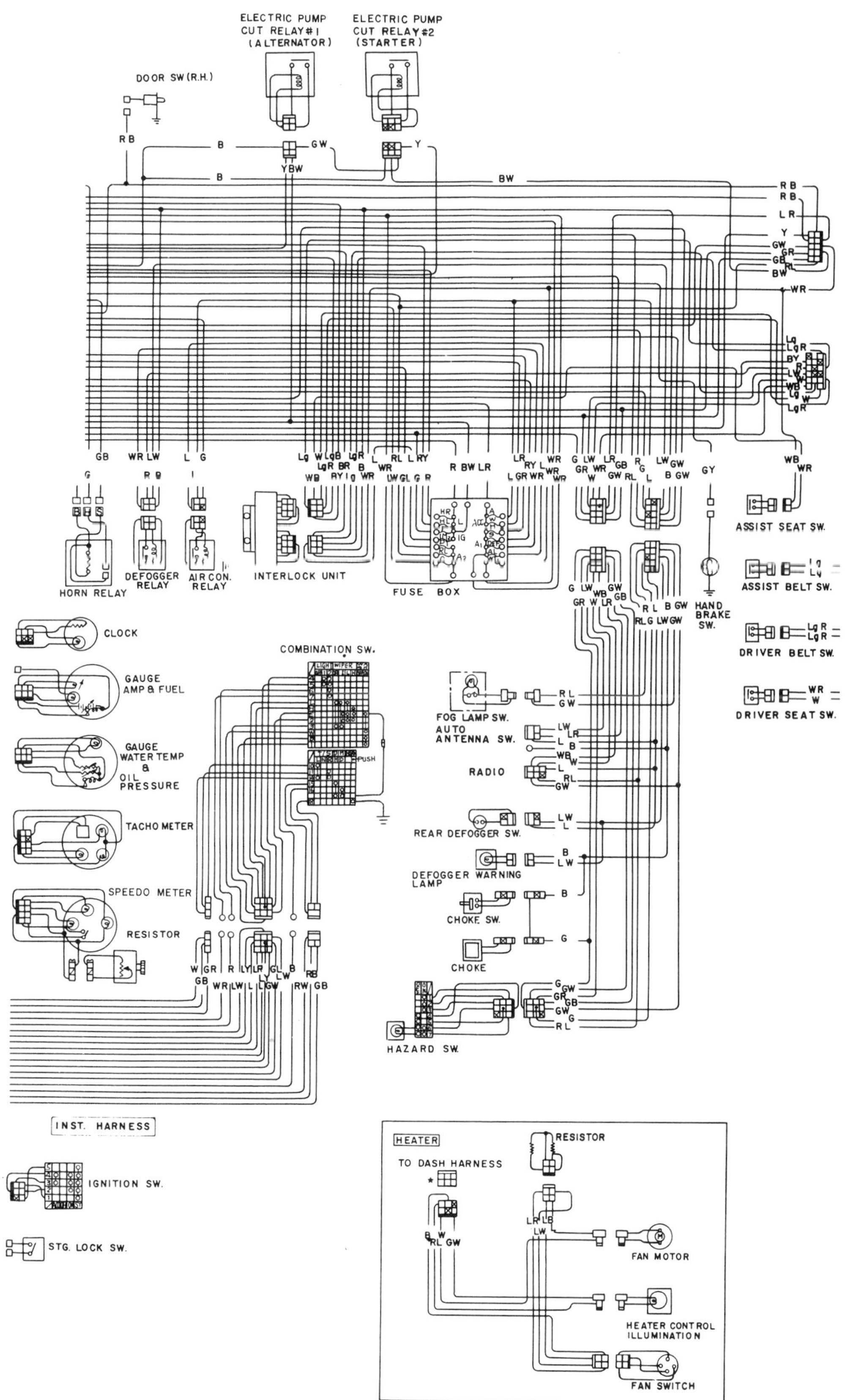


260-Z, automatic transmission

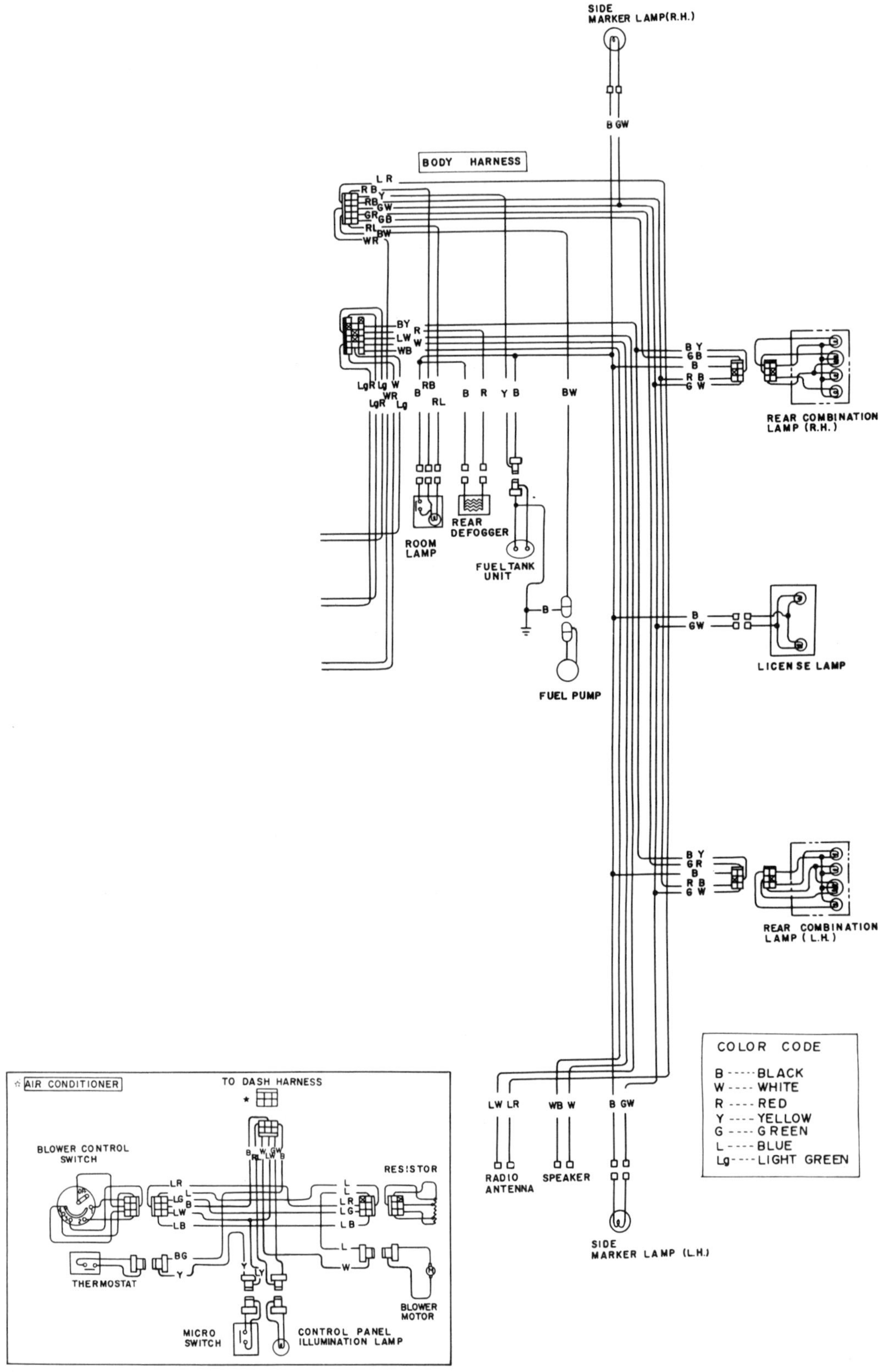


260-Z, automatic transmission

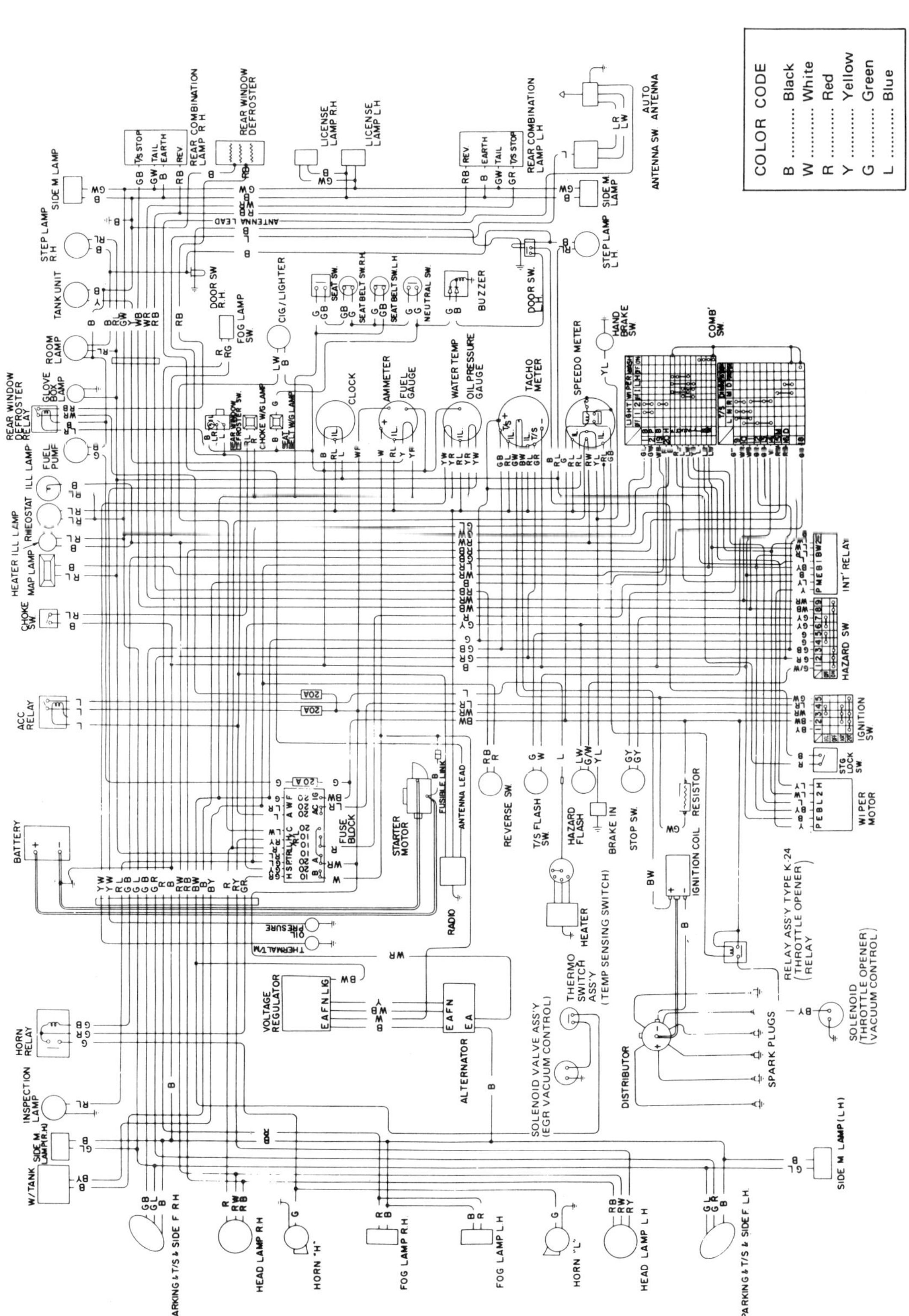


240-Z, 1973 manual transmission

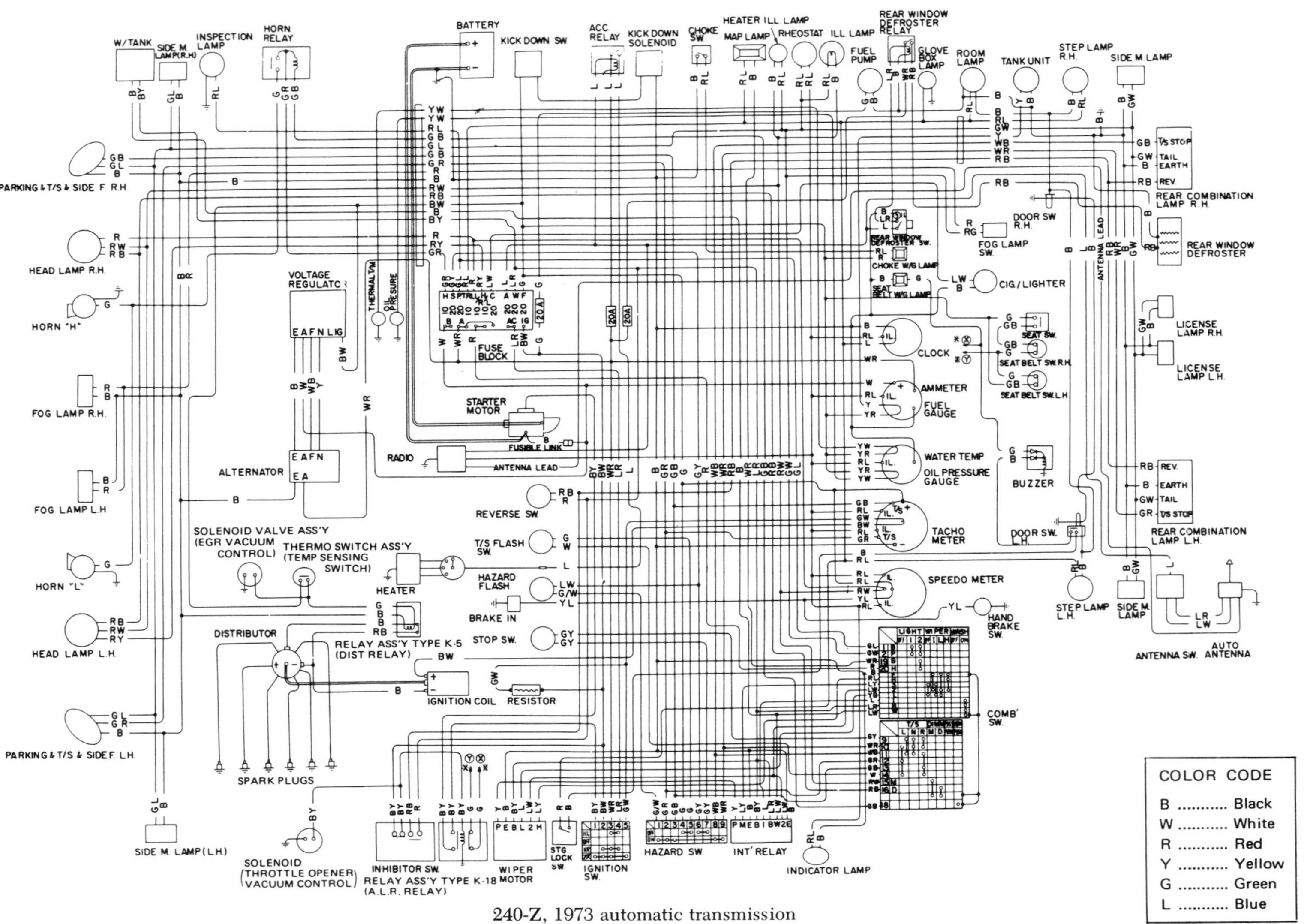


240-Z, 1973 automatic transmission

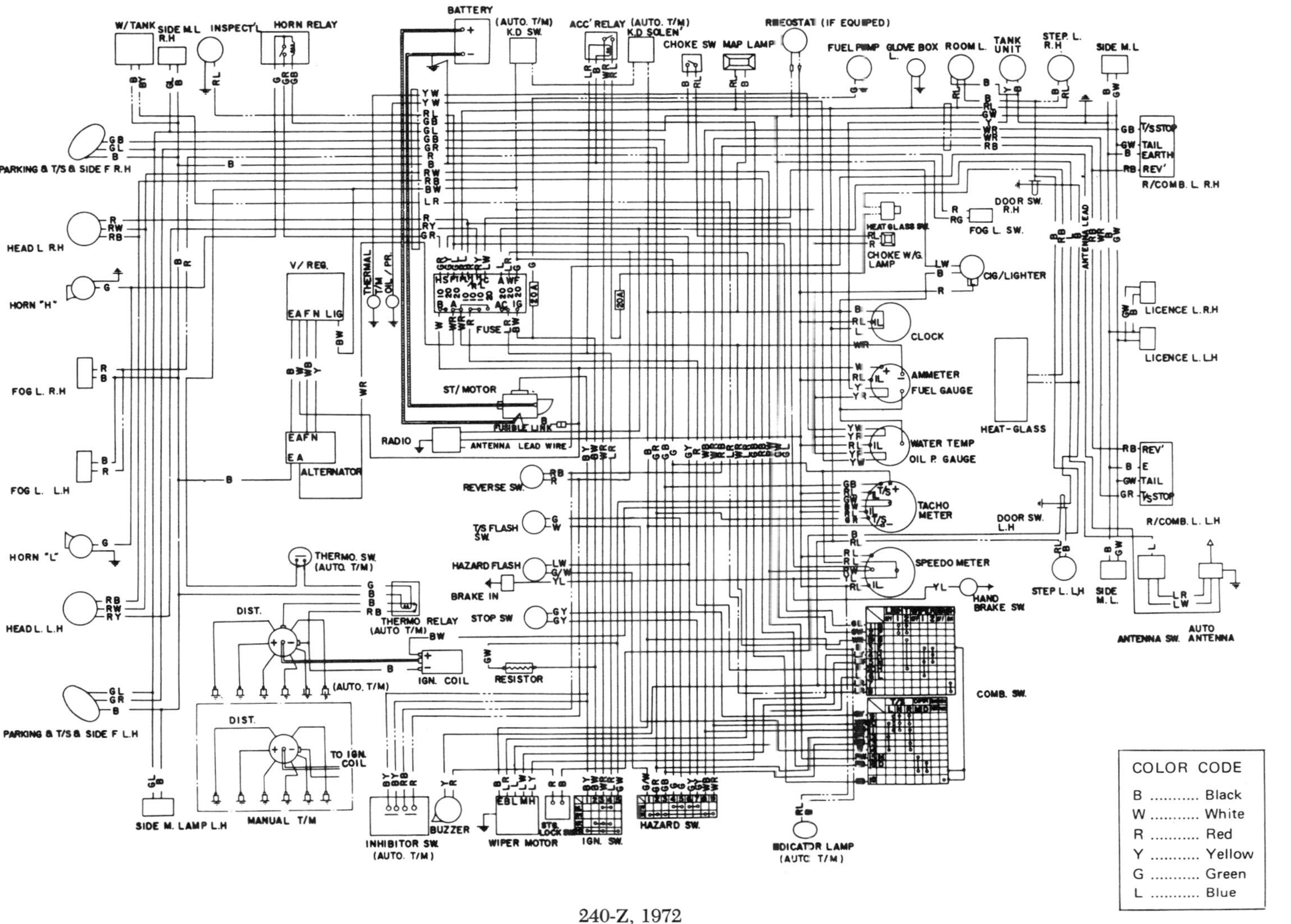
BATTERY
(AUTO. T/M) K.D SW.
ACC' RELAY
(AUTO. T/M) K.D SOLEN'
CHOKE SW
MAP LAMP
RHEOSTAT (IF EQUIPED)
FUEL PUMP
GLOVE BOX L.
ROOM L.
TANK UNIT
STEP. L. R.H
SIDE M.L
W/TANK
SIDE M.L R.H
INSPECT'L
HORN RELAY
PARKING & T/S & SIDE F R.H
HEAD L. R.H
HORN "H"
FOG L. R.H
FOG L. L.H
HORN "L"
HEAD L. L.H
PARKING & T/S & SIDE F L.H
SIDE M. LAMP L.H
V/REG.
ALTERNATOR
THERMAL T/M
OIL/PR.
FUSE
ST/MOTOR
FUSIBLE LINK
RADIO
ANTENNA LEAD WIRE
REVERSE SW.
T/S FLASH SW.
HAZARD FLASH
BRAKE IN
STOP SW
THERMO. SW. (AUTO. T/M)
THERMO RELAY (AUTO T/M)
DIST.
IGN. COIL
RESISTOR
(AUTO. T/M)
TO IGN. COIL
MANUAL T/M
INHIBITOR SW. (AUTO. T/M)
BUZZER
WIPER MOTOR
STG. LOCK SW.
IGN. SW.
HAZARD SW.
INDICATOR LAMP (AUTO T/M)
COMB. SW.
HEAT GLASS SW.
CHOKE W/G. LAMP
CIG/LIGHTER
CLOCK
AMMETER
FUEL GAUGE
WATER TEMP
OIL P. GAUGE
TACHO METER
SPEEDO METER
HAND BRAKE SW.
HEAT-GLASS
DOOR SW. R.H
FOG L. SW.
DOOR SW. L.H
STEP L. L.H
SIDE M.L.
ANTENNA LEAD
T/S STOP
TAIL
EARTH
REV'
R/COMB. L. R.H
LICENCE L. R.H
LICENCE L. L.H
R/COMB. L. L.H
ANTENNA SW.
AUTO ANTENNA
COLOR CODE
B ........... Black
W ........... White
R ........... Red
Y ........... Yellow
G ........... Green
L ........... Blue

240-Z, 1972

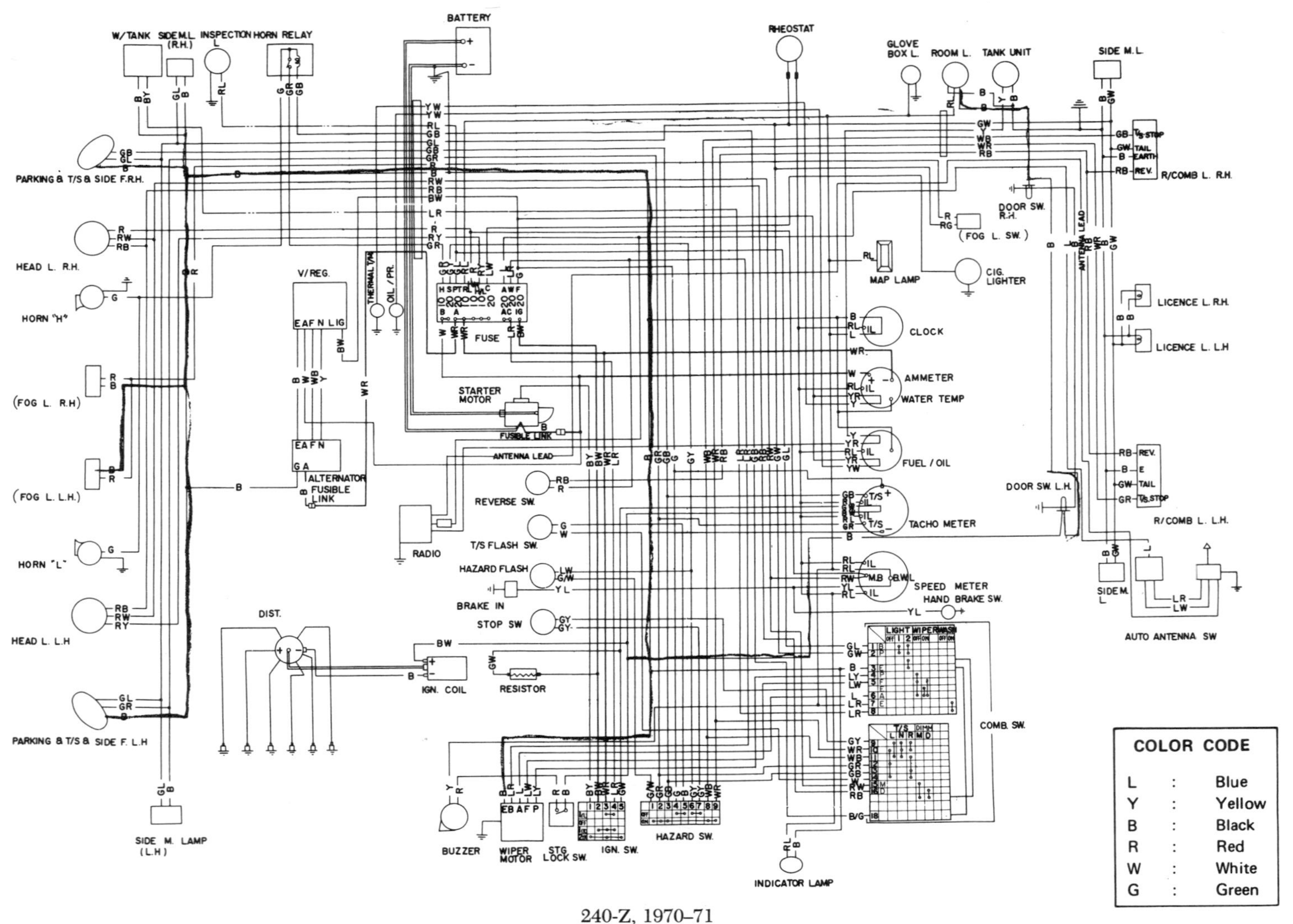
W/TANK
SIDE M.L (R.H.)
INSPECTION L
HORN RELAY
BATTERY
RHEOSTAT
GLOVE BOX L.
ROOM L.
TANK UNIT
SIDE M.L
R/COMB L. R.H.
DOOR SW. R.H.
(FOG L. SW.)
CIG. LIGHTER
MAP LAMP
LICENCE L. R.H.
LICENCE L. L.H
CLOCK
AMMETER
WATER TEMP
FUEL / OIL
TACHO METER
SPEED METER
HAND BRAKE SW.
DOOR SW. L.H.
R/COMB L. L.H.
SIDE M. L
AUTO ANTENNA SW
PARKING & T/S & SIDE F.R.H.
HEAD L. R.H.
HORN "H"
(FOG L. R.H)
(FOG L. L.H.)
HORN "L"
HEAD L. L.H
PARKING & T/S & SIDE F. L.H
SIDE M. LAMP (L.H)
V/REG.
THERMAL T/M
OIL / PR.
FUSE
STARTER MOTOR
FUSIBLE LINK
ANTENNA LEAD
ALTERNATOR
FUSIBLE LINK
RADIO
REVERSE SW.
T/S FLASH SW.
HAZARD FLASH
BRAKE IN
STOP SW
DIST.
IGN. COIL
RESISTOR
COMB. SW.
BUZZER
WIPER MOTOR
STG. LOCK SW.
IGN. SW.
HAZARD SW.
INDICATOR LAMP
COLOR CODE
L : Blue
Y : Yellow
B : Black
R : Red
W : White
G : Green

240-Z, 1970–71

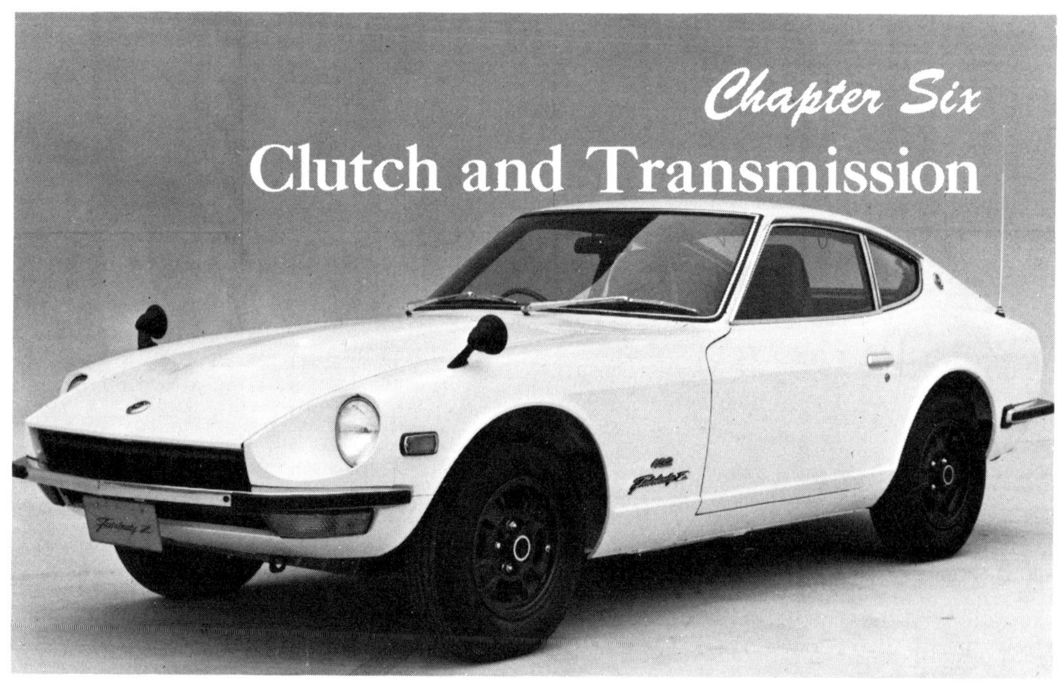


## Manual Transmission

**Neutral Safety Switch Removal and Installation**

1. Disconnect the lead wires (green with black stripe and green with white stripe) at the connectors.

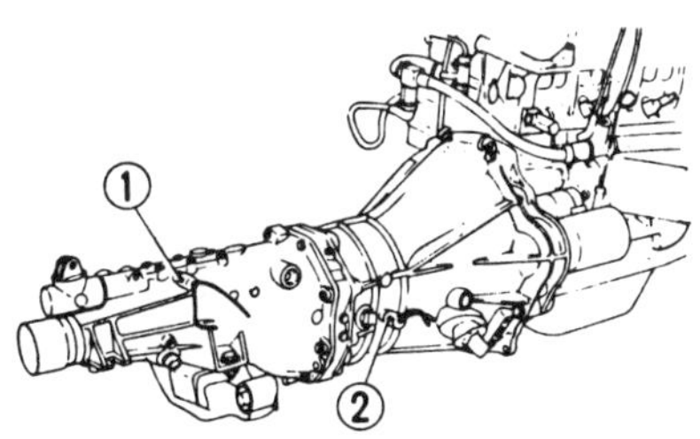

Neutral safety switch (1) and back-up switch (2)

2. Unscrew the neutral safety switch from the transmission rear extension housing and remove it.
3. Install in reverse order.

**Removal and Installation**

1. Disconnect the battery negative cable and the accelerator linkage to the carburetor. Drain the transmission oil.
2. Remove the five screws holding the console in place. Remove the choke control wire from the console. Disconnect the wiring harness and remove the console.

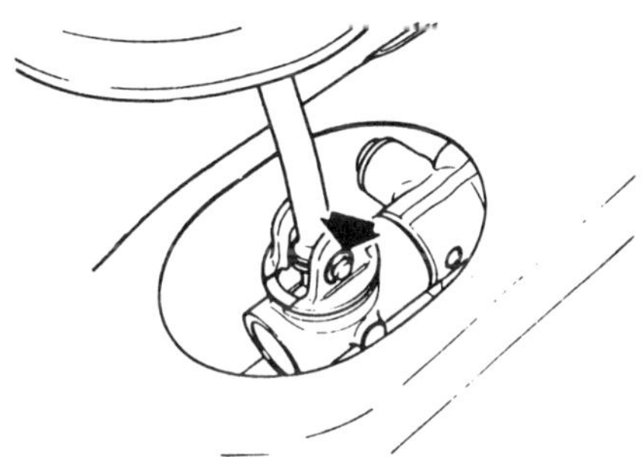
Disconnecting the gearshift lever

3. Put the transmission in Neutral and remove the C-ring from the gearshift lever pin. Then, remove the pin and remove the gearshift lever.
4. Support the vehicle on safety stands or a lift.
5. Disconnect the exhaust pipe at the front.
6. Disconnect the back-up light and neutral safety switch wires.
7. Remove the clutch operating cylinder.
8. Disconnect the speedometer cable at the rear extension housing.
9. Remove the resonator and muffler hanger bolts.
10. Scribe matchmarks on the rear of the driveshaft and on the companion flange.
11. Remove rear driveshaft bolts, pull the rear down, and then draw the drive-

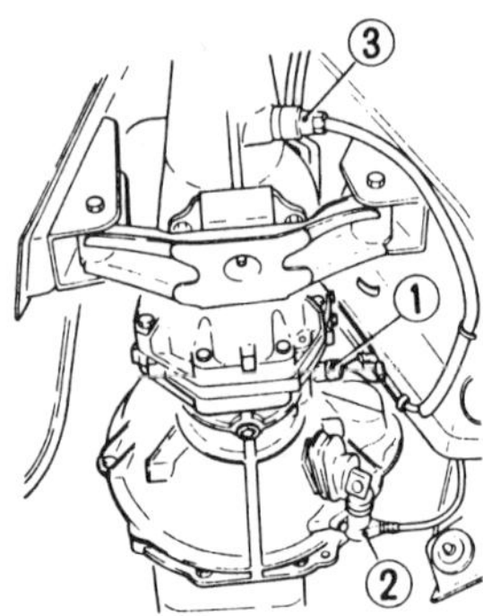

The underside of the transmission

1. Neutral safety switch
2. Clutch slave cylinder
3. Speedometer

shaft sleeve yoke out of the transmission. Draw the shaft out carefully so as not to damage the spline, yoke, or transmission oil seal. Plug the opening in the transmission with a clean rag.

12. Support the engine under the oil pan with a jack. Place a wood block between the jack and pan.

13. Place a jack under the transmission.

14. Remove the nut atttaching the engine to the rear crossmember. Remove the crossmember atttaching bolts and remove it.

15. Disconnect the wiring and remove the starter motor.

16. Remove the bolts holding the transmission to the engine.

17. Slide the transmission slightly to the rear, then slowly downward, and remove it.

On installation:

1. Clean the mating surfaces of the engine and transmission case.

2. Lightly grease the clutch disc and mainshaft splines.

3. Reverse the above removal procedures.

4. Refill the transmission to the level of the filler plug with the recommended oil.

## Clutch

The clutch consists of a driven disc splined to the transmission mainshaft and a pressure plate which is bolted to the engine flywheel. When the clutch pedal is released, the pressure plate moves toward the flywheel and sand-

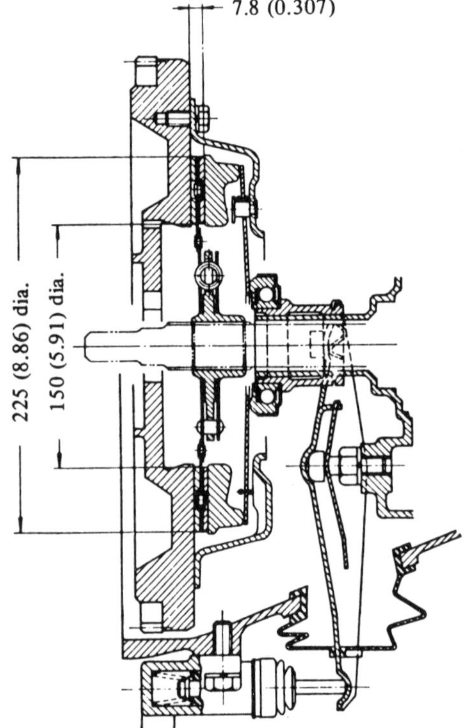

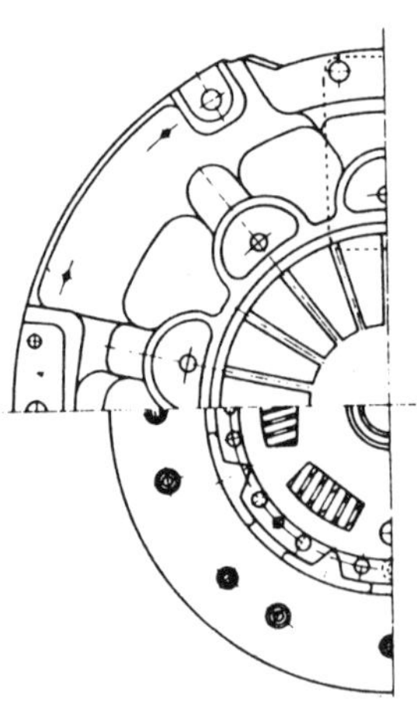

The basic construction of the clutch

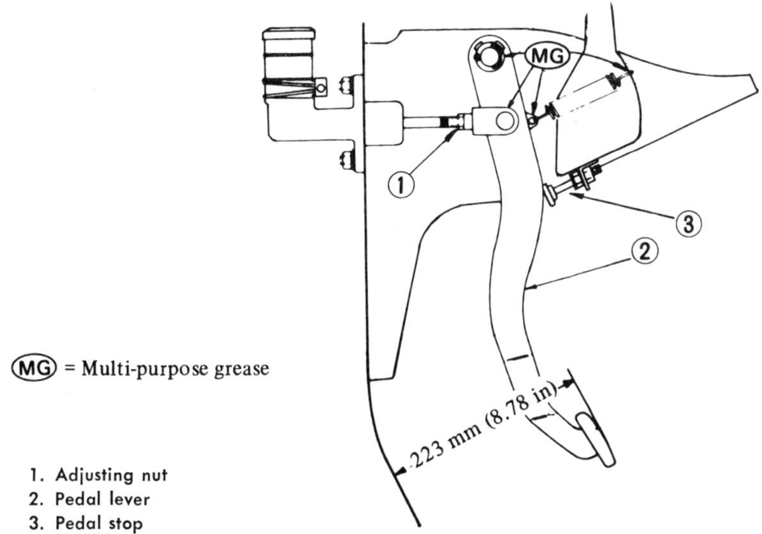

Adjusting clutch pedal free-play

wiches the driven disc between itself and the flywheel, thus providing smooth engagement, but a solid drive connection.

**Pedal Height Adjustment**

1. Loosen the locknut and screw the pedal stop in as far as it will go so that the pedal is free to move out as far as possible.
2. Loosen the master cylinder pushrod locknut and adjust the rod so that the pedal height above the floor is 8.9 in. (226 mm). Tighten the pushrod locknut.
3. Screw the pedal stop back out until the pedal height is 8.78 in. (223 mm) and tighten the locknut.

**Removal and Installation**

1. Remove the transmission as described above.

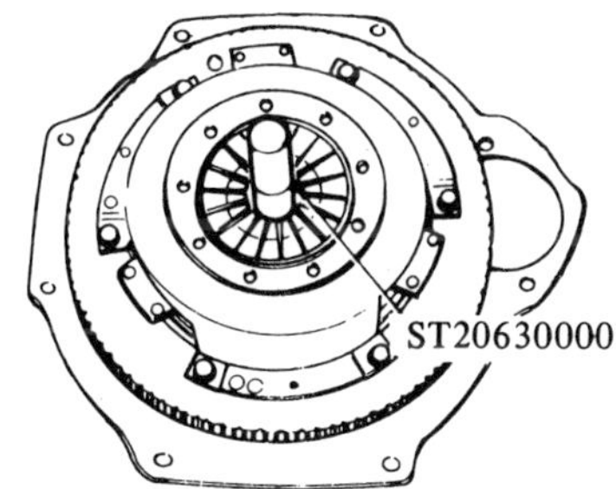

Supporting the clutch assembly

2. Insert a clutch aligning bar or similar tool all the way into the clutch disc hub. This must be done so as to support the weight of the clutch disc during removal.
3. Loosen the pressure plate-to-flywheel bolts evenly, one turn at a time, until all spring pressure is released.
4. Remove the bolts and pull the pressure plate and disc off the flywheel.

To install:

1. Lightly grease the transmission mainshaft and clutch disc splines. Slide the disc onto the shaft and then wipe any excess grease from the clutch hub and mainshaft. *Be careful to keep grease off the clutch lining.*

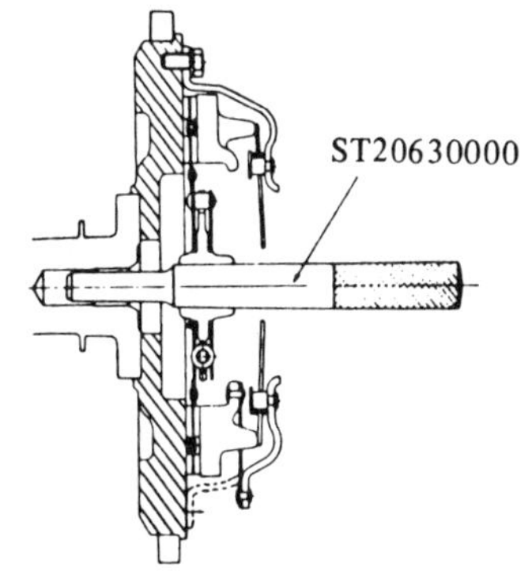

Installing the clutch cover

2. Insert an aligning tool through the clutch disc hub, into the flywheel, and position the pressure plate on the flywheel.
3. Start the mounting bolts, then tighten them evenly, one turn at a time. Make sure that the dowels which align

the pressure plate fit properly and allow the plate to go flat against the flywheel. Torque the bolts to 11–16 ft lbs (1.5–2.2 kg-m).

4. Remove the aligning tool. Install the transmission as described above.

## *CLUTCH MASTER CYLINDER*

### Removal and Installation

1. Remove the pushrod clevis pin. Disconnect the tube going to the slave cylinder and drain the fluid.
2. Remove the mounting bolts and remove the cylinder from the car.
3. On installation, reverse the above procedures.
4. Bleed the system as described below.

### System Bleeding

1. Fill the master cylinder with the recommended fluid to the proper level.
2. Clean any dirt from the bleeder screw on the slave cylinder and install a bleeder hose. Submerge the free end of the hose in a container of brake fluid.
3. Have someone depress the clutch pedal slowly. Loosen the bleeder screw as the clutch starts moving down and retighten it before the clutch stops moving downward.
4. Have your assistant release the clutch pedal, then repeat Step 3 until the fluid in the bleed hose is bubble-free. Keep your eye on the fluid level and refill the reservoir as necessary.
5. When all air is bled, refill the master cylinder, tighten the bleeder screw snugly, and remove the bleeder hose.

### Overhaul

1. Remove the dust cover. Remove the stopper ring.
2. Remove the pushrod and piston assembly.
3. Remove the spring seat. Remove the piston cup and discard it. Wash all parts in brake fluid.
4. Check the cylinder for uneven wear/or damage and measure the clearance between the piston and cylinder. The clearance should not be more than 0.0059 in. (0.15 mm). If defects are found, replace master cylinder.
5. Replace the piston cup.
6. Inspect the dust cover, oil reservoir, cap, and replace parts as necessary.
7. Inspect the return valve springs and replace if broken or weak.
8. Inspect the hose and tube. Replace parts as necessary.
9. Reassemble the master cylinder, reversing Steps 1–3. Dip the piston cup in brake fluid and coat the piston and cylin-

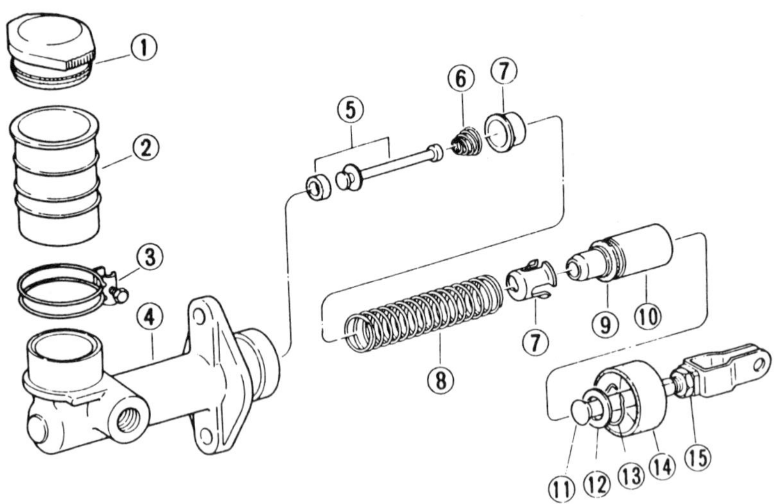


Exploded view of the clutch master cylinder

1. Reservoir cap
2. Reservoir
3. Reservoir band
4. Cylinder body
5. Valve assembly
6. Valve spring
7. Spring seat
8. Return spring
9. Piston cup
10. Piston
11. Pushrod
12. Stopper
13. Stopper ring
14. Dust cover
15. Nut

der with fluid before installing. Make sure that the piston is facing the right way!

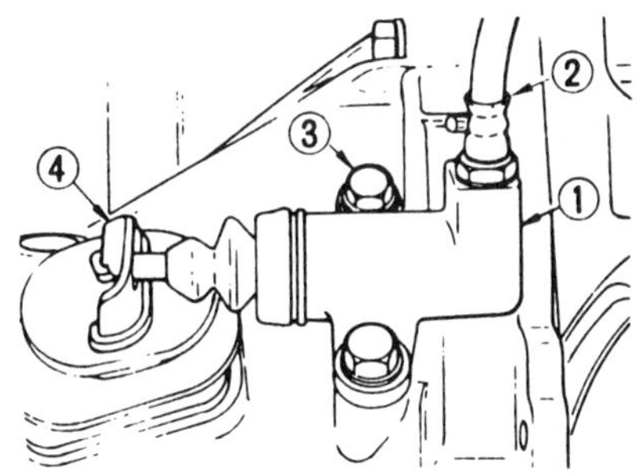


Master cylinder mounting

1. Clutch master cylinder
2. Clutch hose
3. Mounting bolts
4. Withdrawal lever

*CLUTCH SLAVE CYLINDER*

**Removal and Installation**

1. Remove the return spring. Detach the line going to the master cylinder and drain the fluid.
2. Remove the mounting bolts and remove the cylinder.
3. To install, reverse the above procedure and then bleed the system as previously described in "Clutch Master Cylinder System Bleeding."

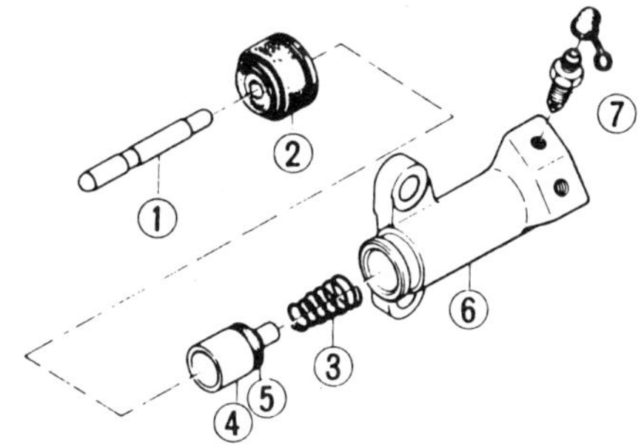


Exploded view of the clutch slave cylinder

1. Pushrod
2. Dust cover
3. Piston spring
4. Piston
5. Piston cup
6. Operating cylinder
7. Bleeder screw

**Overhaul**

1 Remove the pushrod and dust cover.
2. Remove the piston and piston spring.
3. Remove the bleeder screw.
4. Clean all parts in brake fluid and inspect for damage. Check the piston and cylinder for excessive wear or scoring. The cylinder must not be worn beyond 0.7500 in. (19.05 mm).
5. Replace the piston cup. Dip it in brake fluid first, and be sure that it is installed in the right direction.
6. Check the dust cover for damage and check the return spring for a break or weakened condition
7. Assemble the cylinder in the reverse order of Steps 1–3, dipping the piston in brake fluid and also coating the cylinder with it.

## Automatic Transmission

**Pan Removal**

1. Remove all pan mounting bolts.
2. Remove the pan slowly, keeping it level to avoid spilling fluid. Drain the fluid.

To install:

1. Clean the gasket surfaces of both the pan and the transmission.
2. Use a new gasket.
3. When tightening mounting bolts, go back-and-forth in a criss-cross fashion, tightening the bolts evenly to 3.6–5.1 ft lbs 0.5–0.7 kg-m).
4. Refill with Dexron ® fluid and check the level as described in Chapter 1.

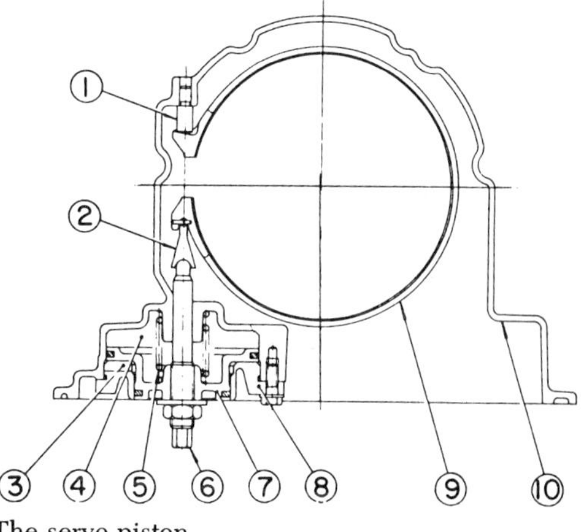


The servo piston

1. Anchor end pin
2. Band strut
3. Apply
4. Release
5. Return spring
6. Band servo piston stem
7. Band servo piston
8. Servo retainer
9. Brake band assembly
10. Transmission case

### Brake Band Adjustment

1. Remove the oil pan as previously described.
2. Loosen the locknut on the piston stem and torque the stem to 8.7–18 ft lbs (1.2–2.5 kg-m).
3. Loosen the stem exactly two turns and tighten the locknut.
4. Replace the oil pan and refill the transmission as described above.

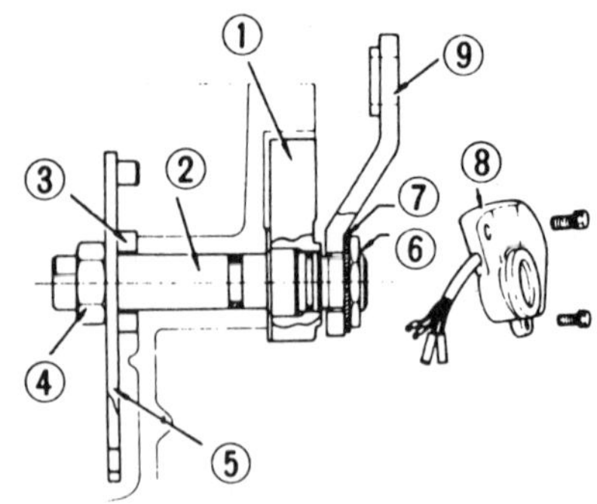

The construction of the inhibitor switch

1. Inhibitor switch
2. Manual shaft
3. Washer
4. Nut
5. Manual plate
6. Washer
7. Nut
8. Inhibitor switch
9. Range selector lever

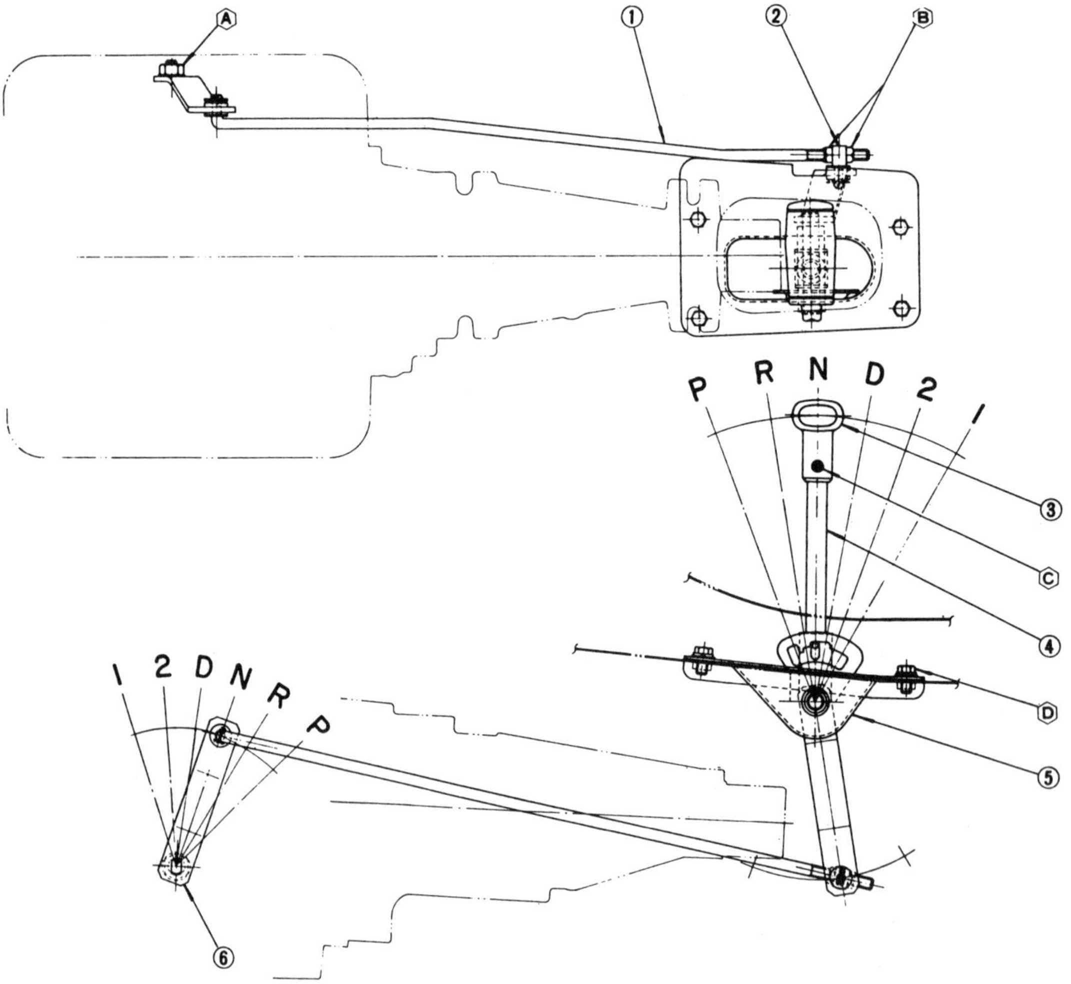

### Neutral Safety Switch Adjustment

1. Apply the brakes and check to see that the starter works only in the "P" and "N" transmission ranges. If the starter works with the transmission in

Transmission control linkage—1973–74

1. Selector rod
2. Joint trunnion
3. Control lever knob
4. Control lever assembly
5. Control lever bracket
6. Selector range lever

Tightening torque (T) of bolts and nuts kg-m (ft lbs)
A=3.0 to 4.0 (22 to 29)
B=0.8 to 1.1 (5.8 to 8.0)
C=0.2 to 0.25 (1.4 to 1.8)
D=0.8 to 1.1 (5.8 to 8.0)

gear, adjust the switch as described below.

2. Remove the fastening nut of the range selector lever and the bolts which hold the switch body in place. Remove the machine screw under the switch body.

3. Put the manual shaft in the "N" position by moving the selector lever so that the slot in the shaft is vertical and the detent mechanism clicks.

4. Align the screw hole with the internal rotor pin hole and insert a 0.059 in. (1.5 mm) pin to ensure and retain alignment.

5. Install the switch bolts, pull out the pin, and put the machine screw back into the hole. Install the range selector lever nut.

6. Test again as in step 1. If the switch does not work, replace it.

### Shift Linkage Adjustment

1973–74

1. Loosen the adjusting nuts ("B").
2. Set both transmission control lever and range selector lever in the "N" position.
3. Tighten the adjusting nuts so that they both just touch the trunnion ("2").
4. Tighten the nuts. Test the shifter for proper operation.

1970–72

1. Loosen the trunnion locknuts at the lower end of the control lever. Remove the selector lever knob and console (see "Manual Transmission Removal and Installation").
2. Put the transmission selector in "N" and put the transmission shift lever in the Neutral position by pushing it all the way back, then moving it forward two stops.
3. Check the vertical clearance between the top of the shift lever pin and transmission control bracket ("A" in the illustration). It should be 0.020–0.059 in. (0.5–1.5 mm). Adjust the nut at the lower end of the selector lever compression rod, as necessary.
4. Check the horizontal clearance ("B") between the shift lever pin and transmission control bracket. It should be 0.020 in. (0.5 mm). Adjust the trunnion locknuts as necessary to get this clearance.
5. Replace the console with the shift pointer correctly aligned. Install the shift knob.

### Checking Kick-Down Switch and Solenoid

1. Turn the key to the normal ON position, and depress the accelerator all

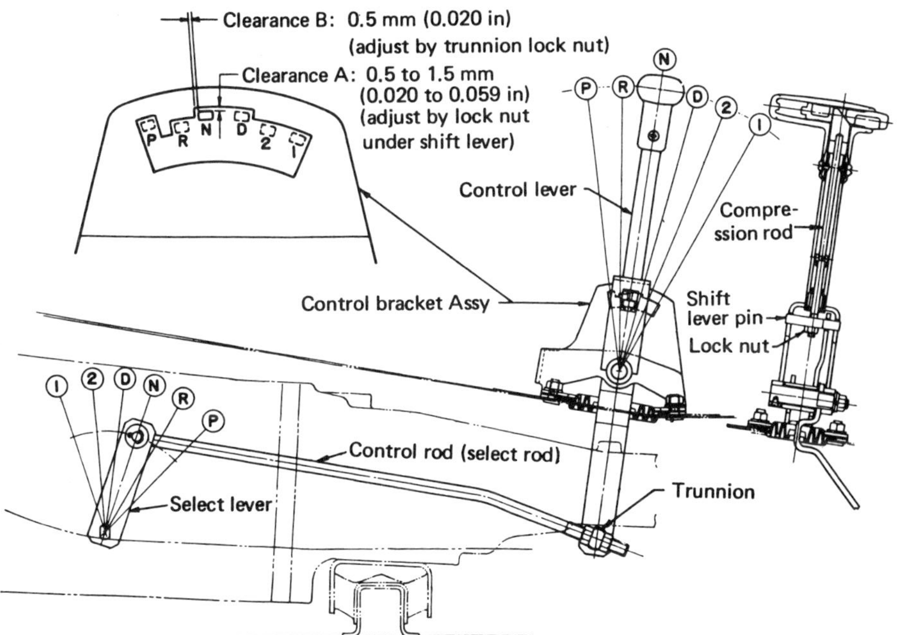


Transmission control linkage—1970–72

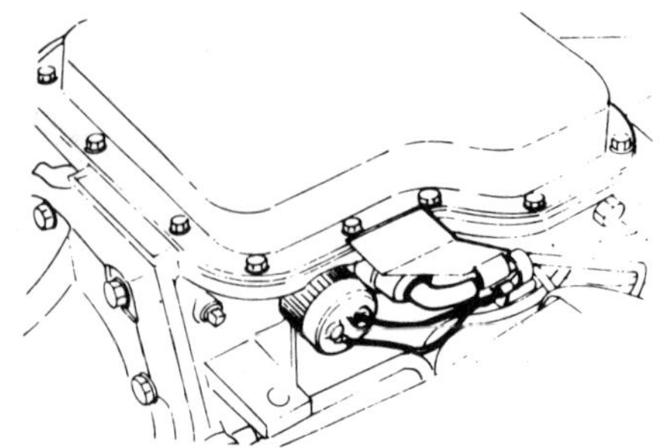

Location of the downshift solenoid

the way. The solenoid in the transmission should make an audible click.

2. If the solenoid does not work, inspect the wiring, and test it electrically to determine whether the problem is in the wiring, the kick-down switch, or the solenoid.

3. If the solenoid requires replacement, drain a little over 2 pts (1 liter) of fluid from the transmission before removing it.

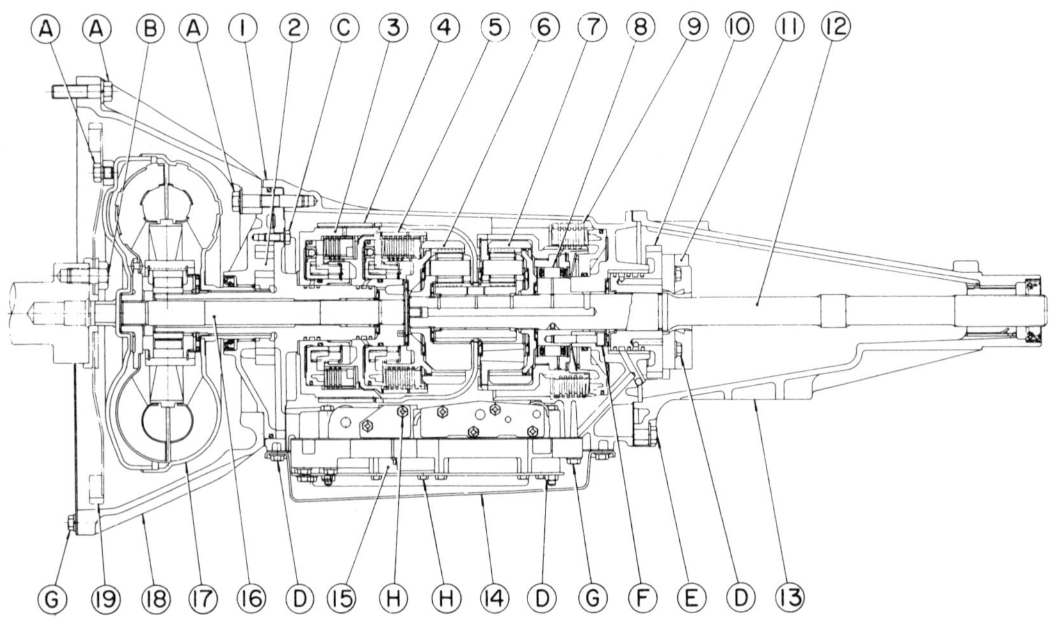


Cross-section of a Datsun automatic transmission

1. Transmission case
2. Oil pump
3. Front clutch
4. Band brake
5. Rear clutch
6. Front planetary gear
7. Rear planetary gear
8. One-way clutch
9. Low and Reverse brake
10. Oil distributor
11. Governor
12. Output shaft
13. Rear extension
14. Oil pan
15. Control valve
16. Input shaft
17. Torque converter
18. Converter housing
19. Drive plate

Torque in ft lbs:

A. 29–36
B. 101–116
C. 4.3–5.8
D. 3.6–5.1
E. 14–18
F. 9.4–13
G. 4.0–5.4
H. 1.9–2.5

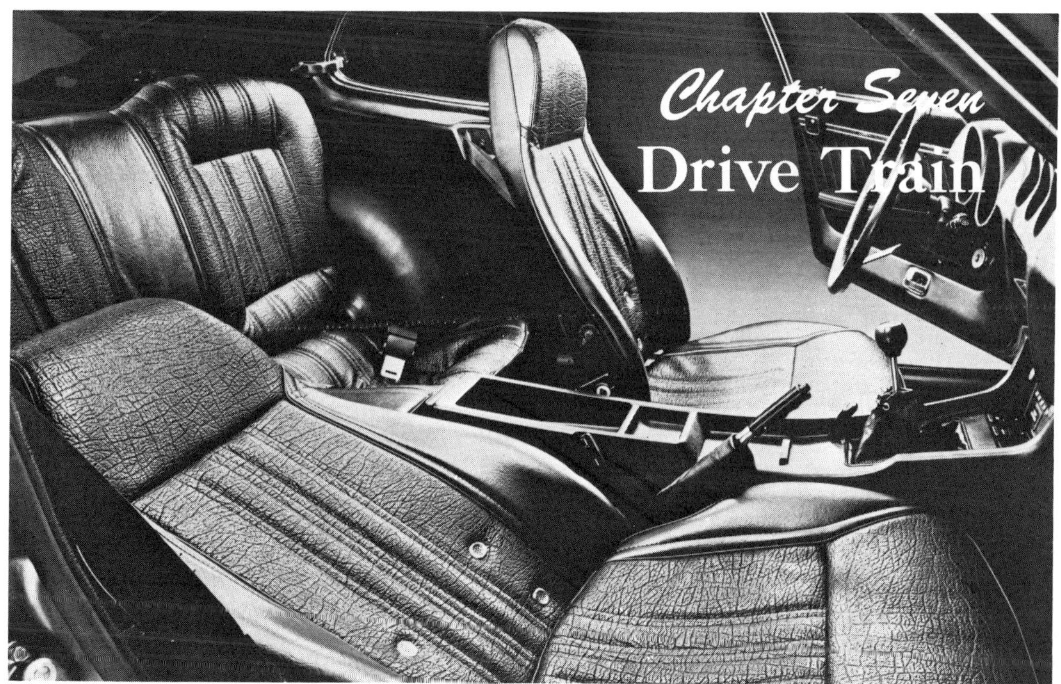


# Chapter Seven Drive Train

## Driveline

*DRIVESHAFT AND U-JOINTS*

**Removal and Installation**

1. Raise the car on a lift. On 260-Z models, remove the muffler and resonator mounting bolts. On earlier models, remove the resonator.
2. Scribe matchmarks on the rear of the driveshaft and the companion flange.

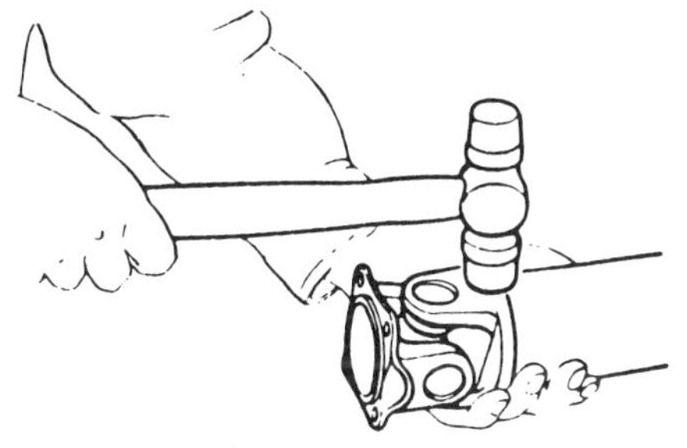

Removing U-joint bearings

3. Remove the bolts and nuts from the companion flange.
4. Pull the rear of the driveshaft downward and pull the splined portion at the front out of the transmission. Plug the hole in the transmission extension housing.
5. To install, reverse these procedures, oiling the splines before assembly. Make sure that the marks made in Step 3 align. Torque the flange bolts to 18 ft lbs (2.5 kg-m).

**U-Joint Overhaul**

1. Clean all parts in a safe solvent.
2. Mark the driveshaft and joint so that they can be reassembled in exactly the same position.
3. Remove the snap-rings with a screwdriver.
4. Lightly tap the base of the yoke with a soft hammer and remove each bearing race.
5. Check the spider bearing journals for dents or brinell marks. Make sure that the yoke holes are not worn.
6. Check the snap-rings, bearings, and seal rings. Replace parts as necessary.
7. Check the shaft tube for dents or cracks, and replace if necessary.
8. Assemble in reverse order. The needle rollers may be held in the races with grease. Reusable bearings should be carefully packed with grease.
9. Install snap-rings that are equal in thickness opposite each other. Choose thickness so that play will not exceed 0.0008 in. (0.02 mm). See the following chart.
10. Check that the frictional resistance of the joint does not exceed 9 in. lbs (10

kg-cm) on 240-Z models, or 13 in. lbs (15 kg-cm) on 260-Z models.

## Snap-Rings

| *Thickness in. (mm)* | *Color* |
|---|---|
| .0787 (2.0) | White |
| .0795 (2.02) | Yellow |
| .0803 (2.04) | Red |
| .0811 (2.06) | Green |
| .0819 (2.08) | Blue |
| .0827 (2.10) | Brown |
| .0835 (2.12) | Unpainted |
| .0843 (2.43) | Pink |

### *STUB AXLE*

#### Overhaul

1. Remove the U-joint yoke flange bolts on both sides. Remove the axle.
2. Remove the U-joint spider from the differential side. See the previous section.
3. Remove the snap-ring from the sleeve yoke plug. Remove the plug with snap-ring pliers.
4. Compress the shaft and remove the snap-ring from the stop.
5. Remove the stop.
6. Disconnect the rubber boot and carefully pull the shaft out of the yoke, retaining the balls and spacers.
7. Inspect the boot and O-ring of the yoke plug and replace them if damaged.
8. Check the shaft for bending, cracks, excess wear, or distortion.
9. Check the steel balls and sleeve yoke for damage, wear, or distortion.
10. Inspect the U-joint as described in Step 10 of the previous section and replace as necessary.
11. Thoroughly clean grease from the sleeve yoke, ball rolling grooves, and oil groove, and clean with a safe solvent.
12. Measure the driveshaft play (as shown in the illustration) with the shaft fully compressed. The assembly must be replaced if play exceeds 0.0039 in. (0.1 mm).
13. Assemble the axle in the reverse order of disassembly, ensuring that the yokes are correctly aligned, and that all balls and spacers are installed in the right order.
14. Grease the ball rolling and oil grooves with multipurpose grease. Also

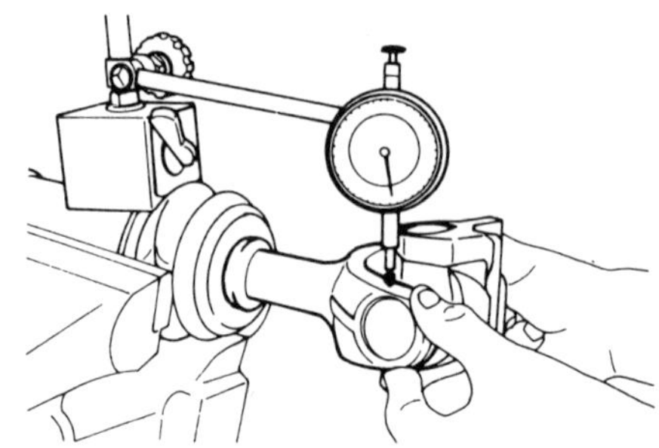

Measuring the play in the driveshaft

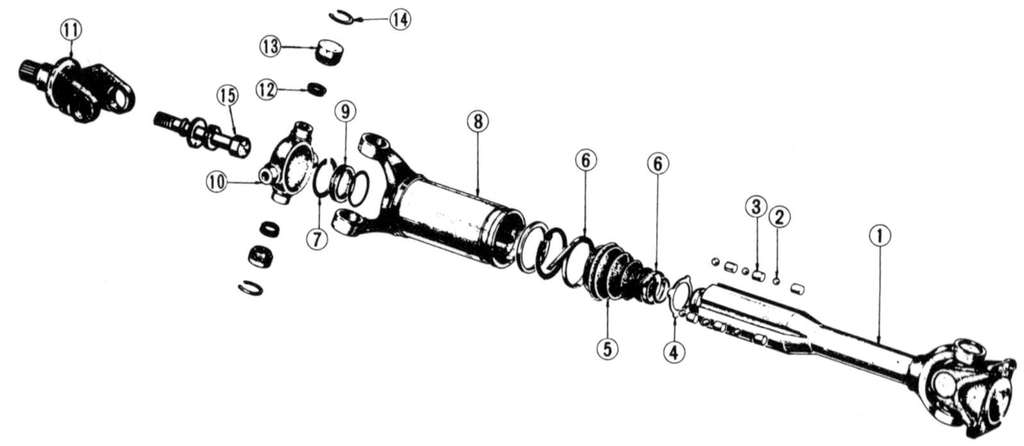


Exploded view of stub axle

1. Driveshaft
2. Driveshaft ball
3. Ball spacer
4. Driveshaft stop
5. Rubber boot
6. Boot band
7. Snap-ring
8. Sleeve yoke
9. Sleeve yoke plug
10. Spider journal
11. Slide yoke
12. Oil seal
13. Needle bearing
14. Snap-ring
15. Side yoke fixing bolt

fill the area behind the driveshaft itself with grease.

15. Select a suitable snap-ring and assemble the U-joint so that the play does not exceed 0.0008 in. (0.02 mm). See the following chart.

16. Bolt the axle back in place.

## Snap-Ring Thickness—In. (mm)

| In. | (mm) |
|---|---|
| .0583–.0591 | (1.48–1.50) |
| .0594–.0602 | (1.51–1.53) |
| .0606–.0614 | (1.54–1.56) |
| .0618–.0626 | (1.57–1.59) |

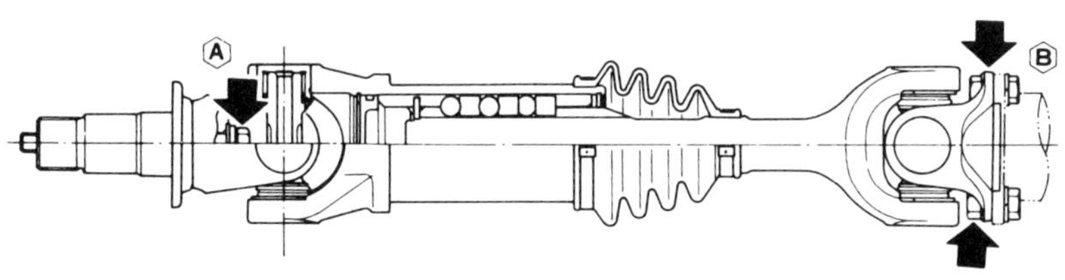


Tightening torque:

Ⓐ : 5.0 to 6.0 kg-m (36 to 43 ft-lb)

Ⓑ : 3.2 to 4.3 kg-m (23 to 31 ft-lb)

Stub axle bolts and their torques

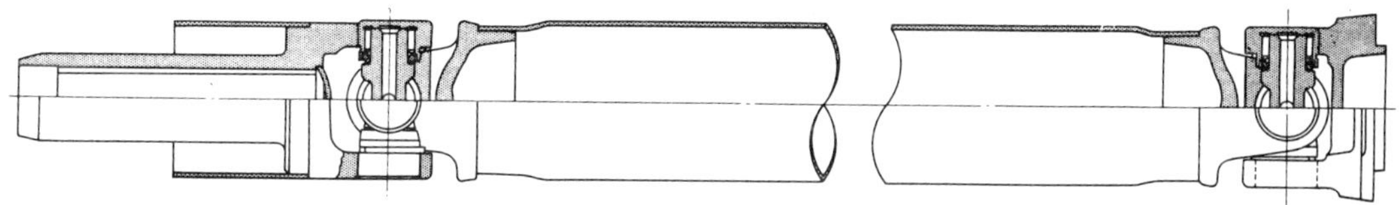

Cross-section of a driveshaft

# Chapter Eight
# Suspension and Steering

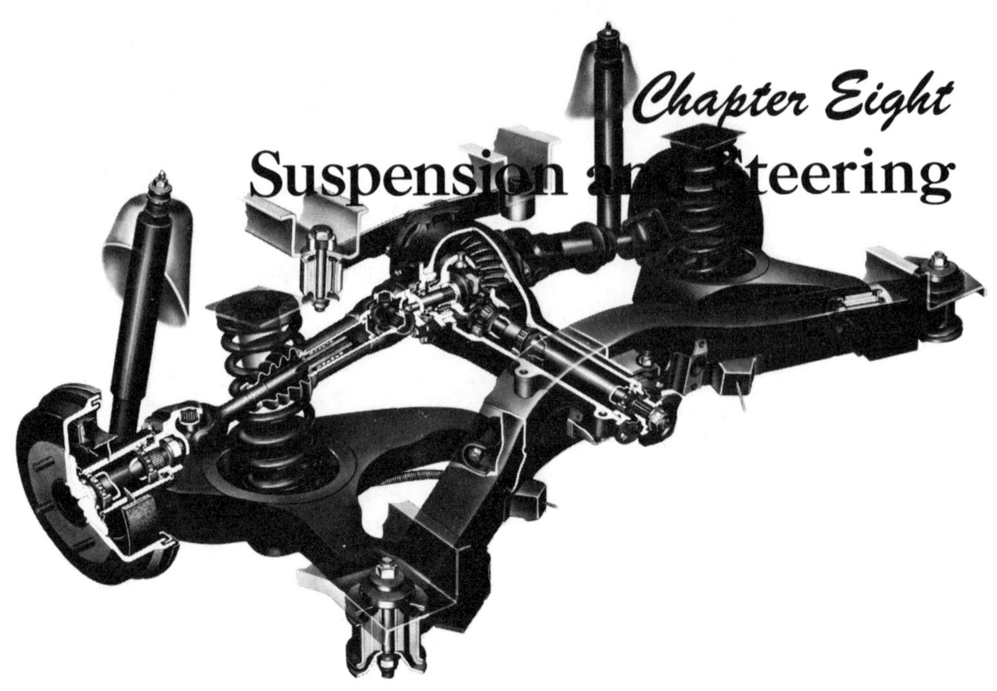

## Front Suspension

The 240-Z and 260-Z front suspension system is of the MacPherson strut type. The strut used on either side is a combination spring and shock absorber with the outer casing of the shock actually supporting the spring at the bottom and forming a major structural component of the suspension. The wheel spindle is welded to the bottom of the strut, a strut mounting thrust bearing at the top, and a ball joint at the bottom allow the entire strut to rotate in cornering maneuvers.

A rubber-bushed transverse link connects the lower portion of the strut to the main front crossmember via the ball joint, thus allowing for vertical movement. Compression rods connect the outer ends of the transverse links to the chassis at points in front of the outer ends, thus preventing excessive fore-and-aft movement.

A stabilizer bar connects the outer ends of the transverse links with points on either side of the chassis so that cornering roll will be minimized with minimal harshness in the normal operation of the suspension.

### *SPRINGS AND SHOCK ABSORBERS*

#### Testing Shock Absorber Action

Shock absorbers require replacement if the vehicle fails to recover quickly after a large bump is encountered, if there is a tendency for the vehicle to sway or nose dive excessively, or, sometimes, if the suspension is overly susceptible to vibration.

A good way to test the shocks is to intermittently apply downward pressure to one corner of the vehicle until it is moving up and down for almost the full suspension travel, then release it and watch the recovery. If the vehicle bounces slightly about one more time and then comes to rest, the shock absorbers are serviceable. If the vehicle goes on bouncing, the shocks require replacement.

### *STRUT REMOVAL AND INSTALLATION*

The struts are precision parts and retain the springs under tremendous pressure even when removed from the car. For these reasons, several expensive special tools and substantial specialized knowledge are required to safely and effectively work on these parts. We rec-

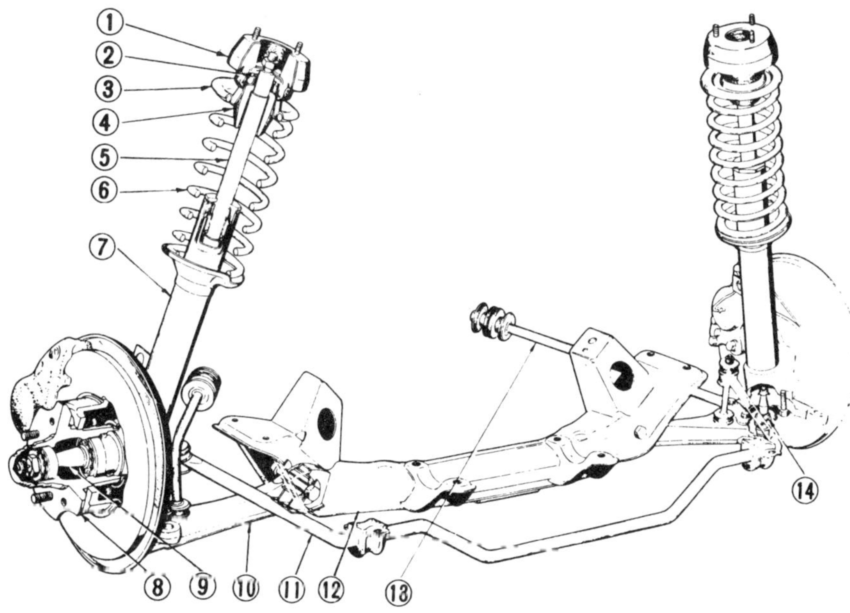


The front axle and suspension system

1. Strut mounting insulator
2. Strut mounting bearing
3. Upper spring seat
4. Bumper rubber
5. Piston rod
6. Front spring
7. Strut assembly
8. Hub assembly
9. Spindle
10. Transverse link
11. Stabilizer
12. Suspension member
13. Compression rod
14. Ball joint

ommend that if spring or shock absorber repair work is required, you remove the strut or struts involved and take them to a repair facility which is fully equipped and familiar with the car.

1. Jack up the car and support the chassis with stands as shown in Chapter 1.
2. Remove the hub nuts and remove the wheel.
3. Remove the splash board.
4. Loosen the brake hose connection. Remove the hose locking spring, pull the plate off, and remove the hose from

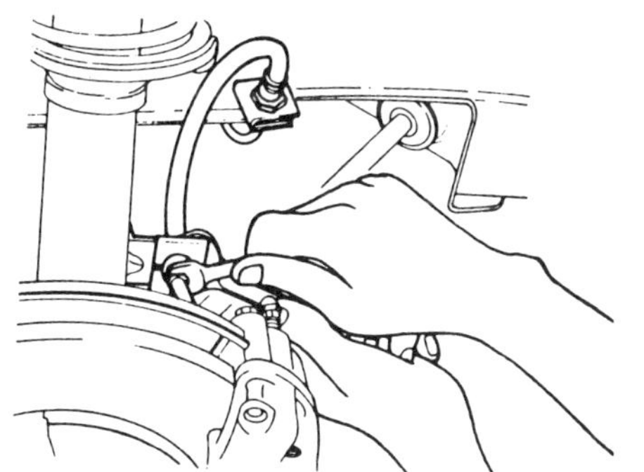

Location where brake hose should be disconnected

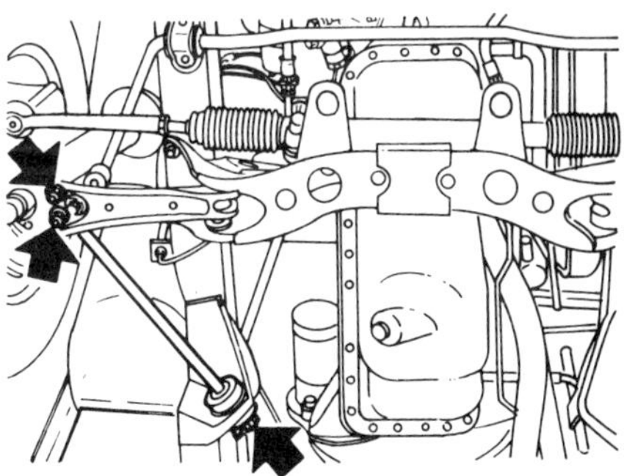

Disconnect compression rod at arrowed points

the strut assembly bracket. Cap the hose so that dust cannot enter.

5. Disconnect the stabilizer bar and the compression rod at the transverse link.
6. Loosen and remove the knuckle arm bolts (bold in the illustration).
7. Separate the strut from the ball joint. Remove the strut securing nuts at the top.
8. Remove the strut.

To install:

1. Inspect all bushings and replace as necessary.

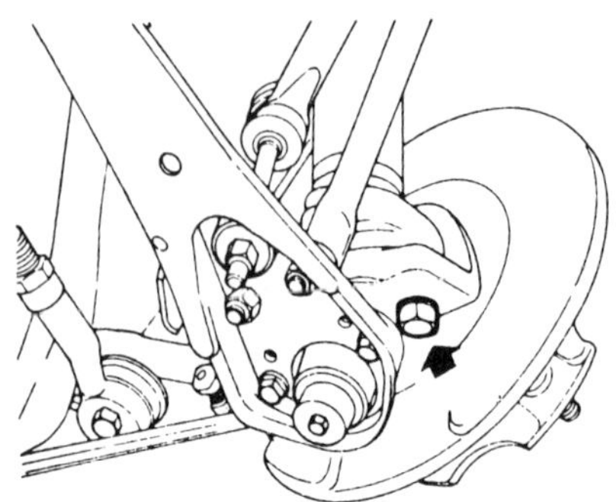

Location of knuckle arm bolts

2. Reverse the removal procedures, using the following torque figures:

a. Strut securing nuts (at body): 18–25 ft lbs (2.5–3.5 kg-m)

b. Knuckle arm bolts: 53–72 ft lbs (7.3–10 kg-m)

c. Compression rod nut: 44–51 ft lbs (6.1–7.1 kg-m)

d. Stabilizer installation bolts: 8.7–19.5 ft lbs (1.2–2.7 kg-m)

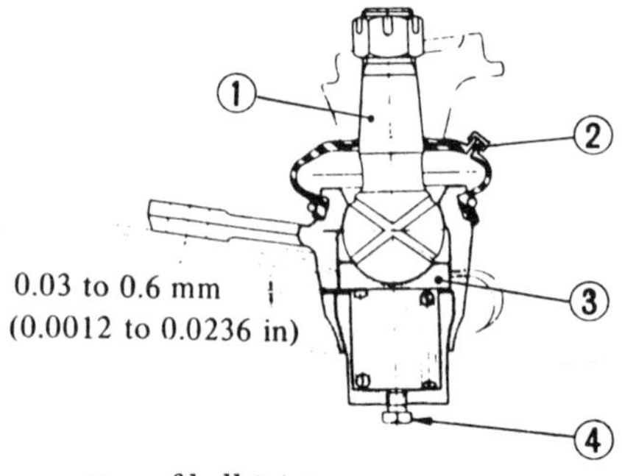


Cross-section of ball joint

1. Ball stud
2. Grease bleeder
3. Spring seat
4. Plug

## *TRANSVERSE LINK AND BALL JOINT*

### Ball Joint Inspection

1. Put the vehicle on a lift so that all weight is removed from both front wheels.

2. Apply downward and upward pressure to the outer end of the transverse link, avoiding any compression of the spring.

3. Measure the play between the link and the bottom of the strut which effectively is the axial play in the ball joint. If play exceeds 0.0236 in. (0.6 mm), replace the ball joint as later described.

### Removal and Installation

1. Jack up the car and support the chassis as shown in Chapter 1.

2. Remove the hub nuts and the wheel.

3. Remove the splash board.

4. Disconnect the stabilizer bar and the compression rod at the transverse link.

5. Loosen and remove the knuckle arm bolts (bold in the illustration).

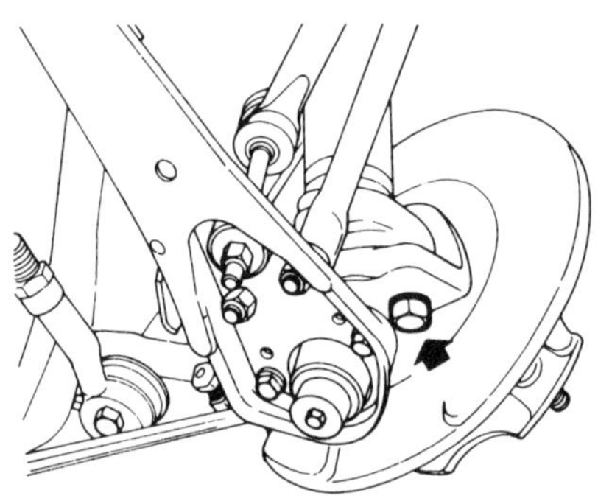

Location of knuckle arm bolts

6. Loosen and remove the transverse link mounting bolt and separate the link from the crossmember.

To remove the ball joint from the transverse link:

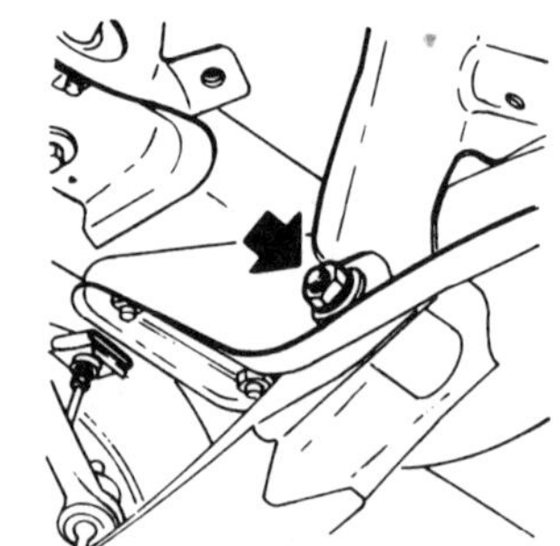

Location of transverse link mounting bolt

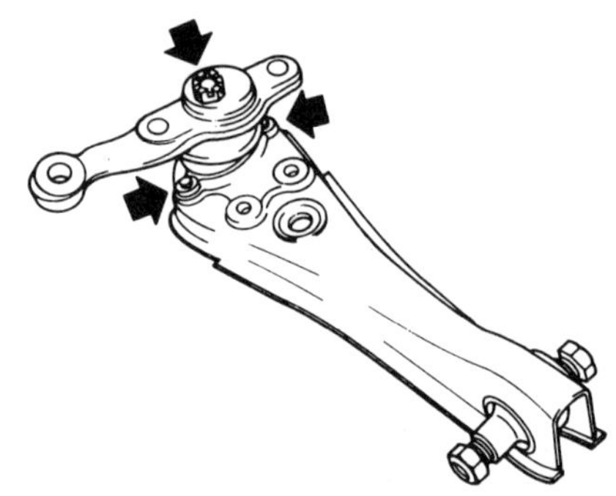

Two lower arrows show bolts removed in removal of knuckle arm

7. Remove the cotter pin from the castellated nut. Remove the nut and remove the knuckle arm from the ball joint.

8. Remove the ball joint installation nuts (arrowed) and remove the joint from the link.

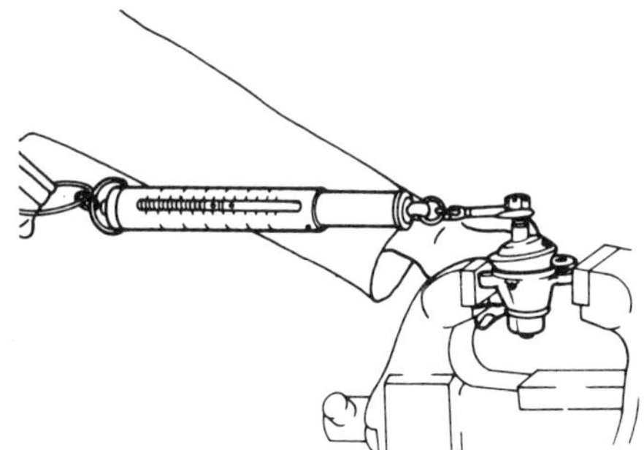

Measuring torque required to rotate the ball joint

To inspect ball joint and bushing:

1. Check axial end-play (see above) which should be 0.0236 in. (0.6 mm) or less.

2. Mount the joint lower part in a vise. Apply pressure with a spring scale at the cotter pin hole on the top of the ball stud. It should take 0.28–1.25 in. ozs (20–90 gr-cm) to force the joint to rotate. Replace the joint if it does not pass both tests, or if the dust cover is cracked.

3. Inspect the bushing for melted or cracked areas where it is adhered to the inner or outer tubes. If there is any doubt about its condition, take it to a properly equipped shop for pressing out with the proper tools and further inspection or replacement.

To install ball joint and transverse link:

1. Reverse the removal procedures, torquing the ball joint bolt to 44–51 ft lbs (6.1–7.1 kg-m), the ball joint castellated nut to 39.8–54.2 ft lbs (5.5–7.5 kg-m), and the transverse link mounting bolt just enough to permit weight to be placed on the suspension.

2. Lower the car to the ground and put the standard load inside (2 passengers). Torque the transverse link mounting bolt to 80–100 ft lbs (11.1–14.0 kg-m).

*FRONT END ALIGNMENT*

Alignment should be performed after it has been verified that all parts of the steering and suspension systems are in good condition. Tire pressures must be correct with tires cold.

Camber and caster angles are determined by the basic geometry of the suspension, and cannot be adjusted except through repair of faulty or bent components. Ride height also is nonadjustable and if the car is not level, a replacement spring of appropriate length must be substituted for a weak one.

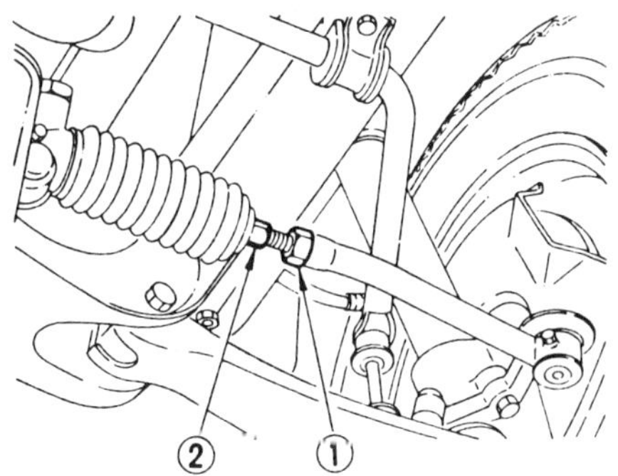


Location of locknut (1) and adjusting nut (2) for toe-in

Steering angle and toe-in are adjusted at the side rod. Loosen the locknut (1) and turn the adjusting nut (2) first to get proper steering angle (33° ± 30′—in; 31.7° ± 30′—out). Then, adjust both side rods equally in or out to get proper toe-in. The standard length of side rod between the adjusting nut and steering ball joint center is 10.846 in. (275.5 mm) on 260-Z models and 10.89 in. (276.6 mm) on 240-Z models.

## Rear Suspension

The rear suspension is also of the strut type with the springs and shock absorbers combined into a single unit. The wheels are located by being borne by spindles welded onto the struts. The struts are attached to the body at the top via a rubber bushing and to the transverse links at the bottom via bushed hinges. The links are hinged to crossmembers at front and rear and front and rear portions of the link are far enough apart that the compression rods required on the front suspension are not necessary.

The axle shafts have U-joints at either end and thus do not support the car in any way. The differential housing is supported by the crossmember at the front,

## Wheel Alignment

| Year | Model | Caster | | Camber | | Toe-in in. (mm) | Steering Axis Inclination | Wheel Pivot Ratio (deg) | |
|---|---|---|---|---|---|---|---|---|---|
| | | Range (deg) | Pref Setting (deg) | Range (deg) | Pref Setting (deg) | | | Inner Wheel | Outer Wheel |
| 1970–72 | 240-Z | 2°55′ ± 30′ | — | 50′ ± 30′ | — | .079–.197 (2–5) | 12°10′ ± 30′ | 32.5° ± 30′ | 31.9° ± 30′ |
| 1973 | 240-Z | 2°55′ ± 45′ | — | 50′ ± 45′ | — | 1/16–7/32 (1.59–5.56) | 12°10′ ± 30′ | 33° ± 30′ | 31.7° ± 30′ |
| 1974 | 260-Z | 2°54′ ± 45′ | — | 46′ ± 45′ | — | .079–.197 (2–5) | 12°10′ ± 30′ | 33° ± 30′ | 31.7° ± 30′ |

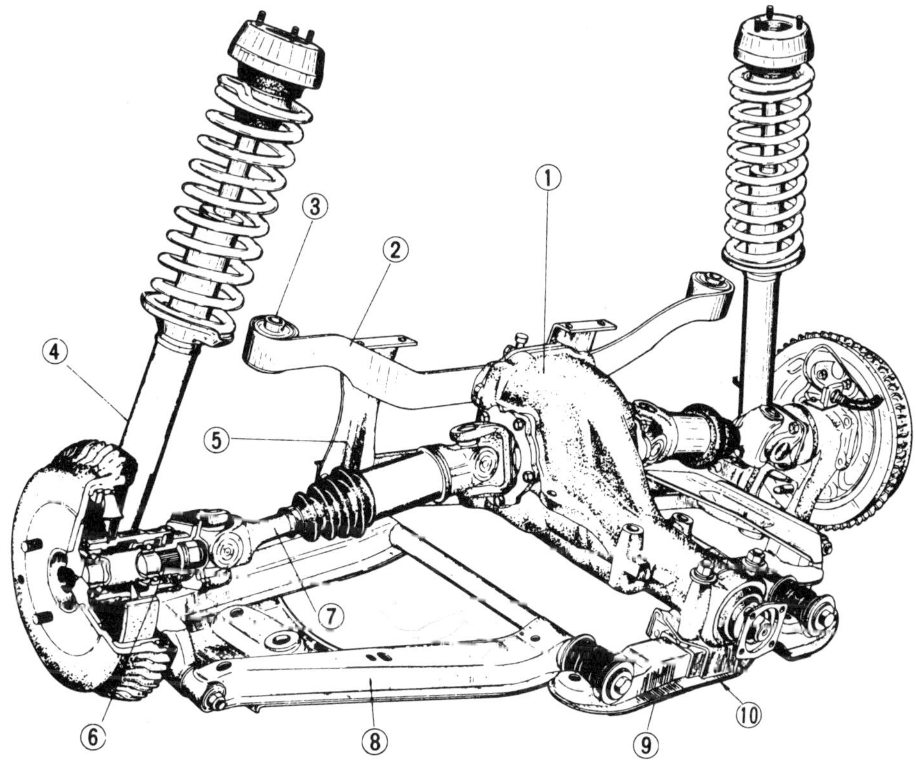

The rear axle and rear suspension

1. Gear carrier
2. Differential case mounting rear member
3. Differential case mounting rear insulator
4. Strut assembly
5. Link mounting brace
6. Rear axle shaft
7. Driveshaft
8. Transverse link
9. Differential case mounting front member
10. Differential case mounting front insulator

and by a horizontal leaf spring at the rear. The suspension is entirely independent except for the use of a stabilizer bar.

## *SPRINGS AND SHOCK ABSORBERS*

### Testing Shock Absorber Action

Shocks require replacement if the vehicle fails to recover quickly after hitting a large bump or if the vehicle sways excessively with a change in steering wheel position.

A good way to test the shocks is to intermittently apply downward pressure to one corner of the vehicle until it is moving up and down for almost the full suspension travel, then release it and watch the recovery. If the vehicle bounces slightly about one more time and then comes to rest, the shocks are serviceable. If the vehicle goes on bouncing, replace the shocks.

## *STRUT REMOVAL AND INSTALLATION*

The struts are precision parts and retain the springs under tremendous pressure even when removed from the car. For these reasons, several expensive special tools and substantial specialized

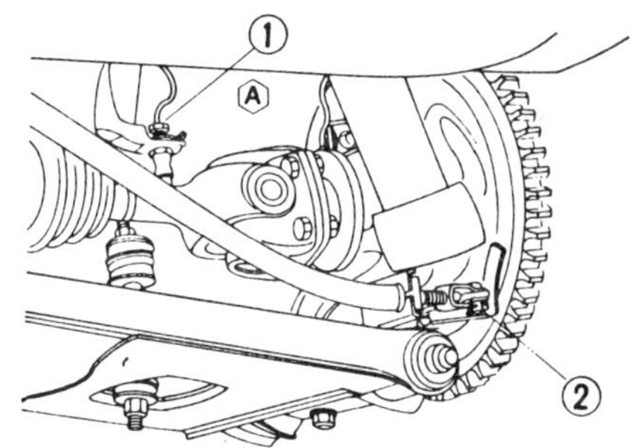

Tightening torque:

Ⓐ : 1.5 to 1.8 kg-m (11 to 13 ft-lb)

Where to disconnect brake line (1) and brake side linkage (2)

knowledge are required to safely and effectively work on these parts. We recommend that if a spring or shock absorber repair is required, you remove the strut(s) involved and take them to a repair facility which is fully equipped and familiar with the car.

1. Loosen the wheel nuts, jack the car up, and support it on stands as shown in Chapter 1.

2. Remove the wheel nuts and wheels. Disconnect the brake hose at (1) and the linkage at (2).

3. Disconnect the stabilizer bar at the crossmember and transverse link.

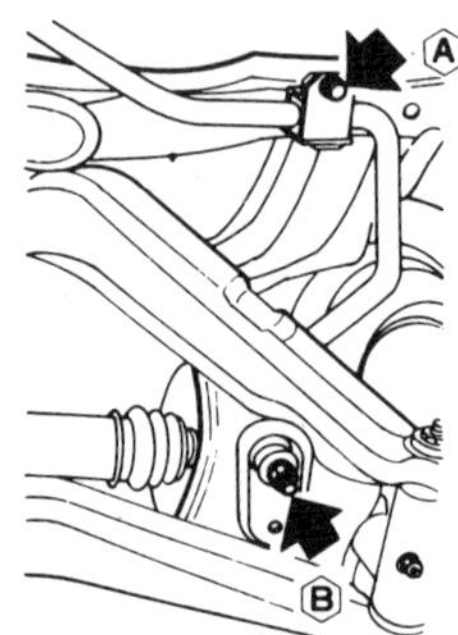


Arrows show bolts removed in removal of stabilizer bar

4. Remove the transverse link outer spindle self-locking nuts (2), and the spindle bolt (1). Pull the spindle out and separate the transverse link and strut.

5. Disconnect the driveshaft at the outer end.

6. Place a jack under the lower end of the strut. Remove the strut installation nuts from inside the passenger compartment. Lower the strut carefully with the jack.

To install:

1. Inspect all bushings and replace as necessary.

2. Reverse the removal procedures, installing the spindle so that the shorter length, when measured from the locking bolt notch, is toward the front.

3. Use the following torque figures:

Strut installation nuts: 18–25 ft lbs (2.5–3.5 kg-m)

Driveshaft U-joint bolts: 36–43 ft lbs (5.0–6.0 kg-m)

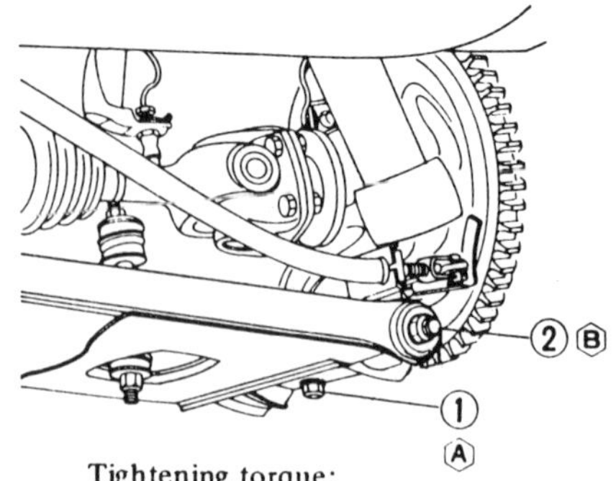


Location of transverse link lockbolt (1) and nuts (2)

Link spindle locknuts: 54–69 ft lbs (7.5–9.5 kg-m)

Link spindle lock bolt: 7.2–8.7 ft lbs (1.0–1.2 kg-m)

Stabilizer bar at link: 8.7–12.3 ft lbs (1.2–1.7 kg-m)

Stabilizer bar at crossmember: 7.2–8.7 ft lbs (1.0–1.2 kg-m)

Brake line connector: 11–13 ft lbs (1.5–1.8 kg-m)

4. Fill and bleed brake system.

### *REAR SUSPENSION ADJUSTMENTS*

The rear suspension is not adjustable for wheel alignment. However, alignment should be checked periodically and repairs made to defective or bent parts, as necessary.

## Steering

### *STEERING WHEEL*

#### Removal and Installation

1. Disconnect the battery negative terminal.

2. Depress the horn pad, turn it counterclockwise, and remove it.

3. Remove the steering wheel nut.

4. Install a puller, threading the anchor screws into the holes provided for this purpose in the wheel.

5. Turn the center bolt of the puller counterclockwise until the wheel comes off.

To install:

1. Apply grease to all portions which will slide together during installation.
2. Put the punch mark on the top of the column shaft and install the wheel in a straight-ahead position.
3. Torque the steering wheel nut to 36–51 ft lbs (5–7 kg-m).
4. Turn the wheel through the whole range of the steering system and make sure that it does not grab.
5. Install the horn pad, reconnect the battery, and test the horn.

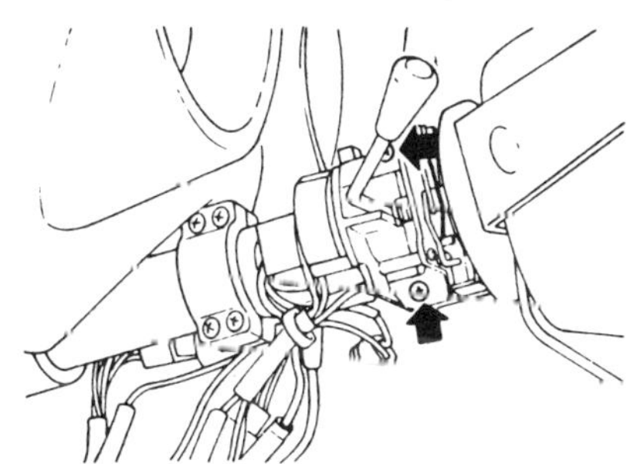

Arrows show screws which must be removed in combination switch removal

### *COMBINATION SWITCH*

**Removal and Installation**

The combination switch operates the lights, wipers, windshield washer, turn signal, and dimmer switches.

1. Disconnect the negative terminal from the battery.
2. Remove the screws which hold the shell cover halves together and remove them from the column jacket.
3. Disconnect all six electrical connectors.
4. Remove the two screws which hold the switch to the column jacket.
5. Separate the switch halves (without disconnecting the connector which connects the two halves electrically) and remove the switch.

To install:

1. Reverse the above procedures, ensuring that the location tab inside the turn signal switch lines up with the hole in the jacket of the steering column.

### *IGNITION SWITCH*

**Removal and Installation**

1. Remove the screws holding the shell cover halves together, separate, and remove the cover halves.
2. Disconnect the lead wires at the connector located at the bottom of the steering lock.
3. Remove the screw which holds the switch to the steering lock, and remove the switch.
4. Install in reverse order of the above procedure.

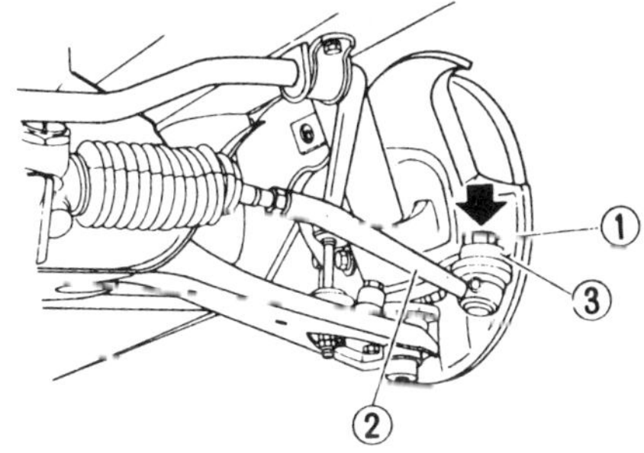


Arrow shows location of outer ball stud nut (1). (2) indicates the side rod, and (3) the knuckle arm

### *SIDE ROD AND STEERING BALL JOINT*

**Removal and Installation**

1. Raise the car, put it on stands, and remove the front wheel(s).
2. Remove the splash board.
3. Remove the cotter pins and nuts which hold the ball studs in the knuckle arms (arrowed).
4. To remove the ball studs, strike the knuckle arm boss with a copper hammer, backing up this force with a large hammer held against the opposite side of the knuckle arm. *Do not strike the ball stud head or any part of the side rod.*
5. Loosen the side rod locknut and unscrew the rod from the steering system.

To install:

1. Reverse the above procedures, torquing the ball stud nut to 40–55 ft lbs (5.5–7.6 kg-m).
2. Check the steering angle and adjust the toe-in.

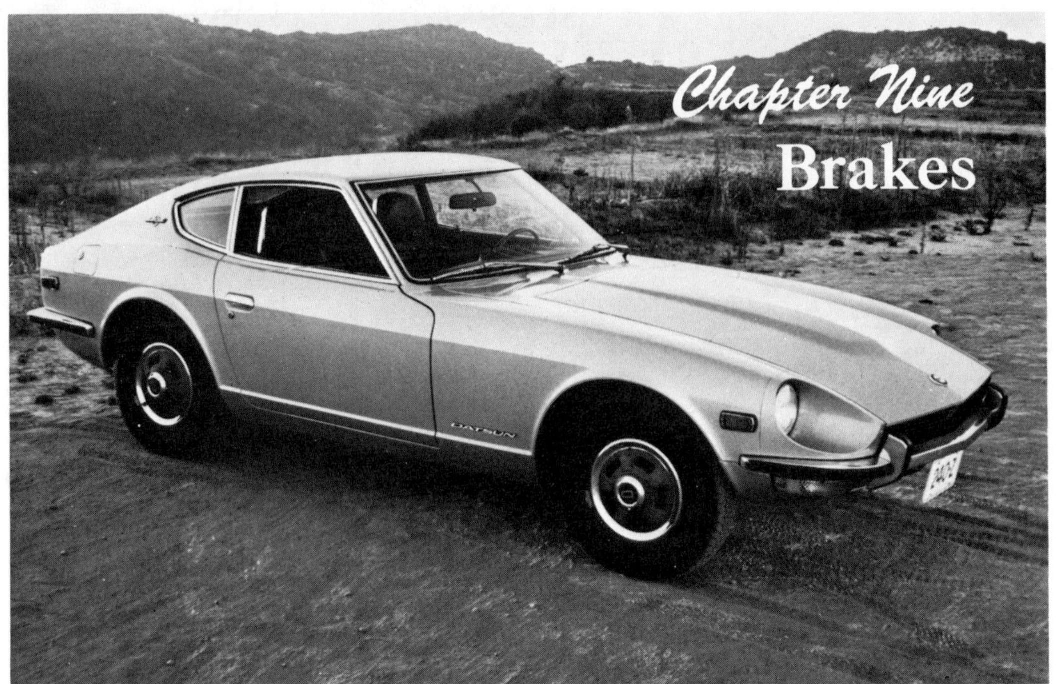

# Chapter Nine
# Brakes

Datsun 240 and 260-Z automobiles are equipped with a vacuum-assisted, proportioned braking system employing discs on the front and finned aluminum drums on the rear. The vacuum-assist cylinder is 6.0 in. in diameter on 1970–72 vehicles, and 7.5 in. in diameter on 1973 and later models. The disc brake calipers are the two-piston type, and the rear brakes are self-adjusting, leading-trailing type. The handbrake is mechanical, employing cables for actuation of the rear drum brakes.

The master cylinder is a dual cylinder design so that failure of either the front or rear brakes causes the brake system at

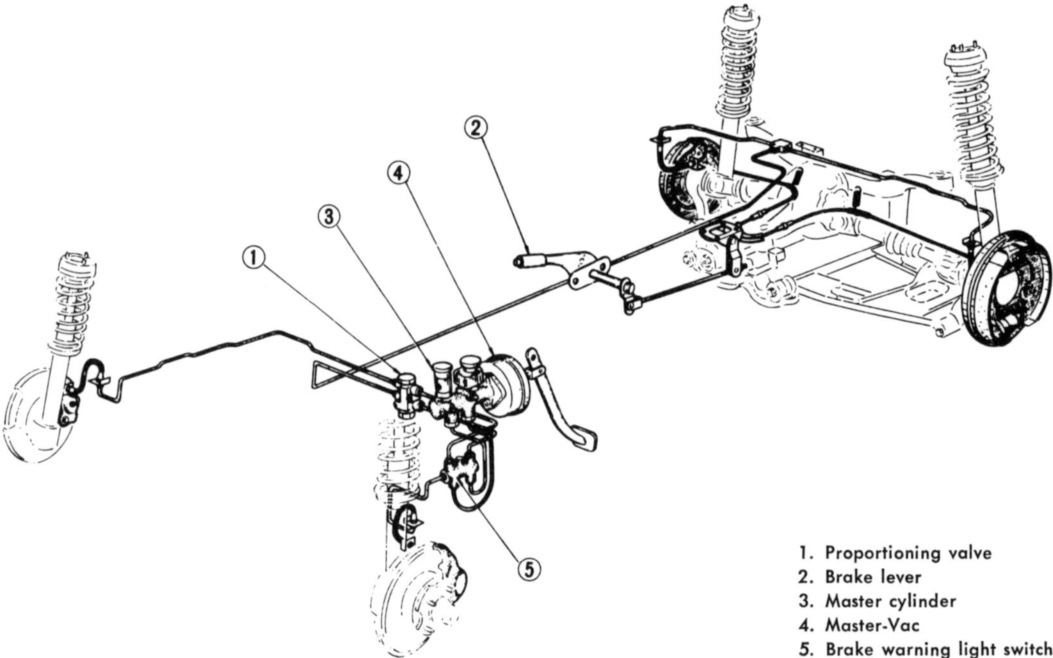


The brake system (1973–74)

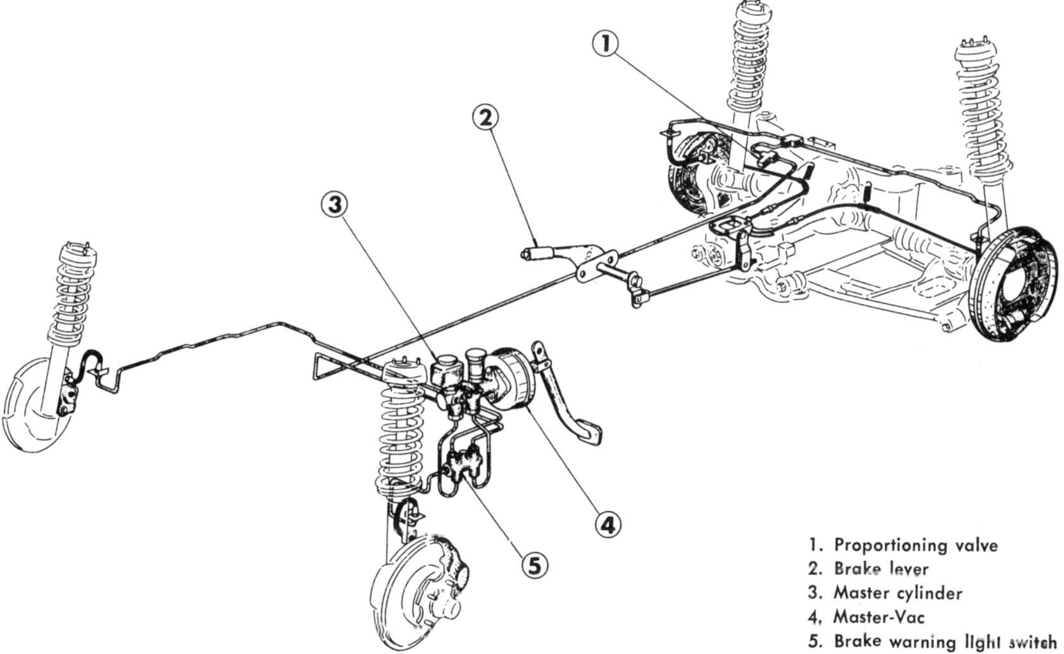


The brake system (1970–72)

the opposite end of the vehicle to be sealed off at the master cylinder and continue to operate normally.

The "Master-Vac" assist system employs manifold vacuum against a diaphragm to assist in application of the brakes. The vacuum is regulated to be proportional to the pressure placed on the pedal.

The system also incorporates a warning light which is operated by a hydraulic electric switch which connects the front and rear hydraulic systems. If pressure in one system is not counterbalanced by pressure in the other, as when a leak has caused it to be sealed off at the master cylinder, the switch piston is forced to one side and closes the warning light switch.

Ordinarily in a hydraulic brake system, application of pressure at the master cylinder causes equal pressure to be built up at all wheel cylinders or caliper pistons at the wheels. While this is appropriate during normal braking, weight transfer from the back wheels to the front under very hard braking lessens rear brake pressure requirements. Stable braking cannot be achieved if the rear wheels cease to turn as tire tread will track only if it is rolling along the road. As a result, a proportioning valve is used. The valve permits equal pressure in all parts of the system until system pressure reaches a certain point. Then, through the motion of sprung pistons in the valve, rear brake pressure is throttled and maintained at a reduced percentage of front brake pressure.

In 1970–72 models, the proportioning valve is located in the rear of the main brake line going to the back of the car, while in later vehicles, it is located in the engine compartment and links the front and rear systems.

## Brake System

### *PEDAL ADJUSTMENT*

1. Loosen the locknut and turn the pushrod clevis to get a pedal height of 8.11 in. (206 mm). If necessary, loosen the locknut and adjust the pedal stop back and out of the way so that it has no effect on pedal height. Tighten the pushrod locknut.

2. Adjust the stop back until height becomes 7.99 in. (203 mm). Tighten the stop locknut.

3. Check the stop lamp switch to ensure that the end surface of the installa-

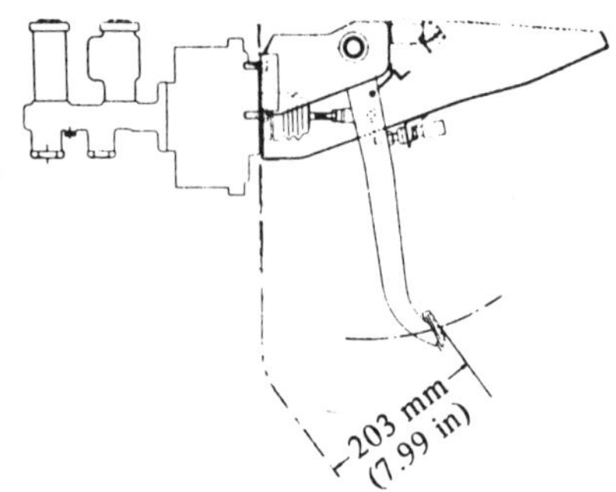

Adjusting pedal play

tion screw is flush with the bracket. The lamp should go on when the pedal is depressed 0.59 in. (15 mm) and should go off when the pedal is released.

## Hydraulic System

### *MASTER CYLINDER*

#### Removal and Installation

1. Disconnect all brake tubes at the master cylinder.
2. Remove the installation nuts and separate the master cylinder from the Master-Vac.
3. To install, position the master cylinder on the Master-Vac and install installation nuts, torquing to 5.0–8.0 ft lbs (0.8–1.1 kg-m).
4. Install the brake lines, torquing to 11–13 ft lbs (1.5–1.8 kg-m).
5. Bleed the system, as described in "Brake System Bleeding." Check for leaks.
6. Adjust brake pedal height, as previously described.

#### Overhaul

1. Drain the brake fluid from the master cylinder.
2. Remove the stop screw.
3. Remove the snap-ring and remove the primary and secondary piston assemblies and associated parts.
4. Remove the check valve caps and remove the check valves.
5. Thoroughly clean all parts in brake fluid and carefully inspect them for wear. Check the cylinder and piston for scoring, and replace the entire unit if piston clearance exceeds 0.0059 in. (0.15 mm).

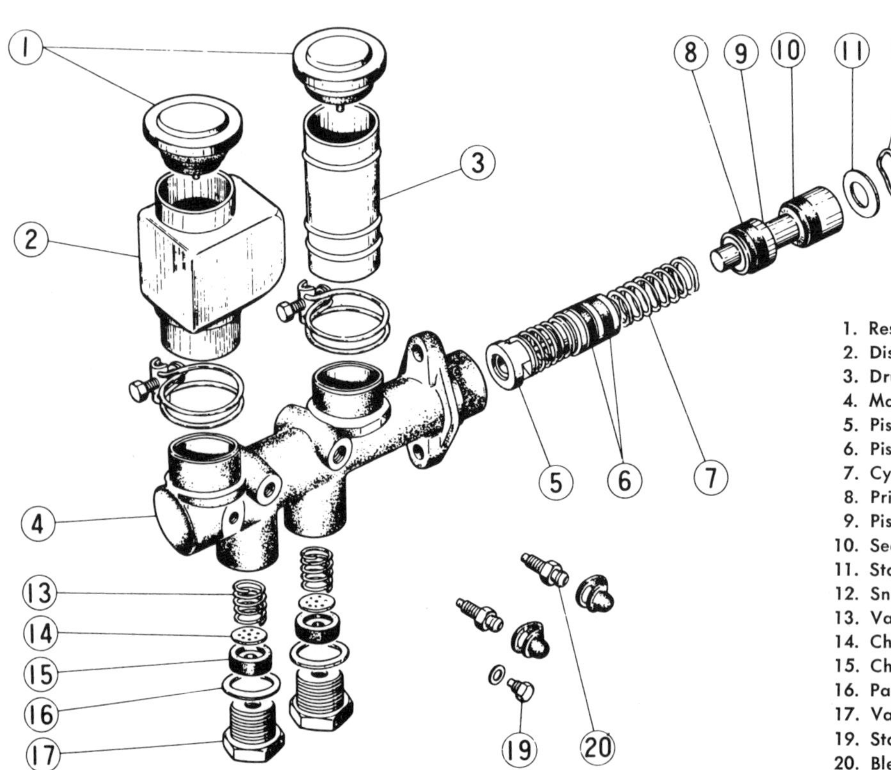


1. Reservoir cap
2. Disc brake reservoir
3. Drum brake reservoir
4. Master cylinder
5. Piston assembly (A)
6. Piston cup
7. Cylinder spring
8. Primary piston cup
9. Piston assembly (B)
10. Secondary piston cup
11. Stop
12. Snap-ring
13. Valve spring
14. Check valve assembly
15. Check valve assembly
16. Packing
17. Valve cap screw
19. Stop bolt
20. Bleeder

Master cylinder (1970–72)

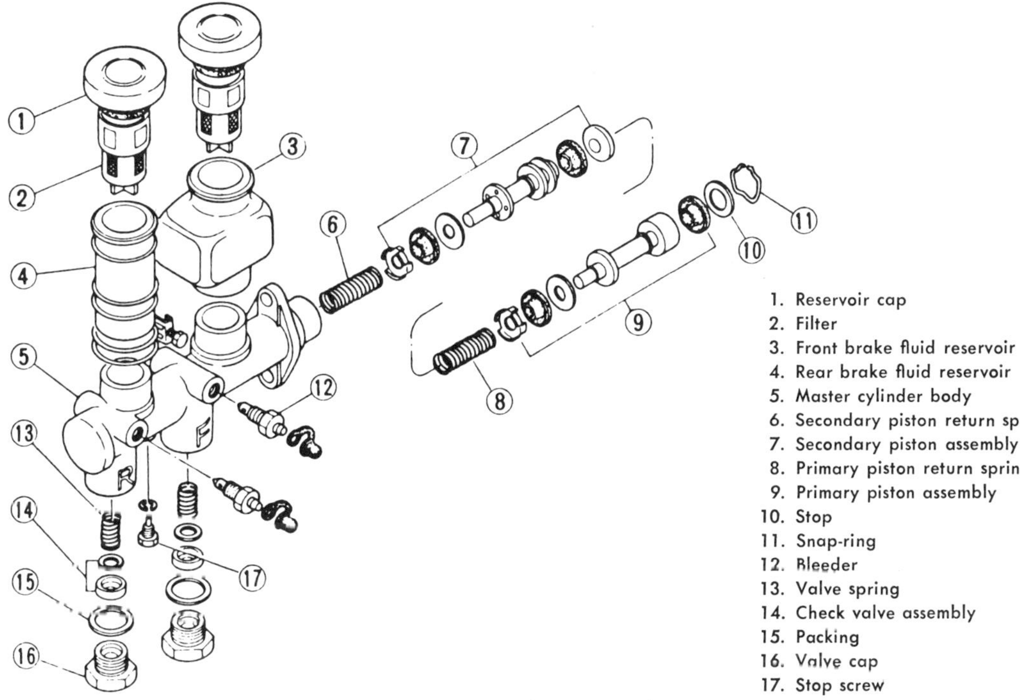


Master cylinder (1973–74)

6. Replace the piston cups, packing, and valves.

7. Inspect the return springs carefully for wear or breakage and replace if necessary.

8. Reassemble the master cylinder in the reverse of disassembly order, coating all parts with brake fluid. Torque the stop screws to 2.9–3.6 ft lbs (0.4–0.5 kg-m), and valve caps to 58-65 ft lbs (8–9 kg-m).

9. Install the master cylinder to the Master-Vac, torquing the mounting nuts to 5.8–8 ft lbs (0.8–1.1 kg-m).

10. Install the brake lines at the master cylinder, torquing to 11–13 ft lbs (1.5–1.8 kg-m).

11. Bleed the system.

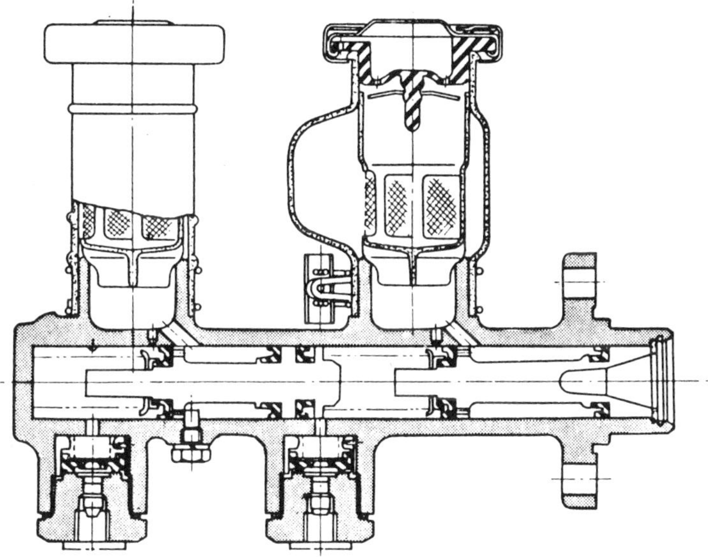

Master cylinder cross-section

*PROPORTIONING VALVE*

### Removal and Installation

1. Disconnect the brake lines at the valve.
2. Remove the mounting bolt and remove the valve.

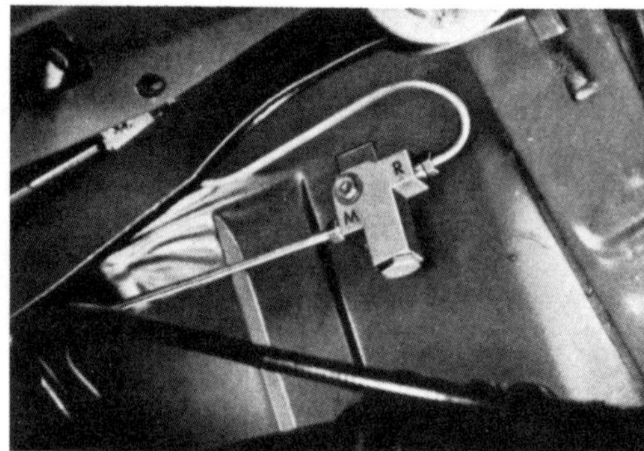


Proportioning valve (1970–72)

Note: Identification for inlet and outlet is facilitated by an arrow mark.

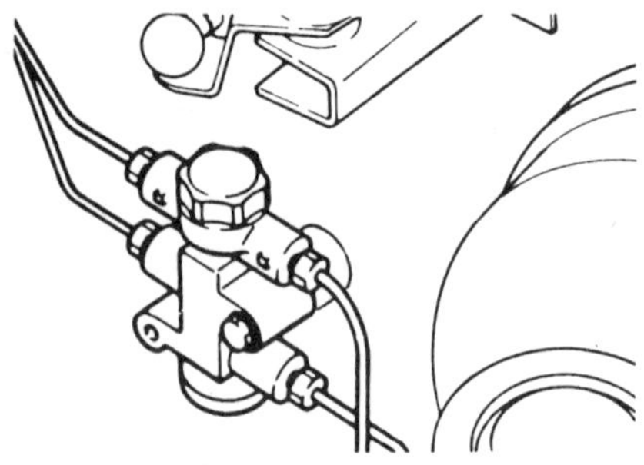

Proportioning valve (1973–74)

To install:

1. On 1970–72 models, the "M" faces toward the master cylinder and the "R" toward the rear brakes. On 1973–74 models, the "F" faces the front brakes, and the arrow faces the rear brake side.
2. Install the mounting bolt, connect the lines, and bleed the system.

*BRAKE WARNING LIGHT SWITCH*

This assembly is unrepairable, and must be replaced as an assembly if problems occur. Replace it by simply disconnecting the brake lines, then connecting them to the new valve, and then bleed the system.

*BRAKE SYSTEM BLEEDING*

1. Clean all dirt from around the reservoir caps. Remove the caps and fill reservoirs with new brake fluid. Watch the fluid level in the reservoirs during bleeding and keep it full or nearly full.

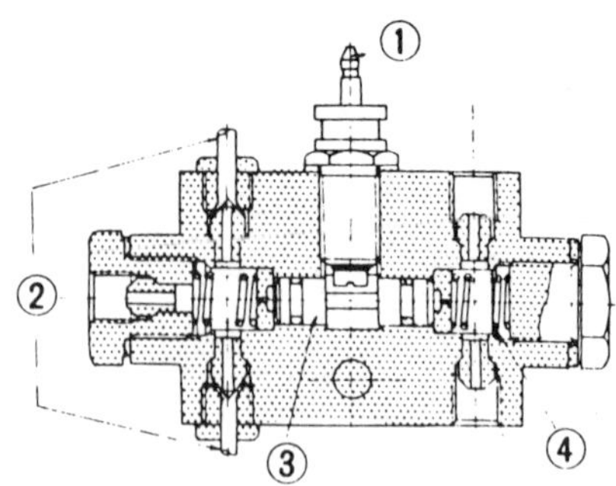


Cross-section of brake warning light switch

1. Wire terminal
2. Brake tubes
3. Valve assembly
4. Piston load spring

2. Bleed each rear wheel and then each front wheel as follows:
   a. Clean off any dirt from around the bleeder valve and connect a hose. Place the other end of the hose in a container of brake fluid.
   b. Have someone pump the brake pedal several times and then hold it down.
   c. Open the valve and bleed air until the brake pedal approaches the floor. Close the valve before the pedal bottoms out.
   d. Have your assistant allow the pedal to return slowly, and then repeat Step "b."
   e. Repeat Steps "b," "c," and "d" until the stream of fluid coming from the hose is no longer white and is entirely free of bubbles.

## Front Disc Brakes

*DISC BRAKE PADS*

### Inspection

1. Clean the pad with a safe solvent.
2. Check the pad for:
   a. Heavy saturation with fluid or grease.
   b. Friction material thickness of less than 0.079 in. (2 mm) or overall thickness of less than 0.295 in. (7.5 mm).

If either "a" or "b" apply, replace *both pads* with a new *set.*

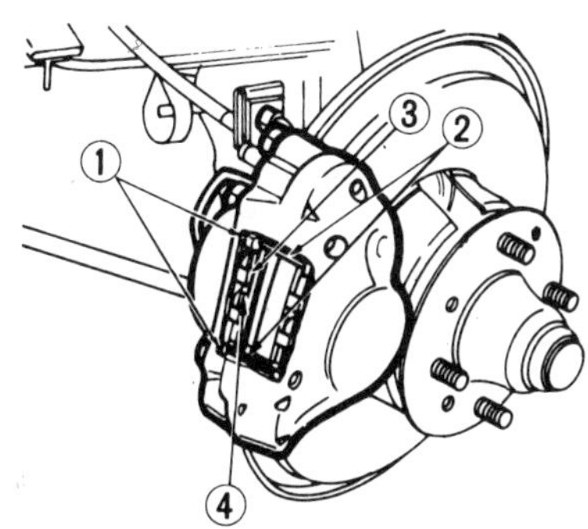

Parts of the front disc brake

1. Clip
2. Retaining pin
3. Anti-squeal spring
4. Pad

## Removal and Installation

1. Raise the front of the car and support it securely.
2. Remove the clip, retaining pin, and anti-squeal spring.
3. Remove the pad and anti-squeal shim.

To install:

1. Clean all caliper and pad locating parts.
2. Loosen the master cylinder "F" reservoir cap. Force the piston back into the cylinder to accommodate the greater thickness of a new pad.
3. Install the pad and anti-squeal shim. The shim arrow must point in the direction of forward rotation. Install the anti-squeal spring and retaining pin, and secure them with the clip.
4. Depress and release the brake pedal several times.

### *DISC BRAKE CALIPERS*

## Removal and Installation

1. Remove the pads, as previously described.
2. Disconnect the brake line, remove the caliper installation bolt, and remove the caliper assembly.

To install:

1. Put the caliper in position and install the installation bolt.

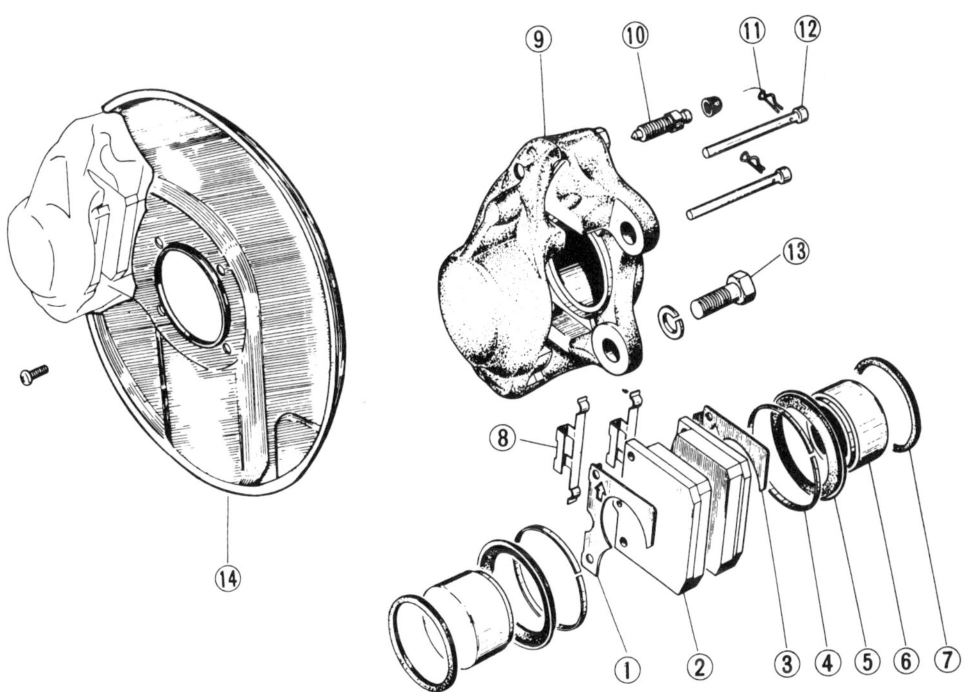

Parts of the front disc brake

1. Anti-squeal shim (right-side)
2. Pad
3. Anti-squeal shim (left-side)
4. Retaining ring
5. Dust cover
6. Piston
7. Piston seal
8. Anti-squeal spring
9. Caliper assembly
10. Bleeder
11. Clip
12. Retaining pin
13. Caliper mounting bolt
14. Baffle plate

Figure shows brake line (1) and installation bolts (2)

2. Reconnect the brake line. Bleed the system, as previously described (bleeding of only the disconnected line should be necessary).

**Overhaul**

1. Clean the caliper assembly of all accumulated mud and dust.

2. Remove the retaining rings. Remove the dust covers.

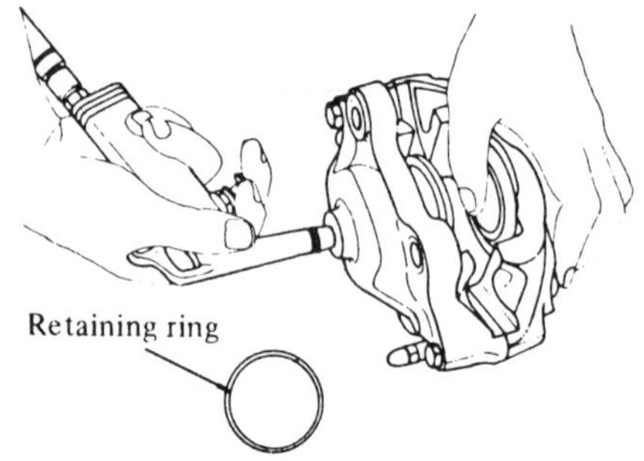

Removing caliper piston

3. Hold one piston with a finger so that it will not come out and gradually apply air pressure to the brake line fitting. This should cause the other piston to come out, but if the piston you are holding begins moving before the other, switch your finger over and remove the more movable one first.

4. Carefully push the other piston out.

5. With a finger, carefully remove both piston seals.

6. Thoroughly clean all parts in brake fluid.

7. Inspect, as follows:

a. Check cylinder walls for damage or excessive wear. Light rust, etc. should be removed with fine emery paper. If the wall is heavily rusted, replace the caliper assembly.

b. Inspect the pad, as previously described.

c. Inspect the piston for uneven wear, damage or any rust. Replace the piston if there is any rust, as it is chrome plated and cannot be cleaned.

d. Replace piston seals and dust covers.

8. Coat the piston seal with brake fluid and carefully install the piston seal.

9. Install the dust seal onto the piston. Coat the piston with brake fluid. Install the piston and seal assembly and install the retaining ring.

10. Repeat Steps 8 and 9 for the other piston.

*BRAKE DISC*

**Removal and Installation**

1. Raise the vehicle and support it securely. Remove the front wheel. Remove the caliper as previously described.

2. Pry off the hub cap with two flat bladed screwdrivers.

3. Remove the cotter pin. Remove the wheel bearing locknut.

4. Remove the hub and rotor and wheel bearing and seal as an assembly from the spindle. Remove the seal and bearings from the hub.

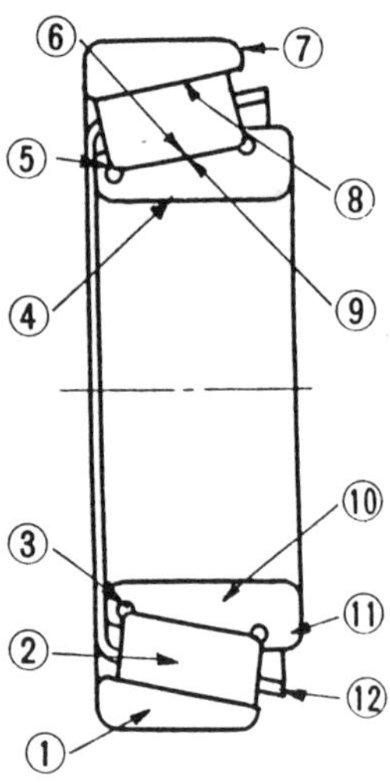

Wheel bearing

1. Outer race
2. Roller
3. Small collar
4. Collar surface
5. Inner race fitted surface
6. Inner race surface
7. Outer race fitted surface
8. Outer race surface
9. Roller rolling surface
10. Inner race
11. Large roller
12. Supporter

5. Remove the bolts holding the rotor to the hub and remove the rotor.

To inspect the wheel bearings:

1. Remove all old grease with solvent.
2. Put the bearings back in position in the hub, and slowly rotate to check for smooth rotation. Check for roughness, burrs, discoloration, or other defects. If any defects are noted, supply new parts and remove and replace the outer races, as later described. Otherwise, go on to the installation procedure.

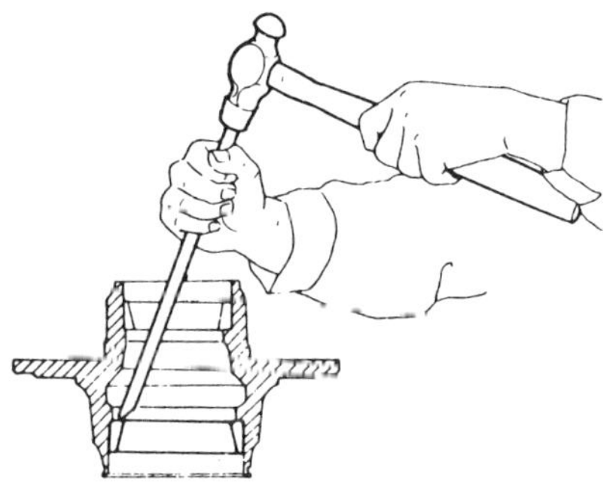

Removing outer race

3. Utilizing the two grooves inside the wheel hub, tap each outer bearing race to remove it from the hub.
4. Install the new outer races with a drift, as shown.

To install:

1. Install the rotor onto the hub, install the mounting bolts, and torque to 28–38 ft lbs (3.9–5.3 kg-m).

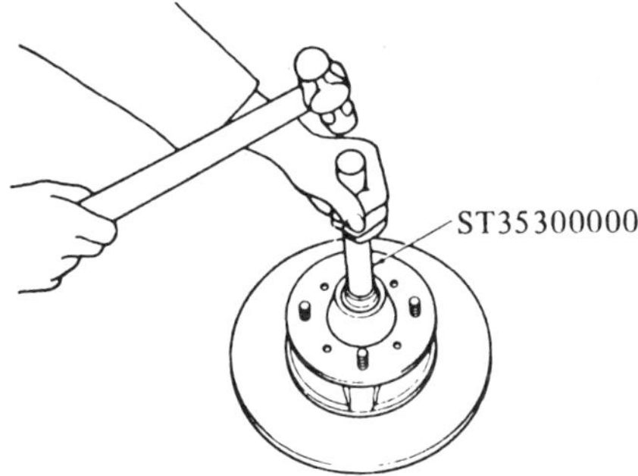


Installing outer race

2. Carefully reassemble the bearings and seal in the hub, employing a new seal if leakage was noted during disassembly.
3. Fill the spaces between the rollers and the pocket in the seal lip with wheel bearing grease. Fill the hub and hub cap with grease as indicated in the illustration.

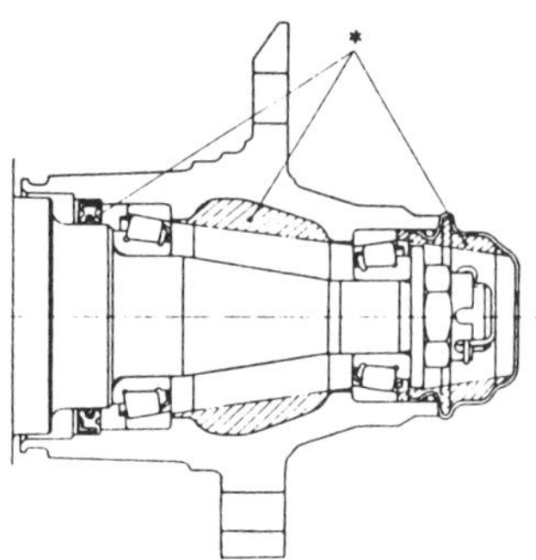

Greasing points in hub assembly

4. Coat the spindle shaft and threads, the seal, and the locknut with bearing grease.
5. Install the inner bearing and seal onto the spindle.
6. Install the hub and outer bearing onto the spindle.
7. Install and tighten the locknut to 18–22 ft lbs (2.5–3.0 kg-m). Turn the hub back and forth several turns to seat the bearing, and retorque the locknut to the same figure.
8. Turn the locknut back out at least 60° and up to 75° until the nut is aligned properly for the cotter pin.

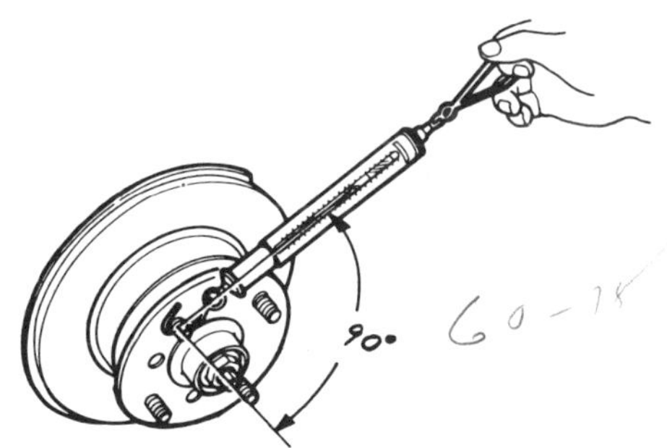

Measuring wheel bearing rotation torque

9. Rotate the hub back and forth several times, then measure the starting torque at the wheel hub bolt with a spring scale. It should be 3.5–7.4 in. lbs (4.0–8.5 kg-cm) with new parts or 0.9–3.9 in. lbs (1.0–4.5 kg-cm) with used parts.
10. If the torque is correct, install the cotter pin and hub cap.
11. Replace the caliper, and bleed the hydraulic system. Replace the wheel.

**Inspection**

1. Remove the wheel. Remove the caliper as previously described.
2. Mount a dial indicator so that deflection at the center of pad contact sur-

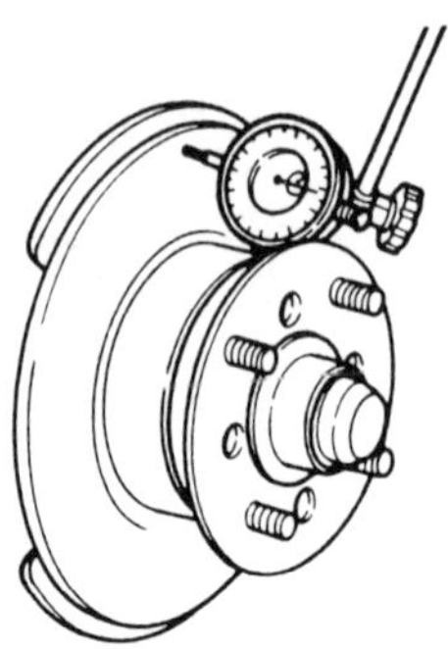

Measuring rotor deflection

face can be measured. Maximum deflection is 0.0079 in. (0.2 mm). If necessary, adjust the wheel bearing.

3. Measure the thickness of the rotor all the way around with a micrometer. Maximum variation should be 0.0012 in. (0.03 mm) or less with a used rotor, or 0.0028 in. (0.07 mm) when new.

4. If the rotor is machined, thickness must be 0.413–0.492 in. (10.5–12.5 mm).

*WHEEL BEARINGS*

**Adjustment**

1. Support the vehicle securely. Remove the wheel. Remove the hub cap.

2. Remove the cotter pin, and loosen the hub locknut fully.

3. Follow Steps 7–10 of the "Brake Disc Installation" procedure.

4. Install the wheel and lower the vehicle.

**Removal, Installation, and Packing**

Follow all steps of the "Brake Disc Removal and Installation" procedure except Step 5 of the removal procedure and Step 1 of the installation procedure, which involve removing the disc from the hub.

## Rear Drum Brakes

*BRAKE DRUMS*

**Removal and Installation**

1. Raise the vehicle and support it securely.

2. Remove the wheel. The brake drum may now be removed. If the drum will not pull off readily, proceed as follows:

   a. Remove the handbrake clevis pin from the wheel cylinder lever and disconnect the handbrake cable;

   b. Remove the plug from the adjusting hole in the drum, and, using a screwdriver, remove the adjusting lever from the adjusting wheel;

   c. Turn the adjusting wheel in a downward direction, using a screw-

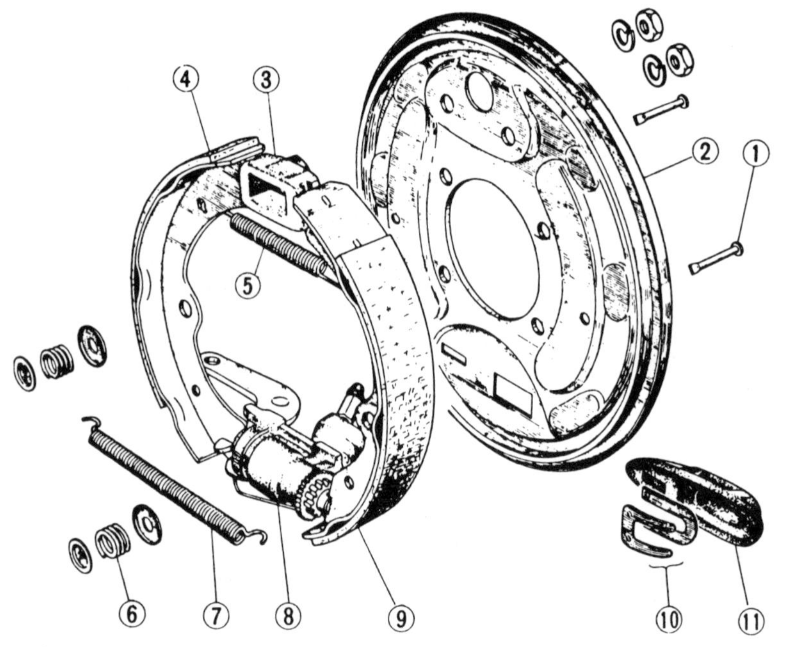


Disassembled view of the rear drum brake

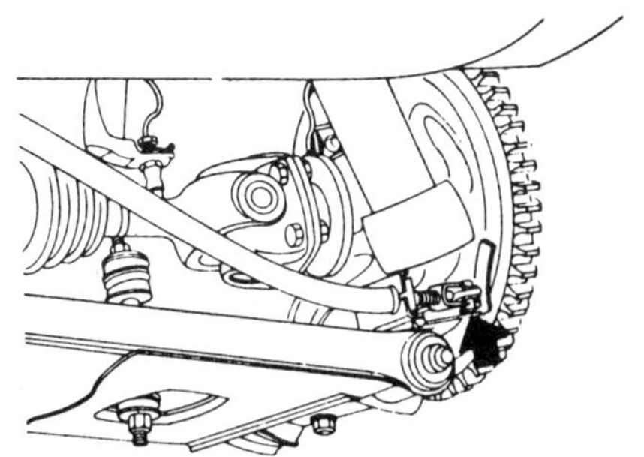
Disconnecting the handbrake cable

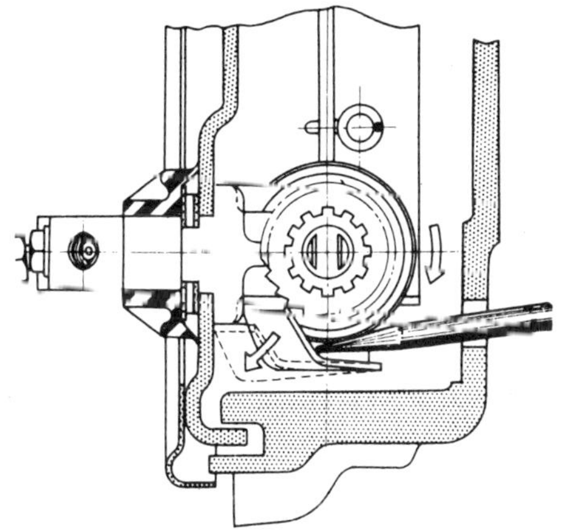
Turning the adjusting wheel

driver until the drum is movable. Remove the drum.

To install:

1. Install the drum onto the wheel studs.

2. Using a screwdriver and going in through the adjusting hole, turn the adjusting wheel in an upward direction until the brake shoes lightly touch the drum.

3. Reconnect the handbrake cable with the clevis pin. Operate the handbrake until the adjusting mechanism no longer clicks.

4. Install the adjusting hole plug making sure that it is installed so that the inner lip is on the inside of the drum all the way around.

5. Install the wheel and lower the vehicle.

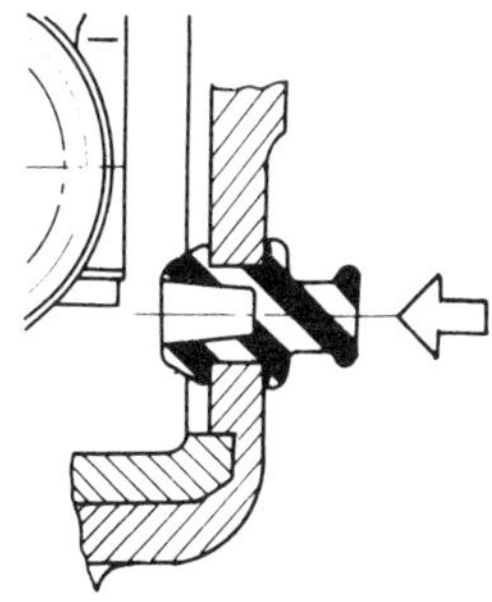
The adjusting hole plug

**Inspection**

1. Inspect the drum for uneven wear, wear in steps, or scoring.

2. The drum may be machined until it reaches the wear limit shown in the "Brake Specifications" chart. The drum requires machining if the inner diameter is more than 0.0020 in. (0.05 mm) out-of-round.

## *BRAKE SHOES*

**Removal and Installation**

1. Remove the brake drum as previously described.

2. Remove the anti-rattle springs.

3. Remove both brake shoes together.

To install:

1. Apply grease to the adjusting wheel and to the threaded and sliding portions of the adjust screw.

2. Apply multipurpose grease to the backing plate, anchor block, and sliding portions of the wheel cylinder, carefully avoiding getting any grease onto the lining surfaces.

3. Install the shoes. Install the anti-rattle springs and return spring.

4. Install the drum, and adjust the adjuster mechanism, as previously described, under "Brake Drum Removal and Installation."

## *WHEEL CYLINDERS*

**Removal and Installation**

1. Remove the brake drums and shoes, as previously described.

2. Disconnect the brake line (1), and remove the dust cover (2).

3. Drive out the locking shim (3) toward the front and remove the other shim by pulling it to the rear.

4. Remove the cylinder.

To install:

1. Apply grease to the cylinder, backing plate, and shims. Also apply grease to the wheel cylinder lever fulcrum.

2. Put the cylinder in position and install shims in reverse of the removal procedure. Install the dust cover.

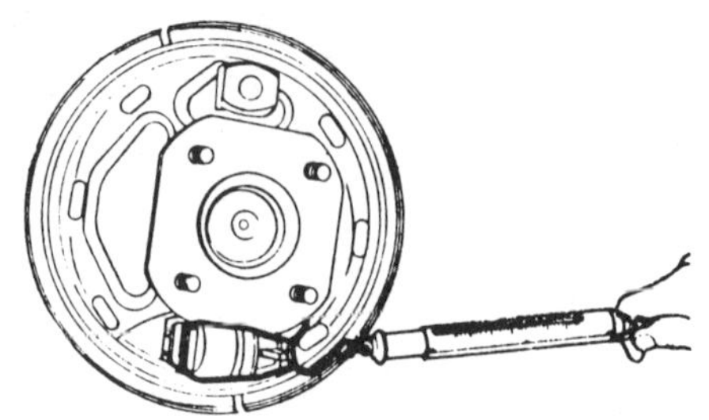
Measuring wheel cylinder sliding resistance

3. Measure the sliding resistance of the cylinder with a spring scale. It should be 4.41–15.43 lbs (2–7 kg).

4. Reconnect the brake line, install the brake shoes, install the drum, bleed the hydraulic system, and adjust the adjuster as previously described.

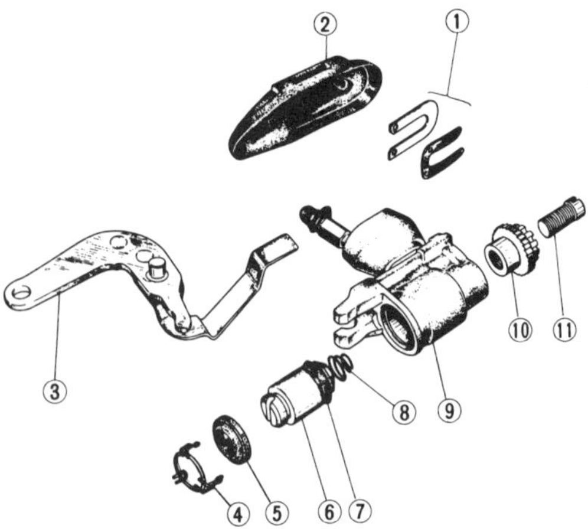
Wheel cylinder components

1. Retaining shim
2. Dust cover
3. Wheel cylinder lever
4. Retainer
5. Dust cover
6. Piston
7. Piston cup
8. Spring
9. Wheel cylinder
10. Adjust wheel
11. Adjust screw

**Overhaul**

1. Remove the dust cover retainer and remove the dust cover.

2. Pull the piston out. Remove the adjusting wheel and screw.

3. Thoroughly clean all parts in brake fluid. Check the cylinder and piston for scoring. Replace any damaged parts.

4. Replace the piston cup. Replace the dust covers if they are torn or excessively softened.

5. Inspect both return springs and check their free length. Black springs should be 4.80 in. (122 mm) long. Green springs should be 4.740 in. (120.4 mm) long. Replace springs if necessary.

6. Apply brake fluid to the piston cup and dust covers and assemble the wheel cylinder in reverse order of disassembly.

## Parking Brake

*CABLE*

NOTE: *The driveshaft must be removed, as described in Chapter 7, to adjust or replace the handbrake cable.*

**Adjustment**

1. Release the handbrake fully and block the vehicle wheels.

2. Loosen the locknut at the rear of the front rod.

3. Measure the dimension between the wheel cylinder lever pin hole centers and their respective buffer plates.

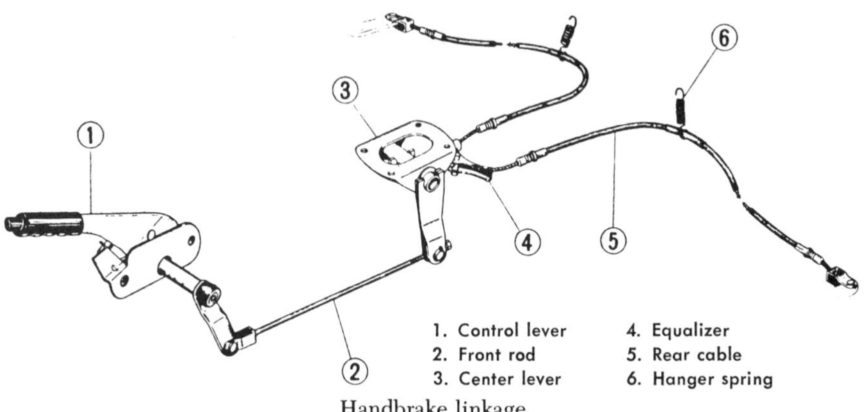
1. Control lever
2. Front rod
3. Center lever
4. Equalizer
5. Rear cable
6. Hanger spring

Handbrake linkage

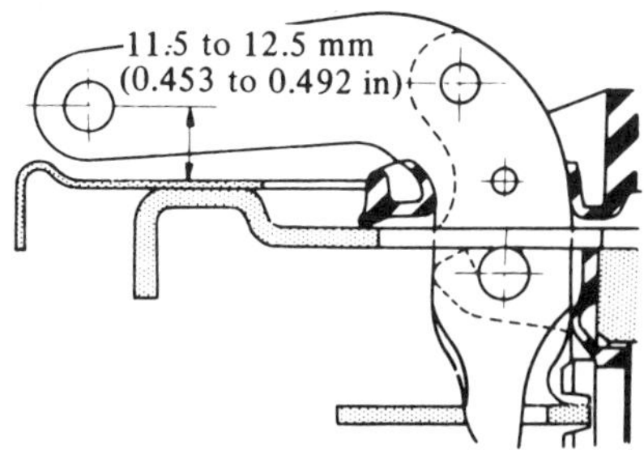


Handbrake adjustment dimensions

4. Rotate the front rod to bring the dimension to 0.453–0.492 in. (11.5–12.5 mm) on both sides.

5. Tighten the locknut at the rear of the front rod.

### Removal and Installation

1. Remove the hanger spring and clevis pin located at (3).

2. Remove the clevis pins at both wheel cylinder levers.

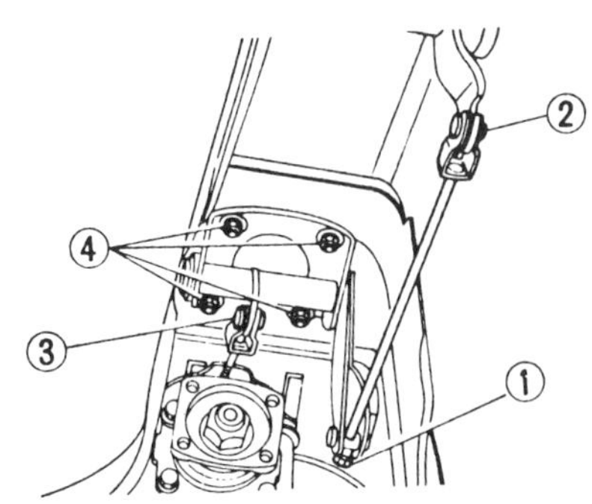


Illustration shows handbrake locknut and adjusting nut (1), clevis pins (2, 3), and brake handle mounting bracket bolts (4)

3. Remove the cable retainers at the wheels and disconnect the cable from both hanger springs.

4. Remove the retainers at the forward (equalizer end) and remove the cable.

To install:

1. Reverse the above procedures.

2. Adjust the cable, as previously described.

## Brake Specifications

All measurements are given in in. (mm)

| *Year* | *Model* | *Master Cylinder Bore* | *Wheel Cylinder Bore* | | *Brake Disc or Drum Diameter* | |
|---|---|---|---|---|---|---|
| | | | *Front* | *Rear* | *Front* | *Rear* |
| 1970–71 | 240-Z | .8748 (22.22) | 2.1252 (53.98) | .8748 (22.22) | 10.67 (271) | 9.04 (229.6) |
| 1972–74 | 240-Z, 260-Z | .8748 (22.22) | 2.1252 (53.98) | .8748 (22.22) | 10.67 (271) | 9.055 (230.0) |

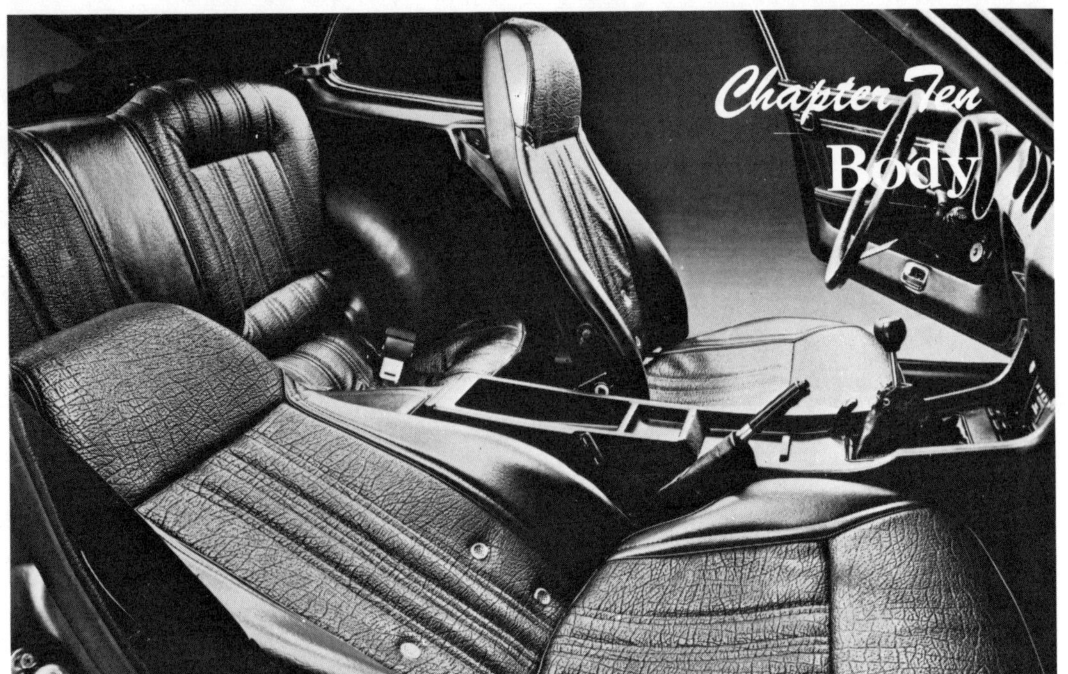


## Doors

### Removal and Installation

260-Z

1. Disconnect the battery ground cable.
2. On left-side door, remove the following parts (with door open):
   a. Turn signal and hazard flasher units.
   b. Hood release bracket.
   c. Side ventilator control bracket.
   d. Fastener.

On right-side door, remove the following parts (door open):
   a. Junction block.
   b. Fuse block.
   c. Side ventilator control bracket.
   d. Relay bracket.
   e. Ignition interlock unit.
   f. Fastener.

3. With the door wide open, support the door on a jack or stand, protecting the finish with a rag.
4. Loosen the bolts which attach the hinge to the door and remove it.
5. Reverse the procedure to install either door.

240-Z

1. Disconnect the positive battery cable, and the driver's side horn relay on the instrument panel side (left door only).
2. Remove the hood latch control installation bracket.
3. Remove the instrument panel side trim.
4. Open the door wide and support it with a jack or stand, using a rag to protect the finish.
5. Remove the door hinge bolts from the body side. Remove the door.
6. Install the door by reversing the above procedure. Torque the hinge bolts to 7–8 ft lbs (0.9–1.1 kg-m). If necessary, grease the hinge pins before installation.

*DOOR PANELS*

### Removal and Installation

1. Open the door and remove the lock knob by unscrewing it.
2. On 260-Z models, remove the arm rest securing screws and remove the arm rest. The screw from the tip end of the arm rest may be removed after first prying the cover out with a regular screwdriver.

On 240-Z models, remove the assist strap by prying the cover up at either end and removing the mounting screws. Also, remove the arm rest.

3. Remove the door handle escutcheon cover and screw, and remove the escutcheon.
4. Remove the regulator handle secur-

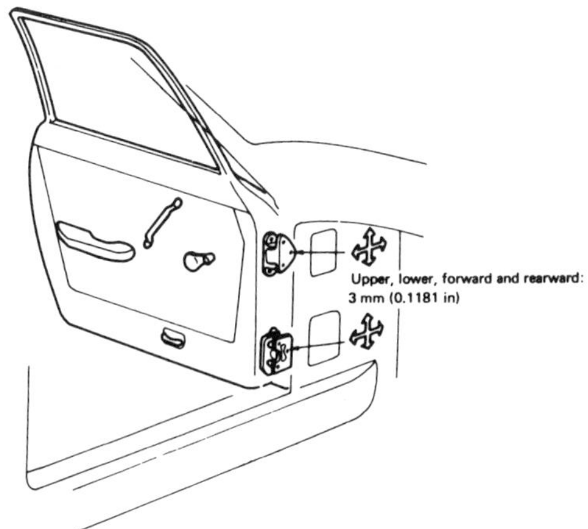

Adjusting door hinges

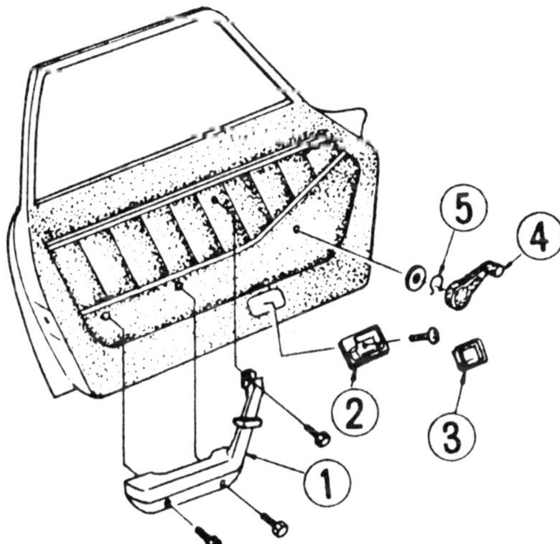
Parts to remove in removal of door trim panel

1. Arm rest
2. Escutcheon
3. Cover
4. Window regulating handle
5. Retaining spring

ing spring and remove the handle and washer.

5. With a regular screwdriver, pry the panel retaining clips out of the door, and remove the panel.

6. On 260-Z models, remove the water sealing screen from the door.

On installation:

1. Install a new water sealing screen if the old one is damaged or suspected of leaking. On 240-Z models, the screen is glued to the inside of the door panel.

2. Reverse the removal procedure, installing the window regulator so that it will point forward when the window is all the way up.

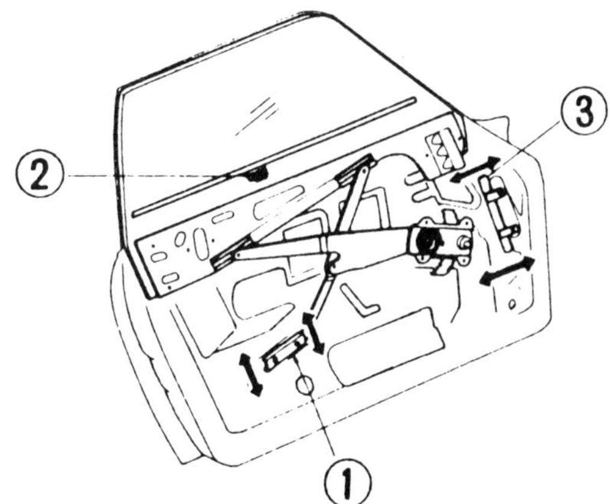
Adjusting window glass

1. Guide channel 2. Glass bumper 3. Front sash

## *WINDOWS*

### Adjustment

1. Remove the door panel as previously described. Raise the window all the way and loosen the guide channel adjustment attaching screws.

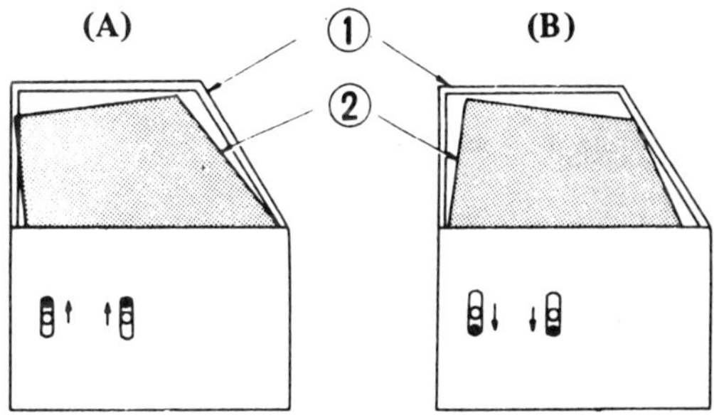

The top of the glass (2) must be parallel with the sash (1)

2. Adjust the position of the glass so that it is parallel with the top rail of the door sash and tighten the guide channel adjusting bolts.

3. If the glass moves back and forth excessively, loosen the bolts and move the front sash forward or backward as necessary. Tighten the bolts.

4. Install the door panel.

## *LOCKS*

### Removal and Installation

1. Open the door and remove the door panel.

2. Remove the sash.

3. Remove the key cylinder rod from the key cylinder.

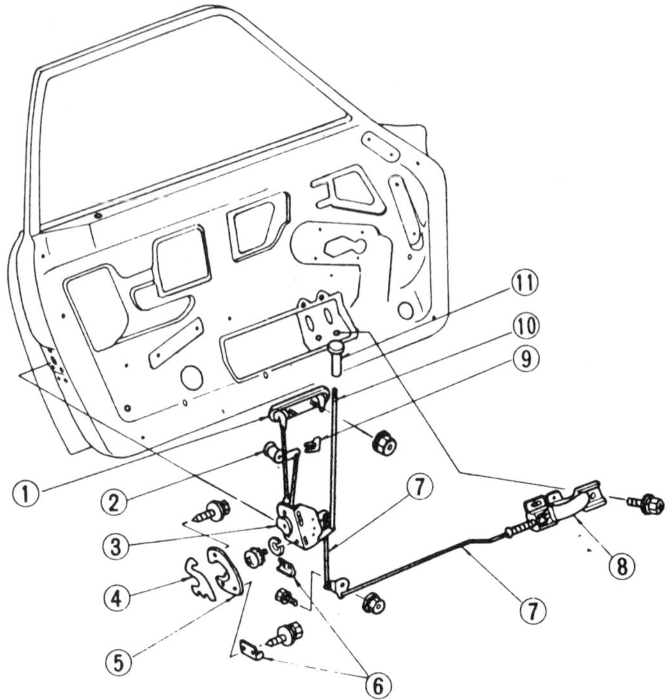


The parts of the door sash mechanism

1. Outer handle
2. Key cylinder
3. Door lock
4. Striker shim
5. Striker
6. Dovetail
7. Remote control
8. Inner handle
9. Clip
10. Knob rod
11. Lock knob

4. Remove the remote control rod from the main lock unit.

5. Remove the remote control side bellcrank and the inside lever installation screws, and remove the remote control mechanism from the opening on the inner panel.

6. Remove the installation screw for the main lock unit, remove the outside handle rod from the opening on the main lock unit, and remove the main lock unit.

7. Remove the key cylinder retaining clip and the key cylinder.

8. Remove the door handle attaching nut from inside the door and remove the outside handle.

9. Check return springs, actuating levers, and all other parts for excessive wear or bending, and replace faulty parts.

10. Install door lock parts in reverse order, carefully applying multipurpose grease to all surfaces where mechanical loads are present.

# Hood

## Alignment

260-Z

1. Loosen the bolts attaching the hood to the hood hinges and move the hood fore-and-aft until it fits flush with the headlight cases and side gaps are equal. Retighten the bolts.

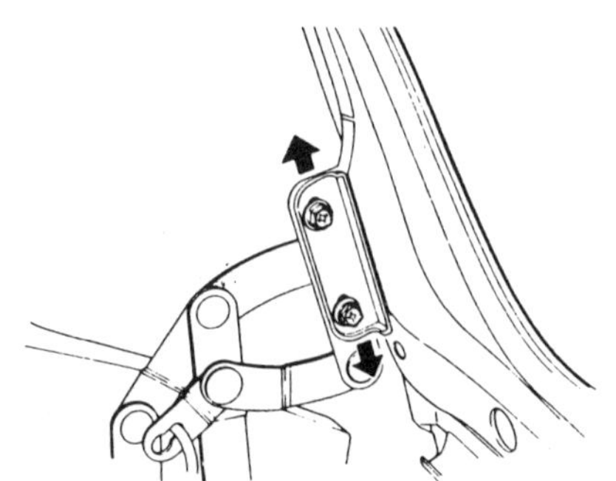

Location of the hood attaching bolts

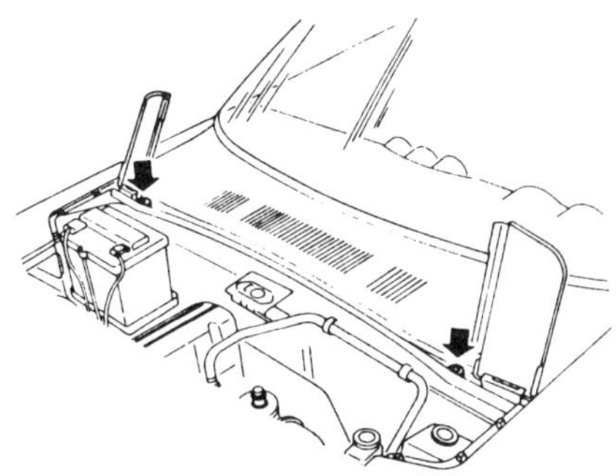

Where to adjust hood bumper height

2. Loosen the hood bumper locknuts, and lower the bumpers until they just contact the hood when it is closed. Then proceed with the following lock adjustment.

### Lock Adjustment

240-Z, 260 Z

1. Loosen the hood lock attaching bolts, and move the lock back-and-forth or from side-to-side until the lock will fit smoothly into the female fitting in the cowl. Tighten the attaching bolts.

2. Loosen the locknut of the dovetail bolt on the hood lock and adjust it until the hood is flush with the cowl when closed. Tighten the locknut.

3. On 260-Z models, raise the hood bumpers until the hood is just flush with the cowl and tighten the bumper locknuts. *Make sure that the hood lock still closes fully.*

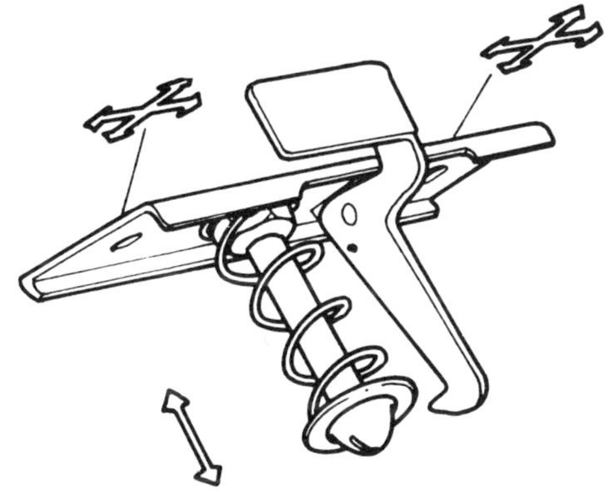


Adjusting the hood lock

## Trunk Lid

### Alignment

1. The clearance between the trunk lid and roof should be 0.138–0.217 in. (3.5–5.5 mm). If necessary, add or subtract shims to achieve this, and make the rear of the trunk lid fit flush with the rear fender.

2. Loosen the trunk lid hinge attaching bolts. Move the lid up-and-down to achieve a flush fit with the roof, and from side-to-side to achieve an equal gap on either side. Tighten the bolts.

## Fuel Tank

### Removal and Installation

1. Disconnect the battery negative cable.

2. Remove the fuel tank drain plug and drain all fuel.

3. Disconnect the gauge unit cable and outlet or outlet and return hose(s) at the tank.

4. Remove the nuts from the two tank securing bands and lower the tank slightly.

5. Disconnect the three ventilation hoses used on models with evaporative emission control and the fuel tank filler pipe. Remove the tank.

6. The tank should be checked carefully for cracks or dents which might cause leaks, and be replaced if necessary.

7. Install in the exact reverse order of removal. Be careful not to kink hoses or overtighten fittings when reconnecting. The fuel filler hose must be connected after the tank is mounted in place.

# Appendix

## General Conversion Table

| Multiply by | To convert | To | |
|---|---|---|---|
| 2.54 | Inches | Centimeters | .3937 |
| 30.48 | Feet | Centimeters | .0328 |
| .914 | Yards | Meters | 1.094 |
| 1.609 | Miles | Kilometers | .621 |
| .645 | Square inches | Square cm. | .155 |
| .836 | Square yards | Square meters | 1.196 |
| 16.39 | Cubic inches | Cubic cm. | .061 |
| 28.3 | Cubic feet | Liters | .0353 |
| .4536 | Pounds | Kilograms | 2.2045 |
| 4.546 | Gallons | Liters | .22 |
| .068 | Lbs./sq. in. (psi) | Atmospheres | 14.7 |
| .138 | Foot pounds | Kg. m. | 7.23 |
| 1.014 | H.P. (DIN) | H.P. (SAE) | .9861 |
| —— | To obtain | From | Multiply by |

*Note:* 1 cm. equals 10 mm.; 1 mm. equals .0394″.

## Conversion—Common Fractions to Decimals and Millimeters

| Inches | | | Inches | | | Inches | | |
|---|---|---|---|---|---|---|---|---|
| *Common Fractions* | *Decimal Fractions* | *Millimeters (approx.)* | *Common Fractions* | *Decimal Fractions* | *Millimeters (approx.)* | *Common Fractions* | *Decimal Fractions* | *Millimeters (approx.)* |
| **1/128** | .008 | 0.20 | 11/32 | .344 | 8.73 | 43/64 | .672 | 17.07 |
| **1/64** | .016 | 0.40 | 23/64 | .359 | 9.13 | 11/16 | .688 | 17.46 |
| 1/32 | .031 | 0.79 | 3/8 | .375 | 9.53 | 45/64 | .703 | 17.86 |
| 3/64 | .047 | 1.19 | 25/64 | .391 | 9.92 | 23/32 | .719 | 18.26 |
| 1/16 | .063 | 1.59 | 13/32 | .406 | 10.32 | 47/64 | .734 | 18.65 |
| 5/64 | .078 | 1.98 | 27/64 | .422 | 10.72 | 3/4 | .750 | 19.05 |
| 3/32 | .094 | 2.38 | 7/16 | .438 | 11.11 | 49/64 | .766 | 19.45 |
| 7/64 | .109 | 2.78 | 29/64 | .453 | 11.51 | 25/32 | .781 | 19.84 |
| 1/8 | .125 | 3.18 | 15/32 | .469 | 11.91 | 51/64 | .797 | 20.24 |
| 9/64 | .141 | 3.57 | 31/64 | .484 | 12.30 | 13/16 | .813 | 20.64 |
| 5/32 | .156 | 3.97 | 1/2 | .500 | 12.70 | 53/64 | .828 | 21.03 |
| 11/64 | .172 | 4.37 | 33/64 | .516 | 13.10 | 27/32 | .844 | 21.43 |
| 3/16 | .188 | 4.76 | 17/32 | .531 | 13.49 | 55/64 | .859 | 21.83 |
| 13/64 | .203 | 5.16 | 35/64 | .547 | 13.89 | 7/8 | .875 | 22.23 |
| 7/32 | .219 | 5.56 | 9/16 | .563 | 14.29 | 57/64 | .891 | 22.62 |
| 15/64 | .234 | 5.95 | 37/64 | .578 | 14.68 | 29/32 | .906 | 23.02 |
| 1/4 | .250 | 6.35 | 19/32 | .594 | 15.08 | 59/64 | .922 | 23.42 |
| 17/64 | .266 | 6.75 | 39/64 | .609 | 15.48 | 15/16 | .938 | 23.81 |
| 9/32 | .281 | 7.14 | 5/8 | .625 | 15.88 | 61/64 | .953 | 24.21 |
| 19/64 | .297 | 7.54 | 41/64 | .641 | 16.27 | 31/32 | .969 | 24.61 |
| 5/16 | .313 | 7.94 | 21/32 | .656 | 16.67 | 63/64 | .984 | 25.00 |
| 21/64 | .328 | 8.33 | | | | | | |

## Conversion—Millimeters to Decimal Inches

| *mm* | *inches* | *mm* | *inches* | *mm* | *inches* | *mm* | *inches* | *mm* | *inches* |
|---|---|---|---|---|---|---|---|---|---|
| 1 | .039 370 | 31 | 1.220 470 | 61 | 2.401 570 | 91 | 3.582 670 | 210 | 8.267 700 |
| 2 | .078 740 | 32 | 1.259 840 | 62 | 2.440 940 | 92 | 3.622 040 | 220 | 8.661 400 |
| 3 | .118 110 | 33 | 1.299 210 | 63 | 2.480 310 | 93 | 3.661 410 | 230 | 9.055 100 |
| 4 | .157 480 | 34 | 1.338 580 | 64 | 2.519 680 | 94 | 3.700 780 | 240 | 9.448 800 |
| 5 | .196 850 | 35 | 1.377 949 | 65 | 2.559 050 | 95 | 3.740 150 | 250 | 9.842 500 |
| 6 | .236 220 | 36 | 1.417 319 | 66 | 2.598 420 | 96 | 3.779 520 | 260 | 10.236 200 |
| 7 | .275 590 | 37 | 1.456 689 | 67 | 2.637 790 | 97 | 3.818 890 | 270 | 10.629 900 |
| 8 | .314 960 | 38 | 1.496 050 | 68 | 2.677 160 | 98 | 3.858 260 | 280 | 11.032 600 |
| 9 | .354 330 | 39 | 1.535 430 | 69 | 2.716 530 | 99 | 3.897 630 | 290 | 11.417 300 |
| 10 | .393 700 | 40 | 1.574 800 | 70 | 2.755 900 | 100 | 3.937 000 | 300 | 11.811 000 |
| 11 | .433 070 | 41 | 1.614 170 | 71 | 2.795 270 | 105 | 4.133 848 | 310 | 12.204 700 |
| 12 | .472 440 | 42 | 1.653 540 | 72 | 2.834 640 | 110 | 4.330 700 | 320 | 12.598 400 |
| 13 | .511 810 | 43 | 1.692 910 | 73 | 2.874 010 | 115 | 4.527 550 | 330 | 12.992 100 |
| 14 | .551 180 | 44 | 1.732 280 | 74 | 2.913 380 | 120 | 4.724 400 | 340 | 13.385 800 |
| 15 | .590 550 | 45 | 1.771 650 | 75 | 2.952 750 | 125 | 4.921 250 | 350 | 13.779 500 |
| 16 | .629 920 | 46 | 1.811 020 | 76 | 2.992 120 | 130 | 5.118 100 | 360 | 14.173 200 |
| 17 | .669 290 | 47 | 1.850 390 | 77 | 3.031 490 | 135 | 5.314 950 | 370 | 14.566 900 |
| 18 | .708 660 | 48 | 1.889 760 | 78 | 3.070 860 | 140 | 5.511 800 | 380 | 14.960 600 |
| 19 | .748 030 | 49 | 1.929 130 | 79 | 3.110 230 | 145 | 5.708 650 | 390 | 15.354 300 |
| 20 | .787 400 | 50 | 1.968 500 | 80 | 3.149 600 | 150 | 5.905 500 | 400 | 15.748 000 |
| 21 | .826 770 | 51 | 2.007 870 | 81 | 3.188 970 | 155 | 6.102 350 | 500 | 10.685 000 |
| 22 | .866 140 | 52 | 2.047 240 | 82 | 3.228 340 | 160 | 6.299 200 | 600 | 23.622 000 |
| 23 | .905 510 | 53 | 2.086 610 | 83 | 3.267 710 | 165 | 6.496 050 | 700 | 27.559 000 |
| 24 | .944 880 | 54 | 2.125 980 | 84 | 3.307 080 | 170 | 6.692 900 | 800 | 31.496 000 |
| 25 | .984 250 | 55 | 2.165 350 | 85 | 3.346 450 | 175 | 6.889 750 | 900 | 35.433 000 |
| 26 | 1.023 620 | 56 | 2.204 720 | 86 | 3.385 820 | 180 | 7.086 600 | 1000 | 39.370 000 |
| 27 | 1.062 990 | 57 | 2.244 090 | 87 | 3.425 190 | 185 | 7.283 450 | 2000 | 78.740 000 |
| 28 | 1.102 360 | 58 | 2.283 460 | 88 | 3.464 560 | 190 | 7.480 300 | 3000 | 118.110 000 |
| 29 | 1.141 730 | 59 | 2.322 830 | 89 | 3.503 903 | 195 | 7.677 150 | 4000 | 157.480 000 |
| 30 | 1.181 100 | 60 | 2.362 200 | 90 | 3.543 300 | 200 | 7.874 000 | 5000 | 196.850 000 |

To change decimal millimeters to decimal inches, position the decimal point where desired on either side of the millimeter measurement shown and reset the inches decimal by the same number of digits in the same direction. For example, to convert .001 mm into decimal inches, reset the decimal behind the 1 mm (shown on the chart) to .001; change the decimal inch equivalent (.039″ shown to .000039″).

## Tap Drill Sizes

| Screw & Tap Size | National Fine or S.A.E. Threads Per Inch | Use Drill Number |
|---|---|---|
| No. 5 | 44 | 37 |
| No. 6 | 40 | 33 |
| No. 8 | 36 | 29 |
| No. 10 | 32 | 21 |
| No. 12 | 28 | 15 |
| 1/4 | 28 | 3 |
| 5/16 | 24 | 1 |
| 3/8 | 24 | Q |
| 7/16 | 20 | W |
| 1/2 | 20 | 29/64 |
| 9/16 | 18 | 33/64 |
| 5/8 | 18 | 37/64 |
| 3/4 | 16 | 11/16 |
| 7/8 | 14 | 13/16 |
| 1 1/8 | 12 | 1 3/64 |
| 1 1/4 | 12 | 1 11/64 |
| 1 1/2 | 12 | 1 27/64 |

| Screw & Tap Size | National Coarse or U.S.S. Threads Per Inch | Use Drill Number |
|---|---|---|
| No. 5 | 40 | 39 |
| No. 6 | 32 | 36 |
| No. 8 | 32 | 29 |
| No. 10 | 24 | 25 |
| No. 12 | 24 | 17 |
| 1/4 | 20 | 8 |
| 5/16 | 18 | F |
| 3/8 | 16 | 5/16 |
| 7/16 | 14 | U |
| 1/2 | 13 | 27/64 |
| 9/16 | 12 | 31/64 |
| 5/8 | 11 | 17/32 |
| 3/4 | 10 | 21/32 |
| 7/8 | 9 | 49/64 |
| 1 | 8 | 7/8 |
| 1 1/8 | 7 | 63/64 |
| 1 1/4 | 7 | 1 7/64 |
| 1 1/2 | 6 | 1 11/32 |

## Decimal Equivalent Size of the Number Drills

| Drill No. | Decimal Equivalent | Drill No. | Decimal Equivalent | Drill No. | Decimal Equivalent |
|---|---|---|---|---|---|
| 80 | .0135 | 53 | .0595 | 26 | .1470 |
| 79 | .0145 | 52 | .0635 | 25 | .1495 |
| 78 | .0160 | 51 | .0670 | 24 | .1520 |
| 77 | .0180 | 50 | .0700 | 23 | .1540 |
| 76 | .0200 | 49 | .0730 | 22 | .1570 |
| 75 | .0210 | 48 | .0760 | 21 | .1590 |
| 74 | .0225 | 47 | .0785 | 20 | .1610 |
| 73 | .0240 | 46 | .0810 | 19 | .1660 |
| 72 | .0250 | 45 | .0820 | 18 | .1695 |
| 71 | .0260 | 44 | .0860 | 17 | .1730 |
| 70 | .0280 | 43 | .0890 | 16 | .1770 |
| 69 | .0292 | 42 | .0935 | 15 | .1800 |
| 68 | .0310 | 41 | .0960 | 14 | .1820 |
| 67 | .0320 | 40 | .0980 | 13 | .1850 |
| 66 | .0330 | 39 | .0995 | 12 | .1890 |
| 65 | .0350 | 38 | .1015 | 11 | .1910 |
| 64 | .0360 | 37 | .1040 | 10 | .1935 |
| 63 | .0370 | 36 | .1065 | 9 | .1960 |
| 62 | .0380 | 35 | .1100 | 8 | .1990 |
| 61 | .0390 | 34 | .1110 | 7 | .2010 |
| 60 | .0400 | 33 | .1130 | 6 | .2040 |
| 59 | .0410 | 32 | .1160 | 5 | .2055 |
| 58 | .0420 | 31 | .1200 | 4 | .2090 |
| 57 | .0430 | 30 | .1285 | 3 | .2130 |
| 56 | .0465 | 29 | .1360 | 2 | .2210 |
| 55 | .0520 | 28 | .1405 | 1 | .2280 |
| 54 | .0550 | 27 | .1440 | | |

## Decimal Equivalent Size of the Letter Drills

| Letter Drill | Decimal Equivalent | Letter Drill | Decimal Equivalent | Letter Drill | Decimal Equivalent |
|---|---|---|---|---|---|
| A | .234 | J | .277 | S | .348 |
| B | .238 | K | .281 | T | .358 |
| C | .242 | L | .290 | U | .368 |
| D | .246 | M | .295 | V | .377 |
| E | .250 | N | .302 | W | .386 |
| F | .257 | O | .316 | X | .397 |
| G | .261 | P | .323 | Y | .404 |
| H | .266 | Q | .332 | Z | .413 |
| I | .272 | R | .339 | | |

# ANTI-FREEZE INFORMATION

## Freezing and Boiling Points of Solutions According to Percentage of Alcohol or Ethylene Glycol

| Freezing Point of Solution | Alcohol Volume % | Alcohol Solution Boils at | Ethylene Glycol Volume % | Ethylene Glycol Solution Boils at |
|---|---|---|---|---|
| 20°F. | 12 | 196°F. | 16 | 216°F. |
| 10°F. | 20 | 189°F. | 25 | 218°F. |
| 0°F. | 27 | 184°F. | 33 | 220°F. |
| −10°F. | 32 | 181°F. | 39 | 222°F. |
| −20°F. | 38 | 178°F. | 44 | 224°F. |
| −30°F. | 42 | 176°F. | 48 | 225°F. |

Note: above boiling points are at sea level. For every 1,000 feet of altitude, boiling points are approximately 2°F. lower than those shown. For every pound of pressure exerted by the pressure cap, the boiling points are approximately 3°F. higher than those shown.

## To Increase the Freezing Protection of Anti-Freeze Solutions Already Installed

| Cooling System Capacity Quarts | Number of Quarts of **ALCOHOL** Anti-Freeze Required to Increase Protection | | | | | | | | | | | | | |
|---|---|---|---|---|---|---|---|---|---|---|---|---|---|---|
| | From +20°F. to | | | | | From +10°F. to | | | | | From 0°F. to | | | |
| | 0° | −10° | −20° | −30° | −40° | 0° | −10° | −20° | −30° | −40° | −10° | −20° | −30° | −40° |
| 10 | 2 | 2¾ | 3½ | 4 | 4½ | 1 | 2 | 2⅓ | 3¼ | 3¾ | 1 | 1¾ | 2½ | 3 |
| 12 | 2½ | 3¼ | 4 | 4¾ | 5¼ | 1¼ | 2¼ | 3 | 3¾ | 4½ | 1¼ | 2 | 2¾ | 3½ |
| 14 | 3 | 4 | 4¾ | 5½ | 6 | 1½ | 2½ | 3½ | 4½ | 5 | 1¼ | 2½ | 3¼ | 4 |
| 16 | 3¼ | 4½ | 5½ | 6¼ | 7 | 1¾ | 3 | 4 | 5 | 5¾ | 1½ | 2¾ | 3¾ | 4¾ |
| 18 | 3¾ | 5 | 6 | 7 | 7¾ | 2 | 3¼ | 4½ | 5¾ | 6½ | 1¾ | 3 | 4¼ | 5¼ |
| 20 | 4 | 5½ | 6¾ | 7¾ | 8¾ | 2 | 3¼ | 5 | 6¼ | 7¼ | 1¾ | 3½ | 4¾ | 5¾ |
| 22 | 4½ | 6 | 7½ | 8½ | 9½ | 2¼ | 4 | 5½ | 6¾ | 8 | 2 | 3¾ | 5¼ | 6½ |
| 24 | 5 | 6¾ | 8 | 9¼ | 10½ | 2½ | 4½ | 6 | 7½ | 8¾ | 2¼ | 4 | 5½ | 7 |
| 26 | 5¼ | 7¼ | 8¾ | 10 | 11¼ | 2¾ | 4¾ | 6½ | 8 | 9½ | 2½ | 4½ | 6 | 7½ |
| 28 | 5¾ | 7¾ | 9½ | 11 | 12 | 3 | 5¼ | 7 | 8¾ | 10¼ | 2½ | 4¾ | 6½ | 8 |
| 30 | 6 | 8¼ | 10 | 11¾ | 13 | 3 | 5½ | 7½ | 9¼ | 10¾ | 2¾ | 5 | 7 | 8¾ |

Test radiator solution with proper tester. Determine from the table the number of quarts of solution to be drawn off from a full cooling system and replace with concentrated anti-freeze, to give the desired increased protection. For example, to increase protection of a 22-quart cooling system containing Alcohol anti-freeze, from +10°F. to −20°F. will require the replacement of 5½ quarts of solution with concentrated anti-freeze.

| Cooling System Capacity Quarts | Number of Quarts of **ETHYLENE GLYCOL** Anti-Freeze Required to Increase Protection | | | | | | | | | | | | | |
|---|---|---|---|---|---|---|---|---|---|---|---|---|---|---|
| | From +20°F. to | | | | | From +10°F. to | | | | | From 0°F. to | | | |
| | 0° | −10° | −20° | −30° | −40° | 0° | −10° | −20° | −30° | −40° | −10° | −20° | −30° | −40° |
| 10 | 1¾ | 2¼ | 3 | 3½ | 3¾ | ¾ | 1½ | 2¼ | 2¾ | 3¼ | ¾ | 1½ | 2 | 2½ |
| 12 | 2 | 2¾ | 3½ | 4 | 4½ | 1 | 1¾ | 2½ | 3¼ | 3¾ | 1 | 1¾ | 2½ | 3¼ |
| 14 | 2¼ | 3¼ | 4 | 4¾ | 5½ | 1¼ | 2 | 3 | 3¾ | 4½ | 1 | 2 | 3 | 3½ |
| 16 | 2½ | 3½ | 4½ | 5¼ | 6 | 1¼ | 2½ | 3½ | 4¼ | 5¼ | 1¼ | 2¼ | 3¼ | 4 |
| 18 | 3 | 4 | 5 | 6 | 7 | 1½ | 2¾ | 4 | 5 | 5¾ | 1½ | 2½ | 3¾ | 4¾ |
| 20 | 3¼ | 4½ | 5¾ | 6¾ | 7½ | 1¾ | 3 | 4¼ | 5½ | 6½ | 1½ | 2¾ | 4¼ | 5¼ |
| 22 | 3½ | 5 | 6¼ | 7¼ | 8¼ | 1¾ | 3¼ | 4¾ | 6 | 7¼ | 1¾ | 3¼ | 4½ | 5½ |
| 24 | 4 | 5½ | 7 | 8 | 9 | 2 | 3½ | 5 | 6½ | 7½ | 1¾ | 3½ | 5 | 6 |
| 26 | 4¼ | 6 | 7½ | 8¾ | 10 | 2 | 4 | 5½ | 7 | 8¼ | 2 | 3¾ | 5½ | 6¾ |
| 28 | 4½ | 6¼ | 8 | 9½ | 10½ | 2¼ | 4¼ | 6 | 7½ | 9 | 2 | 4 | 5¾ | 7¼ |
| 30 | 5 | 6¾ | 8½ | 10 | 11½ | 2½ | 4½ | 6½ | 8 | 9½ | 2¼ | 4¼ | 6¼ | 7¾ |

Test radiator solution with proper hydrometer. Determine from the table the number of quarts of solution to be drawn off from a full cooling system and replace with undiluted anti-freeze, to give the desired increased protection. For example, to increase protection of a 22-quart cooling system containing Ethylene Glycol (permanent type) anti-freeze, from +20°F. to −20°F. will require the replacement of 6¼ quarts of solution with undiluted anti-freeze.

# ANTI-FREEZE CHART

## *Temperatures Shown in Degrees Fahrenheit*
## *+32 is Freezing*

| Cooling System Capacity Quarts | Quarts of **ALCOHOL** Needed for Protection to Temperatures Shown Below | | | | | | | | | | | | |
|---|---|---|---|---|---|---|---|---|---|---|---|---|---|
| | 1 | 2 | 3 | 4 | 5 | 6 | 7 | 8 | 9 | 10 | 11 | 12 | 13 |
| 10 | +23° | +11° | −5° | −27° | | | | | | | | | |
| 11 | +25 | +13 | 0 | −18 | −40° | | | | | | | | |
| 12 | | +15 | +3 | −12 | −31 | | | | | | | | |
| 13 | | +17 | +7 | −7 | −23 | | | | | | | | |
| 14 | | +19 | +9 | −3 | −17 | −34° | | | | | | | |
| 15 | | +20 | +11 | +1 | −12 | −27 | | | | | | | |
| 16 | | +21 | +13 | +3 | −8 | −21 | −36° | | | | | | |
| 17 | | +22 | +16 | +6 | −4 | −16 | −29 | | | | | | |
| 18 | | +23 | +17 | +8 | −1 | −12 | −25 | −38° | | | | | |
| 19 | | +24 | +17 | +9 | +2 | −8 | −21 | −32 | | | | | |
| 20 | | | +18 | +11 | +4 | −5 | −16 | −27 | −39° | | | | |
| 21 | | | +19 | +12 | +5 | −3 | −12 | −22 | −34 | | | | |
| 22 | | | +20 | +14 | +7 | 0 | −9 | −18 | −29 | −40° | | | |
| 23 | | | +21 | +15 | +8 | +2 | −7 | −15 | −25 | −36° | | | |
| 24 | | | +21 | +16 | +10 | +4 | −4 | −12 | −21 | −31 | | | |
| 25 | | | +22 | +17 | +11 | +6 | −2 | −9 | −18 | −27 | −37° | | |
| 26 | | | +22 | +17 | +12 | +7 | +1 | −7 | −14 | −23 | −32 | | |
| 27 | | | +23 | +18 | +13 | +8 | +3 | −5 | −12 | −20 | −28 | −39° | |
| 28 | | | +23 | +19 | +14 | +9 | +4 | −3 | −9 | −17 | −25 | −34 | |
| 29 | | | +24 | +19 | +15 | +10 | +6 | −1 | −7 | −15 | −22 | −30 | −39° |
| 30 | | | +24 | +20 | +16 | +11 | +7 | +1 | −5 | −12 | −19 | −27 | −35 |

+ Figures are above Zero, but below Freezing.

− Figures are below Zero. Also below Freezing.

| Cooling System Capacity Quarts | Quarts of **ETHYLENE GLYCOL** Needed for Protection to Temperatures Shown Below | | | | | | | | | | | | | |
|---|---|---|---|---|---|---|---|---|---|---|---|---|---|---|
| | 1 | 2 | 3 | 4 | 5 | 6 | 7 | 8 | 9 | 10 | 11 | 12 | 13 | 14 |
| 10 | +24° | +16° | +4° | −12° | −34° | −62° | | | | | | | | |
| 11 | +25 | +18 | +8 | −6 | −23 | −47 | | | | | | | | |
| 12 | +26 | +19 | +10 | 0 | −15 | −34 | −57° | | | | | | | |
| 13 | +27 | +21 | +13 | +3 | −9 | −25 | −45 | | | | | | | |
| 14 | | | +15 | +6 | −5 | −18 | −34 | | | | | | | |
| 15 | | | +16 | +8 | 0 | −12 | −26 | | | | | | | |
| 16 | | | +17 | +10 | +2 | −8 | −19 | −34 | −52° | | | | | |
| 17 | | | +18 | +12 | +5 | −4 | −14 | −27 | −42 | | | | | |
| 18 | | | +19 | +14 | +7 | 0 | −10 | −21 | −34 | −50° | | | | |
| 19 | | | +20 | +15 | +9 | +2 | −7 | −16 | −28 | −42 | | | | |
| 20 | | | | +16 | +10 | +4 | −3 | −12 | −22 | −34 | −48° | | | |
| 21 | | | | +17 | +12 | +6 | 0 | −9 | −17 | −28 | −41 | | | |
| 22 | | | | +18 | +13 | +8 | +2 | −6 | −14 | −23 | −34 | −47° | | |
| 23 | | | | +19 | +14 | +9 | +4 | −3 | −10 | −19 | −29 | −40 | | |
| 24 | | | | +19 | +15 | +10 | +5 | 0 | −8 | −15 | −23 | −34 | −46° | |
| 25 | | | | +20 | +16 | +12 | +7 | +1 | −5 | −12 | −20 | −29 | −40 | −50° |
| 26 | | | | | +17 | +13 | +8 | +3 | −3 | −9 | −16 | −25 | −34 | −44 |
| 27 | | | | | +18 | +14 | +9 | +5 | −1 | −7 | −13 | −21 | −29 | −39 |
| 28 | | | | | +18 | +15 | +10 | +6 | +1 | −5 | −11 | −18 | −25 | −34 |
| 29 | | | | | +19 | +16 | +12 | +7 | +2 | −3 | −8 | −15 | −22 | −29 |
| 30 | | | | | +20 | +17 | +13 | +8 | +4 | −1 | −6 | −12 | −18 | −25 |

For capacities over 30 quarts divide true capacity by 3. Find quarts Anti-Freeze for the 1/3 and multiply by 3 for quarts to add.

For capacities under 10 quarts multiply true capacity by 3. Find quarts Anti-Freeze for the tripled volume and divide by 3 for quarts to add.

## Datsun Distributors

National Headquarters:
Nissan Motor Corporation, U.S.A.
18501 S. Figueroa St.
Carson, California
P.O. Box 191
Gardena, California 90247

Boston Regional Office:
777 West St.
Mansfield, Massachusetts 02048

Chicago Regional Office:
51 Shore Drive
Hinsdale, Illinois 60521

Dallas Regional Office:
13405 N. Stemmons Freeway
Dallas, Texas 75234

Denver Regional Office:
11000 E. 45th Ave.
Denver, Colorado 80239

Jacksonville Regional Office:
8743 Western Way
Jacksonville, Florida 32216

Los Angeles Regional Office:
137 E. Alondra Blvd.
P.O. Box 260
Gardena, California 90247

New York Regional Office:
400 County Ave.
Secaucus, New Jersey 07094

Norfolk Regional Office:
151 Harbor Drive
Portsmouth, Virginia 23705

Portland Regional Office:
9575 S.W. Schools Ferry Road
P.O. Box 23327
Portland, Oregon 97223

Hawaii:
Datsun of Hawaii
The Hawaii Corporation
711 Kapiolani Blvd.
Honolulu, Hawaii 96813